DEPRESSION IS A CHOICE

DEPRESSION

IS A

CHOICE

Winning the Fight
Without Drugs

A. B. CURTISS

HYPERION · NEW YORK

IMPORTANT CAUTION TO OUR READERS

Because of the unique circumstances that may apply to each individual reader, as well as other factors, the publisher and author cannot guarantee that the information and advice discussed in this book are appropiate and accurate for every reader. For that reason, readers are strongly cautioned to consult a pyschiatrist, psychologist, medical doctor, or other professional advisor before making any medical decisions. This book is not intended to replace professional advice.

Library of Congress Cataloging-in-Publication Data

Curtiss, A. B.
    Depression is a choice : winning the battle without drugs / A. B. Curtiss.
        p.   cm.
    Includes bibliographical references and index.
    ISBN 0-7868-6629-2
    1. Depression, Mental.   2. Depression, Mental—Alternative treatment.
3. Curtiss, A. B.   I. Title.

    RC537 .C875   2001
    616.85'27—dc21

                                                            2001016909

First Edition

10   9   8   7   6   5   4   3   2   1

To my husband, Ray, the lovely man who has stuck by my side through thick and thin, good and bad, crazy and sane.

ACKNOWLEDGMENTS

I wish to thank my brilliant chief editor, Leigh Haber, whose insight and enthusiasm will always be enough to overcome the busiest of schedules. Thanks especially to Sofia Shafquat for her intuitive and discriminating editorial work on the structure and form of the final manuscript; and the able editorial assistance of Liza Nelligan, Nira Brand, and Barbara Villasenor during the early phases of this lengthy project. I am grateful to my literary agent, Sandra Dijkstra, who shepherded this book toward its destiny in that excellent and swift manner that only she knows how to do. Many thanks also to my daughters, Demming Forsythe and Sunday Arvidson, and my daughter-in-law, Paula Curtiss, for their helpful comments.

A big thank you to my wonderful network of fellow therapists and writers, whose advice and enthusiasm have made all things possible—Bob Holt, Gene Kira, Victor Villasenor, Terry and Lynn Badger, Wanda Belmont, Bonnie Robison, Patty

Weech, Dick Brown, Karen Black, Christa Zohn, and Gary Lungen. I am most grateful to my neighbor Steve Psomas and my son, Wolf Curtiss, for their computer troubleshooting. Thanks and a big hug for my friends Bobbi Janikas, Pat Pangburn, CeeCee Wainwright, Susan Fisher, Gail Griffith, Cris and Jon Fleming, Judy and Taylor Hines, Kay and Bob Fisher, Helen Cyr Hock, Helen Lee Fletcher, Dottie Myers, Loretta Strang, David and Maryanne Forward, Elizabeth and Bill Wood, Carmen Torrent, Claudia Melendez, Jane Jacobsen, Ron and Olga Seibert, R. Lee and Lynn Hammet, Bill Ellenberger, Lois and Paul Grunder, Mary Jacobsen, and Rosie and Bob Stubbs for their unflagging interest and loving support reaching down the years and across the different roads we have taken. Thanks and hugs to my mother, Bert, who was very helpful with proofreading and very encouraging with enthusiasm, and another big thank you to my brother Deane, whose comments were extremely helpful for organizing my original ideas into book form. Kisses and hugs to my sisters-in-law Judy B., Miriam B., and Jeanne Cramer, and my aunt, Lucy Baukney, for their continuing interest in all my writing projects. Thanks to my nephew Curtiss Lapoint, who is a great fan of all my efforts. I could not have done without the help and guidance of the rest of my family either—Ford Curtiss, Deane and Shelli Curtiss, Dave Arvidson, and Kyle Forsythe. Thanks and kisses to my grandchildren who are an indispensable cheering gallery: Solmar, Blueray, Harmony, Peregrine, Summer, Cutter, Tanner, Mavrik, and Ayla Ray. I am grateful most of all to my dear husband, who is such a good sport he put up with the writing of the book and remodeling the house at the same time.

CONTENTS

WHAT IF . . .

Prozac is not the best answer to depression?
You could discover the real cause *of depression?*
You could fight a battle of wits with your depression and win?
Depression is "catching" instead of genetic?
You could *pull yourself up by your own bootstraps?*
You could *cure depression by an act of will?*
Futility is only a feeling, *not reality?*
You could learn to think *your depression away?*
You could "pull the plug" on depression any time you wanted?
Depression is a choice?

DEPRESSION
IS A
CHOICE

Help! I'm falling into the whirlpool again of a thousand
   thinking, sinking thoughts.
Uh-oh. I'm caught, plunged to the central core of my despair.
Oh, it is rock-bottom here, on the stones on which I break
   myself. I hate depression, this horribleness. For lifetimes
   maybe I have hated it, this prison of myself, where I keep the
   crazy one locked up screaming, screaming, screaming
   to jump off my mind and splatter sanity.
Well, it's visiting hours now, throw down the doors to solitary!
I am here to meet my dark, dark self
   and make a student's study of my agony!
Death, Madness, is that you hiding there? I don't care.
Here, I'll throw you a bone, Me! Take what you want.
We can all sit down to the tea of me, us old enemies,
   we can chat.
Not to negotiate myself, I only wish to visit and know myself at
   last, the pain and worst of it. I have no other hope.
I play the wounded hunter here in the jungle of my soul, hiding
   in the grass to watch my beasts come down to water.
No drugs now to sleep them off of me. They can drag me under
   easily.
No? Nobody comes to my darkness here but me?
And my pain. Listen, pain, you beast from Hell, I surrender, do
   your worst.
I will not whine, this time, that I be saved (from what, I never
   knew),

Or do one thing to make this better. I'm going to sit and look at
   you, and watch you, pain, like any other show.
Watch for what? Perhaps I'll never know.
Maybe there is no what, *but I* know *this watching is real.*
Something is breaking, but it's not my heart.
Something is dying, but there is no part of me that's gone.
I am all right. I'm still right here.
It's very quiet, sober as a shadow now with no adrenaline.
I'm feeling free and nothing's happening.
I think the pain has died instead of me.
That's interesting, without the pain, madness is a laugh.
It doesn't bother me at all. Can it be I've birthed myself at last?

—CHILDREN OF THE GODS

One

JOURNEY TO A CHOICE

The moment I felt depressed, it never occurred to me to do anything else but be depressed. The progression from a feeling of depression to being a depressed person was a foregone conclusion that I never questioned.

Depression always ends. Not because of Prozac. Not because of psychotherapy. Not because of psychoanalysis or shock treatments. Depression always ends because it is in the very nature of depression to end. The only question is, how can we get it to end sooner, the way we want it to, instead of later, which we hate?

The answer is that we have to learn to think about depression in a different way. But it is not going to be enough to simply consider new ideas from a safe distance. We have to get down on our hands and knees with a magnifying glass and crawl around inside of the beliefs we have for so long relied on. It is not going to be enough to consider *what* we think. We have to consider *how* we think because the problem of depression lies in the very gears of our thinking process.

To do this we must entertain some rather esoteric ideas that we cannot so easily dismiss with our ready-made answers.

There are wonderful clues in ancient paradoxes, like koans: What is the sound of one hand clapping? These clues can reach beyond our normal considerations to some uninvented part of us that we are not normally in touch with. They help us learn to think sideways, intuitively, restructuredly—all the better to match wits with our depression.

Depression makes us fear that we will never be truly happy because we see how our happiness can be blown away in an instant, like straws in a hurricane, and absolutely nothing remains to comfort us in our anguish.

We need not be afraid. We do not need comfort. It is not true that all our happiness has fled and what we are suffering is the pain of its loss. Our essential capacity for happiness is not something we can get back or acquire, no matter how hard we try, because it is our natural state. What happens is that depression covers over our natural state and tricks us into thinking that we don't have it anymore. When we properly address our depression, it relinquishes its hold upon us, and we find ourselves once again in the bedrock of our infinite okayness. Practically speaking, *happiness is unlearned depression*.

Our essential happiness is not conditional. Conditional happiness cannot pass for essential happiness any more than being serially grateful for disparate things can pass for a state of infinite and abiding gratitude. Conditional gratitude, where we see something that causes us to be grateful, is not the same as essential gratitude, where being grateful causes us to see something. Conditional happiness, the temporary excitement of having what we want, is not the same thing as essential happiness, the transcendent awareness that we can want what we have. Conditional happiness is a feeling that comes and goes. Essential happiness is our original state of well-being that is always available to us. It is not quantitative despite the fact that we think it depends upon some quantity of things or feelings we must have.

Depression is not quantitative, either, despite the fact that psychiatrists have labeled it a disease and divided it up into various classifications and diagnoses. Depression, like essential happiness, is *qualitative*. But depression is not our natural state, it is a state of alarm. When I began my career as a psychotherapist in 1987, I was as deeply afflicted with depression as anybody else who walked through my door looking for help. But no more. I have come to see depression in a revolutionary way, which has totally eliminated the whole idea of it as a disease in my life. After suffering with it for decades; after watching my brother struggle with the same ravages of manic depression that killed my father, I know, now, that it doesn't have to be that way.

There are 17 million people suffering with depression who are all seeking an answer to their hurt and pain.[1] Ten years ago, as a result of my work as a cognitive behavioral therapist, my struggles with my own severe mood swings and my experiences with patients who came in for therapy, I discovered the real cause of depression. I haven't "been depressed" since that time.

This book is not an orthodox book on depression. The trouble with orthodox books is that we agree with them. We seldom do things we agree with because agreement makes us feel so comfortable that it is easy to substitute our knowledge for our action. There is simply no movement without resistance, as physics tells us. That's why we bounce a ball on the hard floor instead of a pillow. That's why we do exercises. Because we seldom agree with them. Exercises make us feel so uncomfortable that we end up doing them out of some kind of spite, and they take us galaxies beyond anything we intellectually agree with.

There's a good chance you won't agree with even the title of this book. You may find it uncomfortable, annoying, confronting, outrageous, even dangerous. How can depression be a choice? You may want to argue with this book, fight with it, wrestle it to the ground. Good. The quickest path to change is through our resistance to change. And there is nothing we less want to change than our own long-held opinions and the process of how we think. It is human nature. But sometimes the very act of defending some deeply held idea causes us to look at it more closely. We see a flaw. I have sat down at my desk in a furious rage to write down all the one-two-three points that "prove I am in the right"; only to find, as I read over my own words, the surprising clue to my culpability.

The other problem with orthodox theories about depression, in addition to the fact that we agree with them, is that at some point they all depend upon some faulty but *hidden* premise that no one thinks to ferret out because everyone is so caught up in the admiration of the excellent logic employed. We are all subject to this touch of intellectual arrogance.

The hidden premise in psychiatry and psychology, upon which both disciplines depend entirely, and without which all of their diagnoses and treatments would disappear in a puff of smoke, is that the persona and the self (the mind and the self) are one and the same. This is based upon Freud's model of the unconscious mind, which has never been scientifically proven but has always been taken as a "given."

"Ultimately our troubles are due to dogma and deduction," warns historian, philosopher, and educator Will Durant. "We find no new truth because we take some venerable but questionable proposition as the indubitable starting point, and never think of putting this assumption itself to a test of observation or experiment." So I do not depend upon my logic as proof that I am right. I am sure my ideas work because I have already freed myself from depression, and I have lived in a calm state of cheerful sanity for more than ten years. My logic does not proceed from a disease in search of a *possible* answer. My theory starts with the answer I have already found and goes backward to see how I did it.

You may, at this very moment, be suffering from depression yourself, or someone you love may be fighting their own terrible battle with it. What I say in this book does not come from the abstract notions of some lofty and idealized therapist's pulpit. It comes from my soul's-depth experience of the very pain you may now be suffering. It is a pain that I think I can help you negotiate because I have learned how to negotiate my own pain.

Sometimes you may not so easily follow my thinking, but my intention in the pages ahead is to be your true companion, trying to make myself understood not by telling you how you must have been doing something wrong to be feeling so bad, or to list all the ABCs of what you *should be* doing and thinking. We get depressed not because we are doing something wrong but because there are a few essential things we have never been taught how to do at all. Thanks to some new advances in neuroscience, which have pointed out the way, we can all learn how to do these things.

In the coming chapters I will illustrate for you the progress of my own education and how it has served me, my own errors of thinking, and what I have done to correct them. I will pass on to you precepts rooted in ancient wisdom as well as some rather esoteric philosophical concepts, which I have found helpful. I will also tell you stories about incidents in my own life, and then link all of these up with current scientific research.

I now have the tools I need to handle depression. But they are not tools you can so easily hand over, ready-made, to someone else. They are tools that only emerge into being by entertaining small ideas and applying them to your life. Depression is essentially a trick of the mind. First, we can learn how this trick works so that we will not be fooled by it so easily. Then, we can develop our own tricks to protect us from this life-disturbing strategy of the mind gone wrong.

The solution to depression lies waiting on almost every page of this book. One person will click with an idea in the first chapter and think, "I get it." Someone else will read to the very last chapter before something will spring to life for them. Another may read the book, put it back on the shelf, and later a situation will occur and they will connect it with something they have remembered and, click, click, click. They will get it.

The secret to depression is very much like the secret of learning how to read. And isn't it simple and easy when we know how? And isn't it seemingly impossible for those who remain illiterate? And how many of us could have learned how to read on our own, without anybody teaching us? And who has ever tried to teach us about depression?

For those of us who experience it, depression is like living your own death. As successful as I was in many other aspects of my life, I was often paralyzed by a chronic despair. I spent half my life locked in a joyless, painful, coffin of the mind. I learned about depression from the inside of it, from the pain, from the helplessness, and from the hopelessness.

One day, when depression began its periodic and pitiless attack upon me, I decided to fight back, *mentally*, and found that I had the power all along to escape from depression; I just didn't know it. I discovered that I had a choice. I did not have to meekly give way to my painful feelings. I could battle them for precedence and win!

If the three most important things in real estate are location, location, and location, then the three most important things in mental health are perception, perception, and perception. It is our perception of depression that is the problem more than the low level of serotonin that seems to cause all the trouble. When we are born, our perceptions are very limited. We have not even differentiated our own self from the world that surrounds us. As newborn infants we must learn to distinguish our own legs from the ceiling.

We all transcend this first enmeshment when we learn to distinguish our body from the universe at large, as well as from other bodies. For many of us, this is as separated as we get.

Our soul remains merged with the self, and our self remains merged with the mind. I cannot yet see through that "one-way mirror" of the soul that enlightened ones such as Buddha describe. I keep company with that larger part of humanity; those of us who, like moons in a cosmic midnight, know not the sun to which we owe our luminous existence. But I have transcended my enmeshment with my mind enough to be able to free myself from depression as an act of will.

Please note that I say "free myself from" depression. Yes, the feeling of depression is caused by a chemical imbalance in the brain, but "disease" or "medical illness" is not the name of the situation. It is neither necessary nor possible to "cure" the primal impulses of depression or mania, which are merely extensions of the fight-or-flight response—our most basic defense mechanism. What we need to cure is our *reaction* to them.

Most people think we can't do that. Most people think that what creates our perceptions and the behavior of depression and manic depression lies within the workings of our unconscious mind and is therefore not accessible to will. I found this to be incorrect. We simply have to learn how to *use* our mind, instead of thinking we *are* our mind. This is the meaning of that old maxim: The mind makes a wonderful servant but a terrible master.

With a push from the New Age spiritual movement, we now understand the *body-mind* connection; that the mind can have a powerful effect over illness and healing in ways we once didn't think were possible. But we have not yet grasped the *mind-self* connection; that the self is supposed to direct the mind to manage our health, thinking, feelings, and behavior. The mind-self connection is the key to depression. If the self does not choose to direct the mind, the mind may bury the self in all sorts of varieties of negative thinking and mood disorders. In the absence of any conscious direction by the self, the mind can direct itself right into mental illness.

Johann Wolfgang Goethe, German poet, dramatist, and philosopher, was clearly referring to this same idea when he wrote, "Where a man has a passion for meditation without the capacity for thinking, a particular idea fixes itself fast, and soon creates a mental disease." Yes, depression is strong and painful, and we can get very focused on it when we get into that downward spiral. But we don't have to. We can cure our easy habitual reaction to depression, which is to succumb to it, and as an act of will regain our lost equanimity.

That is because we can improve the mind. We don't improve the self. Rather, we more or less uncover the self or don't uncover the self, use the self or don't use it. Human beings don't just know something, we also know that we know it. *What* we know (mind) may change as to improvement, but the awareness *that* we know (self) is not a matter of improvement or gradation, it is a matter of either/or, it is a matter of asleep to it or awake to it.

This means that the understanding that we are painfully depressed can awaken us to the hidden point of choice; it need not abandon us at the edge of despair. Where is choice hidden? *Choice is hidden between the awareness of the self and the use of the mind.* Choice lies eternally and changelessly between the "I am" and whatever else may follow it to complete any sentence (such as "I am depressed").

In order to exercise this choice we must learn to "split the atom" psychologically. That is, we must be able to separate out the "I am" from the "I am angry" or the "I am" from the "I am depressed" so that we can understand we are not those things; and in fact, we are much more powerful than depression or anger. It is simply a matter of educating and training our minds so that anger and depression are no longer in charge of us. We are in charge of them.

For many of us, depression is the fight of our lives. We can win that fight. We can do whatever we have to do to win. We can read anything that can help us. If we don't understand it at first, we can study it. We can encourage ourselves into a belief that we can get better, which is just a little bit stronger than our belief that we can't. All that we need to begin is our earnest desire to understand. It is the strongest force in the world because understanding is not just a possibility, it is our destiny.

I may still struggle with the chemically based *impulse* to depression. But I no longer get depressed. I may still be *momentarily overtaken* by depression, but I can no longer be taken over by it. My struggle with depression is different now, and on a more conscious level. The battle is not limited to the lower brain states of emotional pain and my *reactive* behavior to that pain, for I have learned to call upon the higher brain functions of reasoning, intelligence, and creativity that now come to my aid.

I have game rules, boundary lines, and acquired skills for play, such as there must be in any endeavor where we find our creature selves pitted against nature for survival. The end result is that I have domesticated "the Beast," which I had once thought must forever feed upon me at will. And like an old sea captain whose experiences have toughened him into a worthy adversary of the mighty ocean he sails, at times, and from a respectful distance, I too regard my own unfathomable "deep" with an awe not unmixed with affection. Depression, well encountered, has many virtues.

But depression no longer has the authority to intrude itself upon my daily life. I am not claiming, however, that I *control* depression. This would be a foolish attempt, like trying to control electricity, or the ocean, or nature. We do not seek to control these great imponderables. We do not dare to grab them by the throat and throttle them until they do what we want. We observe them, and respectfully learn their principles so that we can have a safe and proper relationship with them, and make good use of what they have to offer us.

By studying depression in this manner, I have learned to control my response to it based upon my understanding of its principles, and the discovery and exercise of what precautions I must take in order to "command" it. There is no other way. Cutting, shocking, or drugging depression out of our brain is like wrestling with lightning; we will only harm ourselves. The right way is not to gain complete control over depression but rather to gain complete control over our reaction to depression. It is a very simple solution. Unfortunately, in the beginning, for those of us who have a habit of going deep into depression, it is also very difficult to do.

It was the difficulty of managing their terrible pain of depression that most often brought people into my counseling office in search of some commonsense therapy for a failed relationship with their spouse, or their boss, or their child. Slowly I began to sense a pattern in the unconstructive, almost passive, way in which we were all living our lives.

It seemed to me that my problem, and everybody else's, lay in the lack of clarity and directedness in our everyday thinking, especially when depression hit. We all had an extreme dependence on a very vague reality, thinking things and doing things in a certain way, not based upon any clear, conscious investigation or choice, but simply because we have always thought it or done it that way.

For instance, if I were at a party and a feeling of depression came over me, I always excused myself as soon as possible, went home, and crawled into bed. The moment I *felt* depressed, it never occurred to me to do anything else but be depressed. The progression from a *feeling* of depression to *being* a depressed person was a foregone conclusion that I never questioned. But a dedicated, long-term, systematic study of my habits, especially those habits that I employed automatically whenever I got depressed, opened my eyes to some entirely new possibilities.

The first thing I discovered was that I had never clearly

understood that sleeping in my clothes, staying in bed for days, sighing a lot, and talking in a weak, sad voice were habits, choices. I thought they were reality, my life, *the behavioral necessities that came automatically with the paralyzing pain of depression.* The psychiatrist I went to as a woman in my thirties also believed that. He suggested drugs. But drugs had not greatly helped my brother or my father with their manic depression, so I refused drugs, hoping something better would come along. I was not to find that "something better" for fifteen years, not until after I became a psychotherapist myself.

I would like to say I had a brilliant theory that transformed my life. But it was not like that at all. Looking back I can pretty much piece everything together, how one thing led to another and how, therefore, it all came about. But it wasn't so much a matter of creating fundamental ideas. It was more like fundamental ideas kept coming and dragging me along by the scruff of the neck. And when I still didn't get it, since there is nothing more patient than potentiality, they would come around in another disguise so I could discover them all over again in a different and hopefully more promising context. Sometimes I was not a quick student, but anyone who ever knew me could see that I was tooth-and-claw tenacious.

It may seem that I was always quick because I relate to you, in the coming chapters, incidents of "instant" success. But I know that any such instant was the shining victory to a great siege of unknowingness that went before, much of it so unknowing that it would be difficult for me to reconstruct it. There will always be connections between my breakthroughs and my awareness of unknowingness, but they are not always easy to catch. Most breakthroughs are not so much a case of truth being revealed as ignorance being dissolved. This is a level of experience about which one can say nothing, and yet something of meaning has nevertheless been conveyed.

Perhaps it has been a help to me, as well as a scourge, that even as a child I was often introspective. When I was ten I had an experience that started out as a kind of playacting that all children turn to when they are bored and lonely, but it transformed into something much more significant than that; a deep awareness that I was alone in my ultimate responsibility for myself. Even though I denied it for years as an adult, I was always being pulled back to this essential core.

I can remember staring dreamily and intently at myself in the full length mirror on the back of the bathroom door, a little girl in white cotton underpants, hair still damp from a summer bath. I realized that I could not really see myself in the mirror all at once, the way I could see other people when I looked at them. I could see any one of my features clearly but I somehow couldn't focus on my complete image in the mirror or carry it in my mind like I could carry the complete images of other people. I could recognize myself when I looked at the mirror, but when I turned away I could not reconstruct myself in my mind. This did not frighten me, but it started me thinking some rather odd thoughts.

I found that my image would disappear when I stared intently into my own eyes for a long time. At a certain point, only the staring would be left to stare back at itself. Then I began trying to see through the eyes in the mirror that were looking back at myself so I wouldn't disappear, and this is what I thought: I am going to remember this exact moment forever. I am going to remember always that I am now ten years old. I am always going to remember myself. I am going to grow up and, when I do, I am going to remember this time and come back and keep myself company so I won't be so lonely.

For some reason this thought has been a great comfort to me, beginning at that exact instant, and continuing for all of my life. I might forget it for years at a time and then it would come back to me. There was something very important and solid and real about this thought. Even today it gives me a sense of being ageless and timeless.

When I lost this sense of core self in the busyness of growing up and mixing it up with life, I found two remarkable teachers to help me salvage my ship of self-responsibility when it foundered. Osho was an Indian guru who is now widely published. Dr. Allan Anderson was the sage I encountered in graduate school at San Diego State University. And I must credit all those books that jumped off the shelf as I rummaged through old bookstores or foraged through garage sales.

I first sensed Dr. Anderson was no ordinary teacher when I found that two students in one of his courses were quantum physicists who had driven from Los Angeles to San Diego three days a week *for ten years* to audit his classes! Sometimes the physicists were able to illustrate some small point for the class such as the "myth of continuity" with descriptions of their experiments on quarks.

And here is one book incident: Just before I entered graduate school, we moved to a new house from the rented quarters we had been in since our big move from New Jersey to California in 1983. I got lost trying to meet with a real estate agent and found myself at a small psychic community book sale where I proceeded to buy the whole lot, whatever wasn't a Harlequin romance or a Louis L'Amour Western. I took a chance on everything else, even Greek history, feathery handwritten journals of "sidereal theory" (whatever the heck *that* is, I thought), Chang Tsu, Sankaracharya, and Karl Menninger.

The paperbacks were only 25 cents each, and I had been supplying myself with what often turned out to be disappointing paperbacks from the drugstore at four or five dollars *per* to feed my longtime reading habit during the year and a half my own books were in storage. You can well imagine the metaphysical treasure trove I thus came by.

The lot included some volumes on *The Metaphysical System of Hobbes,* a various assortment of Yogananda, Krishnamurti, Rudolf Steiner, L. Ron Hubbard, Edgar Cayce, Mary Baker Eddy, Martin Heidegger, and George Gurdjieff. For one dollar per hardback I grabbed up an odd accumulation of Carl Jung, Max Picard, Erich Fromm, R. D. Laing, Alfred Adler, Ludwig Wittgenstein, and Alan Watts. There were a couple of anthropology and astrology textbooks. There were also some wonderful old 1890s to 1930s books on hypnotism and astronomy, and a "scientific study" of the Mind, not the human mind per se but what one author referred to as the "cosmic Mind," of which the human mind was "but the reflection."[2]

The books on hypnosis were especially interesting to me. One little gem, called *The Practice of Autosuggestion*,[3] was dedicated "To all in conflict with their own imperfections." I loved that! Another, *Hypnotism: Its Facts, Theories, and Related Phenomena*[4] acknowledged Jean Louis Agassiz, an American naturalist, who said, "Every great scientific truth goes through three stages: First, people say it conflicts with the Bible. Next, they say it has been discovered before. Lastly, they say they have always believed it."

In graduate school I took the courses required for my Master's degree in the departments of Psychology and Counseling Education, which were quite politically correct for the liberal-minded 1980s, with the emphasis on multiversity, personal freedom, self-actualization, and the various Freud-derivative psychotherapies. At the same time I also indulged myself in courses from the more traditional Department of Humanities, which expanded my interest in classical literature and philosophy. It was here that I was introduced to *The Tarot*,[5] *The I Ching*,[6] *Tao Te Ching*[7] and the writings of Nisargadatta Maharaj,[8] Heraclitus[9] and Meister Eckhart.[10]

My continuing interest in hypnosis led me to study the latest research in neuroscience and brain mapping. There have been remarkable advances in just the last few years in the knowledge of the architecture of the brain by neuroscientists such as V. S. Ramachandran[11] and Antonio Damasio,[12] knowledge that was not available to Freud and William James at the time these respective fathers of psychoanalysis and psychology formulated their theories.

My growing familiarity with neuroscience, hypnosis, and the more esoteric philosophies slowly began to color some of my attitudes about psychiatry, psychology, and the practice of psychotherapy. I began to see that the stronger a therapy emphasized feelings, self-esteem, and self-confidence, the more dependent the therapist was upon his providing for the patient ongoing, unconditional, positive regard. The more self-esteem was the *end*, the more the *means*, in the form of the patient's efforts, had to appear blameless in the face of failure. In this paradigm, accuracy and comparison must continually be sacrificed to acceptance and compassion; which often results in the escalation of bizarre behavior and bizarre diagnoses.

The bizarre behavior results from us taking credit for everything that is positive and assigning blame elsewhere for anything negative. Because of this skewed positive-feedback loop between our judged actions and our beliefs, we systematically become more and more adapted to ourselves, our feelings, and our inaccurate solitary thinking; and less and less adapted to the environment that we share with our fellows. The resultant behavior, such as crying, depression, displays of temper, high-risk business, or romantic ventures, or abandonment of personal responsibilities, which seem either compulsory, necessary, or intelligent to us, will begin to appear more and more irrational to others.

The bizarre diagnoses occur because, in some cases, if a "cause disease" (excuse from blame) does not exist, it has to be "discovered" (invented). Psychiatry has expanded its diagnoses of mental disease every year to include "illnesses" like kleptomania and frotteurism. (Do you know what frotteurism is? It is a mental disorder that causes people, usually men, to surreptitiously fondle women's breasts or genitals in crowded situations such as elevators and subways.)

The problem with the escalation of these kinds of diagnoses is that either we can become so adapted to our thinking and feelings instead of our environment that we will become dissociated from the whole idea that we have a problem at all; or at the least, the more we become blameless, the more we become helpless in the face of our problems, thinking our problems need to be "fixed" by outside help before we can move forward on our own.

For 2,000 years of Western culture our problems existed in the human power struggle constantly being waged between our principles and our primal impulses. In the last fifty years we have unprincipled ourselves and become what I call "psychologized." Now the power struggle is between the "expert" and the "disorder." Since the rise of psychiatry and psychology as the moral compass, we don't talk about moral imperatives anymore, we talk about coping mechanisms. We are not living our lives by principles so much as we are living our lives by mental-health diagnoses. This is not working because it very subtly undermines our solid sense of self.

Uncorrupted, unconditional, positive regard is powerful; it is called love. However, in order to gain their power of authority as an agent of change, the psychotherapist and the psychiatrist must first pay unwitting homage to the Great Dread Disorder. If the disorder is not more powerful than the patient, there is no need for a psychiatrist to cure it. So the disorder is what *really* gets the regard, not us. The unconditional positive regard for the patient is necessarily shallow because this hidden loyalty to the disorder relegates the patient to second class in power and importance not only to the psychiatrist but to the patient's *own anguish*. Our whole society is now in a state of learned helplessness which psychology has taught us.[13]

In contrast to the undue reverence for mental illness as a prime determinant of behavior, which I found in the psychological sciences, was a denial of dignity and authority to disease, which I found in the work of Emil Coue in the 1890s. Coue was a French pharmacist who introduced a psychotherapy based upon hypnosis, which in those days was called "suggestion." Coue "tactfully teased some of his patients, giving them an idea that their ailment was absurd, and a little unworthy; that to be ill was a quaint but reprehensible *weakness*, which they should quickly get rid of."[14] Here was the idea that it was *our ignorance and weakness* causing our problems, not some overwhelming, powerful outside force. The solution was that we were to become informed and strong. And the implication was that it was doable.

It was thinkers like Coue who seemed to point solidly in the same direction I had tentatively begun to travel in my determined effort to "cure" my depression. I did, at first, hope to cure depression, thinking it was an affliction. Later, I saw the goal more clearly as coming to a "right relationship" with my depression. What proved correct was my initial decision that heroic effort and self-responsibility were the proper ways to head. Perhaps I chose this way because I had already begun to give up on my existing idea of happiness as being either not achievable or a bad bargain, I wasn't sure which.

I was encouraged to this understanding about "happiness" by the ancient mystics who warn us to beware of all desire, of wanting something else other than reality; of wanting something else other than what is. I found I was now willing to commit myself to a slightly revised version of the old Victorian adage "Be good, my child, and let who will be clever": "Be good, my child, and let who will be *happy*." When we are able to question our frantic search for our skewed idea of happiness, we turn away from the complications of wanting something other than what we have now got; and then there is only the one and simple path ahead.

On this path I encountered Ovid, the Roman poet, who claimed, "The most potent thing in life is habit"; and the Duke of Wellington, who maintained, "Habit is ten times nature"[15]; and Dryden, who warned, "First we make our habits, then our habits make us." My subsequent experience coincided with these philosophers rather than contemporary psychologists and psychiatrists. I found that the positive habits that I formed consciously as an act of will could override the bad habits that I had formed autonomically as coping mechanisms.

And though it was the foundation on which I developed the counseling techniques I was now using to help others, I found I needed something beyond traditional cognitive behavioral therapy in order to help myself. So when I worried that my life was becoming so complicated I couldn't see where to begin to make changes, I consulted the *I Ching*, which counseled: "If you wish to be rid of something, it is sufficient to simply withdraw from it in your heart."

I began to explore pertinent relationships, relative to depression, among the disciplines of anthropology, sociology, psychology, hypnosis, neuroscience, philosophy, and ancient wisdom. I was drawn especially to a salient connection between psychology, neuroscience, and moral principle. The insights that came from making this connection so transformed my perception of reality that when I applied this new thinking to my life, I was able to cure myself of thirty years' worth of manic depression. Not immediately of course, but over a period of two or three years.

Supported by the linking principles of all these disciplines, the now more open-eyed observations of my own behavior, and subsequent theory and practice, a new way of managing depression began to take shape. I started calling my ongoing developmental process "Directed Thinking" when it was so aptly nicknamed by one of my patients.

Although Directed Thinking can be learned, it is not so much a system that may easily be encapsulated, like a twelve-step program. It is a description of my own personal quest to a cure, and the insights that led me, indirectly, to a different relationship with my mind. I do not know how to give you the truth about depression, but I can describe for you exactly the journey I took where the truth about depression found me.

It is not necessarily a journey from point A to point B because many important insights were the hindsights of experience before they became the foresights of theory. Thus my journey was sometimes from point G to point B, so it lacks the linear continuity that is generally the stuff of a learn-step-one-then-go-on-to-step-two self-help text. But this is good. We don't learn psychological lessons deductively, in a linear way. They generally sneak in the back door when we're least expecting them. I love this story about accidental learning that Susan F. told me.

She was an elementary school music teacher who was teaching her first grade class the notes of the scale by letting them tap on glasses filled to different levels with different colored water. She ran out of colors and mixed the blue and red to differentiate the last glass. At the end of the class, when she asked the children what they had learned about music, one child raised his hand and said, "I learned that red and blue makes purple."

Though Directed Thinking is basically an inductive process, there is still the temptation to impose standards of deductive reasoning in the reporting of it, which can result in a "foolish consistency"; that old "hobgoblin of little minds," about which Ralph Waldo Emerson[16] warned us.

For instance, I might say at one time that pain may not be as real as it seems and another time that pain may be our most trenchant reality, two inconsistent ideas when compared to one another. But these two ideas are less truths to be disputed than they are different-colored lenses through which to see ourselves. In the same sense I may refer to happiness as our original givenness, or a will-o-the-wisp that is dangerous to pursue. An Eastern guru would say it this way: If you want to see the moon, do not debate directions with the finger pointing to the moon, simply look where the finger is pointing.

We want the truth about depression. The problem is that the horizon of any truth may be seen differently from a north or a south view. Truth itself may not be one way but we can only apprehend truth one way, from one direction, from where we stand at the moment. The French writer and diarist Anaïs Nin said, "We don't see things as *they* are, we see them as *we* are." The old sages understood this. The reason their sayings often seem meaningless is due to their penchant for answering the questioner instead of his question. Instead of directly answering our question, real wisdom indirectly gets us to change our stand and then we see that it was our question that had been meaningless.

In the pages to come I present to you the kaleidoscope of my own journey. At any point some idea may become so clear to you that it could totally change your stand, the way you look at things. This is what happened to me. I was given an "answer" to depression that lies beyond any medical cure for it. As a result of this new understanding, although I still experience the same wide mood swings that used to devastate me, I now remain a calm, stable, sober, and cheerful person.

Two

THE MYTH OF EASY

I have found it generally true that when I acknowledge that something is not easy I seem to get about it with a better attitude. Perhaps acknowledging that something is difficult somehow calls up the will to do it.

Some of the principles that underlie Directed Thinking have long been known by shamans, winning coaches, and motivation gurus. These concepts are often taught in Indian ashrams, seminars, and courses costing thousands of dollars. I have been to such an ashram. I have taken those courses and attended those seminars. Many of the precepts of Directed Thinking I discovered by trial and error as I struggled to put general theory into specific practice. Some of the most powerful exercises I simply stumbled over and bumped into by accident as I was groping about in the dark trying to save myself. I was not a natural-born philosopher; I learned by terror.

The process of Directed Thinking requires no belief system. It requires dropping a belief, the one that tells us we are the helpless victim of our moods and our feelings. Once I discarded this useless idea, I was able to apply simple but powerful principles and techniques to my life with immediate results. The idea was not to become some glazed-eyed Pollyanna, but simply to avoid the paralyzing pessimism that kept me from living my life.

The first task was to dispel two widely accepted myths. One: It is simply not true that we have to think any thought that happens to bubble up in our mind. Two: It is simply not true that some of our feelings may be so strong that we are compelled to act them out just because they "chemical up" in our brain. Not only is it not *necessary* to live this way, it is not *appropriate* to live this way. Depression may indeed be a slippery slope, but I found I could install handrails and footholds, even automatic step-in elevators.

The age-old principle that was crucial in helping me dispel those two deeply rooted myths is this: The continual refusal to see the unreal ("we are helpless") is the necessary condition for seeing the real ("we are self-responsible"). This principle is embodied in the parable of the rope and the snake: Walking up the stairs of his back porch at night a man is frightened by the sudden appearance of a snake coiled on the step ahead. He jumps back in horror and alarm; but suddenly someone lights a lamp, and he laughs to see the "snake" is only an old rope. The continual refusal to see the snake is the necessary condition for seeing the rope. Focusing on the "snake" is called anxiety.

Living in a continual state of anxiety is the easiest thing in the world. We don't have to exert ourselves in any way. We just collapse into anxiety and let it take us, mindless and weak-willed, wherever it is going. We can run away from the "snake" in fear and calm our nerves by picking up any one of hundreds of different addictions or medications to distract us or deaden our body so it doesn't feel the fear. We can play the Ain't It Awful game and find a group of "snake" survivors so we can tell everybody about our horrible snake experience and listen to the stories about their snakes.[1]

Or we can light the lamp of our own awareness and "be a light unto ourselves." We can turn on our awareness when we remember where the switch is. The switch is in our earnest desire to know what is. Most of our anxiety is very shallow because it is the fear of what isn't, an illusion, like the rope "snake." So what is reality then? Reality is a pure act of attention to what is at hand. What *seems* like a snake may be a rope, but we will not *know* that it is a rope unless we refuse to succumb to our fear that it is a snake. We should question all behavior based upon the idea that the rope is a snake. We should question depression.

When we are overcome by depression, there are concepts, thought processes, and small mind-tricks that can get us out of the worst of it without dulling our mind and personality with drugs. These concepts are not just for the low-grade blues and sadness that dry us up and render us temporarily purposeless and stale on life. They are equally effective with the sudden onset of what I call the "great chemical dump" that suddenly wrests our mind from the security of its normal moorings and pitches us headlong into the timeless dark and lifeless void of depression.

We do not have to stay there! As the old Chinese proverb reminds us: we cannot prevent the birds of sadness from flying over our heads but we must not let them build a nest in our hair. We can learn to distinguish between impulse and volition, between feelings and principles, so that our fear remains a necessary wake-up call, which ends in some chosen action instead of ending *in itself,* the condition of self-terror we call depression.

The American Psychiatric Association puts both depression and manic depression (now called "bipolar disorder") in the category of "mood disorders" in the *Diagnostic and Statistical Manual of Mental Disorders*, the diagnosis "Bible," although they separate them into two distinct diagnoses (unipolar depression and bipolar disorder) within that one classification (mood disorders).[2] However, there is no difference in the symptoms of depression between depressives and manic-depressives.

We are much more familiar with the different garden varieties and gradations of depression than with the varieties and gradations of mania, although such gradations of mania are also classified in the diagnostic "manual." The reason they are classified is not because people seek help for them, but because these symptoms of mania so often show up in people seeking help for depression. Manic depression is only *quantitatively* different, not *qualitatively* different, from unipolar depression.

We do not generally seek help for less severe mania because it is not painful for the person who has it. As a matter of fact, just the opposite. A little mania feels quite wonderful. But low-key mania is no more healthy for us than low-key depression. And low-key mania is plenty painful for the people around us who bear the brunt of it. With low-key depression we are very sensitive to our own feelings, we are self-critical and unaccepting of ourselves, we don't think we are important or worthwhile, and we worry about things we didn't even do. When we are suffering from low-key mania we are very insensitive to the people around us, blame them for our problems, yell at them, criticize them, and think *they* are unimportant.

The general public is much more aware of depression than mania because we are more than willing to buy drugs to lessen the pain of even a little depression for ourselves, and the pharmaceutical companies who know this are bombarding us with ad campaigns and infomercials about every little nuance of anxiety and depression, with a different pill for each nuance.

Pharmaceutical companies are not interested in run-of-the-mill mania because no one is going to buy a pill for that. We generally do not recognize our own mania while it is in progress because it is never painful for us in the way that depression is. There is a great unrecognized problem with mania that is causing a great deal of violence and alienation in our society. But it may be that events like the 1999 shooting at Columbine High School will sooner or later call attention to long-overlooked mania. Directed Thinking also works for mania.

What is Directed Thinking exactly? And how does it work for depression? Directed Thinking is a combination of awareness, understandings, formula thinking, and mind tricks applied to depression; my own and others'. I kept and enlarged upon what worked and discarded what did not work. Directed Thinking is not based upon Freud's psychological model of the unconscious mind; it is based upon the neurosurgeons' mapping of the physical brain.

The tenet of philosophy upon which Directed Thinking is based is this: As human beings we are not forced to function from instinct; we may choose to function from reason—freedom of the will. But here is the really important point. This is not just an ancient philosophical concept, neuroscience shows us how freedom of the will works physically, in the brain.

Neuroscience tells us that the higher mind, which is responsible for our reason, language, and other rational cognitive faculties, is located *in a different part of our brain* from our primal mind, which is the seat of our instincts, irrational impulses, feelings, and emotions, such as excitement, fear, anxiety, and depression. Further, neuroscience has demonstrated that as an electrode can stimulate a part of the brain and elicit a thought, so also can a particular thought elicit neural activity in a particular part of the brain.

Part of the development of Directed Thinking was to determine which particular thoughts activate more intense neural activity in the area of the upper brain, which contains reason, language, and creativity (but not depression). Once increased neural activity is stimulated in the upper brain, as a natural result there will be less of the painful neural activity (depression) in the lower brain. Just like any other machine, our brain comes with a finite amount of "horsepower."

The physiological capacity for depression lies in only *one* part of our *two-part* mind, the primal mind, from where emanate our instincts and automatic defense mechanisms of pain and fear. This lower-brain primal mind was the first to evolve and it is responsible for maintaining the sympathetic mode, known as the fight-or-flight response; wherein the body is tight, anxious, and ready for action. From the upper-brain higher mind we produce reason, language, and creativity. It developed later in the evolutionary time scale and can be used to initiate activity that will direct the body back from a sense of urgency into the parasympathetic mode, the more relaxed mode where we are no longer anxious and therefore available for more laid-back, slower-paced activity and tissue repair.

If we are depressed we are functioning from instinct, from our lower-brain primal mind. We believe that we are a prisoner of depression and are helpless to come out of it. We forget we have a choice, that we can function from reason, *from our upper-brain higher mind*, which is in a different part of the brain and which does not contain depression.

Depression is essentially the quality of being stuck in the sympathetic mode and situated, neural-activity-wise, in the primal mind of the lower brain. Happiness, in the sense of infinite okayness, is the quality of being stabilized in the parasympathetic mode and not cemented, neural-activity-wise, in the lower brain.

Directed Thinking is the process by which, as an act of will, we choose particular and specific thoughts to switch the focus of our attention—and thus mind functioning—from our lower-brain primal mind to the upper-brain higher mind. In this way we can escape the painful and traumatic *feelings* of depression, which are caused by the temporary chemical imbalance of the fight-or-flight response, while at the same time allowing this chemical imbalance to right itself through the homeostasis brought about by new thoughts and new actions; without the necessity of introducing outside chemicals.

We always have the choice of which part of our two-part mind to use. However, we may have to learn how to exercise that choice. I found it helpful to remember that it is *easier* to remain depressed and focused in the primal mind and *harder* to direct my thinking to the higher mind. This seems like a very small point to make but I have found it generally true that when I acknowledge that something is "not easy" I seem to get about it with a better attitude. Perhaps acknowledging that something is difficult somehow calls up the will to do it.

For example, last month I decided to lose some weight and committed myself to drinking eight glasses of water every day. At first, when I would think it was about time for another glass but I would be in the middle of some chore, I would put off getting a glass of water with the thought that it was an "easy enough thing to do" and I could always "catch it later."

After several days I realized that "later" usually turned out to be "not." By evening I had only drunk two or three glasses of water. I changed my mind and decided that it is *hard* to drink eight glasses of water a day. Now when I think it is about time for my next glass and I don't feel like it right now because I'm doing something else I say to myself, "It's *hard* to drink eight glasses of water a day so you better do it RIGHT NOW." I realized that what is easy about drinking eight glasses of water a day is *not doing it*.

I call this "The Myth of Easy": how simple things like drinking eight glasses of water, diets, and exercise, for the very fact of being thought "easy," are therefore almost impossible to accomplish because we don't call up the earnest determination that guards us from the don't-feel-like-it primal-mind temptations away from higher-mind goals. My son's bedroom is always messy because he thinks it's easy to keep it clean. My bedroom is always neat as a pin because I know how hard it is to keep things picked up.

To make the switch out of depression is also deceptively simple, like drinking eight glasses of water a day. The danger lies in the very perception that these techniques might be thought easy. So Directed Thinking involves technique, mind tricks, and most important of all, the commitment to name and do the "harder thing." Depression is a place in the brain we get to. We do not have to stay there. We do not have to "kill" depression. We can simply withdraw from it to a level of mind at which it does not "operate." It is a matter of choice.

The further difficulty with depression, of course, is that the feelings are so overwhelming that we can get lost in them before we know it. Therefore, to take any action at all in the face of such a painful, paralyzing, fearful thing, we must be prepared, *in advance*, with knowledge and technique. And we must make use of some abiding principle or imperative.

But it is important to understand "principle" not just in the traditional sense of ideas, as in religion and philosophy. We must understand principle in the sense of *physical and psychological survival*, as in anthropology, sociology, neuroscience. We must have on our side something as strong as our brain chemistry in order to move successfully against it. To be fully effective this force must also have a reference to some common ground that connects us with the rest of humanity. The main problem with depression is that we lose a necessary sense of our reciprocal moral obligation to others while we're in it. There is no force stronger than moral obligation, which is our commitment to a combination of belief, imagination, and moral imperative.

Let me illustrate the idea of moral imperative by my first firewalk, that mainstay of traveling hypnotists and motivational gurus. It was in the summer of 1996. The fire had been built and raging for an hour or so. The facilitator declared that the temperature in the coals, now spread out in a glowing bed ten feet by thirty-five feet, was about 1200 degrees and therefore ready.

The facilitator offered the customary firewalk warnings and instructions as we all signed waivers absolving him of all responsibility in case of burns or other injury. He further told us that it often helps to make the walk in the name of something really important to us and suggested that we walk across in the name of world peace.

I was tenth in line and the first one, so far, who had not ever "walked before." Those in front of me went the course with some dispatch. Suddenly it was my turn. I hesitated, my knees weak as Jell-O. The drums continued to beat a steady rhythm. Nobody hurried or hassled me. The person behind me seemed to be in no great haste either. I searched myself for something to screw up my courage. World peace? Nope, that was not going to work. Stopping world hunger? Nice, but it's not going to get me across those glowing red coals!

For what *would* I give my all, my life? For this is finally what courage comes down to every single time, doesn't it— total commitment to some moral imperative? At the risk of your very life! Would I walk across those coals for wealth? Fame? Perfect Health? Enlightenment? My family? That's it, I thought. I would give my life and brave hell itself to keep my family safe, and without hesitation I proceeded across the coals in the name of, in the absolute love of my family—with nary a burn.

My fear that I might miss an opportunity, albeit a symbolic one, to do something that might keep some member of my family safe was greater than my fear of walking over the coals. Getting out of depression is like walking across burning coals, simple but very difficult unless you know the technique and can call upon some moral principle.

No, I am *not* saying that to cure depression we have to be able to walk across burning coals. I myself would not know how to help anyone else do that, though hundreds of thousands of people, including children, have been taught the simple hyp-nosis techniques of the firewalk.[3] The power of the fire is great. The power of the mind is greater.

This is the whole point of the firewalk—the limitless power of the human mind. My mind. Your mind. The power of our mind is already within us. That is why depression seems so overwhelming. The lesson of the firewalk is this: The great power of our mind can work *for* us or *against* us. That great power can mire us in terrible, painful depression, or we can learn to *direct* that same power of mind that is now agonizing us to help us avoid depression. We can do it even though psychologists and psychiatrists tell us that we cannot.

Psychologists tell us that depressed people have a short attention span and can't concentrate as well as "normal people." I found this to be a myth that disappeared when a wise person suggested to me that I didn't have to believe it if I didn't want to. If our attention span is so short, how come our depression is so long? The answer is that we unknowingly concentrate on our depression. We are actually causing what seems to be happening to us. We can learn to stop doing that.

When we get hunger pangs we don't panic. We go into the kitchen and choose between the Wheaties and the chocolate-chip cookies. Depression pangs are caused by the concentration upon thoughts that we are in pain. Why choose these thoughts when we can choose other thoughts? But, you will insist, the pain is caused by the chemical imbalance in our brain and we are forced to think these thoughts because the pain is too great to ignore. And my response is this: Jerome Kagan, a professor of psychology from Harvard University says, "no single biological state *by itself* can define pleasure or pain because we have to make a judgment about our feelings before we can experience them."[4]

The biochemically based feeling of fear that makes facing the knife of a mugger so desperate and traumatic is the exact same feeling of fear, physiologically speaking, that makes a roller coaster or a bungee jump so exciting and fun. In the absence of any other clues to the contrary, someone can plunge our hand into a bucket of ice cold water, tell us it is boiling hot, and we will feel like our hand is burning and pull it out in pain. Someone's leg can be amputated and the person will still feel pain where the leg used to be. Someone can be paralyzed and *think* they are moving a hand, which, to any other onlooker, remains absolutely motionless. So much for the mind's connection with objective reality![5]

Neuroscientist V. S. Ramachandran, with his groundbreaking book *Phantoms in the Brain*, shows "how the brain is continuously updating its model of reality in response to novel sensory inputs." The brain's connections are extraordinarily labile and dynamic, says Ramachandran. "Perceptions emerge as a result of reverberations of signals between different levels of the sensory hierarchy, indeed even across different senses. The fact that visual input can eliminate the spasm of a nonexistent arm and then erase the associated memory of pain vividly illustrates how extensive and profound these interactions can be."[6] Evidently we do not speak to ourselves without an answer but we may not hear it.

The fact that a judgment has to be made about our feelings *before* we can experience them seems to be borne out by Ramachandran's research with phantom limbs. This principle is the basis for medical hypnosis in open heart surgery. The patient is concentrating upon the thought, I am fine and feeling comfortable. He could just as well be thinking: My God! They are cutting into me. The PAIN! The PAIN!

The reason that both medical hypnosis and Directed Thinking works is because we can only think one thought at a time and we can choose any thought we want. This is also the basis for the mantra in transcendental meditation. Thoughts are as available to us as the air we breathe and they are a matter of our choice. We can choose the thoughts that access the part of the brain from which we want to function—the primal mind of instincts, feelings, and depression, or the higher mind of reason, cognitive faculties, and creativity, where there is no pain or depression. Thinking is like breathing in another respect. We can both breathe and think *on purpose*, by conscious choice; or we can cease to bother about our breathing or our thinking, and both will simply continue *autonomically*, on their own.

Thoughts are generated in two ways, chosen or unchosen. And different thoughts access different parts of our brain. If a man sees a shadow on the ground and thinks SNAKE he's going to access a particular part of the brain. If he looks at a *Playboy* centerfold and thinks BREAST he's going to access another part of the brain. Why don't we choose the thoughts that access the part of the brain that does not contain depression, thus restoring our lost equanimity? Because we have not learned how to do it.

We have learned, instead, to succumb to depression and wallow around in the lower primal mind. It is accidental learning brought about by following the easy path of least resistance; by choosing the negative of inaction rather than the harder, positive, active choice—to do something. To refuse to choose is a choice in itself, albeit a negative one. And to refuse to choose causes us to believe that we have no choice.

But whatever we have learned we can unlearn. Yes, depression is a chemically based automatic reaction; this need not frighten us. If we think the thought "lemon" we will also cause a chemically based automatic reaction called salivation. We do not have to cut out our tongue, or take Prozac to keep from salivating. We can simply stop thinking the thought "lemon." The way we stop thinking the thought "lemon" is to think some other thought. Thoughts cause the chemistry of salivation and thoughts can uncause it. Thoughts cause the chemistry of depression and thoughts can uncause it.

The reason depression always ends is that unchosen thoughts will progress on their own, little by little, hit or miss, into a line of thinking based upon learned associations that will result in a shift of neural activity, sooner or later, neuron by neuron, from the lower-brain primal mind to the upper-brain higher mind. Then, at that point, activity and thinking based upon higher mind reasoning can result in different thoughts causing different chemistry, and the primal mind, therefore, may go from fearful to more positive feelings.

The advantage of Directed Thinking over random thinking is that we can make the switch from lower-brain primal mind to upper-brain higher mind almost immediately, any time we want, just by repeatedly choosing our own thoughts. Also, we can directly access particular principles rather than allowing the *arbitrary* access of principles, which may have a closer connection than necessary (by learned association) to primal-mind fear.

We can override negative thoughts and frightening shadows any time we wish, *even if we don't know what they are*, by consciously choosing positive or neutral thoughts as soon as we notice we are feeling bad. Stressful and anxious thoughts will not be able to accomplish themselves at our expense.

It's not that we access the higher mind so that it can control the lower mind. What happens is that as long as our attention is engaging the higher mind, our attention will necessarily disengage from the lower mind simply because of that concentration. *We have only one attention.* If it is focused on "Row, Row, Row Your Boat," it can't be focused on "I'm so depressed."

Using a mantra or phrase, even a nursery rhyme, and repeating it over and over breaks the preoccupation with the feelings going on in the lower brain because more neural activity starts concentrating in the upper brain. Many of my patients use a to-do list, which they write in the evening and put on their bedside table. The list commits them to some simple structured activity that they follow when they wake up in the morning, no matter how bad they feel.

Any physical activity works—jogging or doing small chores. Don't dismiss these seemingly simplistic solutions. Nursery rhymes and small chores seem ridiculously inconsequential but, you will be surprised when you first try them, they are not so easy to implement. Singing a nursery rhyme per se is a very simple thing. But singing a nursery rhyme *instead* of concentrating on our depression is very hard at first. Any of these small mind tricks are hard at first, *but they all work*. They are all doable. The only thing that doesn't work is the easy thing, doing nothing.

There is another aspect to Directed Thinking that involves more than just the switch from the lower-brain primal mind to the upper-brain higher mind, which brings the resultant fairly immediate relief from depression. Directed Thinking depends on a *deliberately* educated, rather than an *accidentally* educated, higher mind.

Directed Thinking depends upon chosen principles, rather than feelings, to fund behavior. It does not do us much good to make the switch out of the painful depression of our primal mind if all we have waiting for us in our higher mind is a well-thought-out plan to get a gun and shoot up the local schoolyard or a scheme to attract attention by appearing nude at our next-door neighbor's hot-tub party.

This narcissistic, antisocial behavior is based upon principles also, but these kinds of principles will not empower us, they will ultimately throw us back into the primal mind with renewed and even more painful feelings of impotence, guilt, shame, fear, and rejection because these principles have no healthy common-ground connection with society. These principles are based upon *feeling* good rather than *doing* good (and therefore doing well).

The anthropological contribution to Directed Thinking is the evolutionary principle of survival of the fittest. The "fittest" human being is the one who learns how to get along well with, and therefore gets reciprocal support from, the society in which he lives. Marcus Aurelius said it this way: "That which is not in the interest of the hive cannot be in the interest of the bee."

Depression is not a mental-health crisis, it is a behavioral crisis brought about because psychology and medicine, unduly influenced by pharmaceutical companies, are mainly disconnected from other important disciplines. This was brought home to me again recently when I attended an all-day seminar on panic disorders sponsored by the Anxiety Disorders Association of America (funded by a grant from Pfizer). During this eight-hour series of lectures and comments by a succession of psychiatrists and therapists who were helping their patients overcome agonizing fears and stultifying behaviors, depression among them, I never once heard the word *courage*.

This is the downside of modern psychology. Psychology will not be able to help us with our depression or manic depression if it does not reconnect itself with ideals like courage, honor, integrity, moral authority, moral principle, and moral judgment, which are all *relational* principles that keep us safely connected with our fellows. We can successfully manage our depression by maintaining our reciprocal connection with people, and our reciprocal moral obligation to them; with the result that we do not become "lost" within ourselves in a never-ending, unremitting sense of isolation.

But we seem so afraid these days of the words "moral" or "sin," as if these relational words belong solely to the discipline of religion. When the last brick of the last church has crumbled into dust on this planet, as long as two human beings still remain (or maybe even two monkeys, according to some anthropologists), they will still be able to sin against each other, or relate to one another based upon some common-ground imperative.[7]

Since I am a psychotherapist, my family members are not above coming to me for free counseling even though I have told everyone that I am not the family counselor, I am the family grandmother. I had one such recent anxious petitioner who told me he feared he was having a mental breakdown and could I please get him into some kind of counseling because he thought he might be losing his mind. (In a psychologized society we all start thinking "mental illness" when we are overwhelmed because it's *easier* than getting to work to overcome our weaknesses.)

When John said that his upset was caused by a totally harmless but totally outrageous and weird lie he told another family member that had gotten way out of hand and caught up with him, I told him that he wasn't losing his mind and he didn't need any counseling. I told him that he had simply done something wrong. He needed to fess up, apologize, make amends, and be more responsible to direct his thinking so he wouldn't succumb to temptation and lie again, and take the easy way out, since he now knew he was vulnerable to it.

John said he lied because he just wanted to look better than he was. We all have that problem. There isn't one among us who hasn't told a stupid and weird lie at some point in our lives to make ourselves look better. Psychological counseling is not going to help us. Self-esteem is not going to help us; failure is. The highest self-esteem in the world will never measure up to the strength of character gained by braving the righteous scorn of our fellows with nothing but our own pitiful truth in our hand. This is what the word "moral" means.

I wish I had understood this when I was young. I wish I had known something of Directed Thinking. I certainly knew plenty about depression. Coming out of depression was always like coming back from the dead for me.

The syndrome was always the same: I am happy. Then, for no apparent reason, my heart sinks as a wave of the most agonizing gloom washes all the good feelings right out of me. At the first warning fibrils of despair, my okayness wilts like paper in the rain. Then I begin to leak away. I hang on as long as I can. But I will soon go, all of me; slow at first; then a free fall into the painful, dead nothingness that folds me into itself.

There were probably only four or five days in my whole first year at college that I wasn't depressed, hog-tied by my unhappiness during the day, at night my sleepless anguish tormented by the *brrong-brrong-brrong* of the library clock tolling every cheerless hour until dawn. My boyfriend and I decided we would date other people while I was living away from home. I wasn't used to being alone, I was always in a panic. I began to think that there was something terribly wrong with me, something that hinted of shame, something defective, not normal. And I couldn't let anybody find out.

There is one scene I often think back upon. One Saturday while in college, like a walking zombie, I had begrudgingly searched out the prop room behind the theater to join other freshmen who had been frantically conscripted to finish some costumes in time for the Christmas play. My Great Pain was with me, as usual, carefully disguised in bright red lipstick and a soft blue sweater. I, who was so aching to be popular, had failed to make the choir, failed to be nominated for any class office, and failed to have a date for the weekend.

Total ignominy, I thought. Look at me now. Me, who dated one of the most popular boys in high school, who was vice president of my senior class, who won a scholarship to college, and now this is how low I've sunk, sitting here on the floor in a circle of "losers" making ridiculous costumes. A friendly hand passes me a six-foot-long mouse tail made out of gray cloth. I am supposed to stuff this with cotton batting! Are they serious? I force my death mask to flash a fake smile as I think to myself, if this is supposed to make me feel better, it is not working! I look for the first opportunity to escape and rush back to rebury my pain in my room.

Oh, ye gods that be, could I have just that one day back! In my ignorance, I didn't know that it was perfect, and that I was fine the way I was; with the sunshine streaming in the windows to warm the old oak floors we sat on; and the pleasant Christmas music and chatty girls I ignored in my misery. At that stately Victorian campus, instead of languishing in despair, I could have hiked the nearby mountains, read any book, taken up the guitar, studied the stars, made any friend, visited with any wise professor, been happy. Why didn't I? What prevented me?

Depression prevented me. The same depression that now prevents millions of people from leading their own exciting and wonderful lives. I don't really want to re-do that day in the theater prop room; it is precious to me just the way it is. Because I like where I am now, I also treasure all the roads it took to get me here. And that old familiar pain that stunted and blighted my early life no longer has power over me.

Because of the extraordinary breakthrough with my own depression and the help I have been able to give others, I have been urged to put some of my insights and techniques down on paper, to "tell the real truth" about depression—that there are certain habits of mind that cause all the trouble, and we can change those habits and discover the perfectly all-right person trapped inside the frozen agony.

In this sense we are all like Michelangelo's statue of David, of whom the artist said, "David was already there, perfectly formed in the marble. All I had to do was chip away everything that was not David." The answer to depression is to chip away everything that is *not us!* Our mind and our persona are not us. Neither are they our prison nor our executioner. *They are our responsibilities.*

This book is part theory and part a memoir of my journey to an understanding of the relationship between the self and the mind, and the difference between living according to feelings and living according to principles. I invite you to go along with me and learn what I have learned; and witness the changes this learning wrought in my life. Sometimes you will come across a new idea, as I did; and you will be able to apply it to your life immediately, as if it were the long-sought missing piece to the jigsaw puzzle of your own search. Sometimes you will struggle with a new concept that is unclear to you, as I did; before something else in a later chapter will suddenly "bring it home."

It will take time. The most critical insights are so subtle and seemingly insignificant that at first they can just slip right through our fingers. Our greatest obstacles to truth are the particular concepts cemented into our minds by decades of use. These concepts are both the windows and the security from which we view our world. We normally don't feel the need to break down the walls for a clearer look. But it is these very concepts that get us into trouble because they cause us to not see things that ultimately make our walls come tumbling down.

This need not be the end. The secret to our strength lies in owning our weakness; for only in this state of humility will we be soft, fertile ground for the seeds of understanding to take root. I learned, finally, that the quality of my life depends not upon its *activity* but its *directivity*. I learned that the lower road of primal-mind feelings is always easy, and to choose the upper road of higher-mind principles is always hard, but doable. I learned to keep my feet firmly planted on common ground and not lose the connection with my fellows that protects me from painful self-absorption.

By constantly reminding ourselves of some basic principles, our lives can be filled with the things we care deeply about, instead of the things we fear most. We will need courage to go forward in the face of our depression and our anxiety, but this has always been so. It may be that our whole existence is nothing more than a cosmic firewalk.

Three

ALL IN THE FAMILY

My little ones asked me why I looked so mad all the time. "I'm not mad," I would reassure them. "What makes you think I'm mad?" I guess to a child, sad and mad look very much the same. There may be some wisdom in that.

I was always a ticking time bomb of depression that could go off at any moment. Even on a day like this. It had snowed a rare eighteen inches in Washington, D.C., and I love the snow. The first few flakes of any snowstorm fall directly into my heart. My husband and I are spending the weekend with another couple, our best friends. Between us we have a gaggle of preteens who are busy building a snow fort outside, while we four adults are toasting our toes in front of a cheery fire, chatting cozily.

The snow is still sifting down from a billowy gray sky that looks like it was painted long ago on Chinese silk. A beautiful day. A perfect day. My husband throws back his head and laughs at his buddy's joke. I too am smiling broadly. Then the smile slides off of my face as I feel my inner self suddenly give that downward jerk. In a nanosecond everything good is gone. I am submerging into that empty pain, sinking helplessly into myself, going further and further away from everybody. Faster and faster I am sucked into that alternate universe of agonizing, utter loneliness called depression. They don't notice. They are laughing and passing me the cheese and crackers and they don't know I am no longer here. I have gone to misery.

I spent many years in depression. I have a lot of company. Recently I was counseling a woman whose thirty-two-year-old son was suffering a "major depression." She said sadly, "I tried to tell him just to get up and get going, and pull himself up by his own bootstraps. But he said, 'Mom, don't you think I would if I could? I don't *want* to feel this way. I can't help it.'"

I can remember feeling that bad. Depression periodically drew aside my regular world as if it were an imaginary curtain, leaving me the yawning pit of a lethal, brutal, solitary despair into which I was eternally falling. I had to grab for my children as I fell by them in the darkness, as they would momentarily appear like little ghosts in the distance. I would swim to them out of the undertow of black nothingness just long enough to attend to their needs, and then sink back into the paralysis of my pain.

I can remember that my father used to feel bad too—so bad he couldn't get up and go to work. "I can't help it," he would sigh in that deadlike, hollow voice I learned to dread as a child. Both my father and my brother were diagnosed with manic depression. At the age of thirty-four I too finally sought help from a psychiatrist and had my own diagnosis of manic depression, which, for many years, I refused to accept. I didn't want to believe such character traits were hereditary because my family was quite odd and I had a passion to be "normal." Plus the fact that we often refuse to accept things when we don't know what to do about them.

My father's various psychiatrists gave him only temporary relief from his anguish. The public-relations firm he worked for tolerated his down times and nervous personality for years because they profited from his obvious talents when he was up. But ultimately his mood swings made him so undependable that, at the age of fifty-one, he was fired. It was the end of his career. My brothers and I were grown by then and my mother divorced him in disgust. During their weather-beaten thirty-two years together, my mother maintained a steady if not eloquent opinion on the subject of my father's depression—"more of his same old crap."

During periods of depression, my father would lie in the drawn-shade dark of his bedroom where he chain-smoked and read historical novels day and night. There was no television in those days; *we* were the center of our rooms. Late mornings my father might come downstairs to the kitchen and fix himself some coffee to the tune of heavy sighs and a soulful "Oh, my God!" or two. Evenings I would bring his food up on a tray. Feeling abandoned and frightened and missing his up-time storytelling and fun, I tiptoed around what we used to call my father's "migraines," until we learned it was manic depression.

But not my mother. When my father was depressed my mother did not tiptoe, and she never closed a door if she could possibly manage to slam it! She walked loud, very loud—a sound I learned to dread as a child. My heart froze when I'd wake at four o'clock in the morning to the heavy pound and squeak of my mother's worn tennis shoes on the old wood staircase. I knew she was mad at my father when she got up that early—every quick, overburdened step of hers a deliberate stab of criticism at his malingering.

It was only a matter of time before her high-pitched screaming would begin its reign of terror over the quiet morning. There was always something to trigger it; a missing pair of scissors, or the toy she tripped over because "nobody ever puts anything AwaYY AROUND HEEEERE;" or the laundry detergent that was all gone, or the fact that my father was driving her "CrAAAzyEEEE."

My mother never believed my father was really ill. She believed that he was a weak, immature, selfish person who just refused to get up in the morning and go to work like everybody else. In the 1940s and 1950s there wasn't any media attention or literature on manic depression and its occurrence in highly intelligent and creative people. As this connection started to be made, psychiatrists like Kay Redfield Jamison began to call manic depression the "genius disease." My brother calls it that. My mother, bless her irreverent heart, has always stuck to "crap."

By now many well-known people have come forward with stories of their depression and manic depression, including TV journalist Mike Wallace, actor Rod Steiger, and author Kathy Cronkite. Actress Patty Duke, before drug treatment, used to scream and fly into uncontrollable rages at her family. William Styron's *Darkness Visible*, the book about his depression and drug therapy, was a best-seller. Another best-seller, *An Unquiet Mind*, details psychiatrist Kay Redfield Jamison's own struggles with manic depression and her subsequent reliance upon drug therapy.

These authors and my brother similarly describe their bouts with depression as a living hell foisted upon them, out of the blue, through no fault of their own, and at odds with what would otherwise be successful, fulfilled, happy lives. I am not convinced of the *foisted upon* and *through no fault of their own* parts. The *out of the blue* and *living hell* parts I do buy, but only in the context that we all live in hell who take ourselves and our feelings too seriously, who exhibit, as C. S. Lewis describes in *The Screwtape Letters*, "the ruthless, sleepless, unsmiling concentration upon self which is the mask of Hell . . . where everyone is perpetually concerned about his own dignity and advancement."[1]

My father's living hell of depression periodically tortured him his whole life. Not that he didn't enjoy some good times. A slight, handsome man with blond hair and blue eyes, he always dressed well. He had some business success, and some years of a minor-celebrity status moonlighting as a nightclub singer in Washington, D.C. He patented an invention he hoped would make him a million—it didn't. He had a couple of affairs, and spent a great deal of time with his newspaper buddies at the Washington Press Club, where he played poker and drank until dawn. And he was fun for us children. When we were little, he made up fairy tales and sang us gentle, loving songs.

My father told us stories about Lincoln and John Wilkes Booth, the Gutenberg Bible, the discovery of mercury. He regaled us with fantasies of our future wealth as we "royalty in disguise" sat around our dinner table, which he had made by covering half the top of an old Ping-Pong table with a piece of blue linoleum. "Oh, it will be wonderful for you children," he'd fairly twinkle; as my grumbling mother cleared away the dishes as noisily as possible, muttering her disclaimers: "Meanwhile somebody has to do the work around here."

But nobody could daunt my father when he was up and onto the next can't-fail, get-rich-quick scheme. "We'll have a mansion with a guest house," he would proclaim joyfully to our delight, "a pool and tennis court, and twin yellow Cadillac convertibles side by side in the driveway. One for me"—he would pause grandly—"and one for your mother."

As we grew older, my father had fewer and fewer good moments. He missed my mother after the divorce, and once we were grown, he couldn't dream through us anymore. He would come out of one depression only to go into another. Shortly after his divorce, he married a woman who was very nice to him, much nicer than my mother had ever been. But in just a few years he began a slow but insidious slide into catatonic depression.

At first he stopped visiting friends or going to the movies. He gave up his daily walk and took no further interest in his little dog. He refused to go to the doctor and bullied my step-mother into covering for him when anyone expressed concern. He sat all day in a rocking chair. Falling further into depression, he would get out of bed only for meals. Then he ceased to change his clothes or bathe. Finally, when he refused to eat and became too weak to prevent her, my stepmother gently picked up his sixty-five-pound body in her arms and drove him to the hospital for the last time.

Meanwhile my father's ills began to be visited upon my equally talented brother, a successful journalist in New York City. He was economics editor for a well-known business weekly before he was thirty. He hobnobbed with secretaries of state and headliners like Aristotle Onassis and Alan Greenspan. He progressed to *Fortune* magazine, where he had a string of cover stories.

But my brother also began an escalation of screaming tirades at the editors who "ruined" his "brilliant work." Final deadlines became, more often than not, the signal for another major depressive episode. His career was cut short when he was fired, and despite twenty years of psychoanalysis, lithium, Ritalin, and the rest and the best of what the psychological community has to offer, he hasn't been able to work for fifteen years.

My own brain chemistry is such that I still wake up almost every morning of my life in deep despair, although it usually only lasts three or four minutes once I employ some simple mind tricks. I am seldom troubled this way by depression in the late afternoon or evening unless I take a nap. Anytime I take a nap, I am likely to wake up in the black hole. But I no longer panic and fear drowning.

Now I can float to the top and swim for shore, unafraid, regardless of the fact that I do not know how deep the water goes, nor how far away the shore might be. I know, now, that it is neither the water, nor the shore, nor my fear, but only swimming that is the present moment, and the present moment is our only reality. But for many years, and certainly as a child, I was often lost in pain and ignorance.

I spent a lot of time by myself in those days. I'd often climb a favorite elm tree in my yard, where I would sit for hours reading. Or I'd take my book across the road, down by a little stream that still runs today behind the public library built upon that very spot. The elementary school is long gone but I was delighted to find my old reading place still existed despite all the superhighways and new housing developments in the now thoroughly urbanized town of McLean, Virginia.

Where the library now stands used to be a vast field of blue forget-me-nots. For those of you who live in McLean, the house I grew up in is the old white farmhouse with the round front porch columns, directly across the street from the public library. Those columns were a bone of contention between my parents. The year we moved in my father painted the old yellow house white but ran out of paint when he had only one more column to paint. Five years later, when we sold the house, that lone yellow column was still unpainted. My mother, who is now eighty-seven, is still mad about it.

I remember my very first depression, although I didn't call it that. I didn't call it anything in the beginning because I didn't know what it was. But I soon learned to recognize the first sinking feeling that always announced the coming of "the Beast." I was twelve years old. I had experienced sadness before. I remember crying on the playground in the first grade because nobody liked me. I remember staying home sick from school as my parents went off to work and I felt lonely, empty, abandoned, homesick even though I was home. But this was different. This was not sadness. This was something else and more.

This was not just a wave of unhappiness that knocked out my joy. This was a whole ocean that sucked me into itself and ripped the very heart and soul and breath right out of me. I had never felt such terrible pain, and it marked the end of my childhood innocence as much as any rape could have done. And, like a rape, it brought with it a sense of paralyzing shame and guilt. I was afraid to tell anybody, especially my parents. I didn't want anyone to know there might be something wrong with me. That, I was sure, was something I needed to hide from everybody. The need for a good reputation is hardwired into us all, hooked to our survival instinct. To feel defective is to feel devalued and dis-entitled.

Sandy Banks, a columnist for the *Los Angeles Times,* wrote about having to tell her then-eight-year-old daughter that her father had died. Banks said that she knew her daughter would be distraught and was prepared for her to be sad, even angry and disbelieving. But the columnist said, although she fully expected the first tears, she was not prepared for her daughter's first words, which came out in great gulps of choking sobs, "I'll be the only . . . be . . . the . . . only . . . one . . . in the third grade . . . without a father."[2] We do not want to be negatively singled out, the only one left outside the norm, the shamed one; this is the ultimate horror for us all.

I wonder how my life would have been different if I had even the most rudimentary information about some of these things when I was younger. I remember how much I was helped by just a few words from my aunt. When I was twelve, shortly after the onset of my first depression, I was fortunate to have been invited to visit my mother's sister for several weeks during summer vacation when my brothers were sent off to camp. My aunt and uncle and their six-year-old son lived a totally different lifestyle from the chaos at my house. Their place was much smaller than our rambling old farmhouse, but they had nice furniture and the house was always cleaned up. Nobody screamed at you.

My aunt was home all day and had an orderly schedule: breakfast at a certain time, dinner at another, planned outings for the afternoon. My uncle was always home promptly after work, at which time he and I played croquet in the backyard until we were called to dinner. I enjoyed setting the table with dishes that matched, napkins, and pretty silver. They even had a record player—we didn't have one at our house—and I could check out records from the nearby library.

I loved being there but, even so, I got depressed. I never complained, but my aunt spoke to me one day and warned, "You'd better find something to do to cheer up and be happy. If you don't quit moping around here and playing that sad music all the time, we are going to have to send you home early. It's up to you. We'll give you one more day to change your attitude."

My aunt was very blunt and to the point, some might even say cold and unsympathetic. Certainly she was a little hard on Tchaikovsky's *Overture to Romeo and Juliet*. But it was a moment of profound learning for me. This little seed would take important root many years later. I wouldn't be in charge of my feelings for decades, but it was the first time the idea of any kind of choice was attached to my feelings.

At home nobody had ever noticed whether I was happy or sad, much less that I should display one demeanor as opposed to the other. That my aunt believed cheerfulness to be an obligation on my part was proof to me that sadness must be some kind of a personal failure. Also new was the insistence that I fix it immediately, or else.

Up to that moment I had believed that my painful sadness was an irresistible force over which I had no control. I didn't know that the reason it seemed irresistible was that I just hadn't resisted it yet. I did get myself cheerful based upon little more than blind faith that my aunt seemed to think I perfectly well could, and blind terror at the prospect of being sent home a "loser."

I did start to feel better when, as my aunt suggested, I got busy. That all-important visit to my aunt gave me a way to help keep myself more okay. I began to see that creative activity could keep that terrible down feeling more out there, hovering. It was still nearby and threatening, but now I could keep it more at bay.

I learned to embroider and knit at school and my mother taught me to sew. I made applesauce from the apple trees in our backyard as well as lemon meringue pies. I took long rides on my bicycle and sold stationery and religious pictures door-to-door that I sent away for in a magazine. I didn't have any second line of defense once depression set in, so my creativity was mostly preventive.

I read novels. I bought seeds and planted flowers in my yard. I made a writing desk out of an old hospital tilt-top tray I found in the garage and sent my poems off to local newspapers. I wrote a play for a Girl Scout community program in which I had the starring role. I auditioned for a talent contest and sang on a Washington, D.C., radio station.

I was one of those unlucky ones who suffered from depression at a time when the rest of my generation was, on the whole, quite mellow compared to today. My life used to be a roller coaster of depression-mania-depression, which got me some well-deserved put-downs as a young girl, but I didn't really understand what the problem was. And I didn't know the words "depression" and "mania" until many years later.

So I didn't get the message until way late that I was a bit of a neurotic twit thanks to wild, unchecked mood swings and the pervasive narcissism that was my main coping mechanism. I can remember the things I did to impress people. They seldom turned out well. I was always working on my image, on my attempt to keep the outside shell of me picture-perfect calm while my insides were a frightened, churning tumble of jumble.

When I was a child, doing the right thing meant *then* they will like me. I spent most of my effort trying to figure out what *they* would like. I wasn't looking to be *me*, God forbid, I was hoping to be better than that. A *somebody* doesn't try to be somebody. Only a *nobody* tries to be somebody. I looked to my "betters" for clues, but most of the ideas and phrases one picks up in passing are said just to make a point and normal people take them with a grain of salt. I always took things too far.

Even before my first depression, I displayed traits that could be called manic. I think these childhood, out-of-the-norm ways of thinking and coping were a good indication, if not an early manifestation of, the manic depression I was heading for.

It seemed to me then that life was a closed circle, and I was always trying to break in. I very much wanted to be part of the in-crowd in the fourth grade. I overheard some of the popular girls outdoing each other in terms of how much they "just hated" one particular overweight boy in our class. For Valentine's Day I made cards for everybody with a big "I love you" heart, but on the poor child's card who was in his chubby stage, I quite happily made a big black heart that said "I Hate You."

How could I do such a cruel thing? I didn't think of it as cruel. I didn't think of things as right and wrong, but whether or not they would make me look good; whether or not they would be *perceived* as right or wrong by the people I wanted to impress. That is the reason I was so agitated with second thoughts while the valentines were handed out at recess, when I observed that nobody else but me had sent a hate valentine to the "hated" boy. And while everybody else had store-bought valentines, mine were the only handmade ones. Maybe this was not such a good idea after all. What had I done?

I heard a little disturbance from a small crowd of kids near the steps where I was sitting and then I saw the boy head straight for me. I hadn't signed my name but he knew. I was sitting by myself, counting how many valentines I got. He walked up with another boy behind him, his face sweaty and red, his right hand clenched. Without a word he threw the crunched-up hate valentine in my face and walked away leaving me alone, shocked and hurt, everybody looking at me.

I had never imagined that he might get mad at me. I only thought as far as wanting the popular kids to like me. I felt betrayed by them too because I could see in an agonizing flash that they hadn't really meant what they said. I was the fool left holding the empty bag of the day. He had crunched the valentine up into a marble, like a big spitball. (I had used thin typing paper and pencils, which was all I could find at home.) It landed at my feet and I put my shoe over it. When no one was looking, I threw it away. Whew, evidence gone.

I was always getting into trouble like that. At times I was elected president or vice president of my class, but still I felt unworthy. I was always trying to prove something. It was as if there was some blueprint for knowing how to be and what to do, and everybody else but me had a copy of it. But I did have a blueprint, and I would employ it for decades, and it would never work because it was based upon my being totally self-absorbed. I had to be first, special, and right. I craved attention like a junkie. That would get me out of the dead place of the soul. I was hungry for the neon high of excitement. That would get me out of the dead place of the soul.

I guess that's why I almost killed myself doing daredevil tricks on my bike. I would pedal as fast as I could halfway down Carper's Bridge Road, popularly known as "Steep Hill," and then I would take my hands off the bars and raise my arms high over my head in the ecstasy of flying joy, my body electric with fear. I wanted that excitement of being on edge. Living flat, I could be too easily stomped on by depression. I had to keep running, and ducking, and flying, and zigzagging so depression couldn't get a clear shot.

Living on the edge has you studying all those little oddments that are balancing and dancing there along with you that nobody else notices, much less cares about. I delighted in little pieces of information that "told me things." I would put them under my psychic microscope and, as they grew and took shape under my imagination, I would offer them up like I was passing around hors d'oeuvres at a party. They had an odd flavor. Nobody liked them much, I could see that. I would add another garnish, and dash of spice, and try to pass the same stuff off again. It was all I had.

As a teenager helping with the dishes at a friend's house (in the days before automatic dishwashers) I noticed that when her mother quickly emptied the dishpan into the sink, she haphazardly let stay a small bit of dirty water as she refilled the pan with clean water. I announced, with what I felt was great philosophical insight, "MY mother would never do that! She would let all the water out first and clean the pan before refilling it."

The neighbor shot me an annoyed look and cut me off pretty quick, luckily before I got the chance to add my further sterling observation that the reason their house was so neat and mine was always a mess was due to my perfectionist mother putting off housework until she would have the time to do it right. It never occurred to me that my neighbor might not relish a philosophical discussion with a hyper thirteen-year-old about the difference between her housekeeping ability and my mother's as symbolized by the way they emptied their dishpans. I overheard both the parents and kids in this family call me "Clever Arline" behind my back. In case you had any doubt, this was not a compliment!

I'm sure I believed my course of action would lead the other children to admire me greatly. I was the quintessential know-it-all. That's why I was never shy about sharing my manic ideas, however covert I might be about my depression. That's the thing about mania—that sudden godlike, ordained feeling that you want to share with other people; to let them know however so much more clever and knowledgeable than *they* you are, and how, therefore, they should adore you.

Since the age of ten I had been trying to construct a working theory of myself, using whatever scraps happened along, trying to identify myself with "normal" or "better." My own family was a role model for chaotic and odd. My parents both worked and were gone from seven in the morning often until long after dark, leaving us children to fend for ourselves. It never occurred to me to talk about my fears to anybody.

It was around this time that I got the idea of going to church by myself. We went to church as a family only on occasional Easter Sundays, which event was always preceded by a hectic all-day-Saturday shopping spree for new clothes for everybody; a further example of my father's sporadic and bizarre attempts to veneer us with his manic expectations. He was always trying to pretend we were rich. As if the trappings of wealth could pass for it; as if you could *buy* lifestyle. After one such Sunday, I decided I wanted go to church every week. After the service I would hang around the church "elite," the minister's wife and her court, and catch whatever gossip might drift out from beneath their bobbing hats.

Church gossip always seemed more useful to me than the Episcopal liturgy, to which I thought there must be some secret initiation for the privileged, among whom I was not so bold as to count myself; although I always found the hymns inspiring. I also had books and women's magazines. There was hardly anything I couldn't use in some way or another. I was desperate to know how normal people lived.

I often overheard people at church gossiping about my family or pumping my younger brothers for information when we ran into them at the grocery store ("So I hear your father is singing in nightclubs now?"). I felt so helpless and ashamed as I watched them trick my four-year-old brother into spilling all the family guts out into the Safeway aisle ("Your mother isn't home yet?"). I was not so innocent. So in church, after the ladies were through getting what they could out of me in the courtyard, I had no trouble eavesdropping to see what I could get out of them.

I picked up trash and dirty dishes in the most effective ways.

I got positively addicted to gossip and scandal, of which there was aplenty in a small town like McLean, Virginia—with no television, and movies only four days a week at the parish hall of the church, at which time the church organist became the movie ticket taker. Downtown consisted of the elementary school, a Safeway store, a gas station, a post office, a candy store, a drugstore, a lawyer's office, and three taverns. (Yes, yes, I know what McLean, Virginia, looks like today.)

The other way I sought to educate myself was books. I practically lived in the 10-x-12-foot school library until I was twelve. Books were what kept me from being lonely and afraid. I trusted them. I did not trust people. I didn't see my teachers as advisors or counselors; they were just more school furniture to me. And the other adults around me—my family, my neighbors, even the church ladies—were quite frantic with their own lives; at least as I saw them through the eyes of those who gossiped about them. I figured we were just *all* in the dark. The difference was that I was in the dark by myself.

I knew my family was considered strange, that other people had regular furniture. Nobody else had a Ping-Pong dining table and a pile of wallboard stacked on the floor next to it to sit on instead of chairs. The wallboard was for a grandiose plan of my father's to make our sagged-wall house into a showplace. One spring weekend he actually did demolish the wall between the dining room and the living room toward this end, but he never rebuilt the gaping holes, which, from then on, were the defining feature of our interior decoration.

One December my mother grim-facedly refused to put up a Christmas tree anymore unless my father "fixed the god-damned walls first." Was this the push he needed to finally finish our "great room"? Not exactly. The day before Christmas, in what I now recognize as a classic manic episode, he hatcheted a huge mountain of pine branches from the nearby woods.

Then, to the tune of nonstop Christmas carols sung gaily to the fourth verse, as we children joined in to help, and my mother steeled herself to ignore him, my father nailed the thick branches in four-foot-wide swaths over the offending holes—up one wall, across the ceiling and down the other wall. It made the most grand and glorious indoor Christmas trellis, a baronial splendor that by the next spring had become a fire hazard we sidestepped by selling the house and moving.

I liked the idea of moving. Nobody in the new school would know about my past sins. I could pass for perfect. This uppity arrogance and need to impress is pretty typical of both teenagers and manic-depressives. The difference is that manics don't outgrow the smarty-pants phase. This narcissism seems, at first, like just a normal desire to be important to others. But wanting to be important can escalate into a veil over our whole focus on life. Self-importance is a great cannibal; it needs to be fed. If others don't feed it, it will feed on the one who calls it up.

Ultimately the need for attention and the resultant focus on self causes us to be even further alienated from our fellows. A stunt I pulled in graduate school, in my forties I'm embarrassed to say, taught me this lesson in living color.

On Halloween, feeling very high on myself, I put on a long white formal gown that belonged to my daughter, complete with her Junior Princess rhinestone tiara and a plastic magic wand, and went to my classes dressed as a fairy godmother. Nobody else wore so much as a pumpkin-colored T-shirt to commemorate the day. I'll never forget the look of pure alarm I got from my favorite professor, who studiously ignored me after he put his eyes back in. I felt "inappropriate" stamped all over me.

And I remember how much time I had spent in deciding whether or not to dress up. My tools for making such a decision were skimpy. Would this daring act show people how beautiful and unique and fun and exciting I was? Or wouldn't it? To my credit, I found I did have some tools for handling the awk-

ward and embarrassing situation I created for myself. I didn't
know yet that this was just another manic high gone wrong
since I hadn't, at this time, accepted my manic-depressive diagnosis. But what I *can* say for myself is that I decided that I
had committed a terrible gaffe, and I was going to sit right
there in front of everybody I was hoping to impress and stand
the pain of being the immature ass that we could all now see
I was. It was excruciatingly, wonderfully horrible.

The beauty of it is that I had already started to commit to
some principles that gave me a sense of empowerment, such as:
not to try in vain to change reality by wanting other than what
is; that what is happening is not as important as how we are
looking at it, or what we decide to do about it. These principles
enabled me to be more in charge of my life, to welcome the
pain of my social belly flop as a character moment. I was very
aware while it was happening that the pain I felt was some
kind of transcendence, and I threw myself willingly on the
dagger of life.

Dressing in bizarre outfits was not the only way I went on
stage. I had unconsciously been jerking my friends around for
years by forcing a patient-counselor script on them long before
I actually became a therapist, to the tune of the latest self-help
book I was reading. Succumbing to the psychologizing in these
1970s books, I was quite willing to impose upon long-term
friendships for a moment of glory in truth-telling encounter
sessions, which I would initiate, to everyone else's discomfort.

This is what happened with one couple who were visiting
houseguests, a couple who had been longtime friends of ours
from college, a couple who now don't even send my husband
and me a Christmas card anymore. I had just finished reading
Open Marriage. During the course of conversation, I made the
observation that most marriages become stale and dishonest because people don't have the courage to communicate their real
feelings.

The husband remarked that, quite to the contrary, after twenty years of marriage he was extremely happy, that he loved his wife more than when they first married, and his sex life was exciting. I turned to his wife and challenged her to admit, in the name of honest communication versus a "typical" phony relationship, that she didn't feel the same way about sex. "Well," she hesitated, rather embarrassed, "I guess if I have to be truthful about it, I would have to say I can take it or leave it."

It was about this same time, in my mid-thirties, that I began to have some serious problems with depression just like my brother and father. I too began staying in bed for days at a time, with the blinds drawn. I blamed the weather, my husband, my just-a-housewife life. Influenced by both my mother's attitude and my father's and brother's apparent lack of success with the accepted therapy for manic depression, I was wary of medication for my own mood swings. I refused to take any drugs. Instead, for many years I chose the path of denial. As you may imagine, this was not greatly successful either.

I was depressed most of the time. I carried my pain heavily, like a pregnant woman, but I was not growing life. Every cell of my body was diminished by the *thing* I carried within me. I hid it from everybody pretty well I thought. I managed to keep the house presentable. I waxed the oak floors and vacuumed the Oriental rugs. I got my children off to school. Then I could sometimes spend the whole day, until the children came home, suspended in the painful extremis of a surreal gray murkiness into which I would unfocus myself and dissolve into the time spent and another day somehow got through.

I would either crawl back into bed and pull the covers over my head or lie face down and flat on the floor *under* my bed as if I somehow could just sink down and disappear my painful self into some coffin of earthly release. I remember the first time I got under the bed. It was almost like I was choosing a theater set upon which I wanted my statement of despair to be as dramatic as possible, and lying under the covers, all of a sudden, just wasn't enough.

Sometimes I would curl up behind the clothes hanging in my closet like the tragic little mermaid in Hans Christian Andersen's fairy tale, a nude, silent, weeping statue. I guess for many years I was a "closet" depressive. Only my husband and children knew. Though even they didn't know the full extent of it because I generally felt less panicky and desperate in the evening when they were home. I did not believe that I did anything to cause my situation, and I did not believe I could do anything to help it.

My husband coped with an unhappy wife by concentrating on his career, his business friends, and his drinking buddies. My little ones asked me why I looked so mad all the time. "I'm not mad," I would reassure them. "What makes you think I'm mad?" I guess to a child, sad and mad look very much the same. There may be some wisdom in that.

There is a kind of sadness that occurs when we have committed a wrong we deeply regret, a sadness over a loss that we have suffered but have accepted. There is a soft, beautiful, peaceful quality about that kind of sadness. This was not my sadness. I remember checking myself out in the mirror once when my children said I looked mad, and I was shocked to find they were right. I was positively glowering.

There was nothing tranquil about *my* sadness. *My* sadness consisted of eating myself up with chronic anxiety because I wasn't happy. I felt trapped. Denied. There was some vague longing for rescue, or was it coronation that would allow me at last to be "recognized" by one and all as the very special and wonderful "real me" I was sure I was *supposed* to be— if only...? I despaired of life passing me by; I was angry about talents wasted. I felt bereft of some other life I better deserved and should have instead. God knows, I certainly deserved a better husband than the one I had got stuck with.

Somehow I always felt prevented. Of course, in reality, I was the perpetrator of my life, not the victim of it. That was the clue to the effect my sadness had on my family. A victim is always on the lookout, albeit unknowingly, for someone to *blame*. So my husband also experienced my pain as anger toward him. There is definitely something to be learned from the fact that at the same time I was feeling the most helpless and vulnerable victim to myself, I appeared hostile and aggressive to my family.

In my arrogance, I must have been thinking that the members of my family were some kind of indestructible Roman columns that by rights were supposed to support my self-esteem no matter how I might push or rail against them. In those days I couldn't see my family as the gift of some kind of divine grace, the butterfly-fragile consignments to my continuing care and responsibility. I saw only myself as being fragile.

Depression, once I learned its name, served as a very convenient catchall for the whole mess of whatever confusion and terribleness was going on in my life. And since I didn't know anything to do about my depression except to suffer it grossly, I didn't do anything substantial about my life's real problems either. Although I didn't seem to mind dumping it all over my family, I tried to hide my depression from anybody else so that it wouldn't hurt my image.

On one level I was afraid of being *thought* crazy. But on a deeper level, I was terrified that I might really *be* crazy or *go* crazy; that the difference between me and the empty-eyed souls in St. Elizabeth's Mental Hospital might be only the ticking of some clock of fate that had not yet struck the hour of my doom.

At first I both feared and venerated psychiatrists because they *knew*! They alone had the power to stamp a CERTIFIED SANE on my forehead if only I could prove myself to them. But at the same time I had a terror of being found out by them too. Suppose I was unknowingly guilty of some shameful horror that would somehow come out? The monster hiding in my brain might suddenly reveal itself and blow my cover.

Now I realize that all these fears are simply the ordinary paranoia strategies of the primal mind. Now I realize that sane and insane are not something that we are or aren't. Sane and insane are modes of behavior that we *use* or *don't use*. We can become habituated to one mode or the other, but both modes, in the form of choice, are simultaneously available to us at all times. In my early years I didn't know that. I thought my real self was some kind of a crime I needed to hide from everybody.

My mania passed for eccentricity and cleverness and was often a social attribute because I was such a high risk taker. I was always shocking people with my controversial ideas and offbeat solutions to problems. I had some credibility even with my more emotionally stable husband because some of my crazy ideas actually succeeded. He has always thought of me as a can-do kind of person in a crisis, the one who says confidently, "This will work!"

When the toilet floods or the water heater goes out, he yells for me. There is hardly anything I can't repair temporarily with a hammer, duct tape, Elmer's glue, wire, or solder. Mainly, I think, because I believe I can do it. There is a little mantra I use when I get stumped. I say to myself, "I know it is humanly possible to fix this so I must, somehow, be able to do it."

Too bad I didn't have the same I-can-fix-it attitude about depression when I was younger. I understand, now, that it is possible to save myself from depression because I have done it, over and over again for years. I can see, now, that I didn't have to live half my life at the mercy of wild mood swings that propelled me from the depths of despair, when I spent whole days on the floor of my bedroom closet in the fetal position, to heady heights of godlike euphoria, which burned themselves out in wild shopping sprees for expensive clothes I never wore. I believed I was the victim of depression. I did not understand that I was really the victim of my ignorance about depression.

I was equally ignorant about mania and it caused a great deal of trouble with my relationships. The problem with the person who is in the grip of self-importance caused by manic ecstasy is that they are continually alienated because they relegate all the people in their life to a supporting role. And it is how well the other people play this supporting role that is always under scrutiny, not the mania.

It is very hard for those of us who get stuck in me-me-me, either the manic Great Me or the depressive Poor Me, to get out of it. The reason it is hard to get out of Great Me is that we don't think we are being selfish, rude, and bizarre; we think we are being independent, honest, and unique. We don't think we are being critical, unloving, and cold. We think our significant others are boring or inadequate, and therefore not good enough for us. Although we can see clearly the folly of such thinking as it occurs in other people's lives, it is almost impossible to see in our own. We can always "yes, but" our own situation as being unusual and different.

The reason it is so hard to get out of Poor Me is that we don't think we are being defensive; we think people have short-changed us. We don't think we are demanding; we think people don't give us our fair share. When we are really lost in hopelessness we don't think we are slothful and resistant; we think life is futile, so we dive into another depression. There is just no easy way to see ourselves objectively. It is more painful to see ourselves than whatever trouble we make to *avoid* seeing ourselves. But learning to see ourselves objectively by studying the constructs of victimhood, fear, habit, blame, or wonderfulness by which we may question ourselves is a necessary component of Directed Thinking. For people who will not question themselves and their thinking, nothing can be done.

Great Me and Poor Me are manic-depressive, mood-exaggerated self-constructs that die hard. Besides the above-mentioned psychological rationalizations ("I've been shortchanged," "I can't help it") that keep us in our narcissistic coping mode, there are neuroscientific reasons that make it hard to get out of narcissism or, for that matter, any other defense mechanism. As I learned from my hypnosis studies, the mind and its defense mechanisms are all "go" processes, and neuroscience shows us why.[3] There is no "stop" component, which is an inherent part of any mind process. Even walking has no "stop" to it. Walking has to be countermanded by some other "go" process. So in this sense, even "stop" is a go process. There is no "stop walking," which is a component part of walking.[4]

This is both the good news and the bad news. The bad news is that if we don't realize that mind processes are all "go" processes, we will not make any effort to countermand, by will, those mind processes that are getting us into trouble. Without directing our thinking to initiate another go process, there will simply be a random change of unchosen thinking that decides what defense mechanism will bubble up next to determine our feeling, behavior, or Halloween costume.

That's why we can't really just stop a bad habit. The way we stop a bad habit is to substitute a good habit. Instead of giving up coffee, we can switch to light tea, or hot water with a dash of lemon. Not even those stalwart souls who give up coffee cold, with no substitutions, really manage with no substitutions. They simply make "I want no cup of coffee" the positive substitution.

It is great good news really, once we realize that all mind processes are "go" processes. When we find ourselves stuck in some bizarre, unpleasant, or negative thinking or behavior, we can direct another process to begin simply by willing it. If all else fails, instead of continuing to do what we hate doing, or thinking what we hate thinking, we can take a walk and look at the sky, or sing an old nursery rhyme. Any positive or neutral thought repetitively chosen works. This is eminently doable.

I know, *now*, that my father did not have to die in a state of catatonic depression, and my brother does not have to remain dependent on lithium and endless, costly psychotherapy. These days my attitude about depression, the so-called "common-cold" of mental illness, contains a heaping tablespoon of my mother's skepticism. It also contains a flavor of what Dr. William Osler of Johns Hopkins University suggested in his answer to a colleague who once asked how the great doctor would recommend treating the ordinary cold. "With contempt, sir, with contempt."

We are so much larger, and timeless, and light-filled than the dull, leaden darkness to which we have been confined for so long by chains we thought too thick to break. But there is a weak link that has been hidden from our eyes, which we have only to look for to find, and so set ourselves free. The weak link in depression is that we can choose to think something else *other than it*. We have to learn how to do that, of course, but it can be done. I know that it can be done because not only have I learned how to do it myself, I have taught other people how to do it as well. I declined drug treatment for depression for reasons that were unclear to me then, but which have led me safely to a sanity that has eluded other sufferers of manic depression in my family.

Over the years, it seemed to me that the psychiatrists and psychotherapists who were counseling me were intent upon a combination of two ineffective "cures," the psychological equivalent of "hunger wed to thirst." They were either trying to anesthetize me from feeling anything at all, or they were trying to drag me back, kicking and screaming, into a painful, emotional re-experience of my childhood for clues as to what, or who, might be at fault for why I was the way I was. Certainly the past can *explain* the present, but the past can never *take responsibility* for the present. That belongs only to us.

Becoming increasingly dissatisfied with psychotherapists who themselves suffered from suicidal depression, broken marriages, extramarital affairs, and nervous tics, I stopped going to them, went back to graduate school, and became one. And I found a third alternative. The point is not whether we might be, or might not be, at fault for the way we are. The point is that we are always and inimitably the remedy.

Four

THE DEPRESSION
CONSPIRACY

. . . it is we who have a mind, the mind does not have us.

We are being recruited into mental illness faster than the speed of light. The trouble with mental illness is that it is not measles; it is whatever a psychiatrist or psychologist *says* it is. The Justice Department recently stated that people who are swindled by telemarketing fraud and other white collar crimes can develop post-traumatic stress disorder that may require psychiatric intervention.[1] The National Institute of Mental Health recently launched a national television and radio advertising campaign to encourage more people to seek treatment for anxiety disorders, such as social phobia, which the agency described as "frightening mental illnesses" affecting *19 million Americans*.[2]

When its new drug Paxil showed success in treating severe shyness, the pharmaceutical company SmithKline Beecham decided to fund "public service" announcements in a "patient-education" campaign about social phobia to appear on billboards and at bus stops in several major cities.[3] Another patient-education campaign was started in 1994 by Upjohn, in partnership with the Belgian pharmaceutical company Solvay. It was a careful strategy to raise public awareness of obsessive-compulsive disorder in order to stir a demand for their new drug Luvox as a cure for it. To that end, brochures began to appear in doctors' offices, and doctors' discussions of the "disease" began to take place on television talk shows and in news releases. Successful patients on Luvox were coached by public-relations firms in advance of their talk-show appearances.[4]

Upjohn approached Robert Dupont, a prominent George-town University psychiatrist and former head of the National Institute on Drug Abuse, to do a research study of obsessive-compulsive disorder. Dupont's helpful conclusion: OCD, panic disorder, and phobias cost the U.S. economy $46.6 billion in 1990. But fortunately, Dupont averred, the availability of effective drugs could substantially reduce the economic and social burden of "these common and often crippling mental disorders." "The goal is to make the disease better known," says Upjohn public relations director Philip Sheldon, "and make patients seek treatment. Obviously it's not all altruistic—we want to be part of the treatment."[5]

With funding from Upjohn, James Broatch converted an old seed warehouse in Milford, Connecticut, from which he began to run the nonprofit Obsessive Compulsive Foundation for 8,000 members with a hot line that gets thirty calls a day. In some cases Upjohn worked directly with influential patients, such as Mary Hull of Walnut Creek, California, who founded seven OCD support groups. The Celebrity Outreach Agency in Agoura Hills, California, was contacted to be on the lookout for any possible celebrity sufferers who might glamorize the OCD illness. So part of Upjohn's promotion for Xanax was to send Houston Oiler running-back Earl Campbell "on tour" around the country, telling overflow crowds and reporters how he once raced to the hospital with obsessive-compulsive heart attacks that were all in his mind.[6]

First psychiatry sells us a disease, then they sell us the cure. Pharmaceutical companies are constantly trying to expand their markets for drugs that have already been approved for depression by selling them to people with other "problems." SmithKline Beecham, following its educational campaign on social phobia, is now marketing its antidepressant Paxil to those 19 million people suffering from it, since it has received regulatory clearance from the government. (Drug companies can't market approved drugs for additional uses without further testing.) Other drug companies with dollar signs in their eyes are rushing to test their own antidepressants for success with social phobia, also called social anxiety disorder.[7] Not Prozac's Eli Lilly, however. They have just received approval of Prozac for mood swings caused by *severe premenstrual syndrome*.

The current experience with antidepressants seems to be that if you use them to cure depression, you cure just about everything else along with it. Some extrapolate from this that much of mental illness is undiagnosed depression. But I wonder. Are we really *curing* anything? Maybe when our primal-mind defense mechanisms of anxiety and fear, which are supposed to alert us to the fact that we may have a problem, are good and drugged up we don't worry anymore about *whatever* troubles or weaknesses we have.

But the connection between anxiety and Paxil, or the connection between depression and Prozac, will never be either the psychological or the spiritual equivalent of the connection between fear and courage. Drugs will not take us from scared to sacred.

Paul McHugh, Psychiatrist-in-Chief at Johns Hopkins University, appears to agree. He says social phobia is, in 90 percent of cases, simply the "fear of public speaking, an almost universal condition that can usually be overcome by practice. Although people may differ in such qualities as attentiveness and confidence," says McHugh, "it is simply not true that most individuals deficient in these qualities are sick."[8] When did scared become a disease? Or not paying attention? Or depression?

There are some psychologists who agree with me. Keith Johnsgard began to look for something other than pills for his depressed patients and found exercise more effective than anything else. He now takes his patients on walks, which "help them feel better and make them more thoughtful and expressive."[9] When we are depressed we need to do something, anything, just to "get out of ourselves." Greg Tkachuk reviewed dozens of studies and concluded that aerobic exercise works as well as traditional psychotherapy in cases of depression.[10]

In a 1999 study of fifty-six severely depressed people at Duke University, scientists found that three 30-minute workouts each week brought relief equal to drug treatment. A *Psychometric Medicine* study found that 40 percent of patients relying on drugs were stricken with depression again within six months versus only 8 percent who exercised.[11] Dr. Robin B. Jarret in a 1999 landmark study at the University of Texas found cognitive psychotherapy as effective as MAO inhibitors for major depressive disorder with affective features.[12]

Martin E. Seligman heads a research alliance at the University of Pennsylvania that is trying to turn American psychology away from simply treating pathological traits into the nurturing of positive ones. He deplores the fact that in the last fifty years "[w]e became a victimology. Human beings were seen as passive foci: stimuli came on and elicited 'responses,' or external reinforcements weakened or strengthened 'responses,' or conflicts from childhood pushed the human being around. Viewing the human being as essentially passive, psychologists treated mental illness within a theoretical framework of repairing damaged habits, damaged drives, damaged childhoods and damaged brains."[13]

Seligman says that psychology has been too interested in the study of weakness and damage and not enough interested in the study of strength and virtue. Such "pathologizing," insists Seligman, "does not move us closer to the prevention of serious disorders. The major strides in prevention have largely come from building a science focused on systematically promoting the competence of individuals."[14]

A Kansas lawyer says he healed his depression with "the power of work," after being on a steady regimen of antidepressants from Prozac to Serzone for almost five years. He now sells newspapers for a living and says, "The truth is, this job is saving my life."[15] Except for some side effects, he said, drugs "have been my safety net, stopping my free fall into madness." But no more. Not since a friend "threw him a lifeline" after he lost his law practice and offered him a job delivering newspapers. To his surprise the lawyer found the hard physical work cheering. When he left the warehouse to deliver the papers to vending machines, gas stations, and supermarkets he began to "catch glimpses of small joys."

"With friendly greetings and idle conversation," says the lawyer, "these people (customers) whose names I still don't know began to draw me out of my darkness... For all the insight and help I've received from drug therapy and psychotherapy, I still have feelings of worthlessness." But with this new hands-on, physical work, which hard grounds him in the routine workaday world with his fellows, day by day, little by little, the lawyer-turned-paperboy begins to feel more and more "confident."[16]

Obsessive-compulsive disorders don't need drugs any more than social phobia and depression do. Doctors have been noting the differences in brain scans between healthy people and mentally ill people and saying, "See, it's brain disease." But Daniel X. Freedman, a psychiatarist at the University of California at Los Angeles and editor of *The Archives of General Psychiatry*, announced new research in 1992 showing that behavior modification produces metabolic and functional changes in the brains of people with obsessive-compulsive disorder.[17] *Changes in behavior can effect changes in brain patterns.* Since changes in behavior are subject to our choice, this means we can change our brain patterns as an act of will.

Jeffrey Schwartz, also from the UCLA School of Medicine, claims in his book *Brain Lock* that "we have scientific evidence that cognitive-behavioral therapy alone actually causes chemical changes in the brains of people with obsessive-compulsive disorder."[18] Again, this means we can change our brain chemistry as an act of will. This is powerful and pivotal proof for self-responsibility and brings the problems of depression and anxiety back to where they belong—a matter of choice.

But with all this government and media encouragement to treat our thinking problems with drugs and to beat the bushes for mental-illness candidates, the pharmaceutical companies are like sharks in a feeding frenzy and there is blood in the water. Ours. Mood-altering drugs are being marketed directly to the public and people are starting to ask for them by name. According to an August 23, 1999, National Public Radio news report, 50 percent of those who are now coming to the doctor's office for drug treatment are coming as a result of a media ad or an infomercial. "The combination of the misinformed doctors and the misinformed patients leads to a rise in prescriptions being written which shouldn't be written."[19] [20]

Prozac started a nationwide double-page ad campaign in twenty magazines in 1997 to convince people that "depression is a real illness with real causes," and that you can't "just will yourself out of a depression." The really insidious part of this ad campaign was the statement that "depression can make you feel all alone in the world especially when you're around people who think depression is all in your head. Well it isn't. Some people think you can just will yourself out of a depression.

That's not true." The drug company isn't satisfied with just touting its drug dogma; it is conspiring to isolate the depressed person from anybody who might suggest self-responsibility by intimating that such a person is not only wrong, but not really a friend.

We are being sold our own insanity. The sale is very profitable for pharmaceutical companies and psychiatrists and there are few holdouts. As a matter of fact, the drug industry thinks they have the adult drug market so well sewed up that they are now starting to advertise symptoms for us to check out in our children so we can start to bring *them* in for drugs too. A study of 200,000 preschool children shows a 50 percent increase from 1991 to 1995 in the use of Ritalin and antidepressants such as Prozac for two to four-year-olds when there is little or no research showing the ultimate effect of these drugs for such young users.[21] Recently, a teenage boy suffered a fatal heart attack, which was attributed to his long-term use of Ritalin.

Parade magazine is now including children in its national screening program for depression. "In fact," *Parade* is telling parents, "irritability, moodiness and flashes of rage are the key indicators of childhood depression."[22] These used to be the key indicators of a child's immature behavior, which parents were supposed to teach them to grow out of. We are running away from the legitimate anxiety and pain that is supposed to alert us to our problems and personal weaknesses, and in so doing we are in danger of becoming a nation of neurotics, an epidemic of emotional weaklings.

More than 400,000 people have participated in *Parade*'s screening program to recruit depressed people to feed to the pharmaceutical companies.[23] One of the "giveaway signs" of depression according to *Parade* is, "You've made a will and have been thinking about your funeral."[24] One wonders if these list writers have any idea what real depression is. I did not need a list of seventeen clues as to whether or not I might be depressed.

My symptom was a boulder-sized mallet of doom that went WONK, striking me immediately nondead in that I could still drag my lifeless body around with superhuman effort.

Parade dispenses with the "psychiatrists' elaborate classifications of depression" and makes its own classification "for practical purposes." "First," says *Parade*, "is the depression that has an apparent cause . . . Second is the depression that can develop for no apparent reason."[25] There, that should make it good and clear that we should all be running to our doctors, or to one of those 3,000 screening sites on National Depression Screening Day.

I will admit that in the present psychological climate, people's lives can be turned around by the temporary reliance on drugs for severe bouts of depression. People behave in a manner consistent with their own expectations of themselves, and in the last fifty years we have been educated by the medical community to believe that we cannot self-manage depression or mania. It is not common sense to deprive people of medical stabilization during a major depression who have been educated their whole lives to believe they are helpless in the face of it. This is not to say that they could not have managed the same degree of discomfort with some education and practice. But we should not refuse to rescue a drowning person because they have not yet learned how to swim. They could die.

In addition to National Depression Screening Day, there has been a cadre of celebrity sufferers of depression and manic depression touring college campuses, making documentaries, and appearing on talk shows all over the country for the last ten years, whose avowed purpose is to "educate us" that we are not responsible for our depression, and that drugs are our only hope. Kathy Cronkite began a series of lecture tours in 1992 with her book *On the Edge of Darkness*, which consisted almost entirely of conversations with celebrities about their helplessness in the face of depression and their ultimate cure by drugs. Psychiatrist Kay Redfield Jamison began her depression-trek book tours about the same time, upon the publication of her book on manic depression, *Touched With Fire*.[26]

In addition to celebrity sufferers, there are also many psychiatrists who seem dedicated to the sale of depression as a disease to the American public. Because I'm a licensed psychotherapist, I receive notices of psychological symposiums and conferences from all the local universities. I got one a while ago from the University of California at San Diego School of Medicine for a conference on Postpartum Adjustment and Mood Disorders: Assessment and Treatment. There is just the tiniest little tag line at the end of the page which in small print reads: "This program is supported, in part, through unrestricted educational grants from Wyeth-Ayerst, Janssen Pharmaceutica and Eli Lilly & Co." What does it mean—that when you scratch a psychiatrist today, you are very likely to find a pharmaceutical company?

Dr. Lewis Judd of UCSD announced in 1994 that he had "discovered" a mental disorder that causes "significant social disability" in 8.4 percent of the U.S. population. Called "subsyndromal symptomatic depression," it is made up of people who have only two symptoms of depression instead of the five symptoms that are presently required in order to get treated with antidepressant drugs. People with only two symptoms should get drugs too, says Dr. Judd. People who are suffering with the loss of a job or a loved one fit into his new diagnosis.[27]

Is this an example of a compassionate doctor who wants to go the extra mile for humanity? Or is this, as some of Dr. Judd's own colleagues have protested, a "blatant attempt to help Eli Lilly sell Prozac?" Dr. Judd is chairman of the Department of Psychiatry at the UCSD School of Medicine and former director of the National Institute of Mental Health. His research for "subsyndromal depression" was financed with a $1.2 million grant from Lilly.[28]

Such a conflict of interest is becoming more of a problem. The *Boston Globe* reported in 1999 that Dr. Martin Keller, the head of Brown University's psychiatric department and a nationally known researcher on depression, failed to disclose more than $500,000 in consulting fees, most from pharmaceutical companies whose products he praised in journals and at conferences.[29]

The *Los Angeles Times*, after an investigation of thirty-six drug-therapy review articles, has now accused the renowned *New England Journal of Medicine* of violating its own ethics by publishing articles by researchers with drug company ties and not disclosing these conflicts of interest. "The *New England Journal of Medicine* ranks as the world's most influential medical journal, according to the Institute for Scientific Information, which gauges a publication's impact based on how often other publications cite it."[30]

Dr. Sheldon Krimsky of Tufts University has reported that in an investigation of 800 scientific papers he made in 1997, 34 percent of authors had conflicts of interest with financial ties that were not disclosed. Of 210 scientific journals surveyed, *all* of them had such funding, and only 25 percent revealed it. A 1998 study showed that "virtually every researcher publicly supporting the use of new hypersensitive drugs had financial ties to the drug manufacturers."[31] None of these ties were disclosed. According to Dr. Krimsky, due to the growing commercial influences in science, wherein science has a goal of *marketing* knowledge as well as acquiring it, financial-interest disclosure is long overdue.

When people ask what is happening to our principles in today's society, the answer may be simply that principles don't support science or education with media tours and million-dollar grants the way drugs do. I am not personally aware of a single national support group for depression or a national foundation for depression or manic depression that is not funded in some way by a pharmaceutical grant.

Dial up the National Foundation for Depressive Illness (1-800-239-1265) and first you will be told that if you are experiencing "two or more of the following symptoms for a period of two weeks or longer you could be suffering from depressive illness." Next you will be informed that "depressive illness is a physical illness that can be successfully treated with antidepressant medication in nearly 80 percent of all cases." Then follows a list of "symptoms" (such as slowed thinking, loss of energy, and sleep disturbance) so general that any human being alive would have to find at least two of them that would apply and merit a consultation with a physician for drug therapy. Depression.com is owned and operated by Planet Rx.com, an online pharmacy.

Ads appear in most newspapers with quickie quizzes about depression that can qualify almost anybody to be a subject of some local depression study or research trial. One investigation shows that drug companies are paying doctors millions of dollars a year to recruit their own private patients for drug tests, and recruiters who call on these doctors can themselves earn from $500,000 to $1 million a year.[32]

The trouble is that many doctors conducting this drug research have limited experience as clinical investigators, which puts their patients in jeopardy and their data in doubt. The *New York Times* conducted a ten-month investigation that revealed drug testing to be a system "fraught with conflicts of interest; that relies on government and private monitoring that can be easily fooled and that some researchers said is inadequate; and that secretly offers a share of the cash to other health professionals who might influence patients to join a study."[33]

At any given time, UCSD has more than 1,500 clinical trials in progress and Scripps Clinic in San Diego is currently heading up 161 studies.[34] And still there are newspaper ads in San Diego, where I live, to attract even more subjects. Universities and clinics at least have more inherent brakes and more public scrutiny upon the conduct of their research than doctors in more autonomous private practice.

Are doctors bottling up the truth about mental illness along with their pills? Have psychiatrists and pharmaceutical companies unwittingly conspired to fool us into making illnesses out of personal failings we are unwilling to correct, like social phobia and frotteurism? Are depression and manic depression really genetic genius diseases over which we have no voluntary control as the news media, medical community, and celebrity sufferers claim? It is an important distinction because depression doesn't just strike creative geniuses. Depression strikes 17 million ordinary Americans every year.

Treatment for depression and manic depression has varied over the years. In his book *Moodswing*,[35] Dr. Ronald Fieve talks about the "three revolutions" in the treatment of mental ills. Torture was the first "cure." In the Dark Ages, mental disorder was thought to be an invasion of the soul by the devil and his demons, and the orthodox medical treatment then was to exorcize these demons from patients by torturing them.

The first revolution in mental health was late in the eighteenth century when we turned from a reliance upon torture to a reliance upon the uses of compassion and the attempt to control emotion with reason and logic. When that didn't work, we turned to psychoanalysis, which I characterize as *the attempt to extract meaning from emotion*.

The failure of psychoanalysis, which peaked in the 1950s, ushered in the third and current revolution in the treatment of our mental ills—drugs—which I see as *the attempt to construct meaning from positive emotion alone*. Synthetically acquired positive emotion has only recently become the sine qua non of our existence. In the past it was understood that anything profound must have something of sadness about it, to tie it down so that it might more fully realize itself. Thus did *Moby Dick*'s Ishmael remark, upon first seeing the ship *Pequod*: "A noble craft, but somehow a most melancholy. All noble things are touched with that."[36] Yes, without sadness in our lives our souls would have no weight.

Nathaniel Hawthorne, in *The Marble Faun,* posits that sorrow may be "merely an element of human education, through which we struggle to a higher and purer state than we could otherwise have attained." He suggests that we travel "in a circle, as all things heavenly and earthly do," in and out of sin and sorrow, and thus return to our original self "with an inestimable treasure of improvement won from an experience of pain . . . bringing a simple and imperfect nature to a point of feeling and intelligence which it could have reached under no other discipline." Who today would dare to speak of the *discipline* of depression rather than the *illness* of depression?

In his seventeenth-century *Anatomy of Melancholy*, Robert Burton insists that depression is due to the habit of puffing ourselves up with thin, idealized, and unproven self concepts that can't support our weight and ultimately cause us to "crash."[37] We delicately discount the worth of others while indulging in vain and vague imaginings of the value of "our wisdom, our learning; all our geese are swans . . ." It seems, at first, like an odd connection, but arrogance does seem to be one of the underpinnings of depression as well as mania.

Once deep into depression, we can't imagine that we were ever the slightest bit arrogant. But we mistake feelings of helplessness for humility. There is nothing more stubborn and imperious than abject helplessness. Columnist Art Buchwald said that when he was so depressed he considered suicide, his main concern was whether or not his obituary would make *The New York Times!*

It is the continuing media coverage of celebrity sufferers like Art Buchwald, William Styron, Sylvia Plath, Virginia Woolf, and Ernest Hemingway, whose names are coupled with depression and manic depression, that has brought these "ill-nesses" so much visibility and legitimacy—almost to cult status. And it is in the writings of these authors that we find, if not a cure, at least some comfort in knowing that we do not suffer alone.

So why do we suffer? The impulse to self-love is a further elaboration of that goal-seeking instinct with which nature endowed us so that we would meet our basic primal needs for food, shelter, and sex. It is necessary to impel us to any action. Thus the arrogance of talented people like architect Frank Lloyd Wright, movie director Robert Redford, or inventor Henry Ford progresses to forward action and ultimately results in something selfless. But the impulse to self-love can also stagnate in perpetual recurrence[38] instead of inciting us to action, and end fearfully in itself as self-importance and perfectionism, which mires us in a stultifying solitude and despair. The fear is not great in the beginning, hardly noticeable. It can ferment a long time before it suddenly implodes into depression, and so far away from the beginning thoughts that caused the problem that it is impossible to make any specific connection.

Here's how the connection works in general. We want people to think well of what we are doing but our energy can get caught right there, in the desire for reputation. Then fear sets in, the fear that we won't measure up. Tension sets in. We look for relief, for a way out that can lessen the pain of our stress, so we find it harder to *push forward* and risk ourselves in the ongoing task. Thus actor Rod Steiger describes his thinking when he was depressed: "They'll find out I'm weak. They'll find out I'm in pain. I'll look like a fool, an idiot, they'll find out I can't act . . ."[39] When the problem is beneath our level of awareness we are helpless, but once we understand it, we can direct our energy past our anxiety *about the work* into simply concentrating on the work itself.

It is the impulse to self-love that has gotten stuck in fearful self-consciousness that creates much of our agony, and the mythology and politics of depression and manic depression, the so-called "fine madness" romanticized in the lives of artists and authors such as Byron, Charles Dickens, Tennyson, Vincent van Gogh, F. Scott Fitzgerald, Winston Churchill, and Henry James.

Dr. Julien Lieb also links depression and manic depression with artistic intelligence in his book, *Manic Depression and Creativity*. There are dozens of books now echoing each other on the same theme: *Darkness Visible, An Unquiet Mind,* and *A Brilliant Madness*. These books have firmed up the "prevailing wisdom" about depression and manic depression—that they are diseases caused by chemical imbalances in the brain and are best treated by drugs. Further, almost all psychologists and psychiatrists believe that manic depression is genetic since it tends to run in families. Of course, racism, bigotry, poverty, religious beliefs, conservatism, liberalism, optimism and illiteracy tend to run in families as well.

Author William Styron said that his depression came upon him in the form of physical symptoms that "tricked his mind" into believing the "immense and aching solitude" into which he was suddenly plunged.[40] He contemplated suicide, and in his anguish could do little but dwell on the same phrases over and over, "I'm finished, I'm finished, I'm a goner." In an interview after his symptoms had subsided he heard a woman say that depression was caused by self-pity. "I came close to murder," said Styron angrily. "It was one of those idiotic statements that I just cannot tolerate."[41]

When I was depressed I, too, heard people say that depression was caused by self-pity and it helped me keep a lid on myself, out of shame, in front of those people. (Sometimes it is a great source of strength that we do not dare to show weakness in front of our fellows.) Later, as a therapist, I noticed that everyone who believed that depression was caused by self-pity didn't suffer from depression. One of my first investigations was to find out if these people believed such a thing because they didn't get depressed and were simply ignorant of the pain the rest of us had to endure. Or was it the other way around? Was the reason they didn't get depressed directly due to the fact that they had that belief?

I concluded that the reason some people don't suffer from depression is because they *believe* it is caused by self-pity, and therefore they simply refuse to concentrate on how bad they feel and, as an act of will, turn their attention to something else the moment depression falls upon them. It was my first important clue. My second important clue was people who believed that they could be happy if they just "put their mind to it," and acted as if they were happy, whether they felt like it or not.

At first I considered such people stupid, boring, phony, and shallow. Then, when I found I could replicate their experience, I learned from them that the painful strategies of the primal mind can be fooled into "standing down" if we act as if we're happy, and before long we will actually *feel happy*. This is corroborated by other therapists' work. In his book on depression, Terrence Real encourages his patients to do the behavior and let the feelings follow later—to fake it until you make it.[42] Which is really just another way of saying we should choose to fund our behavior by the use of higher-mind principles no matter how we feel, and let the resulting rational and creative thinking effect a positive mood change in the primal mind, sooner or later, as a result.

To be honest, in the beginning my mood control was more clever than wise as I often slipped right over into mania, of which I was sublimely unaware. The important thing about these experiences was that they taught me to question the reality of things that I had always taken for granted. *I began to question the reality of my depression.* This was the paradigm shift in attitude necessary to develop the concept of Directed Thinking.

But please understand that I am not just talking about intellectual conjecture. I experimented with myself by initiating behavior different from the usual just to see what would happen. When I got depressed I did something other than just taking to my bed. Anything else. It is not possible to question the reality of depression without some actual experiences that cause one to question it.

Much later I found the neuroscientific explanation for the positive outcome of these experiences, such as the mood management by those inveterate "happiness thinkers." The mood change comes about because their very specific choice of thoughts or action activates neural activity in the higher mind, thereby causing a lessening of neural activity in the primal mind, where depression is located.

But even without the neuroscientific explanation, simply *questioning* the sovereignty of our moods is an important step. There is a hue and cry lately about the lack of religion in our modern life. But I can tell you from experience that there is no religious zealot more dedicated than one who is converted to helplessness by the Depression Conspiracy. And for those who are devout and practicing Manic-Depressives there is nothing too sacred—propriety, children, job, wife, husband, friends—to be sacrificed upon that altar.

Questioning the reality of depression and manic depression is not usual. As a matter of fact there is a veritable stampede in the opposite direction. "People normally do not like to hear that they have a disease," says psychiatrist Paul McHugh. But lately, with an increasing number of patients, the idea that they suffer from a mental illness is somehow encouraging. "On one hand, it has rendered their life more interesting. On the other hand, it plays to the widespread current belief that everything can be made right with a pill."[43]

Actress Patty Duke wrote in her book, *A Brilliant Madness,* how relieved she was to find she had an illness, how comforting to know that her depression and her behavior had not been her fault. These are the first four words in her book, all in caps: A DISEASE? THANK GOD!"[44] There are powerful economic and social forces urging us to accept this doctor-approved relief from thinking our behavior is our responsibility.

The idea that depression and manic depression are physical illnesses goes unchallenged in the mainstream medical and psychological community, except for a few stalwart souls such as psychiatrists Thomas S. Szasz and, to a lesser degree, Johns Hopkins' McHugh. In Szasz's book, *The Myth of Mental Illness,* he debunks the whole idea that people can be *mentally* rather than physically ill, with *mental* symptoms in need of a doctor's treatment rather than *physical* symptoms.[45]

Dr. Szasz, psychiatry's most dissident psychiatrist, was once dismissed from his university position for insisting that physicians were trained to treat bodily malfunctioning, not "economic, moral, racial, religious, or political 'ills' . . . That doctors were trained to treat bodily diseases, not envy and rage, fear and folly, poverty and stupidity, and all the other miseries that beset man."[46]

Szasz claims that the concept of mental illness came about because it is "possible for a person to act and to appear as if he were sick without actually having a bodily disease."[47] He believes that mental illness is not a useful concept, that it is scientifically worthless and socially harmful because mental illness is not so much a disease as it is a metaphor for something the person is trying to communicate.

"People have been convinced that what are really matters of their individuality are, instead, medical problems," reiterates McHugh. "Restless, impatient people are convinced that they have attention-deficit disorder (ADD); anxious, vigilant people that they suffer from post-traumatic stress disorder; stubborn, orderly, perfectionist people that they are afflicted with obsessive-compulsive disorder; shy, sensitive people that they manifest avoidant personality disorder, or social phobia."[48]

And, insists McHugh, "wherever they look, such people find psychiatrists willing, even eager, to accommodate them or, worse, leading the charge."[49] McHugh at least is questioning much of the present-day diagnosis of social phobia and multiple personality disorders. Even manic depression, admits McHugh, is a *presumed* disease. The presumption, he declares, "carries the implication that some as-yet-undemonstrated pathological mechanisms and etiological agencies will emerge to explain the stereotyped set of symptoms."[50] To me this seems like pretty thin stuff to trust one's life to and yet this disease theory of manic depression is present-day medical orthodoxy.

I attended a recent lecture on attention deficit disorder, a requirement of my license to practice psychotherapy. According to the presenter, Dr. Michael K. Linden, who lectures all over the country to psychologists and psychiatrists on ADD, there is no research presently being done associating the disease with the inadvertent triggering of the fight-or-flight response.

Wouldn't this natural defense mechanism, when it was stimulated by overambitious or fearful thinking, cause the same syndrome as ADD? And, therefore, couldn't this behavior and brain chemistry be changed by changing one's thinking? Is it any wonder that there are no funds for this research forthcoming since there is no money to be made from it? How should we trust the kind of research that only sets out to prove the efficacy of some pill? Why should we trust the doctors who depend upon this research?

Today most people demand a more compassionate attitude than that of psychiatrist Szasz, or even McHugh. We wish to have the sympathy of the doctors and politicians who "understand our pain." The message from the 1999 White House Conference on Mental Illness is accommodating our wish. "One of the most widely believed and most damaging myths is that mental illness is a personal failure, not a physical disease. Virtually every American has a friend, a neighbor or a colleague with a mental illness."[51] This should be a little hint right here that we might be overdiagnosing ourselves.

Five

RESCUE FROM THE
CULT OF DEPRESSION

But anxiety and depression, says Psychiatrist-in-Chief Paul McHugh of Johns Hopkins University, "are routinely differentiated by appearances alone... not on the neurobiological or psychological data."

When I rejected present-day psychiatry's drugs as the answer to my own depression, I found that I had unknowingly rejected its model of the mind as well. If I was going to make use of more established philosophical principles that allowed me to be in charge of my life, such as freedom of will and the primacy of habit, I could not at the same time make good use of Freud's division of the mind into conscious and unconscious, and his further division of the "unconscious mind" into id, ego, and superego.

People say Freud's influence is waning. But it is Freud's theory of the unconscious mind that provides the only basis for mental illness as we know it. Without Freud's theory of the unconscious mind, we could not have the "diseases" of drug addiction, manic depression, social phobia, or frotteurism. The unwitting conspiracy on the part of psychiatrists and drug companies to disenfranchise us of our self-responsibility for our behavior depends entirely upon Freud's model of the unconscious mind.

The insidious consequence of Freud's model is that his concept of an unconscious superego leads to the conclusion that the self is the *creation* of principles rather than the *user* of principles. Freud's concept of the self therefore is some kind of a helpless and hapless *result* and, as classical philosophy has already taught us, "a result cannot have a purpose of its own." Freud's concept of the unconscious ego leads to the conclusion that the self is the *creation* of feelings rather than the *user* of feelings, and even blurs the distinction between the self and feelings, between impulse and will; with the implication that we are responsible *to* our mind instead of being responsible *for* our mind. Depression is not a problem if we do not have to *obey* our mind but, instead, can learn how to *direct* our mind.

I needed a more practical, user-friendly theory for the proper management of the mind. And the consequences of not managing my mind loomed rather large at that time—depression, mania, bankruptcy, divorce, loneliness. I began to assume a model of the mind that acknowledged choice since it seemed to me that this was the only possibility for a self-responsible existence. The only alternative to a self-responsible existence is a dependent one. Interdependence is not a viable third way because a self-responsible existence among one's fellows has to include the principle of mutual cooperation; without which there can be no objective reality. Also, to make use of interdependence one must first have achieved a position of independence.

What worked better for me than Freud's model of the mind was a simpler model based upon neuroscience's two-part division of lower-brain primal mind and upper-brain higher mind: lower and upper brain referring to the physical tissue and place of location in the brain; primal and higher mind referring to the psychic phenomena produced in the tissue. The lower-brain primal mind houses all our instincts (such as the sexual impulse and the nesting impulse) and our instinctive defense mechanisms (such as fight-or-flight response, anger, paranoia, and depression). All our defense mechanism feelings, and those feelings that escalate into the emotions of fear, happiness, guilt, anxiety, and excitement emanate from the primal mind. Our cognitive concepts, on the other hand, are all initiated in the upper-brain higher mind—learned knowledge, verbal and math skills, logic, creativity, reasoning.

The concepts of the upper-brain higher mind and the feelings of the lower-brain primal mind work in concert so that we can see a beautiful piece of sculpture and feel the pleasure of it.[1] But when thoughts and feelings work in concert to pitch us into depression, we can interject new thoughts and change the unwanted feelings as an act of will. We think our way into depression, and we can think our way out of it.

What is the practical use of Freud's division of the mind into conscious and unconscious except as a postmedieval way of saying there can be a "demon" in our mind, making us do something that we would otherwise not do? That our unconscious mind can control us leads to the conclusion that our addictions, for instance, are diseases rather than behavior choices. I found it more responsible and more helpful to think that the mind is never conscious of itself, or unconscious of itself. The mind is basically a thought-thinking, feelings-feeling machine, different thoughts directly accessing different parts of the brain that contain different strategies that fund different behaviors, feelings, concepts, and emotions.

We however, as sentient beings, are conscious or not conscious at various times of what thoughts our mind is thinking. We can choose which thoughts we wish to think, as in deciding upon some project or course of action. Or we can let thoughts randomly occur as the result of circumstance, as when we see someone on the street who owes us money and we autonomically allow thoughts about how badly we have been used to bandy us about. It is we who have thoughts, however; thoughts do not have us. It is we who have a mind; the mind does not have us.[2] The theory that the mind has us, which is implied in the idea of an "unconscious mind," is not a practical working theory because then we "can't help it" and have to live our lives like wimps and slaves to our impulses and our obsessive thinking.

Freud places the self in the mind. But not even the neuro-scientists who are mapping the brain neuron by neuron, nor the quantum physicists who are weighing matter quark by quark, have seen hide nor hair of a "self." Self must exist because, even though we cannot prove its material existence, as psychologist Jerome Kagan insists, "who we are cannot be reduced to mere brain circuits or physiological measures of arousal." The meaning of the Gettysburg Address or Hamlet's Soliloquy, says Kagan, "does not correspond to linear patterns of neural activity in the brain."[3]

Stanford University biologist Paul Ehrlich states that the approximately 100,000 genes in the human DNA could never determine the 100 trillion connections between the neurons in our brains.[4] Neurobiologist Gerald Edelman concurs. "The genome of a human being (the entire collection of an individual's genes), is insufficient to specify explicitly the synaptic structure of the developing brain."[5] There is no scientific evidence that might give us license to assume the self resides in our mind.

The self is a mystery. What we know about the nature of the reality of the self is not so much *what* it is as *that* it is (I am). We mainly know about the self by what it does, rather than by what it is. Someone once asked Thomas Edison to explain what electricity was. Edison's terse reply was, "I don't know what it is. It exists. Use it." This is the same situation with the self. *What* we are, practically speaking, is our decision when we reach adulthood as to what forward actions we will take (I am a doctor, I am good, I am a good mother, I am an honorable man, I am responsible, I am at the mercy of my addictions). If we have not programmed (learned) much of value into our higher mind, or have programmed games instead of knowledge, or if we have programmed wrong ideas (e.g., I have no control over my feelings), our distinctions, or choices, are going to be necessarily limited.

If I had to define "self" I would sooner call it "choice" than "persona." Certainly the idea of self as choice works for depression, and the idea of self as unconscious mind, or self as persona doesn't work for depression. Choice is also mysterious. We don't know where it comes from, but it exists, like electricity, and we can use it. We can choose *which* part of our two-part mind to use, and, in the case of choosing the higher mind, which concept or program to use. Choice exists as a prerogative of the self, not the mind; although the self, through passivity, can abrogate the responsibility of choice to the mind.

That's the thing about choice; we don't have to choose to exercise it. What makes choice difficult for us is that it is something we have to use before we get it, sometimes even before we believe it exists. Remember the movie in which Indiana Jones was able to climb to the Holy Grail by stepping off the face of the cliff *before* the stepping stones appeared? He had to step first, right into thin air, with no assurance that he would not fall to his death. He understood, he *knew* that the steps would materialize beneath his feet *as the physical result* of his stepping forward. This is the human condition as concerns conscious choice. Choice is always an action; it always entails risk and, therefore, always requires courage.

Choice has to do with the how of our existence, not the why of it. Psychiatrists are famous for dwelling on the why of life, which requires no action; as opposed to the how of life, which does require action. So it is no wonder that we go to psychiatrists for the express purpose of their helping us figure out *why* we do something. The most arrogant psychiatrist I ever knew was chairman of the department of psychiatry at a major university. He also had a private practice in which he saw the same eight people every day for one hour each, Monday through Friday, at $200 an hour. He had been seeing the same eight people for ten years when I knew him. Where is the wisdom in spending any time at all figuring out *why* we do something when with the same effort we can choose *how* to do anything we want? What we really need to decide is *how* we are going to get out of bed in the morning, not *why*.

If we know *how* to live, we don't need a *why*. Looking for the why of life presupposes some existential vacuum within us that we need to fill up in order to be okay. We can simply *choose* to be okay. We can do that by understanding it is the primal mind's job to be worried and anxious; not ours. Depression and worry are problems of the primal mind, they do not have to be *our* problems. We do not need to know *why* we are unhappy. All we need to know is *how* we can be cheerful.

Unhappiness, a feeling, is a product of the primal mind. Cheerfulness, a principle of attitude, is a product of the higher mind. We have two different factories and we can choose which one we wish to power up by manning one production line or the other, according to the thoughts we choose to think. "True joy," says Seneca, "is a serene and sober motion; and they are miserably out that take laughing for rejoicing; the seat of it is within and there is no cheerfulness like the resolutions of a brave mind."

We can situate ourselves as a matter of choice in the higher mind. We can bravely situate ourselves as a matter of choice in the *how* of anything. We can look forever and find ourselves in the *why* of nothing. And that is how we can't find ourselves in the psychiatrist's office. Psychiatrists would have us peel away our memories like an onion to get to our essential "core," our essential self. There isn't any such core self that exists in our mind.

That is because the self is not a memory of the mind. The self only exists in its dynamic interchange with present reality. We cannot witness the self as object anymore than we can witness change. We can witness that change has taken place but we can never see change itself. Take a video of a bulb turning into a flower and you will see the result of change, you will not witness some exact moment of change itself. That is because change is not quantitative. Change does not exist in time. Ask any quantum physicist. We can witness the result of self in its response to present reality; but in the absence of this response, there is no self per se that we can witness because the self is not quantitative. It does not exist in time.

So, if we cannot peel ourselves like an onion to find our core self, how can we find it? If we can learn to look fearlessly upon our feelings simply as "inner landscape," and to look fearlessly upon our problems as simply "outer landscape," with time we will be able to find ourselves in that earnest awareness. This kind of objectivity, especially in the face of depression, seems to be discouraged in the doctor's office.

We are not being trained to be objective about feelings, but subjective to the mere possession of them. The surgeon asks, "Is the *arm* still sore?" The psychiatrist inquires, "Are *you* still depressed?" Doctors spend half their time extinguishing the symptoms of depression with drugs, and the other half firing up the cause with their incessant focus on us as the helpless victim of feelings rather than the active and responsible source and guardian of them. Why doesn't the doctor ask, "What exercises are you using now to lessen your passive self-identification and enmeshment with your primal mind?"

Now we can get all philosophical and say that there is no proof of a self, and therefore no proof of will or awareness existing outside of our mind. For practical purposes, I put "there is no self outside of the mind" in the same category with the Eastern philosophy that claims the world is only *maya,* illusion, and doesn't really exist. My brother once told me about a friend who was so steeped in this kind of philosophical thinking that when her newborn baby unnerved her with several hours of incessant crying, she put the baby in a back room for twenty-four hours, closed the door, turned her back, and said, "*You* don't exist." I remarked at the time that I noticed she didn't say, "*I* don't exist."

I prefer a less esoteric and more useable theory of human existence, the more solid "two-by-four" system based on my own experience. Though quantum physics will tell us that a two-by-four is not really a solid piece of wood, just a bunch of energy running around, I still do not want to get hit in the head by one! If a two-by-four exists, the "I" that can be hit by it exists, and therefore the "will" that ducks the two-by-four to keep from getting hit by it also exists. My theory of depression is similar: I found I can suffer depression by *becoming unaware* of my thinking, and not properly managing my thinking. I also found I can manage depression effectively by *becoming aware* of my thoughts and choosing to think different ones.

Those of us who struggle with chronic depression are very much like soldiers whom fate has brought to the front line. This is no time to ask *why* are we here. This is no time to inflict our morose sighs and morbid comments upon our nearest and dearest. This is the time to get up and report for duty. We can either abandon the line and run in fear of death, or we can hold the line and risk death. "No evil propensity of the human heart is so powerful," says Seneca, "that it may not be subdued by discipline."

This age-old philosophical truth is echoed, in the last twenty years, by a group of neurobiologists who are showing us that it is not simply that our moods, feelings, and behavior are the result of our brain chemistry. It is much more complex and reciprocal than that. Our experiences and our actions throughout our lives physically transform and restructure the tissue of our brains. If it were otherwise there could be no such thing as a new habit. We do not have to obey our minds. Gerald Edelman's work, and the studies of synaptic plasticity that won David Hubel and Torsten Wiesel the 1981 Nobel prize in medicine show us that we can functionally construct a mind for our purposes by forcing our brain (our body) to interact with our environment according to our instructions. We do not have to change our brain to get it to behave. We can behave our brain to get it to change.

But with such a show of power sanctioned by society in general and psychiatry and pharmaceutical companies in particular, it is easy to be seduced into believing that depression is so big and so important and so overwhelming that poor little us couldn't possibly just ignore it by screwing up our courage and cheerfully packing the children's lunch boxes.

The mental-health framework that is already in place subtly subverts us. It encourages a mind-set that is as dangerous for our individual physical and mental health as it is for the moral character of our society. The Social Security Income program (SSI), for instance, was set up to serve the "disabled poor," but once people realized that mental illness could be judged on a parity with physical disability, the floodgates for abuse opened. It has been a great incentive for parents to coach their children to misbehave, or fail their school tests; because each child can receive payments of $458 a month or more. A child in Wynne, Arkansas, asked his teacher if doing well on an exam would affect his "crazy check."[6]

Ezola Foster, Pat Buchanan's running mate in the 2000 presidential election, admitted that she had lied about being mentally ill in order to draw money for a year before her retirement as a school teacher in 1997. "I [had] two choices to survive. Since [my condition] wasn't physical, they make it mental, don't they? If I don't have a broken leg or they don't see blood, or I'm not dead, they said I have to be crazy." Her "mental illness" was worked out "between my doctor and my attorney. It's whatever the doctor said, after working with my attorney, that was best to help me."[7]

Estes Thompson, a reporter for the Associated Press News Service recently wrote an article about James Blackburn's new depression book. He was the prosecutor in the Jeffrey Mac-Donald murder trial. The reporter says very matter-of-factly about Blackburn that "[he] still takes his Prozac daily to treat the depression that helped push him to take $234,000 from his law firm."[8] How is it that we do not think it outrageous to blame depression for embezzlement?

The *San Diego Union* reported that Ann Winebrenner, fifty-three, a San Diego Superior Court judge, told her colleagues in 1998 that "she no longer wanted to be a judge." So she stayed home to sell her expensive bead designs on her web site. How could she do that and still draw her approximately $117,000 salary from the government? Disability benefits. Winebrenner says she suffers from anxiety disorders and depression and can no longer work.[9] How is it that we do not think it is outrageous to claim we cannot go to work because we are anxious and depressed?

But anxiety and depression, says Psychiatrist-in-Chief Paul McHugh of Johns Hopkins University, "are routinely differentiated by appearances alone . . . not on the neurobiological or psychological data."[10] The new DSM approach of using experts and descriptive criteria in identifying psychiatric diseases *has encouraged a productive industry.* If you can describe it you can name it; and if you can name it then you can claim that it exists as a distinct "entity" with, eventually, a direct treatment tied to it.[11]

Another problem is that in the early stages of psychiatry, mental ills were treated *mentally* with the "talking cure." Now, however, mental ills are treated *physically* with shock treatments or drugs. Also, the mental-health system today has extended the doctor-patient relationship to include drug companies as well, an unholy trinity that can become an open invitation to embark upon a course of mutual corruption. Why are we doing this?

It can't be because of psychiatry's cure rate. When I entered graduate school in 1984 they told me that all psychotherapies had the same cure rate—one-third of patients got better, one-third got worse, and one third remained the same. With results like these, psychiatrists would be out of business in three months if we held them accountable for the success of their work like we do orthopedic surgeons or auto repair men. We are now aware that welfare as we know it *creates* poverty because people become permanently dependent upon give-away social programs which mire them in subsidized poverty, with no means to insure themselves of financial stability. Could "psychology as we know it" be creating mental illness in the same way?

When people go on antidepressants, their brains begin to produce chemicals to equalize the newly introduced chemical imbalance, and when the antidepressants are withdrawn, depression is worse than ever. When people are convinced they have no power over their thinking, drinking, smoking, pedophilia, shoplifting, or moods, they cease to strive for control over their impulses because it is easier *not to strive*. They become mired in subsidized emotional dependence, with no means to insure themselves of mental stability.

Our mental stability will ultimately come to rest upon either our emotional self-responsibility or our emotional dependence, because these opposite positionings are constantly evolving away from each toward the accomplishment of themselves, according to the principle of inertia.[12] There is no viable third way that the laws of physics would allow.

As Nobel prizewinner Friedrich Hayek has wisely pointed out to us in the field of economics, there is no viable third way for economic security between liberty and coercion. So society must choose either one or the other when they establish the basic principles that will organize their government. "Liberty not only means that the individual has both the opportunity and the burden of choice; it also means that he must bear the consequences of his actions."[13] It was the Welfare State that ended up trying to be a viable third way between liberty and coercion, and has failed, suggests Hayek, because of a "fatal conceit"; an attempt, without sufficient knowledge, to redesign the nature of man according to its own laws.[14]

Psychology has tried to be the viable third way for emotional stability, between self-responsibility and dependence, and it has failed for precisely the same hubris Hayek ascribes to the Welfare State. Psychology, along with the welfare state, has failed for another reason. In trying to be a viable third way between two dynamic and evolving opposites destined to end up one way or the other, self-responsibility or dependence, psychology has succumbed to the principle of inertia, and fails because of physics. The result of this failure upon the character of our society is that weaknesses that might have remained the exception are, more and more, being enabled into the rule.

This is especially true of depression and its pharmacological cures. They are part of the everyday speech and patter at cocktail parties and backyard barbecues. Everybody thinks they have it pegged. A San Diego editor printed a jargon-filled op-ed essay by a fifteen-year-old girl who called for more treatment for the depression causing all the school shootings. She knew all about the chemical imbalance that was "nobody's fault." Everybody can put in their two cents' worth about selective serotonin re-uptake inhibitors and witness for their drug of choice, Prozac or Zoloft. This climate of acceptance is maintained because people are less likely to talk about their own personal experiences with side effects, which often tend to be sexual problems.[15] Those laggers-behind who had doubts about antidepressants begin to believe they are perfectly safe, a powerful incentive to hop on the feel-good bandwagon.

In addition to this more innocent corruption of the actual facts about depression and its pharmacological "cures" there is something else that can dangerously skew the data. Greed can skew the data because greed can diagnose mental illness when greed sees that insurance will cover it. Having good mental-health insurance coverage alone has put thousands of people at risk because it has made them victims of a conspiracy on the part of hospitals and psychiatrists to give them fraudulent but profitable diagnoses.

"In the early 1990s, psychiatric hospitals and addiction centers paid over $500 million dollars in Federal fines to settle charges of profiteering and diagnostic fraud in recruiting patients with generous mental health insurance."[16] I know from personal experience as a therapist of cases where hospitals have gone to court to get temporary custody of a child with a "profitable" insurance policy, against the parents' wishes, and kept the child on drugs until the policy lapsed. In one case the child died before her parents could rescue her. This case is now in litigation. In some states the schools now have court-sanctioned authority to test children for ADD *against their parents' wishes* and can force these newfound "ADD children" to take Ritalin. Similar court-sanctioned testing for depression with mandated use of Prozac may not be far behind.

Psychiatrist and best-selling author Dr. Peter Kramer believes depression is a disease best treated by drugs, although in his book *Listening to Prozac* he delineates many legitimate objections to Prozac. Unfortunately, Kramer brings up these objections in the form of worn-out philosophical straw men who are no match for his glib new sword of psychologized thinking, and counts himself among those who no longer object.

I find Kramer's premise for labeling depression as a "disease" in need of a cure, and his advocating Prozac as that cure, is at heart a false one. He tells us that Prozac can purge depression, guilt, anxiety, fear, panic, grief, shame, and self-consciousness from the persona. He supports such pharmaceutical personality makeovers because there are "no adverse physical side effects." Yet the loss of sexual desire as delineated in *Prozac Diary* by Lauren Slater, a psychologist and one of the first people to go on Prozac ten years ago, may be typical of long-term users. And Kramer glosses over the fact that his patients on Prozac are no longer so compassionate about helping out their needy family members.

Any possible adverse spiritual effects of eliminating what have always been considered essential human traits of anxiety, guilt, and fear, Kramer dismisses by predicting that such "negative" traits, now that Prozac has come along, will soon cease to be thought of as essential traits and will be considered simply *pathological ones*. This is contrary to all ancient wisdom, which warns that as we cannot rid the world of evil, neither should we maim our darker passions but, instead, direct them to serve our will by "compelling them to yield their vigor to our moral nature."[17]

I find Kramer's willingness to rid the human persona of grief, fear, guilt, depression, and anxiety a grave philosophical error that does not recognize the existential difference between success and wisdom. We are not defined, either individually or culturally, by our humdrums but by our extremes, our excesses. Do we really want to cure ourselves of Janis Joplin and Vincent van Gogh? I think not. We have to go beyond where we think we should be in order to see where we are. It is not what we do right, but in pulling back from wrong directions that most solidly defines us. When out of our own experience we can say with authority for ourselves, THIS and NOT THAT.

We are defined by error in much the same way that a master carpenter is trained to expertise by the mistakes he makes as an apprentice. Unfortunately our feel-good society is frightened by error because error always involves pain. We certainly want to get rid of all pain for our children, for instance, though we would do better to allow our children terrible disappointments in their early years so we could help them undergo and master such disappointments. This is the way we develop character, that most necessary piece of equipment for meeting life's inevitable traumas.

When my two older boys were seven and four, we took them to their grandparents' home for Christmas dinner. Shopping for his six grandchildren, my father's last minute efforts had come up short, with only four of some spectacular battery-operated *Star Wars* machine-guns that erupted in magical fire sparks and loud rat-a-tat-tats at the touch of the trigger. The other four cousins got these splendiferous toys; my two boys got the two substitute plain brown cars that just rolled around on the floor and didn't do anything.

Oh, my boys eyed those guns with envy and despair. I took them aside and told them very matter-of-factly that naturally I understood that they were disappointed, but they had to be polite and grateful for what they did get; and be good sports about it because that's just what people did under these circumstances. "Every dog has his day," I said, "and this is not your day." I could tell how hurt they were but they obeyed me and were courteous, if not ecstatic, and played with their cousins nicely.

When I became psychologized ten years later in the rearing of my last two children, I suffered with terrible guilt that I had done wrong by the first two on that long-ago Christmas Day. I determined that had I been a good mother, I should have insisted that their grandfather apologize to them for his thoughtlessness and take the guns away from the other children so mine wouldn't be hurt and have their self-esteem damaged. Or, if all else failed, I should have marched my whole family off in a huff, in support for my sons who were "being treated cruelly." I asked my two boys, now grown, if they remembered that incident and the younger said, "Only vaguely." But the older boy said "Oh, yes, I remember it very well.

"As a matter of fact," my son laughed good-naturedly, "when I got my first job in college I went out and bought myself one of those guns just for the heck of it." But, you see, he resolved it all for himself. I didn't do it for him. So now, rethinking it again, *more* years down the road, I was right in the first place to have helped my boys stand up strong under the disappointment and unfair treatment, instead of trying to fix the unfair treatment. I didn't know it at the time but I now think that, in introducing them to moral struggle at this early age, I was teaching them nobility. The grief, fear, guilt, jealousy, depression, and anxiety that one has suffered and come to a right relationship with are to be found beneath any measure of nobility. Nobility always rides a dark horse. Would it not be a philosophical error to sacrifice nobility for Prozac?

Kramer's eagerness to rid us of these aforementioned traits seems to me to be a grave sociological, anthropological, and neuroscientific error that does not recognize their necessity to the decision-making process inherent in the "human career." The specter of Phineas Gage raises his ghostly finger in admonition.[18] He was a twenty-five-year-old munitions expert who set charges for railroad construction. In the summer of 1848, being distracted for only a moment, he caused an accident that sent a one-inch-thick, four-foot-long iron rod right through his head, landing part of his brain more than 100 feet away.

He never lost consciousness and seemed to recover fully. However, though his upper-brain, higher-mind intellect and reasoning were left intact, the area of the brain that was the seat of his lower-brain, primal-mind emotions was destroyed. He could still read, do math, and carry on an intelligent conversation just as before the accident, but Phineas Gage became uncharacteristically self-indulgent, aggressive, and socially uncaring, given to offensive outbursts of profanity. He had so little capacity for decision-making, discipline, and deference for his fellow man that he was never able to work again. Is Prozac doing to modern man *psychologically* what that long-ago blasting accident did to Phineas Gage physically?

Maybe this lessening of the capacity to care that antidepressants provide us, so we don't suffer painful feelings, is alienating us from our fellow man in ways we don't realize. There are numerous cases in the courts in which the defense for those accused of murder is that they were on Prozac or Paxil.

Kip Kinkel, a young school shooter, was on Prozac. Eric Harris, one of the Columbine school shooters, was on the antidepressant Luvox.[19] "There have been more than 160 lawsuits against Eli Lilly which blame Prozac for violent behavior. These cases have all been settled out of court, and the confidential settlements allow the pharmaceutical company to avoid admitting publicly that the drug can cause harm."[20] In a trial in Hawaii brought by the children of a man who fatally stabbed his wife and then himself while on Prozac, Lilly testified that violent or suicidal acts are not a side effect of Prozac. But in October 2000, there surfaced disclosures concerning a patent for an improved Prozac, which Lilly purchased three months before the trial. The patent claimed the enhanced Prozac would reduce the *usual adverse effects* of the original including "nervousness, anxiety, insomnia, inner restlessness (akathisia), suicidal thoughts, self-mutilation, manic behavior."[21] The family in Hawaii is now seeking a retrial.

Kramer, and other psychiatrists touting Prozac, tell us that we cannot handle the situation of our own depression. But depression per se is not the situation causing the problem. The situation causing the problem is our *attitude* about depression, and our *habits* when depression hits. My grandmother had more options when depression struck than my mother did. My grandmother dealt with depression as a normal part of her regular life and she had the tacit support of friends, community, and the society at large that expected her to triumph over it. It is only since my mother's generation that psychiatrists have succeeded in gaining almost complete power over how depression is handled in this country. And human beings have a tendency to abuse power when they have it.

It is an American tragedy that the psychiatric and psychological community has conspired to re-label as the "illness of depression" what should more properly be called "the empowering struggle with our human imperfection." These doctors have succeeded in making an illness out of an opportunity by encouraging us to sell our emotional birthright for a pharmacological mess of pottage. The only remedy is for depression to be reclaimed by philosophy, anthropology, sociology, neuroscience, and common sense. We need to stop listening to Prozac.

Another assumption of Kramer's also seems alarming to me. Prozac not only eliminates depression and anxiety, but diffidence and shyness as well, and "refashions" the mind along the lines of more "appropriate" social attributes like boldness and risk-taking, which are the valued traits in a psychologized society geared toward self-actualization. Kramer claims that the person deserves the new, more highly functioning "self" as much as the cosmetically restructured person deserves the new and better body.

But there has never been any proof that the self and the mind, or the self and the persona, are one and the same. No proof even that the self *resides* in the mind or the persona. Only someone who fervently believes in Freud's theory of an unconscious mind could assume that the self and the persona are the same. It seems to me that taking Prozac to eliminate depression is too much like blowing up the town bridge for fear we might jump off it.

Kramer admits only one real problem with Prozac—it "cures" such a wide range of "symptoms" that it increasingly "presents a problem to descriptive psychiatry. Psychiatry has continued to multiply the number of diagnoses—there are now over two hundred." Kramer would address this issue by scrap-ping many of the diagnoses in the *Diagnostic and Statistical Manual of Mental Disorders* and returning to the term " 'neurosis,' a 1950s catch-all category for serious minor discomfort related to depression and anxiety."[22]

This rather arbitrary divvying up of symptoms in order to form new diagnoses is just more evidence that psychiatrists have not proven that depression is a disease at all, much less a genetic one. There are now cracks appearing in the depression-as-genetic-illness supposition as we find studies that show depression is "catching."

A study done recently in San Francisco claimed that the longer Mexican immigrants remain in this country the more likely they are to develop symptoms of depression. The study looked at 3,000 Mexican-American adults in Fresno County and 1,700 people in Mexico City. Another study of 96 pairs of college roommates found that among roommates of the same sex, depression (but not anxiety) was contagious.[23] Could it be that the doctors, the pharmaceutical companies, and the media are causing this burgeoning of depression by encouraging a national mass hysteria?

Studies like these, and my own experience as a cognitive behavioral therapist and a sufferer of manic depression, lead me to a different theory than the orthodox one, more in line with Dr. Szasz and the stalwart challengers. Depression and manic depression are not so much an insanity as they are a strategic abandonment of sanity. I predict a fourth revolution in the treatment of mental illness that relies upon a system of principles and cognitive techniques that will be imposed upon the mind to *direct* it rather than any attempt by psychotherapy or drugs to "heal" the mind itself. Healing the mind to cure depression is rather like trying to fix the engine of our car because it doesn't take us on the right road.

I agree with Dr. Szasz that it is impossible for mental states to be physically "ill." Physical brain damage can eliminate or neurologically impair mental faculties necessary for proper functioning. But when mental faculties are available and not used, as is the case with manic depression, this is not an illness. It is either an ignorance or an irresponsibility.

So, if we wish to be responsible, where do we go to learn the principles we need in order to manage depression? If we go to the doctor's office we are more than likely to get a fistful of pills. Those pills did not help the other people in my family come to grips with their depression although as a result of following a path of principles and discipline, depression no longer has power over me. But depression still has power over millions of people who are turning to the medical profession for help at the same time that depression and suicide are a personal problem for the doctors themselves, perhaps more so than for any other profession.[24]

This may be the reason, and it may not be a good thing, that doctors believe in our suffering as much as we do. Perhaps, in the light of their own well-documented difficulties with it, we should question why psychiatrists have become advocates for drugs in the case of depression and manic depression to the point where Johns Hopkins' Jamison says that she considers it malpractice not to recommend drugs for bipolar disorder. Maybe we should wonder how it came about, when all ancient philosophers say differently, that the last few generations of doctors have determined that mania and depression cannot be cured by an act of will? How could they possibly *know* that?

Are we really the tool of our nature as Freud suggests? Since Freud, psychiatrists tend to treat the real human will as imaginary, and the imaginary symptoms of self-delusion as real. Doctors' well-meant charting, testing, theorizing, storytelling, hushed conversation, and nodding of heads with their patients over these symptoms lends them overwhelming credibility in the patient's mind, to the point of hypnosis. When the doctor says we're sick, we lie down. At the very least, as Nathaniel

Hawthorne put it: "The sick in mind, and perhaps, in body, are rendered more darkly and hopelessly so by the manifold reflection of their disease, mirrored back from all quarters, in the deportment of those about them."[25]

Go into any psychiatrist's office and see the huge encyclopedias painstakingly detailing depression, mania, echolalia, catatonia, hallucinations, nervous tics, mood charts. Where are the references to ethics, self-determination, moral principle, and freedom of the will? Because we can't examine *will* under the microscope, does that mean it doesn't exist? Are the new drugs really more powerful than the age-old principles of character and virtue upon which human society has rested for millennia? Dependence on drugs is spreading beyond the doctor's office. There are warning signs of education by Prozac,[26] law by Prozac,[27] government by Prozac,[28] family by Prozac,[29] and social mores by Prozac. *Mental health by Prozac has already become a reality.*

This is because depression functions much like a cult in the way new people are brought into the fold to advance the depression-as-disease dogma. It is also a national, multibillion dollar industry with political agendas, lobbyists, franchisees, foundations, officers, boards of directors, and antidiscrimination policies. The National Foundation for Depressive Illness in New York sent out a 1998 letter complaining that medical insurance provided for shorter treatment periods and lower disability benefits for depression compared to other ailments (ailments seen as more physiologically based), which reinforce the stigma that depressed people are somehow responsible for their illness.

A worker for a National Mental Health Association's education campaign wears a pin that reads: "Depression is a medical illness, not a weakness."[30] The National Depressive and Manic-Depressive Association, in a January 1998 panel, deplored the fact that family doctors "are not adequately trained to recognize or treat depression... which means that people just get treated for the most common symptoms of depression: fatigue, anxiety, insomnia, loss of weight... instead of the disorder itself." Why don't they get it? *The symptoms* are *the disorder!* There isn't any brain disorder to cure that *causes* the symptoms. Isn't it slightly suspect that the sufferers of depression and manic depression, in tandem with drug companies, feel the need for advertising promotions, including campaign buttons? *Depression and manic depression are the only diseases that ever had to run for office.*

And what is the platform? Depression makes us helpless, fragile, special, we need drugs, allowances must be made for our handicap, and we have legal rights to medical aid, disability payments, and special accommodations at our workplace. Kent Layton, a member of the board of directors of the California Depressive and Manic-Depressive Association, says, "People with depression should not be discriminated against, and their poor on-the-job performance during low periods *should be accepted* rather than measured '*unfairly*' against their better performance during their up times."[31]

Psychologists and psychiatrists offer a complicated logic in their double-columned, thousand-page Bible-like books about cyclothymia, hypomania, circadian rhythm desynchronization, and unsuitable melatonin and serotonin levels. They advocate self-monitoring of anxiety levels to establish agreed-upon categories for gradations of despair to decide drug dosage, all of which comes under the heading of "charting mood disorders." With the same premise, they could logically describe the complications of an automobile with schematic drawings of the internal combustion system and its workings, and a charted diagnosis of all the different kinds of wrecks and when they happened and to whom, and then tell us we are the victims of our cars and deny that we have the power to turn the ignition key on and off.

Mood disorders are simply a needless way to go around in narcissistic circles. It is a dishonest dichotomy that divides into those who are ill and those who are not, whom ancient wisdom has already more properly divided into those who *will* and those who *will not*. The wise men of all ages have always said this, and the politically correct, power-hungry but intellectually passive officialdom has always conspired to maintain the opposite because this dependence insures their empires. Both wisdom and common sense dictate that we are fools when we make a depressive mood into a *conclusion*, much less a disease! Doctors today may disagree, but truth once spoken finds its way all by itself, and it does not care a whit in what vessel it is carried.

Mood disorders will one day look as ridiculous as Female Orgasmic Response Disorder, which is a prime example of the calamities that can occur when you find ignorance in high places, gainfully employed. As late as 1895, doctors were performing clitoridectomies on women who complained of having orgasms because they were "unseemly" for the "good" women of Victorian times. Depression-as-disease will one day go the way of multiple personality disorders, which is now pretty much debunked. I read recently that a psychiatrist was actually convicted of fraud for billing a multipersonality "patient" for group therapy.[32]

The most famous case of multipersonality disorder was made into a best-selling book in 1973, and later into the television movie: *Sybil*. It purported to be a true account of a young woman, a victim of child abuse, who developed alternate personalities who did things without her knowledge. In 1998, some twenty-five years later, the old tapes of the sessions surfaced, and they suggest that the personalities were actually *created* during therapy through the doctor's suggestions to a very pliable patient.

Further, tapes of conversations between Sybil's psychiatrist and the author of the book show that both of them were not totally unaware that they were off the track, and were probably swayed by the fact that the publisher said "there's no book unless we can call it multiple personality disorder." The investigator, however, terms the conspiracy self-delusional and stops short of calling it a deliberate fraud. Either the doctor and the author were more delusional than the patient, or it was a greed-determined diagnosis.[33]

Repressed-memory syndrome is now in the hot seat too, and cases are now being overturned by the courts that were based upon the testimony of psychotherapists who claimed to "uncover" repressed memories from their patients of sexual abuse by their parents. The author of the popular workbook *Courage to Heal* has been sued by a California woman who said she was emotionally damaged because the book made her believe she had been molested when she hadn't been.[34]

Recently a judge in Illinois disciplined a prominent psychiatrist whose patient won a court settlement based upon her complaint that the psychiatrist treated her postpartum depression with repressed-memory therapy, leading the woman to believe she possessed 300 personalities, ate meat loaf of human flesh, sexually abused her children, and served in a cult.[35]

These cases are no more astounding to me than the fact that the government knowingly makes monthly disability payments to people who use the money to buy alcohol and drugs. It is totally against common sense to eradicate a habit by rewarding it. "Oh," says the alcoholic, "I can't stop drinking." "Okay," says the government, "in that case here is some money to buy alcohol." "I'm depressed," says the patient. "Oh," says the psychiatrist, "let me give you some feel-good drugs, and devote my entire $300-an-hour important attention to the slightest nuance of your feeling; and compliment you by telling you that you must be a special person of higher intelligence to be suffering in this way."

This is nothing more than a national insanity. This climate

fosters such inanities as the case of Rickey Higgins, seventeen, who is suing his high school for $100,000 under the Americans with Disabilities Act. The basketball star was arrested for two alcohol-related offenses, including a drunken driving citation for running into a tree, and was kicked off the team. "I think I deserve a second chance." says Higgins. "Most people who are alcoholics think no one will help them, and I'm getting that feeling." "The kid could not control his use of alcohol," said his lawyer. "Because he could not control it, it's a disability and he should not be punished for it."[36]

In such a climate where the bizarre has at times prevailing wisdom, and drug manufacturers are funding most university research, there are huge consequences for both medicine and science. When Yale University announces that a study financed by shampoo maker Procter & Gamble proved that a "bad hair day" is deleterious to self-esteem,[37] clearly science has lost her virtue to commerce.

The huge, important-sounding complications of the mega-buck business of depression can hide from us the plain, small truths of our lives. The plain, small truth about depression is that it has no power if we ignore it and insist upon thinking about something else. This does not mean that we will not suffer and that life will not be hard. I do not know the cosmic answer as to why we suffer and life is so hard. Probably it is supposed to be that way since we have been created with the capacity for will without any requirement that we use it. Maybe without the suffering to inspire our creativity, we'd all still be foraging happily along with the squirrels for nuts and berries to bring home to our cozy stone caves. It is not an easy thing to be a human being.

When we see all the ravages that exist in the world, it doesn't take a rocket scientist to expect that some of it is going to find its way to our doorstep. Even the rich and famous and those who seem to live charmed lives have difficult times and moments when they wonder why they even bother. Successful rock stars overdose on drugs, popular movie stars drink themselves to death, and best-selling novelists put guns in their mouths and shoot their heads off. Is it any wonder that the run-of-the-mill rest of us are often hanging by a thread to the very edges of our lives? Yet men of earlier generations had role models that seemed to be made of sterner stuff. Like the Duke of Wellington, who tells us, "There is little or nothing in this life worth living for, but we can all of us go straight forward and do our duty."

Maybe the closest we will ever get to the truth of it all is something like this: In a world filled with looming uncertainty and pending chaos, and where we may be as accidental as snowflakes, we must nevertheless get up in the morning, brush our teeth, and do our chores, however we feel, and with whatever resources we have. We get up not because we feel like it, but because morning has come. That we have no chores is unacceptable. That the day ahead holds no joy for us does not mean we shouldn't whittle something out of it anyway. Why? *Because to learn to do so is the only real sanity we will ever be able to count on.*

There is no such thing as depression, although there is a *feeling* of depression. Sadness is different from our reaction to it. Most people today think it is the same. Most of us today see no difference between our feeling and objective reality. We can get so highly identified with a feeling that we do not see the difference between it and us; we *feel* sad, we *become* sad; we don't just *feel* sad, we *are* sad. We feel depressed; we *are* depressed. We don't just feel depressed; we are depression itself. The trouble with this kind of identification is that impulses of sadness and depression can come at any time and steal us away from ourselves and then we turn to medical procedures like drugs or electroshock therapy to cure us.

We are not really drugging or stunning the psychological phe-

nomenon of depression; we are drugging and stunning our poor physical bodies. This is neither healthy nor wise. In the same way that we can only achieve a working knowledge of the world by encountering the world instead of avoiding contact with it, we can only achieve a clear understanding of depression by meeting it face to face.

It is our culturally induced over-reaction to a defense mechanism that is the aberration, not depression. It is our quick-fix society, with its hopeless hang-up on cheap happiness and our dependence on drugs and the psychologists and psychiatrists who purvey them, that is the aberration, not depression. Managing our depression will ultimately give us strong mental health in the same way that resisting the temptation to sin will give us strength of character and nobility of purpose. All growth occurs by resistance, by pushing against some counterweight, under stress of some kind. If you want to grow really healthy bean sprouts you weight them down with marbles so they have something to strive against. Even our bones do not grow unless the muscles around them move against them to provide tension and stress.

Psychiatrists cannot rid our brains of depression anymore than ministers can rid the world of evil. And why would we wish to do either one? "The habit of virtue cannot be formed in a closet," said English theologian Bernard Gilpin. "Habits are formed by acts of reason in a persevering struggle through temptation."

The impulse to depression does not have to end in depression. As the medieval mystic Meister Eckhart warns us, "the *impulse* to sin is not sin. Only *consenting* to sin, as in giving way to anger, is sin. Surely, if a just person could wish such a thing, he would not wish to be rid of the impulse to sin, for without it he would be uncertain of everything he did, doubtful about what to do, and he would miss the honor and reward of struggle and victory. Because of the impulse to evil and the excitement of it, both virtue and its rewards are in travail born. The impulse to wrong makes us the more diligent in the exercise of virtue, driving us to it with a strong hand, like a hard task-master, forcing us to take shelter in doing well. The weaker one is, the more he is warned to strength and self-conquest. For virtue, like vice, is a matter of the will."[38]

Further, if we are trying to communicate via our depression symptoms something about ourselves that we cannot otherwise say, as Dr. Szasz suggests is the case in his book *The Myth of Mental Illness*, why would we want the doctors to kill our only messenger? Psychiatrists for some reason have been unable or unwilling to help us encounter depression in a conscious way. They don't seem to be able to help us separate the defense mechanism of depression from the *will of a person,* the physical and psychological phenomenon of depression from the person's chosen behavioral response to it. As we are not our hurt finger, neither are we our depression.

But the trouble is that increasingly, in our culture, we choose to identify with depression. It is strange how quickly we decide to do that. And how slow we are to choose anything else. For years we create, we work, we travel, and yet we still don't feel comfortable in our own skin; we're never really us; we're not "the artist," or "the musician," or "the writer," or "the lawyer," or "the husband." We tell ourselves that we are still searching for an authentic identity, for our core, our "true selves." And yet, let depression hit, and, WHAMMO, we immediately become "the depressed." The enmeshment is complete.

We question the real accomplishments of our life and never question our feelings of emptiness and futility. Why? Because creating is difficult and involves hard work, and if we are true to our calling or our craft we are always working in its service. I am a writer and writing is hard work. It is much easier to get depressed than it is to write. That's the real reason so many famous writers get depressed. It is even harder to write something really good.

My brother is a writer too, and people rightly ask me that if I have cured myself from manic depression why haven't I been able to help my brother? It is a fair question. The answer is that my brother believes in the theories of psychiatrist Jamison, the internationally known expert on bipolar disorder, not me. "I can't help it," says my brother, "it's genetic, it's part of being a writer."

My brother gives me books by "experts" with passages underlined for my edification. Here are a few of his pen-marked offerings from Jamison's *Touched with Fire*: "Other studies of living writers have also found a greatly elevated rate of mood disorders in the artistically gifted."[39] "Modern medicine gives credence to these literary notions of familial madness; the genetic basis for manic-depressive illness is especially compelling, indeed almost incontrovertible."[40] "Three-fourths of the research reports showed a positive correlation between manic-depressive illness and the professional or upper classes."[41]

My brother holds up these enabling theories like a crucifix before him to save him from the hard work of personal growth and return to moral imperatives, such as duty, courage, and discipline, that I propose. You "gotta wanna" do the hard work of self-mastery. Getting up every morning and going to work is hard. Screaming at your family is easier. Meeting your writing deadlines is hard. Ripping off your clothes and running down the snowy sidewalks of New York City in your underwear is easier. Interacting day after day with unfeeling editors, a complaining wife, and a misbehaving child is difficult. Ending up in Bellevue Hospital and passing the time of day with sympathetic psychiatrists is easier.

We hate and despise the agony, and the mess and the utter waste of the path of the primal mind, but it's easier to fall into it than to choose the hard road of the higher mind. By the time these psychiatrists got through with my brother, he believed his problem was that he was the disfavored child in a dysfunctional family. There is no cure for this belief; it's like inoperable cancer.

But it doesn't have to be this way. Depression is just becoming unaware of our thinking, and letting our thinking go off on its own without any direction on our part, which is easy as pie and takes no hard work or discipline at all. We can collapse completely into it in no time, out of laziness or out of ignorance. *The good news is that we don't have to overcome depression, we just have to overcome laziness and ignorance.*

Six

MANIC PANIC

I knew even then, to be safe from that darkness, I had to make my world carefully from scratch every day. I was sure that other people didn't have to do that. They could just live in the world that was already there.

Don't we act, sometimes, like we have two lives? Don't we conduct our day as if our real life is going to occur later and that right now we are just hanging in some kind of temporary working model until we get our *real* life going? Could that be why we often feel anxious, alienated, and powerless?

When we try to reserve two lives for ourselves, we can keep ourselves fooled for a while. But we are really two-timing ourselves. When our life is so full of here-I-am-but-there-I-go busyness, we don't notice that being every place at once is really being no place at all.

The reason our lives don't work is that we are simply too busy for life. We are going faster than the minutes allow. We think that's all right because life is made up of a long time. But it isn't. Life is really made up of brief moments of our being present to it, which means we can easily miss *the whole thing* if we are perpetually distracted. Physicists would say it this way: "Time is imaginary and is indistinguishable from directions in space."[1]

It is odd, isn't it, that we think we won't miss life because we would never waste it by the decade. But life is not made up of decades. Life is really made up of what we are doing right now. We only learn this in hindsight, when we have lost something irrevocable. We don't usually notice that tomorrow never comes. We don't usually contemplate that tomorrow subsists entirely upon the shimmering present moment from which today was supposed to have been made. That's why today seems so sparse we can race right through it. We need to stop racing. Then we can see we have only one life. This one.

Today even regular life has become high maintenance. Our technological advances seduce all of us into the expectation that we should have more time than we do. The hard-ground truth is that every year we amass more possessions, and it takes more time to keep it all up—the lawn, the car, the house, the children, the career, the marriage, the far-flung friends, the lifestyle. We don't realize how overworked we are. The "rewards of the new economy are coming at the price of lives that are more frenzied, less secure, more economically divergent, more socially stratified."[2] Things we used to count on such as job security, predictable pay, and reciprocal employer-employee loyalty are gone. We are practically going naked now in the workplace—stripped down to our bottom-line market value and more and more paid work. "The very character of paid work is becoming more intrusive on the rest of our lives."[3] We are tempted to work longer and longer hours for things we increasingly, therefore, don't have the time to enjoy. And notwithstanding our lowering possibilities, our expectations remain deeply set and ingrained.

A modern American lives like a king compared to the way people lived a couple of hundred years ago. We are used to being royally served; at home by our dishwashers and computers, and at-large by restaurants, theaters, and shopping malls. This has given us a sense of privilege. We enjoy an exaggerated feeling of self-importance in the cosmos.

Mundane daily chores like pumping water, gathering wood for heating and cooking, building a fire, and milking cows (which used to keep us more aware of how dependent we were upon the elements) are now accomplished by machines, or somebody else. No longer farmers, separated from a close working relationship with nature, we have become a nation of executives trying to apportion responsibility rather than take it on personally.

Our attitude is getting closer and closer to the arrogance and impatience of King Louis XIV, of whom the following incident was recorded. The king was walking out of the palace, on his way to a gala, down the front stairs with courtiers in tow. At the same time, the carriage that was to transport him was also driving up and arrived at the bottom of the stairs at the exact moment the king did; without breaking stride, he stepped into it. Annoyed that the carriage was not already at the appointed place *before* he started walking toward it, King Louis complained angrily, "I *almost* waited!"

We also are used to the quick and easy, the fast-o-matic. Set up as we are already, philosophically, to stick some subordinate with the pesky details of life, we are also open to the very easy thing it is to give our mind over to its own autonomic thinking, to let it do its own thing, so we don't have to be bothered.

When our habitual expectation that there should be a pump available when we drive in for gas, or that the bank lines should move faster, becomes our primal-mind *necessity*, we begin to have a chronic stressful feeling of being behind the clock. When we get stuck in traffic, have to meet some deadline at work, or wait too long in a grocery checkout line, since our necessity is being threatened, our fight-or-flight response gets activated unnecessarily, and our chemical balance starts to shift. When checkout lanes and traffic don't go *our way*, we get hostile and aggressive about it. We "manic panic."

"Stress experts say if you're hostile you're more likely to become depressed, and you're more than likely to not have control."[4] It may be that the best time to catch depression is *at the point of mania* instead of waiting until the downward spiral. To do that we have to remember depression is not the opposite of mania, they are two parts of one cycle, both the concomitants of unawareness. When we are depressed we have some sense that we are missing out on our lives. But this is not true of mania. In being overextended and overengaged, we are distracted from noticing how much of our lives we are passing right by.

As the rest of the world partakes of Western technology, more and more people are suffering the stress and manic anxiety that leads to depression. With each generation we're getting more and more depressed, at earlier and earlier ages. The first international study of trends in depression finds that "since 1915, the risk of depression has increased worldwide, nearly doubling for each successive generation."[5]

There have been no such studies on mania per se but newspaper articles on road rage, airline passenger freak-outs, Little League fathers killing one another over the score, and younger and younger murderers suggest it is also on the rise.

Mania is a problem even for the most normal of our daily lives. We lose friends and alienate loved ones when we panic and lash out at them over small crises. We think everyone should help us in these "little pinches," and we are right about that. Everybody is quite willing to help us. But we suddenly-gone-helpless victims of small crises are not sweet and charming in the way we ask for help.

We are often cold, if not mean. We turn rude. We may even scream at our nearest and dearest if they don't move fast enough to pick up the crying baby, or help bring in the gro-

ceries from the car before the ice cream melts, or quiet down
so we can concentrate. We can't see it ourselves but our loved
ones can. We are usually unaware of our low-key mania, which
sometimes erupts into full-fledged manic panic, that part of the
mood cycle that is a kind of halfway house to the depression
that will inevitably follow. Manic panic is a kind of felt entitlement occasioned by the fear of powerlessness.

The fear of powerlessness is a great self-prison. Powerlessness itself is perfectly okay. The trick is unconditional surrender
to the *fear* of powerlessness, which leaves us *knowing* we are
utterly powerless and vulnerable; and feeling the pain and terror that we have been avoiding all our lives that we are lost
and nothing is going to save us.

Knowing we are powerless is light years ahead of *fearing* we
are powerless. If we want real freedom in this life, this is the
place where we will find it. Knowing we are powerless is our
most solid ground, the real human condition that we all try to
avoid seeing at all costs. (You may argue with me here, but
how powerful is a creature who can neither help being born
nor dying?)

When we actually get to this place, when we get to the real
human condition, and simply feel our terror and anxiety instead
of offsetting it onto something or someone, then we see we are
still here and still all right *anyway*. And at this point some small,
positive action might present itself to us. And we might decide
to do it, since, what the heck, in this place of utter surrender
we no longer have anything to lose anyway, and therefore nothing to defend. We are free at last to give a pure act of attention
to what is at hand, which is as close as we are ever going to
get to the "Now" that ancient mystics tell us we are supposed
to live in.

Nathaniel Hawthorne is clearly referring to this idea when
he describes one of the ill-fated characters in *The House of the
Seven Gables*: "With a mysterious and terrible Past, which had

annihilated his memory, and a blank Future before him, he had only this visionary and impalpable Now, which if you once look closely at it is nothing."[6] I agree with the visionary and impalpable part, but I think Hawthorne has not quite grasped Now. Now *appears* to be nothing because, since Now does not come in any anticipatable form, it necessarily disappears in the act of looking for it.

But until such an epiphany concerning *Now* occurs to us, we seesaw from helpless to "in charge of things, by God." Unfortunately, "in charge of" usually refers to others, not ourselves. We who "manic panic" at little things do not have the confidence that we can handle *whatever* comes up in life, moment by moment, without getting upset. So we must control everybody and everything so *that things don't come up.*

We manics are dependent upon everything being the way *we* want it, and we just cave when it isn't. We only want life to come at us one way, *our* way. We spend all our energy preventing life from coming to us as it is, a trapdoor that periodically opens. Of course life continues to come as it is anyway, and all our prodigious effort means only that we are all stuck up with a whole bunch of stress and hard unwillingness. Which will eventually turn into depression.

As a young girl I learned to construct "my-way" manic highs for myself to jump into so that I could escape the terrible lows that were waiting to grab me around every corner of my life. School provided me with plenty of activity. Summers I babysat and made a lot of my clothes.

I can remember in the ninth grade purposely keeping my latest knitting project on my bed so it would be the first thing I thought about when I woke up, before the terrible darkness could have a chance to take hold. I knew even then, to be safe from that darkness, I had to make my world carefully from scratch everyday. I was sure that other people didn't have to do that. They could just live in the world that was already there.

I didn't make a connection then between what I was feeling and my father's chronic unhappiness and dark "headaches." My pain was my personal, unique, shameful failure to be "normal." And I was sure the cure for it was to be smarter, prettier, and more popular than I was. The cure for not being normal was to be *better* than normal. I think I arrived at that remedy because I figured the pain was caused by my not having what would make me happy.

At first I believed I was unhappy because I didn't have a "best friend." Then I believed I was unhappy because I didn't have a "boyfriend." I didn't have them because I wasn't "good enough." If I could just be "good enough" I could get the things I needed to make me happy and then I wouldn't feel bad anymore.

I never told a single person about my secret pain. But, in a way, shame empowered me as effectively as my aunt's remonstrances. I couldn't let anybody "know," therefore I had to go to school, do my homework, play with my friends, and eat my dinner *anyway*. There was a loss of self image because I felt "less than," and my posture started to take on that hunched-over, don't-hurt-me, victim look. But underneath that feeling of "less than" there was a strong determination that nobody should *find out* that I was "less than" if I could possibly help it.

I did a lot of things to prove I wasn't "less than." It was very important for me to be first or best in everything. I desperately needed others to like me. If they liked me, then I would be *saved*. I became a driven, insecure know-it-all and a ruthless social climber, heartless to those I perceived to be unpopular. I strove to disassociate myself with anything or anybody that didn't add to my image of wonderfulness. Wonderfulness would win me friends, and then I would be happy and safe from depression.

I perfected the frantic activity of my school years into a lifestyle of back-to-back projects as a young wife and mother.

My life was hurriedly and haphazardly pitched like a tent upon the two opposing poles of my shifting moods and the wind was always blowing. I was never "at rest." If I wasn't hiding and weeping in a closet, I was marching to my own manic drum upon some public stage or another. Depression was like an enchanted black cloak that would suddenly descend and choke me lifeless. Then it would just as mysteriously lift and I would stumble forward into celestial light and immediately seek out an audience for my latest and greatest terrific idea. Nobody ever knew what I would do next. Neither did I.

I met my husband at a choir practice after school when we were both fifteen. There were a dozen of us choir members waiting for the door to be unlocked and as I was leaning against the door and not paying any attention, when it opened I fell onto the floor. My husband was the one who took my hand and helped me up. It was a prophetic moment, as he has been doing that ever since. I asked him once what he ever saw in me. He said it was just a normal physical attraction at first, but he became fascinated by the fact that I seemed to be able to do so effortlessly all these things that he didn't know how to do.

Once I wrote two ten-page term papers for him in two consecutive nights during the week of my own final exams so that he wouldn't flunk out of high school (including the requisite 3 × 5 cards, bibliography, outline, and footnotes; I told him to rub the cards around on the floor so they would look used). I just stayed up all night two nights in a row. When he took a summer job closing out flower-seed accounts for hardware stores, I was the one who packaged and shipped the seeds back to the company every week. Then I made great Christmas gifts by refinishing the charming old wooden display boxes that the company didn't want shipped back.

And my husband never saw me depressed because he was so popular and good-looking and so much fun and so light-hearted that I was never depressed when I was around him. It wasn't until after we were married that the downsides of our personalities began to emerge and feed on each other—his out-of-control temper and heavy drinking, my depression and unrelenting criticism.

I was probably the worst culprit. My husband would get tired of the fighting and controversy and be ready to mellow out and be friends again. But not me. I could carry on tight-lipped and angry and freeze him out for months at a time over some thoughtlessness on his part that hurt me, that I couldn't get him to talk about so he could change and it could be settled.

I did not know the relevance to me of the word *forbearance*. I did not know the relevance to me of the two poems about deadly arrogance that I insisted all my children learn by heart.[7] Therefore I thought my marriage was something that needed to be fixed and made perfect before I would accommodate myself to it; which is what I must have thought about life as well.

I never thought about my feelings then because, as far as I knew, I *was* my feelings. I didn't realize then that my well-being depended upon my directing my thinking in order that I wouldn't feel bad when periodic depression hit. I thought my well-being was dependent upon my directing the world in order that I might feel good when I got what I wanted.

The thought "I am" by itself was too frightening then. I had to quickly add something else to feel safe—I am a song-writer. I am the smartest one in my class. I am pretty. I am the owner of a school. I am a magazine publisher. I am having fun. But I didn't deeply commit myself to anything; I was always on flyby.

I won a scholarship to Hollins College, a fine women's college, but my good grades simply fed my vanity and widened the gap between me and the other girls. Rather than being grateful for the chance at a college education I could not otherwise afford, I hid in my room when the downs hit and felt outclassed by the wealthier, prettier girls. When I was in an up-mood, I behaved as if my scholarship was the college's anointment of my superior intellect.

My grades were my reputation, and my reputation was my life. I was so obsessive I even memorized quotes from books, including page number, title, author, publisher, and date of publication, or, in the case of Shakespeare, play, act, and scene, so I could upstage my classmates by including actual footnotes in my bluebook essay exams. I could always work the quotes in somehow.

Oddly, these quotes are the very things I remember from all my studies. The one by Hobbes on the state of man being "poor, solitary, nasty, brutish and short" has been a great comfort to me over the years. And I always wondered what my children would think when they read *Macbeth* for the first time after I had been affectionately patting them on the bottom for years as they all piled out of the family car to the tune of "Out, out brief candle."

My connection had always been to books for my education. The books that made an early impression on me as a very young child were stories about heroes. I identified as easily with Hans Brinker and the Hardy Boys as I did with Nancy Drew, not in the way of romance; but in the way of being brave. These images were very helpful when it came time to "make a stand," for I never felt alone—I always had Edmond Dantés with me.[8]

However, I had trouble understanding when it was *time* to make a stand. I was not confused so much about *what* to do as *when* I was supposed to do it, or what kind of thing it was that I should make a stand about. I remember how angry my history professor was for "wasting his time" because I made an appointment to insist he give me credit for a mistake he had made, and change my grade from 97 to 98. He looked at me disgustedly. "What do you want, an A++?" he asked.

Yes, that is exactly what I wanted. It wasn't enough for me to know, I wanted everybody else *not* to know as much. To know was to be safe. Not to know was to be vulnerable—

somebody might think I wasn't wonderful. In fact, for most of my life, I believed that the whole point of human existence was to be wonderful. God knows there is no one more "wonderful" than a manic in full steam.

I refer to this thinking now as my "Miss Wonderful" complex and it is so deep-seated in my personality that it will probably always be my first impetus to action. Now, however, that I realize it is an exaggeration of a legitimate defense mechanism, I can usually call myself into question before I leap off into some kind of precipitous action. "Well, hello there! Miss Wonderful, I presume?"

Years ago I didn't realize Miss Wonderful was a problem. I thought it was a worthy image. Years ago I didn't realize that Miss Wonderful was the personification of my mania in the same way that "Poor Me, the victim" was the personification of my depression.

When my new sister-in-law said I was weird but she liked me anyhow, I took "weird" to be a high compliment to my originality even when she suggested that it was terribly odd that I took a pair of embroidery scissors and painstakingly cut the ragged edges off 200 postage stamps so they wouldn't spoil my perfect wedding invitations. My perfect wedding bouquet had *natural* trailing ivy instead of *artificial* ribbon. The photographer was instructed to not disturb my guests by asking them to, horror of all horrors, pose for him and spoil my perfect reception.

When I had been married about two years and had a six-month-old baby, I started a kindergarten for twenty-six children, ages three to six, in a small community church in rural Florida. Looking back, I can't believe my colossal nerve. Some neighbors asked me to do it because there was no public kindergarten. Why me? Well, why not? I had knocked myself out to impress everybody by volunteering to lead the children's choir the first week I went to church.

Did it matter to me that I couldn't play the piano and didn't know a note of music? Not a bit! I figured I'd teach myself a few chords before the Wednesday afternoon practice, and if worse came to worst I'd simply use the keys as a drum and "keep time." I did learn three chords and found I could play any hymn with them if I just "went silent" sometimes (by waving my arms to direct the choir) when none of those three chords worked.

I figured I could run the school on the same premise. (Mania substitutes for credentials and advisability every time.) I'd get some books from the library and learn how to be a kindergarten teacher. Didn't I have three whole weeks? It was not at all important to me that I had no educational qualifications to teach kindergarten. I saw myself dispensing infinite wisdom to happy little cherubs, and uplifting downtrodden mothers and fathers with the sage parenting advice of a veteran twenty-three-year-old.

Once Miss Wonderful's adrenaline ran down, the great idea of running a school turned into a bona fide commitment and responsibility and Poor Helpless Me went into a depression. I hadn't the slightest idea what I was going to do when I faced a roomful of children. Would they obey me? What would I do if they just took off running in all directions? I was panicked, but my husband, seeing the chance for a little extra money coming in, pepped me up by convincing me that the children weren't smart enough to "organize" against me, and in any one-on-one situation, I had the advantage of size. That was helpful. I got paper and supplies donated by local printers, and playground equipment made by a boat builder. We sang songs to the three chords I had already acquired and, thanks to Providence and dumb luck, in the two years I ran the school nobody drowned in the swamp behind the church or got eaten by the alligators that swam in it.

I would like to relate one success story from my little school. I did not understand the importance of this little triumph at first, although I was always very proud of it. It was not for decades that I finally understood that the value of it lay not in my success but in the lesson that it taught me.

This is the story. To my little school one day a mother brought her four-year-old son who was a genius. She told me in tears that his IQ was 200 and she was warned to put him in a special school, but she wanted to raise him as normal as possible. The problem was that the child was destructive and vicious. He hit other children and pushed them. She said she had to tell me first, because it wasn't fair not to, but she begged me to take him anyway and give him a chance. I saw the situation in terms of another $15 tuition fee.

For the first hour or so I observed the boy. His mother was right. No sooner had some child built a house of blocks than David would knock it down, and when the builder naturally registered his complaint, David would knock *him* down. He pushed children off the slide, he pushed children off their chairs, and he threw sand in their faces. This kid was bone mean. Half the class had been running to me in tears all morning. I called everybody in from the play yard and had them sit at the tables.

"We have a problem," I announced. "David can't help hitting people. Isn't that right, David?" David nodded his head in the affirmative.

"But that isn't fair to the rest of you all because when David hits you or pushes you down, it hurts and it's not fair for you to get hurt, right?" Everybody nodded in agreement.

"So here's what we're going to do. Now, David, I know you can't help hitting and pushing the other children, but from now on I want you to not hit *quite* so hard, and when you push somebody, just give a *little* push instead of a big push. Do you think you could do that?" David nodded somewhat hesitantly but he said he thought he could do that. "And nobody throws sand in my school!" I deepened my voice and rose up on my toes like the wicked dragon from the Northland looking down at David's blue eyes. "Do you understand me? DON'T EVER THROW SAND AGAIN." David nodded; he looked scared to death.

"And for the rest of you, since you know that David can't help hitting you, if he hits you and it doesn't *really* hurt very much, just ignore it." I explained what ignore meant. "Now if David hits you and it really *hurts*, then you come and tell me." We went over it again and again. We did some role playing. I asked a little girl to come up and I told David to hit her, but not so hard it would hurt. The little girl agreed that "it didn't even hurt." We tried having David push a little boy, but not so hard. Again, an agreement that no harm was done.

For the next few days I watched in amazement. David would push a little boy out of line and the boy would lift up a fist to retaliate. Then he would see it was "just David" and he would smile and go back to his play. David would pull a little girl's hair and the eyes would flash until she saw it was "only David" and she would smile at him and go on about her business. David, I noticed, was really calibrating his pushing, pulling, pinching, and hitting so it didn't *really* hurt.

By the end of the week, the children hardly looked up when David bumped into them or knocked down their houses. If they said anything at all it was mostly, "Oh, hi David." And David? His hitting and pushing looked like it was becoming too much trouble. He stopped completely by the end of two weeks and started just playing instead of hitting first and then playing. His mother said she could never repay me for the change I had wrought in her child. Actually, I am rather proud of it still.

What is the lesson? The lesson is that we cannot heal ourselves from our sense of isolation, or learn to live successfully with one another in a group, or even in a marriage, unless each and every one of us in the group lays equal claim to something we all hold equally important. We have to find *common ground*.

In psychology this is called the "in group" feeling as opposed to the "out of group" feeling. In my little school the common ground was David's problem. In most successful marriages the common ground is the commitment. Whenever we lose common ground, we experience alienation and loneliness, which can erupt into depression and mania as we become overly self-absorbed.

My projects were a glorification of self-absorption. They were totally ungrounded and unconnected to anything except my whim to do them. I decided to put together a coupon book when my Air Force husband was ordered to a temporary duty station for two weeks. I got dozens of advertisers; even JC Penney did a coupon for a free beach towel. But I never gave a thought as to how I was going to sell a coupon book once I produced it. I ended up throwing them all in the trash and was too embarrassed to shop in Penney's again for fear someone would recognize me.

This is typical of high-flying manic ideas—they don't come with any built-in follow-through. When the original chemical high wears off, everything looks impossible and then depression sets in.

I started a shopper's guide when we moved to San Juan, Puerto Rico, when my husband, who had become a stockbroker for Merrill Lynch, was promoted to managing the Caribbean region. The guide is still successful decades later, not for me, but rather for my partner who was able to take it away from me because I couldn't be bothered with the mundane legal details of ownership. One month she told all the advertisers that we were changing the name of the guide and she signed all "our" customers up for her own guide. Then she told me she was quitting *our* guide. I was suddenly out of business. I went into a depression.

When the depression lifted three months later, I talked my husband into buying a direct-mail advertising franchise and rented an office. Since I was now going to be a *big advertising mogul*, I decided that all the sewing material I had bought over the years to make clothes was causing a psychic overload.

For years I had been snapping up material by the rolls so I could make anything out of it, short dress or long. If I liked the design and thought it was a bargain, I might even buy it in several colors. I had a whole room that was devoted to my sewing machine, and floor-to-ceiling shelves of ten-yard material rolls.

In typical fashion, I gave up sewing long before I stopped buying material, so I had a lifetime supply of it when I decided I had sewn my last seam. I gave all the material to a neighbor. The advertising franchise followed soon after. The material probably had cost three or four thousand dollars. The franchise cost $26,000 and I ended up just walking away and leaving it to my two salesmen who promised to pay me for it but never did. I knew they wouldn't but, even so, I didn't try to sell the business to anyone else.

The flash-in-the-pan that lived to shine had to glitter it all away again. Even those business ventures that seemed halfway grounded never made any money because I abandoned them before they matured into anything profitable. After several years of back-to-back projects I realized that the $150,000 I got for a house I had just sold went entirely to pay off my old debts. Ten years of hard work and I *lost* money. Plus the fact that I diverted too much of my time and energy away from my responsibilities to my family.

Ultimately all my effort went for nothing because I was so intent on showing people how extraordinary I was, which is essentially distancing behavior, not that of joining and sharing. I did not have a clue as to the virtue and joys that come from being an ordinary person, situated in the mundane, in the everydayness of a regular life. I didn't fully grasp that being an ordinary person takes incredible dedication and courage; that there comes a point where the quotidian sameness that at one time was such a bore is, in fact, the doorway to a cosmic oneness that is quite extraordinary.

But before that epiphany, when I wasn't shining, I thought I was dying. I felt compelled to put into action the merest whim that activated in my brain because it was the only way I felt really alive. Actually, it was even worse than that. I felt obligated to trust anything that occurred to me as an almost noblesse oblige based solely on the fact that my mind had created it. I didn't question what idea came to me, as I had not questioned any feeling that came to me. I felt, I jumped. I thought, I jumped. I followed my most half-baked idea like it was the Holy Grail. I have since learned better.

Manic behavior most often results from a narrow self-focus on our own irrational thinking, which may be perfectly logical, but at the same time totally out of touch with objective reality. Unduly influenced by our potentially destructive compulsive feelings rather than our potentially empowering chosen principles, we withdraw our attention from the better-constructed world that we have been co-creating with our fellows, and focus on some temporary private "inner" world of our own hasty making. This kind of self-conscious self-focus is the exact opposite of self-awareness.

Again, mania is not the antidote to depression that the use of drugs presupposes. Since mania and depression are both the opposite of self awareness, we can't really do anything directly with either one of them. Just like we can't do anything directly with the darkness. Darkness is simply the absence of light.[9] The only thing we can do with the darkness is to turn on the light. The only thing we can do with depression and mania is to "turn on" the self. That is what we are doing with Directed Thinking.

Before I understood all this, however, I threw myself into life like you would meet a wave straight-on at the beach, instead of respectfully turning sideways. So I was always being knocked flat on the shores of my failed projects, bruised and dazed. My husband often said to me that I seemed to have a need for suffering, that I seemed to see myself as some kind of a tragic figure, and he refused to see himself that way. For that reason he avoided me as much as possible for twenty years with customary six-day 6 A.M. to 9 P.M. workweeks and nonstop TV on his day off, for which I hardly blame him. I didn't realize that futility was just a feeling. I took it for reality.

One night I got so depressed on the way home from a neighborhood movie that I told my husband to stop the car because I couldn't breathe, I had to get out. He gave me a funny look, and I insisted, "Please, please, just stop the car." I started to cry. I felt like I was dying. He stopped the car and I jumped out and threw myself into the ditch at the side of the road and began rocking back and forth, hugging myself and weeping.

"I'm so sick. I'm so sick. Can't you see I'm dying. I'm dying. I can't go on without some kind of love." I started retching like I was trying to vomit up my very soul. "Get away from me. Just go away and leave me alone. I just don't care anymore. I just can't do it anymore." Now I ask you, what is a poor husband to do under those circumstances?

He went with me faithfully to see all of my psychiatrists, psychologists, and counselors. I was sure there was some secret about me that they knew and I didn't. And, of course, I wasn't about to tell them the shameful secrets about myself that *only I knew*!

My husband sat in the lobby while I screamed in re-birthing sessions and popped in and out of past lives during hypnotic regression. He hosted encounter groups for weekends at our home when I came under the spell of the current "brilliant teacher" who had us all running around naked (not the children of course, they were visiting friends), who used our pool and Jacuzzi to pocket $300 per person (or about $6,000 per weekend). I was dumb enough to think we were getting a real bargain because, as the hosts, we "saved" $600.

Now, to be fair, I did learn something from these sessions. And so did my husband. The last thing we learned is that there comes a time when you just get tired of trying to improve yourself and decide to give up and be your own mediocre or unhappy self the best crippled-up way you can. My sister-in-law tried to tell me that years ago when she said that the main thing about me was that I had never settled. At the time she said it, I wasn't ever going to settle. I thought settling was a cowardly act that meant you were giving up. It was a crime against nature, a lazy refusal to make something remarkable out of yourself.

And I was exactly the kind of person (if you ever wondered about it) who joins a religious cult. Someone who is past forty and still looking for a sense of identity, someone who spends half their time depressed, someone who wants happiness and true love, someone who believes that they will discover their authentic life if they can just get to the right place, or meet the right person.

One afternoon I walked by a New Age bookstore and saw a small notice in the window about a meditation weekend in Oregon. I went home, called the airline for tickets, and just up and left my family completely for a year to seek enlightenment at the ashram of an Indian guru.

Originally I had gone just for the weekend meditation, but I came home only to dye all my clothes red and tell my weeping eight-year-old son that when he was lonely all he had to do was think about me and I would "visit him in spirit." I told my shocked husband that I would return in a year. I also told him my mind was broken. "All our friends are mad at me for going," I cried, "but if I had a broken *back* and was going into the *hospital* for a year, they'd all be bringing casseroles."

My cousin called my husband and said she would be willing to help kidnap and de-program me. My husband called my youngest brother and together they considered how to commit me to a psychiatric hospital, against my will, so that I could get treatment for the manic depression that had so devastated my father and my other brother. But I beat them to the punch and got a lawyer at the ashram (from the staff of thirty lawyers who were also followers of this particular guru) who told me that I would be legally protected.

When I told that to my husband, he just gave me up for lost. The next time I called home I was terribly hurt to find out that he had told my daughters to take anything they wanted out of my closet. I didn't give a thought to any hurt I might be causing *them*. I returned a year later and when I knocked on the door, they let me in.

I returned a less uptight, less brittle person. I had learned transcendental meditation, learned more about hypnosis and other kinds of thought-processing, all of which helped to give me a more detached and objective view of my emotions and feelings. I still feared depression, but I had started to gather some tools to lessen my self-identification with it, and they were beginning to work.

The only comment my husband ever made about my absence was at the first party we attended after my return to the family, "Well I see they at least taught you how to dance." Of course you may be wondering why my family wanted me back at all.

But, you see, I had put a lot of energy into my family, and had worked very hard for them even though they were often sandwiched between manic projects and depression. It had always been a very thin line of reality that tied me like a kite string to my daily life and kept me from just drifting off into never-never land.

Off and on during the day I would come to and fix dinner or clean the house. A rudimentary schedule on my refrigerator calendar, and habits like reading bedtime stories, taking the children for their medical checkups, braces on their teeth, teacher's meetings, and ritual walks around the block at night after dinner stapled me to some semblance of a normal life.

I may have been a raging manic-depressive but I kept my home neat, I put dinner on the table every night, and I did nice things for my children. When my teenage son wanted to "go West" to work in a uranium mine for the summer because that was the only place that he could earn $8 an hour, I offered to pay him $8 an hour to write his autobiography, which he did complete. He was the student in the family and I thought he had writing talent.

When the children were quite young, I would take them to art shows and encourage their interest by explaining to them that we weren't there just to look at the pictures, we were the judges of the whole show. "Really," they would exclaim with wide-open eyes, "*Us?*" The children would excitedly discuss the merits of all the pictures, and after a few hours they would decide among themselves which picture "won." Then we would ceremoniously present some astonished artist with a $5 check on which was the notation, "Best of Show."

When my youngest son began stuttering at school I cured him by teaching him to stutter on purpose, and then commanding him to "stop that." My theory was that you can't consciously stop doing something that you do unconsciously. When my oldest son brought home all failing grades in the ninth grade and said nobody ever picked him when they chose up sides for teams, I worked with him for years. I was into Zen and Positive Mental Attitude then so these precepts were passed on, and they must have done some good. I remember one conversation with my son at this time about a book called *Zen and the Art of Archery*, and how the archer spiritually first became the bow, then the arrow, and then the target so he couldn't miss. My son said, "So that's how come you always win every argument with me, isn't it? You just become your own point, don't you?" My son did so well that he actually graduated from high school second in his class and even became president of student council; after which time all my friends eagerly sought my advice as to how to straighten out their kids.

The son who wrote his autobiography says that he had a very happy childhood. I was very gratified when he told me that Christmas, which was always a time of terrible depression for me, had been always a happy time for him. The child who overcame his failing grades to become second in his class told me as he left for college, "Mom, I've been high man and I've been low man and I figure I can take either one." The eight-year-old-son I left to go to the ashram, now grown, says that the best thing about me was that I was always very considerate, and the worst thing was that I never planned ahead what I was going to do.

Although it was true I didn't see my children's problems at first, when they were pointed out to me I always got to work immediately to take care of business. The children remember some fun times singing all the children's songs I wrote. I'm glad about that, even though I also remember that when the older children left for school, my two-year-old would cry when I picked up my guitar because she knew she was going to be ignored for the next two or three hours.

With the first three children, I made a conscious effort to keep them separate from my great angst and my grand schemes. If they came into the room while my husband and I were screaming at each other, I would calmly order them out like a strict school librarian with the remark, "Your father and I have the right to argue in private, if you don't mind." I didn't want them to be frightened by thinking our behavior was totally out of control (since I could address them in a calm manner) and I didn't want them to feel any responsibility for our craziness.

There was a lot of craziness between my husband and me in those days, although our arguments were stable enough in that they were always the same. I would scream at him that I wasn't happy with our relationship and we needed to talk about him making some changes NOW! He would yell back that I was a selfish malcontent who was never satisfied with anything, including him, and would slam the door on his way OUT!

When I started a business or remodeled the house, I knew it was for me and not for the children, so I never asked them for help when I bit off more than I could chew (unless I offered to pay them). I never yelled at them and didn't intrude my own personal problems on their lives. I tried to contain the chaos in my head and, as much as possible, I kept our house tidy, the clothes washed, and some orderly schedule of meals.

If there was ever too much work to do I could just work all night with no problem at all. Actually I found I could stay up all night two nights in a row and that I kind of liked the altered state of consciousness, the feeling of unreality that third day, as it was a great relief from depression.

On and off we had full-time help, which I insisted my latest "great idea" was soon going to be able pay for. The problem was that I was hooked on these project "highs" to give my life meaning as much as I was hooked on them to keep me from depression. I was a thoroughly psychologized poster child for self-actualization. Most of my passion was directed to these self-ish pursuits that all ended up as dropped stitches sooner or later when I tired of the details. Sometimes the dropped stitches were my children.

I had no idea that I had lost all connection with my fifteen-year-old daughter (third child) until she ran away (after which event friends no longer asked for my child-improvement lectures). My husband called me in San Juan, Puerto Rico, from our home in New Jersey, and said she had been missing for three days. Why, you may ask, didn't I know? By now I had a nanny and could pursue more far-flung opportunities.

My songs had not sold, so this time fame and fortune was coming my way as the distributor for Pop-Wheels in Puerto Rico. They were clunky elevated sandals that turned into roller skates when you pulled a button on the side. Honest! I was in

all the San Juan newspapers and on television, parading around
in my short shorts and skates. Wasn't I smart? Wasn't I pretty?
Wasn't I going to sell a million of them?

When my husband told me about my daughter, my duty to
my family suddenly reasserted itself, and I dropped everything
and flew back home to look for her. We entered counseling
together, and I resolved to stick closer to home. I started baking
my own bread. I bought a grinding mill and milled my own
whole wheat flour so it would be fresh. I could spend six hours
in the shopping mall to find the "perfect" blouse to go with a
skirt, then come to and, feeling guilty, rush home to my babies.

I rented a small office in order to start a gift-catalog company; I hired myself out as a portrait photographer (I already
had a photo lab in the house so I could develop my own prints).
My oldest son and I "invented" photo-stones. We put an emul-
sion on pieces of marble (free from the local granite works) and
processed photos on them, which we sold as bookends to gift
stores at $40 each.

I was always as busy as a rat in a maze. My life felt no more
solid and real than those empty-eyed theater masks that depict
comedy or tragedy solely by whether the mouth turns up or
down. I reflected the changes in myself and the society around
me no more profoundly than that.

In the end I think the only thing that kept me sane was
befriending people who were in worse shape than I was. I col-
lected them into a kind of foundation or halfway house that
was often the sole support of my self-esteem. For all I know,
the feeling was mutual. Or worse than that. Now that I think
of it, I do recall that after three weeks, one group therapy
session I joined in 1979 decided to change its weekly meeting
to the only evening I said I couldn't attend. I guess they got
tired of Miss Wonderful smiling at grief and not really seeing
it. They knew, better than I, that grief is not to be bested; it is
to be suffered, and mourned, and shared with our fellows. It

is not in "proving ourselves" the champion, but only in the sharing of our mutual human-ness that we become real.

It is hard to tell what was real in those days. In a way, I thought I hadn't gotten to my "real life" yet. Of course when I finally did get to my life I realized that all the "one-day-when," all the "not-quite" and the "not-yet" *was* my life. I have since come to see that what my sister-in-law meant by *settling* is simply to refrain from wrestling life to the mat every single day of our lives to force it to pay up what we think it owes us. Settling is simply a deep understanding that we aren't owed anything. We have already got whatever it is that we are going to get, and the answer to the question, "Is that all there is?" is "YES!"

It took thirty years of my life to get to the amen of this yes. And I believe I was lucky to have refused antidepressants. Although I spent many years in abject pain, it was the pain of depression that finally forced me to my knees, where I could see the failures in my life head-on.

I remember well that day on my knees. It was after our move to California. It was in early afternoon when my children were in school and my husband was at work. I felt that I was going to die from the pain of that emptiness feeding on me. I started rocking back and forth, back and forth like I was trying to bloody birth some terrible demon ripping up my insides. "Please, help me," I cried out to no one by name, but in the general vicinity of Heaven.

"I surrender. I have done everything I can think of and nothing has worked. I have tried my whole life and nothing has ever worked. I don't know what to do. Just tell me what to do. My way has not worked. I will do whatever you say."

I tried to open myself up to whatever might be coming to direct me. Suddenly two phrases from the Bible came to my mind: "Seek and ye shall find, ask and ye shall receive, knock and it shall be opened unto you," and "You shall know the truth and the truth shall make you free." I clung to those two phrases, saying them over and over in my mind. I felt comforted and fell into a deep sleep on the floor where I had fallen. Shortly after that a great store of philosophical and metaphysical books came quite by chance into my possession. My quest had begun. And, though I didn't know it at that moment of desperation, in a year I would be entering graduate school to become a psychotherapist.

Seven

THE NARROW
MOMENT OF CHOICE

It was not the intensity of the onset of depression that made the difference, it was how quickly I chose to take some different action, rather than passively allow myself to go the way of my feelings.

The mind tricks that allow us to slip away from our depression are based upon the simple neuroscientific fact that our feelings are located in a different sector of the brain from our reasoning and intellect. When we are severely depressed, we do not have much neural activity going on in the upper brain. We are completely out of the government of ourselves.

I can remember one late afternoon when I started driving home after leaving my daughter off at a gymnastics class near our home in Ridgewood, New Jersey. It was winter, raining, the streets were getting dark, and I might have turned in the wrong direction when I left the parking lot. After a while I thought I realized my mistake and turned around again. But then I doubted myself and reversed course.

I began to lose all sense of direction. It was as if my thinking just didn't work anymore; the only thing operating was panic. I kept changing my mind and going back and forth and back and forth, driving faster and faster to make up for lost time, squealing my brakes and screaming my frustration at the slow traffic in my way until I was dissolved into hysterical tears and had to pull off the road and call my husband from a gas station. I was two miles from home and did not know where I was. I was very scared, the world seemed unreal and shifting beneath me, and I felt truly crazy.

Writers who suffer from depression are especially horrified to find that our verbal skills fail us when we need them the most. We begin to feel stupid and slow. But, if we make a heroic effort to sit down and write about our depression, we end up concentrating on our writing instead of on our feelings. In calling upon our higher-mind faculties for words to describe our malady, we cause the concentration of neural activity in our lower brain to lessen as we stimulate increased neural activity in the upper brain. The brain manifests a finite amount of neural activity.

This is how our depression always fades with concentration upon the task at hand, one of the benefits of the old-fashioned concept of "duty." We can choose to concentrate on our pain, or we can choose to concentrate on our work. This is the neuroscientific explanation for English poet Letitia Landon's remark: "No thoroughly occupied man was ever yet very miserable."

If we are depressed, we can withdraw from concentrating on our painful feelings and instigate some verbal activity, like reciting a poem or singing a song. Any kind of incessant imaging can create a thought blockade against depression, if we can stick to it for a few minutes, by switching the concentration of neural activity from one brain location to the other. This way we can accomplish a physical brainshift without introducing any outside chemicals.

When depression boxes us in, we can learn to think outside the box. To change channels on TV we use an electric switch.

To change channels in the brain we use a bioelectric *thought*. We *can*, in the sense that we have the choice to do so. Whether or not we decide to make that choice is a different matter.

Depression is daunting, from the inside. From the outside, those who are the onlookers of it wonder why in the heck we depressed can't see that we are really all right, and just get on with it. When we are depressed we can't see we're all right because depression by its very nature contains the built-in conviction that we are *not* all right, that futility is the only reality. Thus it can become a closed and limited universe. Believing in this universe, we will believe we do not have a choice to free ourselves from it. Believing we must remain depressed is a type of self-hypnosis, like watching a movie.

While we are watching a movie, it is not real people who are suffering and causing our tears; it is only shadows of light on a screen. It is the same with depression. It is not objective reality that "nothing's worth anything," or "we're done for"; it is just a temporary painful feeling of hopelessness. But depression is not an on-purpose temporary suffering like a sad or scary movie.

With depression, we can forget we have a choice. So it is necessary to have some pre-arranged trigger to remind ourselves when we go into depression that it is not the pain of some reality, it is only a painful *feeling*, a place in our brain that we are now visiting; but we don't have to stay there if we don't want to. It is also a good idea to have some mind tricks planned in advance so they can be quickly employed. The quicker the better. Depression is more of a "routine" than a disease. And we have acculturated it into a routine that takes precedence over all other routines. In different cultures and in past eras other routines such as duty took precedence over depression. When we decide to slip another routine in on depression it loses its power.

Some of my patients have devised quite effective routines or mind tricks of their own—some at-hand thinking patterns that they can quickly substitute for their regular habit of concentrating on their depression. Adam H. is a college student whose twin brother died in a car accident at the age of fourteen. He told me that when he realizes he is into depression now, he imagines a conversation with his brother who says, "Get up, man, you have to do it for both of us now. Come on. Come on, man, you'll be all right. You can do it. Do it for me. You're the only one who can do it for me now." Adam says he is no longer tempted to stay in bed with depression. He just gets up and goes to work, feeling an obligation to the comforting presence of his brother.

This is not only making use of a mind trick, it is making use of moral imperative as well. Depression isolates us from everybody else. All the advice from philosophy urges us to remain *connected* to maintain ourselves in the world. The smallest thing we grab for to pull us out of depression usually hooks us right back up with the rest of our fellows.

Anthropology echoes philosophy's warning that our social evolution as individuals, as well as our physical survival, depends upon our ability to maintain strong reciprocal connections for ourselves. It is not only genetically through our combined DNA, and emotionally through use of the primal mind, but socially through the use of interactive principles, that the group or family, not the individual, is the embryo of society.

We cannot stand alone, and therefore depression puts our survival at risk because it disconnects us. And there is a converse to that. There is a great deal of evidence that the people who suffer the least with depression are those who live connected lives. When we are depressed we need to move from the almost overwhelmingly strong but not-smart feelings of the primal mind to the intelligent, principled strategies of the higher mind. It is a simple and surprisingly unpromising path we use to get there. In this sense I compare the incredible effect upon our lives of these simple mind tricks to the experience some early explorer might have had traveling along some scrubby little footpath and arriving unexpectedly at the rim of the Grand Canyon. Oh, my God. The beauty. The beauty.

Sharon B. uses nursery rhymes as a path from the primal mind to the higher mind. Nursery rhymes, admittedly, are simple, dumb little things. But they can lead us to the thought-jamming and neural shifting necessary to make the switch out of depression. "In the beginning," Sharon said, "I had to sing them out loud, real loud. Sometimes I even held my hands over my ears as if that would keep the depression from 'getting through.' But later on, as I got used to singing at the very first sign of depression, I could just sing songs in my mind until I got busy and 'into something.'"

Mary J. is a nurse who visualizes her depression as an empty, heart-shaped candy box and one by one she puts little fancy chocolates into the box. "When it's full, I put on the top, tie a red ribbon around the box, and get up."

Here's another wonderful mind trick suggested by the Roman emperor and stoic philosopher Marcus Aurelius: "In the morning, when thou art sluggish at rousing thee, let this thought be present. I am rising to a man's work."

John S. is an engineer. He says he gives himself a "lateral pass" out of depression and helps himself "get going" by visualizing a maze starting with a big arrow that says YOU ARE HERE and then another arrow at the completion of the maze that says GET UP NOW. He's made elaborations on the maze since his first one. What used to be black and white on graph paper is getting more and more, he says, to look like "Technicolor Dragons in the Land of Oz."

My friend Clay E. is a retired hospital administrator. He told me that after his twenty-three-year-old son committed suicide he would sometimes experience an overwhelming feeling of grief and despair that would hit him "like a Mack truck."

One day the phrase "Just be gentle with yourself" occurred to him and he got into the habit of saying it over and over to himself, until his depression faded.

This is a most beautiful technical interception to bypass the painful feelings of depression. Such a simple device but a most powerful and spiritual one. Clay has shared this phrase with many others who have used it to escape from their own despair. It is not simply the *idea* of the phrase that works, however. It is the *use* of the phrase; the thinking of the phrase instead of the thinking of the despair.

T. R., who is a whiz at designing web sites, devised a marvelous trigger to remind himself to move to action when he becomes mired in depression. He once went into a terrible depression that dragged on for months. "One day," he said, "I realized that I had sat in the same chair for three days in my underwear without doing anything except getting up and going to the bathroom. I started to talk to myself, out loud, 'Is this rational?' My answer was 'No, this is not rational.'

"So I got up, got the car keys, and drove down the road to the 7-Eleven. I was still in my underwear, so I did not go in. I waited for a few minutes in the parking lot and drove back home. But I had done *something* other than sit in that chair. It was a victory of sorts. When I got home, I got myself something to eat. I felt better.

"I decided to erect a boundary for myself, a marker to alert me. Now when I realize I am deep in depression I visualize two little red flags, one on either side of my head, just in my peripheral vision. Those red flags tell me to get up and do something, that it is not rational to lie around and be depressed. Get busy. And when I see those red flags, believe it, I get busy."

We never have to suffer depression or mania more than a few minutes. As soon we become aware that we are depressed or manic, we can, as an act of will, replace the accidental, unchosen thoughts that have caused the problem with new, positive, neutral, or commonsense thoughts or actions. We just need to change from the easy *casual thinking*, which got us into trouble, to the harder *causal thinking*, which can get us out of it. Yes, in a sense, "Row, Row, Row Your Boat" is causal in that it can cause a bioelectric brainshift out of the lower-brain primal mind to the upper-brain higher mind.

With Directed Thinking, we always have the option to choose between the reasoning and creativity of our higher mind and the emotional compulsions of the primal mind. We never have to be in the position of not being able to get out of bed, because we can always change the thought "I can't get out of bed" to the thought "I will get out of bed when the second hand gets to twelve."

Choice is the most priceless gift we own. It is the gift of human volition, of freedom of the will. But if no one has ever told us that we have choice, we won't know to make the effort to exercise it. Or maybe we know about freedom of the will as it concerns our ability to refrain from stealing our neighbor's ripe tomatoes out of his garden in the dead of night, no matter how much we want them, but we don't know that freedom of the will can also be used for depression and mania.

Freedom of the will is qualitative, not quantitative. If it exists for stealing tomatoes and ducking a two-by-four, it exists for everything else. The only quantitative thing about freedom of the will is that we can decide to use it, or we can decide to *not* use it. Remember, even *not* choosing is a choice in itself. We are not only responsible for what we do; we are responsible for what we *fail* to do.

Once we are plunged into depression, we cannot for the life of us believe that it is by *our own volition* that we are in such a state of siege and suffering. In fact, it isn't by our own volition that we have become depressed, it is by our failure to exercise our volition *early enough*, at the first warning, to avoid falling into the clutches of hopeless depression.

There is a critical moment of true awareness, an instant of clarity that we all experience before we fall into panic and darkness or when we are struggling with some seemingly insurmountable problem. In our present-day culture, if this moment is talked about at all, it is sentimentalized as the "wee small voice of conscience," or trivialized as "knack" or "hunch." In the rush and busyness of our lives, we have a propensity to ignore what the old mystics called the "moment of divine intelligence," so that we sometimes miss this fleeting, warning instant that invites us to take new and different action.

This narrow moment of choice, which is profound but *not insistent,* is not only important in depression, manic depression, and anxiety attacks, it is important in migraine headaches, road rage, embezzlement, infidelity, suicide, and murder. There is a cautionary but barely perceptible interruption of our flow of ongoingness that comes to us at pivotal times. We can make our claim upon this timeless moment and convert it to our use by expanding our awareness of it, or we can lose it in the surrender to what bent we are already headed for.

It is in this narrow moment of choice that we are given a chance to engage the use of the higher mind instead of remaining in the subbasement of the primal mind. It is a predictive moment in that we can count upon its appearances, but unless we understand its significance, and become alert to it, we can dismiss it out of hand and fail to choose to bring it to "real time." The problem is we don't realize that it is this crucial instant of conscious option that is always the critical event, and not whatever mess is going on in our lives at the moment.

It can mean the difference between sickness and health, happiness and despair, life and death. As English author Samuel Johnson warned, "Men are not blindly betrayed in corruption but abandon themselves to their passions with their eyes open; and lose the direction of Truth because they do not *attend* to her voice, not because they do not *understand* it."

Victor Brancaccio, age seventeen, was convicted in 1995 of

murdering an eighty-one-year-old widow who had criticized the "foul-mouthed" rap music he was listening to when she happened to walk by him. Talking to the police after the murder, the former altar boy said that after his first angry punch at the elderly woman, as he was looking at her broken nose and the blood on her face, he had a fleeting thought. "I should help her, you know, and say I'm sorry; or continue what I'm doing."

Unfortunately he continued to do what he was doing by jumping on her rib cage and bashing in her skull with a toy gun, until the white-haired grandmother could no longer "get him in trouble." In the young man's case, the higher-mind option was quickly passed up. But it is important to note that he remembered the exact moment of choice long enough to comment on it later.[1]

This is an extreme example on the low end of the behavior spectrum. But, qualitatively speaking, it is the same moment of awareness that exists for every one of us. It always comes pure and unaffected by anything we have done in the past. Even if we are the world's worst murderer, the same moment of choice is still available to us that is available to the pope himself. In the worst crush of circumstance we can choose to function from the higher mind of reason, principle, and creativity, or from the primal mind of rote impulse and feeling.

Joe K. told me that his bad temper has caused him a lot of trouble in his marriage and at work. "There are times," he told me, "when some little thing will set me off and I've learned that I have a choice in the very beginning to do something else other than reacting to that very first small thing, even if it's as simple as counting to ten. If I don't turn away from being angry at that first small thing, it snowballs, and I'll be mad at this, and mad at that, and throwing this, and banging that, and my anger will grow and explode and pretty soon I'm completely out of control and can't stop myself."

The trouble with not controlling our feelings, says eighteenth-century English essayist Richard Steele, is that "men spend their lives in the service of their passions, instead of employing their passions in the service of their lives." We cannot escape the stamp of our habitual mind upon our lives; but we can resist it. Principles are the only way to control our response to feelings. Our desire cannot do it, not even the desire to control feelings, because desire is itself a feeling that ebbs and flows. Principles do not ebb and flow. Principles are the solid posts set in cement that we can hold onto to stay the chosen course that feelings would push us from.

It took me many years to learn this lesson about my depression. But finally I did learn to simply turn away from that very first small sinking feeling that was always the lead-in to my inevitable crash. Now, as soon as I feel that first wave, I launch into some mind tricks to switch my attention in another direction. As I got more and more practiced with this, I found I could just as easily handle a full blast of depression as a small wave. It was not the intensity of the onset of depression that made the difference, it was how quickly I chose to take some different action, rather than *helplessly go the way of my feelings*.

There is a point certain in any situation whereupon we can turn one way or the other. We are never without choice at any time, but we can wait overlong to make it. We always have the choice to let our attention drift passively, carried along by rote impulse and random thinking. Or, we can direct our attention to the higher mind by choosing to "work" some goal. If we choose to work some goal, like counting to ten, or getting up and going to work, and insist upon it earnestly, troubling impulses like depression will end in forward action, not end in themselves and "work us."

This is what Ralph Waldo Emerson meant when he said, "Spiritual force is stronger than material; thoughts rule the world." Napoleon made a similar distinction between animal passion and passion directed into creativity when he said,

"Imagination rules the world." On another occasion Napoleon explained how his own passions were under his command. "Different matters are arranged in my head as in drawers: I open one drawer, and close another, as I wish. If I desire repose, I shut up all the drawers, and sleep." Does this seem extraordinary? The power of the ordinary human mind *is* extraordinary.

Most of us don't know that we can direct our mind in this way. We modern-day Americans usually choose to function from feelings, the totally open-drawer policy. Then we get so hooked into the use of primal-mind strategies that it is a Herculean effort to drag ourselves back out. We get so stuck in the throes of a throat-choked, painful, wild-eyed animal state that our lawyers have to start claiming innocence by reason of insanity, and our doctors don't know what to do with us except to drug or shock us out of it.

We get too busy and go too fast, or perhaps we are simply ignorant of the importance of that first feathery warning of despair before full-blown depression sets in, or the significance of that first stab of something behind the eye before we are writhing in pain from our migraines. We neglect to take action when it would have been easier for us, with that first small hint of awareness before we "cook the books" or start the affair, or attack the driver who cut us off.

We can be proactive at this moment of choice and access our upper-brain faculties, or we can be reactive, take the path of least resistance, and our lower brain will automatically pick up the slack with impulse strategies that could ultimately lead us to the hospital or handcuffs.

Artist Yoko Ono had a sign on the wall of her "performance art" gallery that read: "This room slowly evaporates a little bit every day." When I first read about that I looked around at the room I was in and repeated the words over and over to myself. I was astounded how that dumb little phrase slipped right through some immense psychic wall of denial that I had not known was there. It was magical, like a hurricane-tossed straw that has penetrated a brick. We forget that nothing lasts forever. We seldom pause to think what it means that our heart is not going to beat forever. It is only going to beat a finite number of times and then . . . it will stop. How many of those precious beats do we want to spend in road rage, or temper tantrums, or brief, high-risk love affairs? Wouldn't it be nice to think that we were more than just two ends of an alimentary canal? There needs to be some heroic aspect to our anguish, some patience to our torment, some softness to our endurance, or the gods will turn their eyes away and cease to weep with us.

The rest of us may attempt to deny it at times by saying we can't help it. But the great thinkers of the ages understood very well that human beings, whether they are aware of it or not, are *always situated in choice*. Our great philosophers tell us that, as an act of will, we can turn up our awareness by directing our attention to it, or we can let it fade and die aborning.

As Emerson noted, every mind is offered the choice between "truth and repose." We can insist that our mind work toward the fulfillment of a chosen goal or principle, or we can let our mind drift its own way, slipsliding around in some habitual routine, like falling back into sleep instead of getting up and going to work. Each morning when the alarm goes off, there is always a window of opportunity in that half-asleep, half-awake period that every person experiences. We all have the same possibility of conscious choice.

We can wake up to it, get up, face the problems of the day, and experience the good feelings that come with accomplishment. Or we can let our awareness of choice, our knowingness, die down for lack of attending to it at that very critical point. We can shrink away from the clock, put off the day's work again, and feel bad because we have done nothing. This is how we become the tentative, drifting shapes of empty dreams, like hollow men with no guts to them. And it is to this hollow part of us that depression always comes.

I have watched myself do it both ways. I followed the work ethic my parents instilled in me, studied hard in my school years, and always did the best I could at any job I undertook. Yet, year after year, I also went into periodic and lengthy depression, falling headlong into its terror and spiraling pain because I did not know that I had any other choice. The nitty-gritty of it all is that the difference between going on that dark journey, and not going, depends upon a particular choice that is not easy to see unless someone points it out to us.

We can see how we can make a choice between a red or a green bicycle. We can easily see that we make use of bicycles. But choice as it concerns *feelings* is not easy to see. The first thing that we never notice about feelings is that we make use of them; we believe, instead, that feelings make use of *us*. We make use of depression when it comes along instead of refusing to make use of it.

Maureen R. said that the turning point for her with her depression was when she realized that she didn't die from it. If I don't die from it, she reasoned, how bad can it be? At that point, depression was no longer her master; Maureen had taken charge. She could see that as far as depression was concerned, she could simply take a pass. When depression comes, Maureen says, she can feel it coming over her, and she carries on a conversation with it. "Okay, I know you're coming," she says, "I know what this is, and it's not convenient right now, and there are some things I have to do at the moment. I know you're there and I can always check in with you later."

Maureen has learned how to not make use of depression by the device of carrying on a creative conversation, which shifts her neural activity from the primal mind, where depression is, to the higher mind, where it isn't.

"This far I will go and no farther," says Maureen and skirts herself around depression to another place of mind. But for those of us who have not learned how to *not* make use of depression, we go through its motions, we weave and fall with it as if it is some kind of music we are forced to dance to. We could just as well sit out the dance. We just have to learn how to do it.

However, choice as it concerns depression is tricky. It is a very quick, small, and invasive choice; I call it *interstitial choice*. Choice, as it concerns a bicycle is easy to see because a bicycle is only one thing; we are not fooled. Choice, as it concerns feelings, is different. Feeling is like a mental optical illusion wherein two things appear to be one; we can be fooled easily.

There is no way to immediately see through this illusion intellectually, but we have to be *introduced to the concept intellectually*. Then if we just "hang out" with the concept, and do some exercises to help, we will start to get little hints for ourselves in our everyday life so that we can get to the place where choice reveals itself to us; where a new fork in our regular thinking path appears suddenly before us, and we can take a fast sidestep that will make us discontinuous with our depression.

So I am going to relate as clearly as I can how to see through the optical illusion of feeling. First, we have to understand that feeling consists of *two* parts. There is the biochemically based feeling itself, and there is the bioelectrically based we-*know*-we-are-feeling-it. Remember, Jerome Kagan said that in order to experience feelings we must first *judge* our feelings.[2]

The only way it would be possible to employ judgment is if we *know* we are feeling something. Before we *become* happy, we have to know we are *feeling* happy. Before we *become* depressed, we have to know we are *feeling* depressed. Also, there is the further elaboration of *we know* that we know. Ancient wisdom tells us that because human beings are sentient, it not only means that we can know something, we also *know* that we know. *What* we know changes; that we know we know never changes.

We know when we are suffering depression because we are suddenly in pain, and that is a change from *not* being in pain. When things change we notice them. *That* we know we know is not painful, and our attention is never drawn to it because it is not unusual; it never stands out because it *never changes*, and so we never notice it. *Feeling* is one thing. *Knowing* that we are feeling is another thing. *Knowing that we know* is different still again.

There are many kinds of noises. There is only one kind of silence. There are many kinds of fullness. There is only one kind of emptiness. There are many kinds of knowledge, like knowing feelings, but there is only one kind of knowing that we know. As concerns depression, there is a tiny window of opportunity between the *knowing that we feel* and *the knowing that we know*. In a way it is like splitting the atom when we see the space between knowing something and knowing that we know. A veritable explosion of the most powerful opportunity exists in that split, for that is where we will find interstitial choice. Or, to be properly respectful, that is where choice will find us.

We have no trouble choosing between a red and green bicycle. How do we, nitty-gritty speaking, DO choice as it concerns depression? The answer is that the instant we know we are *feeling* depressed we have to remember that there is another place of being where we *know* that we know, and it is this place that gives us the opportunity of choice. From this place we can choose to switch to the higher mind by choosing a positive or neutral thought to *replace* the thought "I know I am feeling depressed." Now we can know a new thought instead of knowing we are feeling depressed.

In this way we interrupt the progression from *knowing* that we are feeling depressed to *becoming* depressed, because we no longer see depression as something that is choiceless. We just need to know some other thought, like the words of a nursery rhyme, instead of knowing that we are feeling depressed. If we choose not to know we are feeling depressed, we can't "get depressed." It is a mind trick.

We cannot know something without knowing that we know it, but we can focus all our attention on the *knowing something* part instead of the *knowing that we know* part because we don't *need to know* that we know in order to feel our feelings. But in order to transcend our feelings we need to focus on knowing that we know, because that is where choice lies.

Steve W., upon first hearing me go through this explanation, told me that it was like having a friend break down for him pop star Michael Jackson's moonwalk dance step. "At first there was no way he could break it down small enough for me to fit my feet in it," said Steve, "but I finally got it anyway just by leaning on it until it kind of fell into me."

We have to "kind of lean on" the place where we *know* that we know until it falls into us. It is also the place of being that is always the same no matter what we are feeling. But it is so obvious and all-enveloping and never-changing, like silence and emptiness, that we have to be alerted to look for it. This is one of those things that the old philosophers clue us in on. Usually we don't even know we are missing this until someone points it out to us. We don't know the relevance to us of this tertiary level of *knowing that we know*; this place where we are always all right.

We never need suffer long if we can change the focus of our attention from knowing *what* we know or feel, to knowing *that* we know or feel it. Mystics like George Gurdjieff call this "self-remembering." Mystic Nisargaddata Maharaj calls it "the witness consciousness." It is not the kind of thing we can do "on the fly" with our usual busyness, trying to accomplish half a dozen things at the same time. We have to come to a complete

STOP. Like learning the moonwalk, it is probably one of the nonbusiest things in the whole world to do; because it is not a matter of effort. It is a matter of being silent and alert and leaning on "a way" until it falls into us.

As to a line of action for depression, a la Steve's image of breaking down a dance step, we can say to ourselves, "Uh-oh, I know I am feeling depressed and I would rather know something else instead of this, so I am going to switch to knowing something else."

Does this seem strange? We are able to say, "I don't want to watch something, or eat something or drink something." Why shouldn't we also be able to say, "I don't want to know I am feeling depressed"?

The way we choose not to know we are feeling depressed is to choose to know something else, like the words of a nursery rhyme, or some phrase like "Just be gentle with yourself." Remember Maureen R.? Instead of knowing she is feeling depressed, she would rather know the things she wants to get busy with, so she focuses her attention on these things, and she respectfully tells her depression she will check in with it later.

This is the simple kind of mind trick that takes care of the problem of depression. The reason we can't say "I don't want to be depressed," the same way we can say "I don't want to bake a cake, or go to the movies," is because we do not do *feelings* directly. The only thing we can do with feelings is to pay attention to them or to detach our attention from them. Directed Thinking accomplishes this detachment by establishing thinking patterns of formula discontinuity with feelings.

The only direct connection we have with feelings is the behavior of judging them, paying attention to them, or ignoring them. Feelings are not under our direct control like behavior. We have to manage feelings indirectly. Or, at least, we have to manage them indirectly as long as they are a problem for us. For some people who are very practiced at simply witnessing their feelings from the know-that-we-know place, witnessing itself is a sufficient mind trick. I myself am not yet at that place. I still find depression so painful and unremitting that I must escape from it using more active mind tricks than simply "witnessing" my pain.

The important thing is that depression cannot maintain its existence except as it is repetitively recorded and reflected in present thinking. The pain cannot think itself. We have to think it. Our mind is like a CD player, our thoughts the CDs. One CD is always playing and others are at the ready. If we don't like the mind's painful CD we can put in another. The pain will echo in us as physical feelings for a short while but, if we insist on putting our CD back in every time it is ejected by the mind, our CD will soon "stick" and the chemicals causing the pain will begin to shift out of alarm mode into painless neutral.

I remember the first time I tried Directed Thinking. I often got terribly depressed and full of anxious worry that would last for days, and sometimes months at a time. I couldn't blame it on anything in particular. Of course I could always get mad at my husband for something.

But basically I would plod along in my gray world, coping and existing, existing and coping, living my shadow existence of quiet desperation where nothing's worth anything. Listening to music, which I normally love, doesn't appeal to me when I am depressed. When I'm depressed, so what if we're on vacation, my children might as well hug a block of wood, my food tastes like cardboard, my soul is permanently stuck in my throat, and my tense sleep provides little rest because I can't turn myself off long enough to relax.

I was never safe from depression, that parallel universe of painful nowhere that would not just lie in wait for me; it would hunt me down like the hound of Hell! It seemed to know I didn't have what I needed to sustain my own life. Well, of course, I did have what I needed and I could have sustained my life as an act of will, but I didn't know that for a very long time. The flowers of my life had always seemed too frail and fragile to stand the regular light of day. I seemed to tear and bruise so easily, my wilted petals creeping back into the solace of their dark roots.

When my little girl was born, after having two boys, I felt like I had won a million-dollar lottery. I was so excited and happy, calling everybody from the hospital about my good luck, looking at little-girl dresses in the newspaper ads, imagining her in knee socks and her first pair of black patent leather shoes. But when visiting hours were over, and the hush of night settled over the ward, and I got out my birth announcements to fill in, the old sinking feeling started to come over me. No, no, I thought, how can it be that there is no joy for me even in this new wonder, my precious little baby girl. But there I went, in just a few seconds, plunged into the deepest despair, weeping, and alone again in my darkness.

Sometimes the taut strain of depression would suddenly snap into the sheer terror of a panic attack. My throat would close, I couldn't swallow properly. My heart would start racing and thumping. I would feel like I couldn't breathe, like I was going to pass out. I can remember at least two occasions when my husband took me to the hospital because I was sure I was having a heart attack. Meanwhile, all this time, I was continually reading self-help and mind-power books like *Psycho-Cybernetics*,[3] *Think and Grow Rich*,[4] *Self Hypnotism the Technique and Its Use in Daily Living*,[5] *Dianetics*,[6] *Knowledge of the Higher Worlds*,[7] *Silva Mind Control*.[8]

One day I thought I was going to die from the pain unless I got some help. My husband was at an all-day meeting. I called my psychiatrist, but except for my scheduled appointment in three days, there were no openings. I became more desperate. I needed help "NOW, TODAY, IMMEDIATELY!!! There must be *somebody* who can help me."

By now I was literally crawling on the floor, weeping, writhing in agony, rolling over and over, smashing myself up against the wall. The pain was unbearable. I would do anything! ANY-THING to get relief. I would even be willing to actually try one of those stupid suggestions and think a positive thought. But I was so distressed that I couldn't even think of a positive thought.

Thrashing and groping around in the muck and mire of my whining and pitiful mind, I succeeded in coming up with "green frog." Not brilliant. I wasn't even sure if "green frog" was a positive thought. But at least I was pretty sure it wasn't a negative one. Anyway, it was the only thought that occurred to me in what seemed like my death throes. So I clung to that thought for dear life.

Every time a resurgent tidal wave of depression engulfed me I would grab onto that thought even tighter, like a life preserver. "Green frog." "Green frog." I wasn't very gentle about it. Like Dylan Thomas's "Do not go gentle into that good night," I did not go gentle into the night of my depression. I went moaning, and complaining, and throwing up and making myself perfectly miserable. I didn't go gentle into thinking "green frog" either. If it's possible to yell a thought into your mind, that's what I did.

I screamed in my mind, "Green frog. Green frog. Goddam-mit. Green frog." Like a dog with a bone, I refused to let go. After about twenty minutes of hanging on to "green frog" I kind of "came to." I noticed that the real panic and pain were gone, and I could breathe okay again. I didn't feel real great, but I didn't feel real horrible either. I felt tentative, tired, a little wary, like the cautious relief after a bad headache has just gone away but might come back any second. My depression didn't seem to be there anymore, but I wasn't about to go poking around for it either. I wasn't sure if "green frog" had anything to do with anything.

But as it turned out, it did. Because I "got into it" really bad a few days later, and again I grabbed for "green frog" since, who knows, maybe it had worked that other time. Again, I started feeling better after about twenty minutes. Then I got better and better at substituting the thought "green frog" for whatever negative thoughts, or thoughts about painful feelings that were bothering me.

Now, when I wake up in the morning with the beast sitting at my throat, in total despair, I find that a "green frog" turnaround is less than five minutes. It works for the solid heavy pain too, the pain that all of a sudden you notice is packed in your chest tight as dirt, filling in your entire body so that there is hardly any room left to breathe. That pain can just soften and break up and evaporate in five or ten minutes. Actually, any neutral thought works as a thought-jamming device to keep the feelings of depression from getting through to my attention. As I found by experimenting. I certainly got depressed often enough to avail myself of the opportunity.

My little "green frog," like any thought can be, acts as a faithful guard at the door of my mind and as long as I think that thought, no other thought may enter. In a way I guess you could say the other thoughts have to remain asleep, potential only, until I open the door by letting go of my chosen thought. It reminds me of a quote of Goethe's, a quote that identifies him for me as a fellow traveler in those dark realms I know only too well: "The passions are like those demons with which Afrasahiab sailed down the Orus. Our only safety consists in keeping them asleep. If they wake, we are lost."

I don't always use "green frog" to distract my attention from a chemical depression or a chemical high, although, out of gratitude, I have an affection for it. Sometimes I use fast counting. I also use counting when I have an adrenaline high and can't get to sleep. If it's not too bad I count backward from 999. If I am really jumping out of my skin, I have to count really fast to begin with (almost like screaming into my mind again), so

I have to start racing through the numbers starting with one-two-three. Pretty soon, lulled with the monotony of the numbers, the counting slows down, gets confused, and disintegrates, and I fall asleep.

Sometimes I can't sleep and I am not patient nor "dutiful" enough to concentrate on counting. If I don't use counting, I can have insomnia. If I insist on using counting, I am always 100 percent successful in getting to sleep. I know this and it does help me to be more proactive when I can't get to sleep. So when I have insomnia and refuse to do the counting I realize I am just being "lazy," doing the *easy* thing even though it's the most agonizing thing. I would guess that most people who dismiss counting out of hand as simplistic and ineffective have no idea how really hard it is to stick to it.

In the morning, in place of "green frog" I might use "Row, Row, Row Your Boat" or "Mairzy Doats," an old 1940s song my father used to sing, to replace the unwilled fearful or obsessive thoughts causing my depression. I recommend a silly song rather than silly words because it is easier to "hang on" to a song without losing concentration.

Remember, I don't need to know what these thoughts are that I am replacing. All I need to know is that if I think neutral thoughts for a time, the depression *always* goes away. I'm still bare-bones basic and unsophisticated about it. I haven't risen to the higher culture of psalms or mystical mantras. But I figure it this way; my mind is as promiscuous as a vacuum cleaner; it will scarf up any old thing. Believe my mind? Do you think I'm crazy! I need to be able to "pull the plug" on it.

As I got better and better at handling my depression and I could be more daring in studying it, I discovered some interesting things about it. The most amazing thing I discovered about depression was that I could not make it worse. No matter how hard I tried to feel worse, I couldn't. Isn't that interesting? The other thing I got a clearer handle on was how my de-

pression had been so situated in my being unaware of and dependent upon rote and autonomic thinking. I learned that any
conscious, on-purpose thinking on my part can take precedence
over autonomic thinking, no matter how silly that on-purpose
thinking might be.

The power does not lie in the magnitude of the thinking or
the greatness of the thought. The power lies in the consistent,
conscious choice of my thought over my mind's autonomic
choice of the thought, "I am depressed." But let me make a
distinction here between Directed Thinking and conscious
thinking. Directed Thinking starts with a conscious choice of
thought. But the concentration upon that thought, by the simple
repetitive choice of it, can cause a self-hypnotic trance, which
reaches deep down into the mind's autonomic processes and
continues to replicate itself by the process of learned association,
neuron by neuron, to alleviate the symptoms of depression, or
to achieve any other chosen goal.

For years I have been studying my own depression so that
I could help myself. But I found I could seriously study my
ongoing symptoms of depression for only about twenty minutes
before the symptoms would begin to break up and disappear.
We have to be careful about studying depression in order to
get rid of it, however, because the "getting rid of it" part—the
"I don't want this" part, which is *fearful thinking*—may replace
the "studying."

I'm always happening upon new defensive-thinking techniques. Such as the "morose meditation." One morning when
I woke up "in the depths" and curled up in the fetal position,
I said to myself, "Well, you don't have to be so morose." And
then I thought, it's gross to be morose. And then the thinking
started to pick up steam by learned association.

It's gross to be morose and lachrymose. I started to think of
all the words that ended in "ose." It's gross to be morose and
lachrymose and verbose and bellicose and comatose and, of

course, one mustn't dose (either "over" or "under")—I congratulated myself on the clever witticism. I got up and looked in the rhyming dictionary to see if there were any more "doses" and saw that I had missed globose. I had to look up the meaning of globose—globular; spherical. Well, that's no good either. I thought to myself, how interesting that you can almost cure your whole life by simply avoiding all the ose's.

It is now about 7 A.M. and my husband is peacefully snoring away and I am having this little morning adventure all by myself. But the thing is that my depression has by now simply evaporated. I put on my jogging shoes and start my forty-five-minute jog. The day seems bright and cheerful. In the past I would have lain in bed, simmering in my depression, despising my husband for sleeping and "not caring about my pain," and going through a checklist of all his faults that were the cause of my unhappiness until my eyes would be nothing but staring daggers of hate into the back of his sleeping head. God, when I think of those days, I imagine the hard-eyed face this man used to have to wake up to. A witch, for sure!! But not any more. I am cured.

We can't get rid of depression *directly* because it is a defense mechanism. It is an autonomic, autonomous phenomenon that, like a cloud, can't be directly manipulated and pushed aside. But, with insistence and concentration, we can override any autonomic depressive thinking. With deliberate thought interceptions, the chemicals relent and the feelings subside and the cloud of depression drifts away.

Billion-dollar industries are much easier to see than truth, which is very small. So maybe it will sound farfetched to some people that the simple use of some neutral thought, like "green frog" or counting, or its like, could replace a multibillion-dollar pharmaceutical industry or the multimillion-dollar psychiatric profession at the task of bringing down our anxiety and depression, or allowing us to sleep at will. But I know that it can.

It is a beautifully simple formula. It has to be simple because I never took any math in school beyond ninth grade Algebra. *What is the formula for the cure of depression?*

d+(cnt)c=e.
Depression plus conscious neutral thinking times concentration equals equanimity.

Wouldn't this formula make a better pin than "Depression is a medical illness, not a weakness" that depression-as-disease advocates now wear? Thinking we are sick has great hypnotic power to actually make us sick. Thinking is part of being a human being. We can no more stop thinking than we can stop eating. To lose weight, we can't stop eating. We eat healthier food—celery instead of potato chips. To have good mental health we can't stop thinking. We just think healthier thoughts—"Don't be so morose and lachrymose and grandiose and bellicose and don't dose (either over or under), ha ha," instead of "my husband is selfish and losing his hair."

It may be helpful to think of the mind as nothing more than an autonomic, thought-thinking machine that, until brain death, is always turned on and operating. Even in our sleep, the mind continues to think thoughts. Our mind machine has many channels that it automatically switches in and out of in a fairly random way, using learned associations between images to establish patterns of thought. At any moment we can interject a new thought of our own conscious choice and intercept the mind's choice. It may take some effort, in the form of concentration, to impose our conscious will over the habitual choice of our mind machine. We may have to learn to bear the suffering of some psychic pain until we get the new system up and going. But, we can do it.

Let us look around for our courage instead of a new "fix" to dull the pain. When our country is at war, we send our eighteen-year-olds to risk their lives fighting for our freedom. They may not be happy about it. We do not think their happiness is the important point. They are afraid. We expect them to conquer their fear. They do not want to get out of bed and go to meet the enemy. We expect them to get out of bed and go to meet the enemy.

How come we ask so much of others and so little of ourselves? Shall we fail to defend in our own mind the freedom we have demanded that others gain for us on the battlefield with their lives? Shall we expect others to be heroic and excuse ourselves from the effort? Isn't all of life a battlefield, and aren't all of us called upon in different ways to prove ourselves worthy of our freedom? Would we really choose to charge a machine-gun nest instead of fighting our depression? Then how come we think our pain is "the worst thing that can happen to us"?

Maybe if we thought someone might shoot us instead of sympathizing with us and taking care of us, we would make the choice to attend to our duty in the fight against our depression, instead of being deserters. I wonder what Tolstoy, who wrote about his own angst with such great respect, would have said to one of his farmhands who couldn't bring in the crops one morning because "he was depressed."

We are not happy. Let us question whether happiness is the important point. We are afraid. Let us conquer our fear. We do not want to get out of bed and go to work. Let us get out of bed and go to work. Let us not, in our weakness and fear, defect from our duty and meekly line up for our Prozac, Xanax, or Zoloft. Let us rather be like the Spartan soldiers who did not inquire how *many* the enemy were, but *where* they were.

Eight

AND THIS IS YOUR BRAIN ON BLAME

Feelings hurt, thoughts don't hurt. Blame is a thought, not a feeling. Blame is the way we avoid and deny fear.

Fear is extremely painful. It is an urgent call for action. We are like cats on a hot griddle, compelled to jump quickly to save ourselves. However, although we have carried our primeval jungle genes intact into the city, it is not always so clear to us what quick move we should make. And, like the cats, we are going to keep hurting until we jump.

But if we jump, we change the status quo, which the primal mind is protecting. The primal mind doesn't want us to jump from our griddle. It is not sure what we will be jumping into—the fire perhaps. So the primal mind is going to make it complicated for us. "DON'T MOVE!" says the primal mind protectively while we are on the hot griddle. This doesn't make sense of course. Which is why nature had to provide us with a higher mind to help us manage this stressful, anxious, painful, fearful, and ultimately self-immolating situation for which the medical profession now proscribes Prozac. Because, unfortunately, we don't always use our higher mind properly.

Stressful, anxious, fearful feelings hurt; thoughts don't hurt, they are much too fleeting. One of the higher-mind devices we use to alleviate the painful feelings (that are not naturally alleviated by jumping into action) is to switch from feeling to thinking.[1] Okay so far. We need higher mind thinking to come up with a plan of positive action. But unfortunately, there are kinds of thinking, such as blame, that lead us to negative or nonaction. Blame is a substitution for feeling the pain of fear. Blame is a substitute for action. Blame is the way we avoid and deny fear. And, vice versa, if there is any blame, ipso facto, there is repressed fear.

Blame is a higher-mind program that is contaminated by primal-mind fear and maintained by our habitual use. Blame is what psychology calls a "first-level" change[2]; the symptoms (anxiety and fear) have been reduced but we are still dependent on outside help (the people we blame). There is a better, higher-mind program that we could choose instead. If we could just "hang" with the pain of some insult or injury to us trusting that the pain won't kill us, and will dissipate with a little time, we could transcend the injury and advance to an increased level of courage and self-awareness. This is a "second-level" change. We are directly handling our situation without outside help, even without any reduction in the symptoms (anxiety and fear) that bother us.

This is how blame works. Instead of moving to take care of ourselves when someone mistreats us (a simple situation in which we could take immediate action), we complicate things by withdrawing our attention away from taking care of ourselves, and we focus instead upon blaming the other person. The upshot of all this is that in most difficult confrontations we are not afraid, the other person is an asshole. Psychology calls this *projection*. Practically speaking, in the world at large, it's called war.

While we are actively projecting our painful feeling of fear into thinking that other things, or other people, are somehow to blame for our plight, our focus of awareness is on something or someone else instead of our fear, and our fear simply disappears from our awareness. But that does not mean it is gone. (It is this stagnant pool of painful feelings that will erupt, sooner or later, into depression.)

We analyze the other person to figure out *why* they are mistreating us, or why they once mistreated us in the past; we criticize their behavior; we look for solutions to *their* problem of being an abusive person; or we simply wait for them to "come around" and change themselves so they won't mistreat us; or so they will give us, finally, that soul-satisfying, groveling-at-our-feet apology for which we have long been holding our breath. These are all complex situations-in-waiting in which we assume all the pain of our circumstance, but have no power and can do nothing to change it. Intelligence is not one of the strategies of the primal mind. And we must not forget that once we are into the process of blaming, we are also into the process of being a victim. It is not possible to do one without being the other. This is the reason it is so destructive to be a person who is always judging others; judging is simply a form of blame. It is not clear to us at the time we are making judgments that we are making ourselves a victim. But we are. And to the extent we are a victim, we are living our lives contaminated, pain-hardened, and depressed by repressed, unacknowledged fear.

Nobel prize–winning poet Joseph Brodsky's 1988 speech to the graduates at the University of Michigan carried this warning: "No matter how abominable your condition may be, try not to blame anyone; history, the state, superiors, race, parents, the phase of the moon, childhood toilet training, etc." If we refuse to blame, we will then experience some fear that can propel us into some appropriate forward action, and we will, to that extent, be free from victimhood.

Blaming is terribly seductive and extremely destructive to our growth as human beings. Whenever we start blaming and to what extent we use it, from that age and to that extent we cease to mature properly. We may be still blaming someone for something that happened to us ten or twenty years ago, or forty. Whenever we stop blaming, we will have to go all the way back and pick ourselves up at that age to do the essential work that we missed. Of course we can advance pretty quickly. Again, it is like learning how to read. If we missed it as a child we have to go back. But once we learn how to read, we can race through a lot of things that a real seven-year-old will have to take slowly, year by year. It's like patching a hole in our sweater. The whole adult sweater of ourselves has been there all the time, but now we no longer have an ugly gap all down the front of us.

This is a problem I have with the ordinary perception of forgiveness. Forgiveness to get rid of blame is really not doing the essential intellectual and experiential work. It is a first level change. It relieves anxiety, but we are still dependent upon the other person in that we think the important thing about forgiveness is what somebody has done to us. When we see blaming for the process trick of the primal mind that it is, and refuse to succumb to it, we reach a whole different level of understanding, and we start living our lives at a different level of maturity. We will see ourselves and our place in the cosmos differently. From a position of choice, which is a second-level change. Once we do this work, we can no longer be victims because blame simply ceases to interest us.

In her second therapy session, Janine M., married to a man with a "bad temper," proudly announced that she had made a "great breakthrough" from victimhood when she convinced her husband to stop breaking glasses on the kitchen floor when he got mad, and got him to break the glasses in the sink instead, where they were so much easier for *her* to clean up!

Sally P. told me that she bought elegant plates at thrift shops for her husband to break when he lost his temper. He complained that he didn't get the same satisfaction out of breaking the old thick, already-chipped kitchen pottery that she tried to foist off on him in an effort to save her good Lenox. I don't remember who cleaned it up, but I have my suspicions.

Compare Janine's and Sally's solutions to Liz R.'s, who tells this story near the end of her therapy program. Liz's husband, in a fit of pique, threw a chair through the family-room window Thanksgiving day. After a rather low-key "Oh, my goodness, what a shame," Liz immediately herded her three young children out the door into the family's only car, calmly informing her husband that she would call him with the telephone number of the motel so he could advise her when the window was fixed and the house would therefore be warm enough for them to return. While delivering these very matter-of-fact and few words, she deftly popped the still-warm but as yet uncarved turkey from its place at the head of the table into a plastic bag to take along for "the children's Thanksgiving picnic."

The manner in which Janine and Sally handled their problem did not change the status quo of their dependence on their husbands to take care of them. A first-level change is usually our first step. Liz, however, transcended her primal mind's fear of taking the bull by the horns. Instead of continuing the soap-opera intrigue of depending on an undependable husband, she bravely assumed the responsibility for taking care of herself *directly*, without knowing for sure what the end result would be. In making this second-level change, we reclaim the power and authority over our own lives, which is only possible when we access the more creative higher-mind functions directly, from the position of courage, instead of indirectly, from the position of fear.

It may be that Liz's husband will make positive changes of his own *in reaction* to the changes his wife has made, changes that will improve their relationship. But those changes will be the husband's changes. This is qualitatively different from what Janine and Sally did in trying to take care of themselves indirectly by trying to change their husbands' behavior. Focusing on what the other person should do for us is an inadequate coping mechanism born of primal-mind fear rather than higher-mind courage. Blaming is always implied when we expect others to take care of us. It has mired millions of women in a chronic state of dependence on the primal mind, whose main strategies are depression, paranoia, and confusion.

We can also see in Janine and Sally's situation how "taking care of someone" out of fear is really a subtle kind of blame. A life of "rescuing" people not only enables them to continue their poor behavior and stunts their growth, it is equally destructive to our own growth.

If we don't wake up to it, our primal mind can get us to fall for some wonderful switcheroos to boondoggle us into maintaining the status quo fearful "security" of the abusive, nonreciprocal, or dead-end relationships that, due to repressed fear, inevitably propel us into depression. We tell ourselves the other person is somehow "our problem" to fix. Sometimes we stay because we fear *hurting* the other person if we leave them. When we focus on feeling guilty, we can avoid thinking about how the other person is responsible for their misdeeds against us and thus is equally or wholly responsible for us leaving them.

Once the breakup of an abusive relationship has occurred or is in the process of occurring, we may experience a major depression. The depression is *not* the result of a long period of abuse suffered at the hands of a cold companion, or a verbally or physically abusive one. The depression is caused by the primal mind wielding its impulse strategies of fear and paranoia at the prospective loss of the security of the status quo.

Also, because the collapse into depression is also a way to avoid the pressing work of one's present reality, depression can be an unwitting strategy to avoid the embarrassment and stress of having to answer to our intimates for our bad choice of mates. People avoid "dumping" on people who have already dumped so heavily on themselves.

What can we do for someone who is employing this option? As firmly and kindly as possible, we can refuse to support them in their distorted idea of reality. We can refuse to be a party to the complaining and blaming by politely switching the content of the conversation from complaints about others to descriptions of the person's own feelings.

For instance, when the person says, "That SOB ruined my life," we can say, "You must feel very scared and vulnerable right now," and encourage the person to talk about these feelings. We don't want to wallow around in feelings and not progress to forward action but, at the same time, we need to acknowledge our feelings so that they can finish themselves. If we make an emotional cutoff from our feelings before they finish, they will hang around to fester beneath our level of awareness and will affect us in covert ways.

After the person has acknowledged their feelings, then we can slowly direct the content of the conversation from lower-brain feelings to upper-brain thinking. What ideas does the person have for action, for task-oriented behavior to help themselves? We might inquire, "So what is the *very first thing* you are going to do?" This makes it more difficult for a person to hide from themselves in their own victimhood.

As long as we are blaming, we are still a victim and the fear is still there, beneath our level of awareness. Fear will continue to influence our behavior by contaminating our reasoning processes. This portion of our behavior will thus be reactive instead of proactive. We will be aggressive, but from the "underdog" position rather than the "top dog" position.

Ironically everybody else always knows when we are afraid. Like an ostrich with its head in the sand, we are the only ones who can't see it in ourselves. It is a painful feeling to be angry; we try to "water down" the pain with thinking that takes the form of blame. Blaming is such an easy slide that we hardly even know we're on it. Sometimes our blaming is totally inappropriate.

Helen G. recently bought a new house. She was quite immersed in her interior decorating and with three young children (three, five, and seven) told me she found it frustrating to keep small fingerprints off the new white walls, and cookie crumbs off the new white carpets. Number one, in her choice of pristine white she has already set up a situation where she is going to be in constant conflict with her children, and it will be a ready-made opportunity to blame the situation instead of more appropriately dealing with the difficult frustrations (fears) in her life, of which there are aplenty.

She is also in conflict with her husband over finances because she wants new furniture, and he is not feeling generous at the moment about giving her the money for it. So when Helen came home from a furniture sale one day, without being able to buy the bedroom set of her dreams, she gathered the children together and marched them all over the house, screaming at them hysterically for each little mark on the wall.

Sometimes our blaming seems perfectly reasonable. Mary K. said she finally confronted her mother about how alone she felt as a child and how sad it was for her that her mother really never "seemed to care much about her." Her mother said, "Well I wish I *had* done things differently."

"Oh," said Mary brightly, "you mean you wish you had been home more, and been more affectionate, and helped me with my homework, and gone to see my school plays?"

"No," said her mother, "I wish I had been more selfish and done more things for myself. I sacrificed my whole life for you and let all my own dreams go down the drain." Mary is forty-two years old and is still trying to trade in her uninvolved, unloving mother for a new one. The only reason we need a mother is if we are still a child. Mary has been living on her own for more than twenty years. By blaming her mother for her inadequacies in the past, Mary can avoid the fear of experiencing her own present ones. Focusing all her energies on improving her mother, Mary's fear is not going to propel her into improving herself.

Mary's error illustrates how it is not rational to make ourselves dependent upon the past by blaming because the past does not have the power to give us anything. An old saying puts it this way: Imagining that the past has any solid relevance to our current reality is like thinking we can push a boat with the wake it has left behind in the water. We cannot ride the past because it does not go anywhere. So we might as well get down off that horse. The past only exists if we think it and when we stop thinking about the past—it disappears. The past can't help us and can't hurt us either.

This is one of the hardest things I had to learn and it took me, literally, decades. For twenty years I never forgave my husband for things I thought he did to me when we were first married. I couldn't even get over the things that happened when we were dating in high school.

I just kept ruminating over the offenses I had suffered and believed that we couldn't do anything about our present relationship until all those old scores were settled. I never gave a single thought to *my* offenses—dependency, repressed fear, selfishness, lack of commitment, and lack of courage. Therefore they did not exist for me. What we do not think about does not exist for us. Which is how, by the way, Directed Thinking works so well for the painful feelings of depression.

One morning I woke before dawn and felt unusually good. I was confused for a minute when I felt around for the old pain and it wasn't there. I decided to get up and take a walk in the park with my new freedom. I walked for about an hour and my head felt as clear as the new snow that lay untrammeled on the path before me. When I got back home I decided to prepare myself for my weekly appointment with my psychiatrist that afternoon by writing a list of all the things people had "done to me" in my life so that he could see, once and finally, that rather than *causing* any of my problems, I was actually doing a brilliant job *in the face* of them.

As soon as the children left for school, I got out a yellow lined tablet and placed it neatly on the cleared-off dining room table. I sharpened a half-dozen pencils, carefully lined them up next to the pad, and began to compose my "proof." (I highly recommend this as an eye-opening exercise.)

1. When I was four my mother "lost it" and woke me in the middle of the night in a fit of rage. Before my terrified eyes, she took a pair of scissors and cut up the birthday dress she was making for me into little pieces which she threw all over the bed, crying hysterically that she would "never sew anything for me again." My crime: My aunt had unknowingly cut up the elastic my mother was going to use for the sleeves in my new dress and set my hair with it so I would have "Shirley Temple" curls for the next day.[3] {At this point I began to weep.}

2. In high school my husband insisted on holding hands in the halls, which was against the rules, and I was kept out of the honor society until my senior year because of it. {I wept some more.}

3. My parents made me go to the college of *their* choice even though I was the one who had to win a scholarship because they couldn't afford to send me. {I got some more Kleenex.}

4. My husband wanted me to run for chaplain of the senior class instead of vice president because he didn't think I was popular enough to win vice president. {I wiped off the yellow pad with some of the Kleenex.}

5. Even though I grew to love my college, my husband still made

me give up my scholarship and transfer for the last two years to his university, as I had originally agreed to do, or he would break up with me. {The bully!}

6. When I graduated from college I was offered a job with Hall-mark. But since I had to move to Kansas City from Maryland, and my husband still had another semester in college, "he wouldn't let me take the job." {The controlling bastard!}

7. The first year we were married I was the one working to support us since he was still going to school, and he "wouldn't let me buy a Christmas tree." {The animal!}

8. When I wanted to go back to college my husband said he would only pay for it if I took something "useful" like account-ing or teacher education, *not* creative writing. {My God, how I have suffered!}

9. My husband wouldn't let me take a YWCA art class on the same evening he went to Rotary Club because he said when he was out, he felt more comfortable knowing I was at home. {He was so mean to me!}

I continued to write in this manner. I stopped weeping and was more or less intent on my project when, about midway into the twenties I had a small twinge of doubt about some of my "proof." I read back over the list and it hit me like a sledge-hammer—except for that small scene as a four-year-old, every single item on that list had been my choice for one reason or another, to have something I wanted.

I could have made a different choice, but I didn't. I was not a *victim* at all, I had done every single thing *to myself*. It was as if a great burden had been lifted from my heart with that understanding, and I felt free as if for the first time. I remember telling the psychiatrist that I felt the scales had fallen from my eyes at last, and like civil rights advocate Martin Luther King Jr., I wanted to shout: "Free at last. Free at last. Great God Almighty, I'm free at last!"

Perhaps the reason I felt so free is that it takes a lot of energy to remain in denial, and once denial is blown, a lot of energy is freed up. But I did not understand, at this time, that knowing I was not a victim was not the same thing as becoming cured of behaving like one. I was not cured of being a victim for I continued for many years to *behave* like one. The intellectual understanding has to come first but that is only the first step. That's just the intellectual degree, then comes the residency and the practice. And we should not feel bad about "settling" for a less than perfect relationship because we are never going to get ourselves perfect.

Generally we try to fix the past because we don't have enough courage to face the fear of interacting with present reality, and by dwelling on the past we never get to present reality. Most of our present reality involves other people, especially if we are a couple, so most of our problems can be blamed on someone else if we are not careful.

It is hard for us to think of our relationship with someone else as our interaction with present reality. We normally think of it as our interaction with that person. But it is helpful to think of it as our interaction with present reality because then we will not put the intentions on it. For instance, if a tree limb fell on us, we would not put intentions on the tree. We would simply take care of our injury. Life is, in reality, no-fault if we consider that any situation is only half ours to handle, up to and including assault and battery. It's not that blaming isn't *justified*. It isn't *helpful* to us.

Here's another odd thing about blaming. In order to be able to blame someone for something, we have to be able to believe that they "owe" us something that we haven't got yet—justice, recovery, happy family, healing, respect, self-confidence, a good education. The more we blame, the more we make ourselves dependent upon something we don't have, something that we unconsciously are waiting around for someone to give us in order to feel "complete," instead of suffering our lack so that our discomfort can propel us to some forward action to improve ourselves.

Blaming a person who has already died is especially fruitless. Then we are dependent on a person who will be letting us down forever. This is a wonderful little prison cell where the primal mind can keep us safe from risk. Ultimately blame ends up in depression because we never can get any satisfaction or closure out of something that is a process and not a need that can be actually filled. Blame is just a process trick of the primal mind that has done an end run around the self and co-opted the use of the higher mind's logic to painstakingly analyze other people's flaws to prevent us from seeing our own.

We can begin to see that it is not the *content* of blaming that is important. It is not important whether or not the blaming is *justified*, which it very well might be. It is the *process* of blaming that is the problem. In blaming we can avoid the painful feelings of primal-mind fear. But we should be using our fear as an impetus to self-directed thinking, which provides the necessary moral struggle with legitimate suffering that we need to accomplish.

One person will blame the reason they didn't get into college on the fact they were black, another because they were white. One person will blame an inflated auto repair bill on the fact they are "just a woman." Another person will blame their failure to get child custody on the fact they are "just a man." We blame automatically, chronically, endlessly. Blaming confuses the issue as we direct our focus on "them" and escape the present reality of the task at hand—which is to take care of ourselves.

For all of us, it is difficult to see how we make ourselves victims. We wrongly think it is some superior state of perfection, rather than our fear, that has us analyzing the imperfections in those "inferior" people who "bully" us, instead of taking care of ourselves more directly. Even when we accept the idea intellectually that we are probably cowardly wimps, it is harder still to catch ourselves in the act of being one.

This is because our lives are not lived by our opinions but

by our habits, which may differ from our opinions without our knowledge. In Dale Carnegie's wonderful classic, *How to Win Friends and Influence People,*[4] he talks about the amazing difference between the way a person really works in the world, and that person's own perception of himself; the discrepancy between a person's *values* and their day-to-day *behavior*.

"Two-Gun" Crowley was a small-time hoodlum who made big headlines in New York City for killing a policeman who walked up to the parked car in which Crowley was sitting with a girlfriend. When the policeman asked to see Crowley's license, he opened fire without saying a word. Not content with emptying his own revolver into the policeman, as the obviously helpless officer lay dying, Crowley grabbed the policeman's own revolver and continued to shoot into his prostrate body. Crowley's explanation of the episode, for which he was sentenced to die in the electric chair, was this: "Under my coat is a weary heart, but a kind one—one that would do nobody any harm. This is what I get for defending myself."[5]

Al Capone, long-time Public Enemy Number One, who murdered dozens of competitors during Prohibition, described himself this way: "I have spent the best years of my life giving people the lighter pleasures, helping them have a good time, and all I get is abuse, the existence of a hunted man." This hard-core criminal actually thought of himself as a public benefactor.[6]

It is hard for all of us to see who we really are because, thanks to the strategies of the primal mind, which can corrupt the higher mind, we are always able to discount or justify the negative aspects of our own behavior. In 1998 a fiftyish cocaine addict from Los Angeles, after blowing his own inheritance, succeeded in begging his wealthy eighty-year-old widowed mother to let him come back home and go into recovery.

Shortly thereafter he was stopped on the highway for erratic driving, and the policeman found the man's dead mother stuffed in the trunk of her own car. Because she had refused to give him money for drugs, he had beaten her to death with a baseball bat, took what cash she had, and was going to dispose of her body, but got high on cocaine first. "I'm not really a criminal," he explained to the judge. "This was just a one-shot deal."[7]

The higher-mind principles of a murderer, a cocaine addict, a depressed person, or a wimp, no matter how excellent and noble, will have no effect on their behavior in the absence of their understanding of how to choose one part of their mind over the other. Without an overall directive strategy by the self (such as Directed Thinking), we will simply be ricocheting back and forth from blaming to victimhood. Little by little we have to move ourselves across the bridge from being a victim to taking care of ourselves. It is a bridge of fear. It takes courage to cross it. We go one step at a time.

Complaining is similar to blaming, a device of the primal mind to stop us from exercising our courage and making positive changes. Courage is very frightening to the primal mind because the mind cannot predict the outcome of a courageous act like it can predict the outcome of a complaint. A complaint does not threaten the status quo because it is always couched in negative terms, some kind of a "no," and our mind is a "yes" mind.[8] A complaint is not a positive suggestion. No action will take place.

As long as we are complaining, the primal mind figures, we are safe from doing anything that might change the status quo. This is how a negative attitude, which is nothing more than a chronic low-grade complaint mode, keeps us from moving forward. It is very efficient because it isn't painful and therefore we don't try to get out of it like we do depression. Neurologically speaking, complaining is the same as blaming—habitual access of higher-mind cognitive faculties by random, accidental thinking based on learned associations stemming from primal-mind fears, not directed by the self and not connected to some common ground of objective reality.

I didn't know what complaining really was until I caught myself doing it all the time. I didn't know that I was secretly counting on having a perfect life and was therefore impatient with a normal, ordinary, mixed-bag life. I am sure that I was influenced in this by a psychologized modern-day tendency to look upon our success as more important than our character, the circumstances that befall us as more significant than how we respond to them. Ancient philosophy tells us that grace means to give something for nothing and it is our grace that ministers to each other's weakness. In a psychologized society one only hears about receiving grace for onself; one never hears about *giving* it to someone else.

Lacking any idea of grace, I didn't know I felt "entitled." I didn't know I was pining like a teenager for a soul mate and not wanting to settle for a struggle. It's odd, really, how we value physical exercise for our out-of-shape bodies yet treat good, honest psychic struggle with our flabby relationships like a plague that must be avoided at all costs. I didn't know I had become a psychic weakling and coward. No wonder I was a sitting duck for depression. I was willing to exercise to build up my body. I *complained* to strengthen my marriage.

When my husband, who had been promoted from San Juan to Wall Street, decided he had had enough of corporate life in the Big Apple and his two-hour daily commute from our home in New Jersey, we moved to California with our two youngest children. The other three children were already more or less on their own. California was not a totally random choice. Two of our children had already "gone west" and although the third child was then in Boston, his wife owned a house in Del Mar to which she had often expressed a hope "to move someday."

Two months after our move to San Diego, I went into a deep depression. I told my husband that I was afraid I was losing my mind, and the rest of me was stretched so thin in opposite directions that I was disappearing in the middle. I thought that I was being cheated out of my own happiness because nobody really loved me for myself, only for "what I could do for them and make *them* happy." I was tired of being "made use of." I wanted to be "fulfilled." I wondered where the real me was. I felt "denied, unfree to be my authentic self." My potential was being stifled, by what I wasn't exactly sure. In retrospect I think I sounded a lot like the man in Billy Joel's 1973 hit song "Piano Man," the man in the bar who was sure he "could be a movie star" if he "could get out of this place."

My husband wasn't too good at listening to these kinds of wibble-wobble, esoteric, and obscure complaints because he always interpreted them as a criticism of himself in some way. Of course that's what complaints are good for—shifting the focus of responsibility away from ourselves. We feel a little better, the other person feels a little worse. My husband would hear me saying *he* didn't love me enough, and *he* was stifling me, and since he was sure he was innocent of any of these dastardly deeds, he felt like I was just beating up on him. So he usually bolted for the office as soon as he was sure I wasn't going to kill myself that day.

And he was right to be leery of my complaints. There is only one reason to complain about anything. We complain when we are trying to fool ourselves about the fact that we are not in full control of our own lives. But not knowing that, we complain and try to drag other people into supporting our conspiracy against ourselves. This is not to be confused with the honest sharing of sadness over some loss. There is a difference between complaining and honest mourning, in which we are accepting, rather than bewailing, our fate.

Complaining is not real communication, it is a game.[9] It's the same game as unhappiness, which is a kind of silent complaint that we mistake for authentic feeling. The payoff of the game is that we get to avoid the present reality that although we can't have or do *some* things, there are other things that we can have or can do. When we alternate blame, complaint, and depression like I used to do, all the bases are covered. We are not connected to our own present reality, and thus are not only lost to ourselves, there is no way for anyone else to connect with us either. So how do we get out of it?

We have to recognize that blaming, complaining, and depression come from primal-mind fear. We need the primal mind, but unless we direct it properly, we crash. Letting primal-mind fear direct our lives is like getting into our car, starting the motor, releasing the brake, stepping on the gas, and not bothering to steer. The primal mind is powerful, not smart. So when we realize the primal mind is in charge, we need to "take the car keys away" and brainswitch to higher-mind intelligence. Feelings are not higher-mind reasoning functions; feelings are primal-mind *defense mechanisms*. They are meant to warn us about our environment, but they can be wrong. Feelings are neither smart nor moral, and they do not have the least modicum of social responsibility. Feelings are like electricity, powerful but dumb. And unless we learn how to handle them both properly, either one of them can kill us.

Before anything else, we have to recognize the value of our primal mind. The primal mind is the place where all impulse and therefore all action begins. Fear is our power base, our gut-energy source, our motor. Again, Damasio said it one way,[10] Hawthorne said it this way: "The world owes all its onward impulses to men ill at ease."[11] Blaming is a way we effectively kill this onward impulse.

But we can always quit our blaming and complaining by getting in touch with the repressed fear that is causing them. All we have to do is make a simple conscious choice between the two activities, blaming or complaining (thinking) and fearing (feeling). Blaming and complaining only occur when fear doesn't progress directly into action.

We can best understand how fear works in our lives by hands-on experimenting. Intellectual theorizing is not enough. Fear comes to us all the time, we just need to be aware of our longstanding habit of ignoring it and be more alert to catching ourselves experiencing it so we can bear the fearful feelings and allow them to dissipate naturally; making sure that they impel us to some forward action by using our courage, instead of emotionally cutting off from fear and later finding ourselves in a steep slide into depression. There is a big difference between motion and emotion. The clue is in the word emotion itself— (e-motion), which means, literally, *no motion.*

Nine

DEPRESSION: THE
SMOKE AND MIRRORS
OF THE MIND

*Depression is just a feeling of helplessness. We are not really
helpless. When we feel like nothing matters, that's just a
feeling. Things and people do matter. When we feel like
we can't go on, that's just a feeling. We can go on.*

This is the problem with laziness: it occurs in present reality.
But the supposed cure for laziness, getting around to doing
something, lies in the future, where no action can take place.
So we spend five times the energy hating the messy apartment,
or the unfinished market study, than we would ever spend
actually attending to them. Laziness is really a time warp in
which we all become Rip Van Winkles to our duty through
hating it. Hate is fear. But we don't know we are afraid. We
are asleep to that fact. The cure for laziness is not "getting
around to it." The cure for laziness is courage. We need to
acknowledge our fear and charge the machine-gun nest of our
time warp by pursuing our chosen goal in the face of our fear.

People ask me all the time how come I'm never depressed
anymore. They want to know "How did I make it?" I remem-

ber asking that same question, many years ago, of a dear friend of mine who had come through a devastating experience of fear. My friend said the most profound thing to me and I have never forgotten it. She sighed quietly and said, "I tried despair and it didn't work."

My friend tried despair for several months. I'm a slow learner. I had to try despair for several decades before I came to the same conclusion. Like John Nash, the genius mathematician who spent thirty years as a schizophrenic wandering the campus of Princeton University before he recovered, I spent thirty years as a manic-depressive wandering around my life. Until I decided I would refuse all thoughts of despair because they were a waste of time and ultimately came to nothing. If I went into despair, nothing changed. I always came out the same way I went in. To do this was difficult, filled with wrong turns and false starts. But, in the end, I was successful.

It is not that the despair itself has changed. I still have the same exact fearful feelings of claustrophobia, panic, anxiety, depression, and mania today that I have always had. These fears have not subsided or altered in any way. It's just that I no longer feel powerless in the face of them. As far as depression is concerned, it is the same "Beast" that still attacks me. The only difference is that I now hold my own against him. It is still an ongoing war. It is not that my old enemy has grown weaker, it is that I have grown stronger. I have become desensitized to my fear of depression and anxiety the way some people have become desensitized to their fear of snakes and spiders. The depression itself has not changed, as the snakes and spiders themselves do not change because we have ceased to fear them.

When depression comes upon me now, what is different is that I know I am not my depression. I know I am not my primal mind. What is the same is that the feeling is still one of endless hopelessness, a dark sinkhole of the self that collapses beneath me at every step—once more I become a vacant soul in a vacant land. There may only be a molecule's difference between the old depression and the new depression, but it has huge consequences.

It is still terrifying and I can still *feel* powerless. But I can say to myself, "Wait, powerlessness is only a feeling, it's just the primal mind doing its thing—terror, fears of inadequacy, addictive impulses to depression." I acknowledge the anxiety in my chest, the tightness in my throat. "It's okay," I say to myself, "I just need to get busy and do the next thing. The pain will pass."

Often the next thing is simply to replace my negative thoughts. Thinking negative or painful thoughts is the human being's most unnecessary, unintelligent and pointless activity. As soon as I realize I am depressed or terribly stressed out about work or a crisis that one of my children is undergoing, or if for any reason I feel hopeless, helpless and discouraged I say to myself, "There is absolutely no good thing that can come from thinking this thought. Even if it is all true, it still doesn't do me or anyone else any good for me to think it. Why should I keep thinking that I feel bad? There is no earthly reason to think this particular thought. Therefore I will think something else."

Instead of "I feel terrible," I will think, "I am feeling better and better." Instead of "My child is suffering," I will think, "My child is getting better and better." Instead of "The house is a mess," I will think, "The house is getting cleaner and cleaner." This is not a housekeeping exercise. This is a mind-keeping exercise to sweep out the thoughts causing me pain. I get right down to business. One. Two. Three. "I'm getting better and better, I'm getting better and better, better and better." It is not a waste of time. What is a waste of time is thinking "This is terrible" over and over and making myself sick.

It is a simple thing to outsmart the mind and get it to think our thought. The hard thing about it is just to get going and actually do it. But we are eminently able to do it because any normal person is smarter than their own bad thoughts or their own painful feelings. Remember; neuroscience has taught us that our feelings and our intelligence are located in two distinct parts of the brain. Depression is extremely powerful, powerful enough to kill us. But it is not at all intelligent and we can outsmart it seven days a week. And this eternal striving helps us grow stonger and more confident.

It is a shocking thing to say but it may be that the first step to human excellence is: first, you ruin your life. I don't think there is any other way. We are fooling ourselves if we think that our ultimate relationship with life is to "do it right." Life is more mysterious than that. Reality has to be a surprise or else we must have manufactured it somehow. It's just at some point, when we begin to wake up to the magic of it all, we can choose to take a deep breath and do things with a little more elegance.

We will always have terrible flaws and limitations. When we accept them instead of trying to assess blame for them, they provide the moral struggle that forges our path through life. We will always have conflict between our behavior and our values. This is how we figure out what our values are. This is how we judge our behavior. We continually adjust our values and our behavior. We are a "work in progress."

If we are unclear about our values, we can look at our behavior choices for *clues* as to what our values might be. For instance: If we put our baby in day care so that we can afford to live in a house instead of an apartment, which do we value more highly, the house or the child? If we refuse to take unfair advantage of our customers, which do we value more highly, being a successful salesman or being a good person? If we take something that doesn't belong to us, which do we value more highly, possessions or honor?

Suppose we have weak values? We can't *heal* our values any more than we can heal our mind. What we can do is choose new values and new thoughts. We can't heal fear and depression just like we can't heal addictions because they are not illnesses, they are impulses. We don't heal impulses, nor can we stop them from occurring to us; we just learn to choose to do something else other than doing them.

The unchosen compulsion to move toward our temptations, impulses, and addictions, which are as biochemically and psychologically unique as fingerprints for every person, provides the impetus by which we are urged to extend ourselves into some kind of chosen, principle-based action. This action is what we call "my life." Between the urge of impulse and the behavior we exhibit, we always exercise our choice, wittingly or unwittingly.[1]

This is the problem with living our lives by psychology, wherein we too often service our feelings, instead of living our lives by principles, wherein we empower ourselves to service our goals. Figuring out *why* we eat too much will not change our behavior. If our behavior is such that we eat things that are not good for us, we don't have to know *why*, we can simply choose to change our behavior. We can access our higher mind to devise a program for a new eating plan that is better for us, and commit ourselves earnestly to making the new way of eating "our habit" instead of the old destructive way.

Psychologists tell us we won't be able to change our habits if we have repressed the fear that caused the habits to develop in the first place. But we can always get in touch with our fear through what we hate—either as in I hate it that I didn't win first place or, I hate it that I can't eat a chocolate sundae. We can simply choose to focus on the fearful feeling *instead* of the hating.[2]

Although we can profitably ignore painful thoughts, we shouldn't ignore painful feelings because these repressed feelings wind us up at a cellular level, and we need to feel and release them so we can unwind. But we don't have to know *why* we feel powerless in order to feel our feelings of powerlessness, while we switch to new thoughts that will result in *different* feelings.

Our mind is not a *why* mind or a *no* mind; it is a *how* mind and a *yes* mind. "Just Say No" doesn't work. There is a huge difference in saying "I will abstain" instead of "I won't use." The mind can't do anything with a why or a no; it can only do something with a how and a yes. That is how trying to say no to a chocolate sundae or our depression doesn't work. The mind can't use a no. The primal mind in its strategy of fear, which causes us to pause with pain, is in effect a no. But other than that there is no neuronal framework that can do a "no."[3] So don't bother giving the mind a command of no. It will simply root around in its learned associations for some kind of a yes it can continue with, like the yes of our compulsion to feel depressed or to eat a sundae.

The reason our yesses, in the form of addictions and compulsions, seem to get stronger is that, as we succumb to them, our behavior forms particular neural patterns we call habits. The first time we do something else other than succumb to our impulses seems harder because we are forging a new neural pattern. But as we choose the new pattern over and over, that too becomes a habit. The old neural patterns don't disappear, but the more recently and frequently used patterns take precedence following the law of inertia.

We are never at the mercy of the fears, impulses, or addictions caused by the primal mind's feelings of powerlessness. No amount of pain or terror or longing can keep us from exercising our choice to function from the higher mind. We are never really weak. We are just not using our higher-mind faculties. As Patrick Henry said, "We are not weak if we make a proper use of those means which the God of Nature has placed in our power."

We have to be careful, however, that we access our higher

mind to maintain our equilibrium by the use of chosen principles that meet our needs *directly* instead of accessing the higher mind for plans that involve manipulating other people to take care of us. For instance, we will still have a weight problem if we choose our higher-mind principle that we'd better be fat so that men won't be interested in us, which some women have created as a way to avoid the advances of men due to their history of sexual abuse as a child. We cannot *eliminate* incorrect principles from the higher mind, but we do not have to use a principle just because we have it. We can simply choose to substitute another principle. Principles that are not consistently chosen tend to take a backseat to those that are.

Whatever problem we have, like overeating, alcohol addiction, or lengthy depression, we can assume that there is some higher-mind logic that supports it, and that the logic contains a false premise due to the contamination seeping up from primal-mind fear by way of learned associations. If we were beaten everyday as a kid with a branch broken off from a pine tree we may find that we have an unreasonable dislike of a decorated Christmas tree. We cannot ever get rid of this thinking, which will be represented somehow in the memory system of our neurons. We can just start from scratch and choose other thinking that will create new positive associations.

But there is no system we can use that will be "the solution" to our life. Our life isn't ever going to be solved. Guilt, frustration, competition, loneliness, mania and depression will never be solved. They form the power base of life, which impels us to risk some sort of action. Our life is to be *lived*, not solved; howsoever it all turns out, thin or fat, rich or poor, depressed or happy, sick or well, and since I'm a writer I always say to myself, best-selling or unread. We don't need to be perfect. Perfect people are like perfect gardens, slightly unwelcoming. We should be like Zen gardens: with the clutter of a dead leaf or a broken twig here and there.

This means we don't need to draw such a big distinction between our latest project being a "success" or a "character moment." We make a problem out of the distinction between having a success and having a failure mainly because of a psychologized emphasis on roles and image rather than goals and mission. We don't have to. A distinct and abject failure, as I have learned from experience, has its own subtle glory. We have not abandoned the path of self-understanding because we do not tromp it under triumphant heels.

Robert L. was telling me that he wondered, when all was said and done, what he had really done with his life. "What do I have to show for it all? What have I really accomplished?" I looked at this handsome, gray-haired man who had raised five children to be good, responsible men and women; who had been successful in business and was now looking forward to a life of retirement and small travels with his wife of some forty years.

I was filled with admiration for him and I simply burst out with, "What have you done with your life? You have lived your life, that's what! You have been successful and you have failed. You have helped people and been helped. You have betrayed people and been betrayed. You have loved and been loved. You have hated and been hated. You have endured terrible despair and experienced great joy. And you have lived every single bit of it. What greater accomplishment could there be than that you have lived your life?"

But we cannot do it all alone, and we don't have to. We can help each other. And we will always have help along the way from the great thinkers and wise philosophers of the past. I learned from people who had successfully met their own fear and learned from it. There have been many times in Western history when to speak your truth was to risk your death. I decided that the words someone spoke when their life was on the line were words that it might well profit me to study: Patrick Henry's "I care not what course others may take, but as for me, give me liberty or give me death;" Marie Antoinette's apology because she stepped on the executioner's foot as she was proceeding to the guillotine. Maybe I couldn't do the guillotine with courage and elegance but surely, I determined, I could do depression.

It is only in sleep that we are controlled by our mind. Our mind operates by thought. When we are awake, we can take over the helm by thinking any thought we want. Why aren't our teachers, lawyers, doctors, psychologists, and judges relaying this message of responsibility?

Carmelina Smith was in jail for stealing $11,615.10 out of a university bookstore cash register. She got caught when she started treating her relatives to spending sprees at the local mall. She blames the welfare system for not giving her what she needed to provide for her two fatherless children; "I couldn't buy my kids milk and Pampers, that's why I did what I did." Now she is trying to get out of prison early and claims she has "seen the light." What did she write to the judge to convince him of her worthiness? "I have come to admit my powerlessness over drugs and drink."[4]

We are not powerless over drugs, drink, or depression. The biggest mistake we can make is to believe that someone or something outside ourselves, or something we are *feeling*, can force us to think or behave in some way other than what we would *choose*. This is never true.

What is true in these cases is that we choose to *not* choose. Our choice of what to do next is always available, it is our only present reality. When we choose to not do anything and unfocus from present reality, we can end up unwittingly in the primal mind. That is because neither the higher mind (a thought-thinking machine), nor the primal mind (a feelings-feeling machine) is necessarily connected with present reality. It is our job as *self* to make sure that our mind is connected with present reality.

If we unfocus from present reality by believing that we need to be in a better mood, or have a better situation before we do something, we can't focus on what we should do. And we can take that concept backward. If we don't know what to do, or are mired in depression, it means, ipso facto, that we are focused on what we would *like* rather than on what *is*. The insistence upon having what is not there means that we are insisting upon something other than present reality. People talk about depression being paralyzing. It seems that we are paralyzed because our focus is not on the present but on the past or the future where no action can take place. This is true even if our desire is as simple and seemingly innocent as, "I don't want to feel this way."

By thinking I don't want to feel this way, we are not accepting reality. *We are putting conditions on reality.* We want reality improved before we do anything. We want things to *get* better, or we want to *feel* better, before we act. It is neither rational, efficient, nor, in the end, successful to try to *change* reality instead of *accepting* it. We feel the way we feel. We don't argue with it. We just get up and do what we are going to do, feeling however we feel, and as a result of that decision we are already separating from the idea that we have no choice.

We are spiritual creatures endowed with the greatest gift—choice. But we forget that. There are all kinds of ways we can refuse to commit ourselves to making a choice. We will wait around in our despair for reality to conform better to our liking before we do anything. We will wait to do something different until we feel differently.

Or we will hesitate to grab for the gold ring of something new and risky because we want to hang on tight to the old and safe: "I want to get married and my boyfriend doesn't, but I don't know if I can get another boyfriend, so I'm going to wait around and see if he changes his mind." "Life does not give itself to one who tries to keep all its advantages at once," warned French premiér Leon Blum. "I have often thought morality may perhaps consist solely in the courage of making a choice."

Decisions are difficult for everybody. Sometimes the best we can do is simply perform the next small task and trust that sooner or later we will take on a direction that makes sense to us. Existence never abandons us without the next thing to do. This would be as unthinkable as looking out in the yard and finding a blank space of nothingness in the middle of the lawn. Or looking up at the sky and seeing a piece missing. I have learned to trust that we always have whatever we need. We are not alone. People of good will are working by our side. We each move ahead on our path with as much grace as we can muster, picking up the burden of our failures, the pain of our suffering. There is no reason, just because we feel bad, to balk and dump our pack on the road like some kind of stubborn donkey.

Caesar Augustus said that he "found Rome brick and left it marble." We, too, expect our lives to be ordered by the certainties of essential progress, high ideals, grand motives, successful careers, and sweeping changes. We find instead that our lives are determined by the surprise of little things. We get depressed. But depression is just a *feeling* of helplessness. We are not really helpless. When we feel like nothing matters, that's just a feeling. Things and people *do* matter. When we feel like we can't go on, that's just a feeling. We *can* go on.

We can always choose to turn away from the feelings of helplessness and futility to the reality and the sanity that lies in a sense of duty and some small task that we can do. Then we can *feel* differently. But not because we want to. We will feel differently because we *did* something different.

We never remember that depression is only a feeling of powerlessness and helplessness. We are not powerless, we just feel powerless so we give up. Depression always wins by default. Depression also wins by *belief*. Rote mind-sets and unwilled self-hypnosis can keep us stuck in all kinds of ignominious status quo so that it can appear to us that we do not have control over our lives. I have carried this tiny phrase of Virgil's since high school Latin because it inspires me to think beyond whatever rough times might be staring me in the face: "They *can* because they *believe* they can." Can't we all do what we *believe* we can do?

Belief, the ultimate product of our imagination, is a very interesting phenomenon. It can work for us or against us. It can imprison us or set us free. For instance, I have just said that we have the ability to choose our own thoughts and thus direct our thinking back out of the self-absorbed private hell of our depression to some common ground of objective reality. Whether this is true or false makes no difference to someone who chooses to believe I am wrong.

A person can say, "I don't believe that you can direct your mind to think anything you want." A person can say, "I don't believe you can change your mood by altering your thinking or behavior." And because of this belief, that person won't make any attempt to direct their thinking or alter their behavior, which nonattempt then completely reinforces their belief that it can't be done.

How should it be that not doing something can satisfy the belief that it can't be done? Because belief is simply a fancy word that means *I don't know*. There is no other rational meaning for the word belief, although the word is used to cover a multitude of psychic sins. We wouldn't, for instance, say that we believe in trees. No, that would sound foolish because we know trees as objective reality. We can only believe something that we can't know as objective reality. Which, in a sense, makes belief a learned defense mechanism, doesn't it? Some kind of protection projection? And learned defense mechanisms can be altered because they can be extinguished by disuse and strengthened by practice.[5]

It is easy to believe that our mind is not under our direction because it requires no effort at all to believe that. All we have to do is *not* direct our mind. What could be easier than *not* doing something? The most interesting thing about belief is that it requires no effort at all to believe anything, which, incidentally, is why it is easy to switch someone out of one belief into another, even an opposite one.

If we decide to support our belief with some action, that is different. But activity to support belief is not belief itself. Belief itself is all process, the content is just secondary. That's why the stronger someone believes in A, the easier it is to get them to switch to believing in B. People fall in belief just like they fall in love, unconsciously, unwittingly, and unwisely. Belief and falling in love are simply headless tentacles of passion thrashing around. They don't much care what they end up getting stuck to. And beliefs are self-perpetuating because, as philosophy tells us, we can't learn what we think we already know.

I was at a writers' club meeting once where one of the members brought a guest, a nice-looking young man in his twenties who complained that he was so depressed he couldn't do anything. He enumerated his ailments in a weak monotone, almost as if he had little real interest in the list himself. He had no friends, no education beyond high school. He "couldn't sleep at night," he "had trouble with his digestion," he "was constipated." Although he was dutifully taking the medicine his psychiatrist prescribed for him, "it didn't do any good." He said his depression was so bad all he could do was "lie on the couch and watch television all day." He lived with his parents and did not have to support himself.

One older member of the group suggested that the suffering young man "do some chores." Another woman interposed, "If all I did every day was lie around and watch television, I'd be depressed too. You say you're too depressed to do anything, but the fact of the matter is that *not doing anything* is why you're depressed." A man suggested, "Get up and exercise every morning for six months and I guarantee that you'll feel better."

"Oh, no," the pale sufferer responded to all with a dismissive wave of his hand, "I don't happen to believe that work or exercise helps depression." And so he won't work or exercise. And guess what? He will be right. Exercise and work will have no effect on his depression. Belief, to the psychologically stuck person, is like tolerance to the alcoholic. Both of their stuck positions are defended (maintained) by denial. As more facts, like more alcohol, are defended against, they have less and less of an effect and the continually defended belief becomes stronger and stronger.

The alcoholic says, "I can't be an alcoholic because I never get drunk, it has no adverse effect on me." He doesn't see that the reason he can drink more than others with less effect is that his body has built up a tolerance for, a resistance to alcohol. Tolerance, the very thing that *makes* him an alcoholic, proves to him that he is not one! Belief, the very thing that is called upon to prevent someone from doing something, becomes the proof that it can't be done.

Belief in this subjective sense should not be confused with the availability of objective knowledge that causes one, in the absence of personal experience, to "believe" that if he jumps out of a forty-story window, he'll die; or, if he sticks his hand in a fire he'll get burned. This is not belief, this is simply fact-based, common-ground, objective reality and common sense.

Beliefs can always be abandoned for the scientific method, and should be in cases where the scientific method can be so easily and safely employed, as in starting a program of exercise to test whether or not it helps our depression, or doing loving things for our spouse to test whether or not our angry feelings change.

Psychiatrists like Kay Redfield Jamison believe that we have no control over our manic-depressive moods. How can this be?

We are not some kind of empty bags that periodically fill up with either pain or joy. The overwhelming feelings of depression lead us to believe we have nothing within us to fall back on. But this is not true. Not one single bit of our extremely complex psyche ever disappears because of our moods. It is just the opposite. It is our moods that come and go. With all its essential capacities for both pain and joy, our mind always remains completely intact and immediately available to us when depression hits. We simply have to remember how to properly access it at this difficult time.

Psychiatrists believe we cannot control our depression or mania without drugs. I have always wondered why they didn't just choose to believe we *did* have control. Belief is such a powerful force because it acts as a stop sign in our lives. Once we come to a belief, like every other stasis in life, it must be maintained. To maintain belief, we must necessarily prevent ourselves from seeking other possibilities to the contrary. But since belief is all process and no content, why not harness it to work *for* us instead of *against* us and believe that we *can* do something instead of believing that we *can't*? Then we will keep looking for new possibilities. The great psychologist William James read a treatise on free will as a young man and decided that his first act of free will would be to believe in it.

Since the magic of believing lies in the fact that we can choose to believe anything we want, why not choose to believe something that would work *for* us? Belief is just a possibility of reality, it is not reality itself because reality is always happening, and belief *never* is happening because belief is always concerned with the future. Belief is always based upon something in the past and it always has implications of future intentions about it. Why be negative about the possible future? What's the point of doing that? The saddest belief of all is that there is nothing we can do to fix what ails us.

So, is that all depression is—that people just *believe* they have to feel bad and so they don't look for ways to feel better? This may be the small, simple truth that is totally hidden by the multibillion dollar complicated industry of depression, the millions of people on Prozac, Xanax, and Zoloft, the thousands of people getting shock treatments, charting their moods, and pulling the blankets up over their heads instead of going to work.

"But," you may counter, "isn't taking Prozac when we feel bad trying to find a way to feel better?" And I will respond by saying, "It's Prozac that feels good, not us." Prozac doesn't make *us* feel good any more than a cherry pie makes us *taste* good. A cherry pie tastes good and when it's gone we don't taste anything. We feel bad, we take Prozac. Prozac feels good and when it's gone, *we* still feel bad!

Managing depression is not generally thought about as something that necessitates instruction, training, and exercise. In ages past, depression was lumped in with other human frailties, which were to be shored up by moral principles. We are sadly lacking in these now.

Fortunately, there are some people who are more aware and insightful. When I asked my sister-in-law if she suffers from depression she said, "Not really, I know it always goes away." And on the news one day a reporter asked a ten-year-old boy whose brother had dropped a five-year-old neighbor out of the window to his death, "Don't you feel bad about that, doesn't it haunt you, make you depressed?" "Well," the boy replied, "there's some things you just learn not to think about." He said his grandmother told him that. That bit of knowledge is worth all the books and all the advice that the entire psychological community ever wrote about depression. And, of course, the way we don't think about something is simply to think about something else.

One of my friends said his twenty-something-year-old son moved back home terribly depressed. He had bummed around for a couple of years, didn't finish college. The first morning, my friend went up to the small attic bedroom where his son lay dormant and inquired of the gaunt, unshaven face what his plans were. "I don't have any plans," he replied. "What does anything matter when you get right down to it? Nothing really means anything, you just die in the end anyway."

"Oh no, you don't pull that kind of stuff on me," said his father. "The world has all the trouble and suffering that it can take. There are millions of people who can't do anything because they're crippled or sick. You're healthy, with a good mind and a lot of talent and training that society has already invested in you. If you don't feel like doing something for yourself, then you can get up and do it for the others."

And what did this depressed 1990s son say to his 1950s father's values lecture? "Okay," said his son. He got up, took a shower, and went to register for classes that very day. He got his degree, shouldered his share of the world's weight, and that was the last anyone heard about *nothing mattering*. To me this is a good example of a commitment to a moral precept being stronger than a feeling, even the feeling we know as depression.

It is absolutely amazing to me that world-renowned psychiatrists are telling us that depression can't be controlled without drugs. Kay Jamison even tours the colleges promoting her books, which "teach" people the symptoms of manic depression, to "catch them while they're young, and get them on drugs so their whole lives aren't 'ruined.' "

That's her belief, and that's what Jamison is teaching people. Personally, I think she's unwittingly *training* young people to be depressed and out of control. Other unwitting "trainers" are those celebrity sufferers who have spoken to thousands about depression. They also tour American campuses to "help" people understand that depression is an illness that *requires drugs,* and that it isn't *our fault* if we scream at our children, refuse to bathe, or can't get out of bed and go to work.

It's hard to say depression doesn't have to be a problem when millions of people are hurting. But that is my own personal experience. I suffered with depression for years, used a lot of self-observation, mental exercises, and mind-tricks to stop suffering, and now I even wonder sometimes that it is necessary to go to all that trouble when one simple little belief will do the trick: the belief that you don't have to pay attention to depression. All you have to do is think about something else and depression always goes away.

But, what about the fact that I still wake up every morning in the depths of despair? one may well ask. I will go back to the cherry pie and Prozac for my answer. I feel good and then I get depression. But I don't feel bad, the depression feels bad, and when it's gone, I feel good. It is not terribly important to me whether I am depressed or not. It is not terribly important to me whether I feel good or not. I don't focus that much attention on feelings. I am not my feelings. Feelings come and go like the weather, but, like the sky, I am always here.

With good feelings or bad, I can still hug my husband and fix him a nice dinner, or play a game with my grandchild, or make a cup of tea and be nice to a friend. That is what is important to me. We can sincerely do these things even when we don't feel spontaneously sanguine about any immediate happiness such actions will bring to us.

I am interested in depression. I have sought among the writings of great teachers to educate myself so that I can encounter it properly and treat it with the respect that such a powerful presence deserves. It may be that depression alone is responsible for our most trenchant connection with existence by interrupting our heedless and arrogant rush through it.

When we are in the fearful pain of depression, the only thing we are interested in is the truth. That's why my friend's son got up and went to work. My friend spoke from a place of great truth the day he said, "If you don't feel like doing something for yourself, then you can get up and do it for the others." That's the virtue of depression. It is only when we are thrust into utter darkness that we start looking for some light; only when we feel utterly abandoned that we know we must risk doing *something*. Then we learn that the only life we ever really have, the only life that we can really claim as our own, be sure of, is the life that we have had the courage to risk, win or lose. In taking this risk, whether we win or lose, we win ourselves.

Ten

FEAR IS A KIND OF INTELLIGENCE

We cannot stop these feelings directly, but we can refuse to be moved by them if they do not accord with our chosen values; or refuse to act upon them, knowing that they are not necessarily objective reality.

Depression has had a mysterious fascination for me and I like to see what it responds to, just so I can learn more about it. However, don't misunderstand me; I don't dream up mind tricks when depression hits me, but before the onset of depression. Once depression hits I simply employ the tactics I have planned and thought about when I am not undergoing it. I am not victorious over depression, I am simply victorious over myself in the face of it. My fascination for depression seems to be unique. Everybody else just wants to know how to get rid of it. The answer is: it goes away by itself when you withdraw your attention from it and pretend it isn't there.

We shouldn't be "killing it" with drugs. No matter how painful our feelings are at times, we need them to connect us to our humanity. Feelings are not like ropes and knives that we can escape from and breathe free. We need the impulse of fear because it is necessary for us to live as social beings. Without fear there is no possibility for human passion. Fear is necessary for us to relate to one another, it provides our most compelling common ground. If we are not capable of fear, we are not capable of being vulnerable and therefore we can't care enough to connect with anyone in an emotional way. In a way, fear itself is a kind of intelligence. The only thing that is incapable of fear is *stupidity*.

Fear makes us uniquely human because it is the basis for compassion and cooperation.[1] Our compassion for others comes from our capacity to imagine our own fear were we to find ourselves later suffering the same situations in which we now see others struggling.[2] Fear is the basis for all personality. Without fear we are mechanical, cold, aloof, and do not need anybody or anything. We have all experienced people who are extremely retarded and seem to have no fear or angst. Without the fear that gives us our human vulnerability to the risk of choice, we become bland and stony-faced shells of nonpersonhood.[3]

It is a hard thing. If we haven't learned to come to grips with our fear, our life is hell because fear can be painful and terrifying, especially when it escalates into depression and panic attacks. But if we are brain-damaged and have lost the capacity for fear, or if we are somehow psychologically *cut off* from the pain of our fear, we are never depressed—but we have no life at all.

It is fear that sparks the psychological internal combustion engine that powers our life. Anthropology tells us that for an organism to survive, even one as advanced as Homo sapiens, nature must provide it with an instinct to seek that which will insure its survival. The self-love that is the extension of our primal needs for food, shelter, and sex is empowered by the fear of not having those basic survival needs met. We are rooted in primal fear. But we are not supposed to stay stuck down in the mud of our roots. We are supposed to flower from our roots.

It is primal fear that is the root cause of our wanting be a friendly neighbor. It is fear that makes us want to prove a difficult mathematical theory, or paint a beautiful picture, or write a wonderful book. All feelings are fear-based, even romance. It is fear that causes us to fall in love. That overwhelming passion of being "in love" is, in reality, the ultimate projection of the totality of our dependent needs. We can see how powerful a force this is once we have fallen out of love, and look back and see, in the cold light of sanity, just who it was that we had been so crazy about.

It is primal fear that we experience in depression. We can learn to ride our fear like we can learn to ride a wild horse, rather than have it stampede and trample us into the ground. But have fear we must! People who experience brain damage that destroys the prefrontal cortices in the lower-brain frontal-lobe region, where depression resides, cannot make any choices or have even the most rudimentary goals that would allow them to hold down the simplest job.

Because they can have no feelings about them, they can make no judgment between two things. In an ironic twist, by being physically incapable of limiting their choice of possibilities, they end up choiceless.[4] For a person who is incapable of the impulse to fear, there is no emotional difference between a vanilla and a chocolate cone, or between a tree and their daughter. These people are never depressed either. But this incapability of feeling due to brain damage should not be confused with the use of Prozac for depression, which "takes the edge off" feelings rather than eradicating them completely.

I listened to a sixteen-year-old girl recently talk about her father who was brain-damaged, similarly to Phineas Gage, in an accident. Now recovered, he could not live an independent life, although he had retained all his motor skills and all his faculties of intellect, language, and reasoning were intact and fully functioning. His only problem was that he was no longer capable of any emotional feeling. He *knew* everything that he knew before the accident, but he no longer cared that he knew it. He always felt good because he was incapable of feeling bad. (More evidence that there is no way we can actually lose our essential core of well-being due to depression.) The father could not feel bad about anything because he was incapable of feeling the pain of fear. Surely, it is no accident that the French word for bread, the staff of life, is *pain*.[5]

"I really miss my dad," the young girl said. It seemed so strange to hear her say that because her father was sitting right next to her. "We used to be so close. He had a wonderful sense of humor and we used to joke around all the time." Now, although her father could understand the *meaning* of a joke, it was no longer emotionally funny to him. It was just facts. Although he could see rationally that he and his daughter were no longer close, he had no way to feel emotionally bad about it. He had no way of being anguished by his own tragedy. Of course he no longer suffered the pain of depression either, but at what cost. The father sat expressionless and stared straight ahead, the emotionally empty shell of his former self. Without fear, time has no psychological meaning to us. Without fear, people have no psychological meaning to us. Without fear, life has no psychological meaning to us. It is all just facts.

This man's emotional paralysis was eerily like something I heard the actor Christopher Reeve say once. Since he no longer had the sensation of feeling in his arms after the accident that left him paralyzed from the neck down, Reeve couldn't hug his children, he couldn't feel them and connect with them physically that way. He couldn't touch and be touched by them, and that's one of the reasons he and his wife decided not to have another baby. In the same way that we can't hug if our arms can no longer feel, we can't choose or love if our mind can no longer feel.

In addition to losing our capacity to feel because of a brain injury, we can also become dissociated and cut off from our feelings psychologically. One quite dramatic therapy session I had was with an attractive young woman, Andrea H., who came in because she "didn't experience normal feelings," and she thought that might be the reason she was "never really happy and excited." She was very intelligent, had a good job in the computer industry, and was quite self-assured. She said her low-key emotional state was mainly a problem with her boyfriend, who complained that she never got enthusiastic about anything, and he took it personally that the things he planned weren't "good enough."

Andrea said she never cried at sad movies, didn't "get all goo-goo" over her friends' new babies like everybody else, and she was worried that maybe she was just coldhearted. She said she had always been this way and but had been seeing a psychiatrist in her home town for almost two years for the "problem." She was "pleased with her progress," and now that she had moved here for her job, she wanted to continue the work with me, plus checkup sessions with her regular psychiatrist during visits back home. My naturally competitive nature wondered what in the world her psychiatrist's idea of "great progress" might be, but instead of asking her that, I asked her how she was feeling at the moment. She threw me a sharp glance and said in a slightly annoyed voice, "I *told* you, I don't feel *anything*. I *never* feel anything."

"Well," I countered, "there must be some word that would explain the relationship you have with your own body."

"Well then," she responded testily, "I guess I would say *numb*."

I asked her where in her body she felt "numb" and she put both her hands on her chest area. I asked her to put both her feet on the ground, close her eyes, and relax (a simple hypnosis technique) and go back to the first time she could remember having this "numb" feeling. Almost immediately she began to cry hysterically and repeat over and over, "No, no, Mommy, no."

I asked her how old she was in this scene that she was

imagining and emotionally "reliving." She said about two years old. I asked her where she was and she said she was on the backseat of a car that her mother was driving. She said she was very scared. She said she was crying and her mother was hitting at her while driving "really fast" and telling her, "Stop crying, stop crying, stop crying this minute, don't you dare cry anymore." After a few minutes I told Andrea to relax again, and that when she opened her eyes and "came back" to being thirty-one years old she would be able to feel normal feelings and cry anytime she wanted to.

When she opened her eyes she was amazed. "I didn't know," she said. I didn't need to point out to her the obvious connection between her mother's command to "stop crying" and the fact that she had disconnected from her feelings. "But now I am happy and excited," she said, beaming. "This is so *wonderful*, I didn't know I could cry like that. I guess I do have feelings after all, like a normal person." She only came to one or two sessions so she wouldn't "lose it again" but she really didn't need to. She had no trouble with expressing her feelings after that first time.

A couple came into my office for psychotherapy because the wife complained that her husband didn't seem to care about anything one way or the other. He seemed to have no feelings about what they did or didn't do. She felt disconnected from him and unloved. The husband was a young man of twenty-six. He related that he had been sexually abused by his father from the age of eight to fourteen. In his first session Joe said that he was a person that didn't have strong feelings, good or bad, except for when he was depressed, and then he tried to commit suicide three times. In answer to my question, he said he certainly didn't feel any fear of any kind. He wasn't exactly sure what fear felt like because he was a marine, and as far as he knew he wasn't afraid of anything.

He was sitting about five feet in front of my desk and his

body language was screaming at me how afraid he was. "With your permission," I said, "I'm going to move my chair closer to you and you tell me if you start to feel uncomfortable at all." I moved my chair to the side of the desk and began to move closer and closer to the young man. When I got to about a foot from him he shouted, "STOP. I'm uncomfortable. I'm uncomfortable." And indeed he was sweating and was quite red in the face. "That's fear," I said. "That feeling of discomfort that you are feeling now is the pain of fear. If you think back to a few seconds ago, you will remember feeling some gradations of that pain as I moved closer. It's a natural defense mechanism to feel fear when a stranger is invading your space."

As children we may have been victims of abuse and our only means of survival was to dissociate ourselves from it psychologically since we couldn't save ourselves from it physically. The way we dissociate ourselves from our painful feelings is by switching to thinking about something else rather than what is happening in our present reality. But dissociating from painful feelings isn't *escaping* from painful feelings. These repressed feelings hang around and drag us down in the form of depression.

By all means, if we have repressed feelings we should dredge them up with therapeutic massage work, exercises, or sad music and finish feeling them. Just because we have fearful feelings does not mean that we should be afraid of them. The trick is to *have* our feelings without letting our feelings have us. We are much more powerful than our feelings and we shouldn't collapse into them as if we were the helpless victims of them.

We need to re-frame our negative thinking about our negative feelings. One way to think about feelings is to see them as a temporary part we have taken in a play and we are "on stage" at the moment. An actor may take on a role and feel himself "become" the part he is playing, but there is always some awareness that he is not "really" the role. That's how we can begin to think about our feelings, and therefore get some objectivity about them instead of becoming their subjectivity.

It's just that nobody ever told us about feelings so they seem more powerful to us than they really are. Some of us are as phobic about our painful feelings as other people are phobic about snakes and spiders. We can desensitize ourselves from our phobia about our fear the same way we desensitize ourselves from our phobia about snakes and spiders—by encountering them at increased levels of exposure.

We have to understand that fear, or its logical extension, depression, is not a disease that needs to be "cured" with drugs. Principles and practice are the keys, not drugs. After all, feelings come and go; it is principles that abide. Wherever it is that we came from, we brought feelings with us; but principles were already here when we arrived. Principles can save us from falling into depression, not by believing in them, but by applying them to our lives. "Let us cling to our principles," counsels poet Edward Young, "as a mariner clings to his last plank when night and tempest close around him."

The difference between principles and emotions is this: Emotions, as somatic impulses, have no inherent good or bad about them, no virtue or vice aspects to them. Not so with principles, which are absolute, either inherently evil, or inherently good. We can't choose what kinds of emotions and feelings impel us. We *can* choose what kind of principles we grab for when we are impelled. Feelings and emotions are never problems in themselves. It is in our succumbing to them that they become a problem. Principles can guard us against succumbing.

Principles can be very simple things. Abiding by the principle of "doing something" when you are depressed is much more powerful than your depression. If you are depressed and you "make yourself take a walk," that is principles-based action. Here is an example of principles-based action from a young woman who posted her solution to a fellow sufferer of depression on an Internet chat group. "When I wake up in the morning, I do this thing called the faces. I make three in front of the mirror. A super goofy one, a mad and angry one. Then I will just smile till it hurts and make the happiest face I can. If I haven't cheered up even moderately I do ten jumping jacks and then I start my day. Sometimes I only feel a touch better, but that is better than nothing. Good luck, and take care, sweetie."

By choosing certain principles, we can use the power of fear to protect ourselves from it. Fear is supposed to *assist* our reasoning, *not overthrow it*. The pain of our fear, a necessary defense mechanism, needs to be powerful enough to assure that its counsel cannot so easily be set aside. But we can make fear of not doing our duty so paramount in our lives that it can deliver us from any fear that would *keep* us from our duty.

This is implicit in the training that every soldier receives. It was the fear for the safety of my family that was stronger than my fear of the burning coals that meant the success of my first firewalk. I walked over those coals empowered by the passion to risk the danger of the firewalk as symbolic protection for my family.

Again, fear is necessary. We should not try to eradicate it from our lives. "It is the strong passions," warns French philosopher Claude-Adrien Helvétius, "which, rescuing us from sloth, can alone impart to us that continuous and earnest attention necessary to great intellectual effort." "The passions are the winds that fill the sails of the vessel," counsels Voltaire. "They sink it at times; but without them it would be impossible to make way." "Even virtue itself," says eighteenth-century English author Anna Jameson, "all perfect as it is, requires to be inspirited by passion; for duties are but coldly performed which are but philosophically fulfilled."

When we decide to get in touch with our fear, we will

probably not have to search very long. We have little fears every day of our lives that we have learned to avoid. Now we can learn to pay attention to them. One of the first little fears I discovered was that I was afraid to make phone calls if I had to tell someone something they didn't want to hear, or if I was expecting some disappointment or rejection of some kind. I began to be aware that I kept putting off phone calls of this type by waiting until "later," or forgetting to call at all, or losing the number. It was less painful for me to blame my noncalling on the fact that I was lazy or forgetful or disorganized than to admit I was afraid. That was because I knew how to handle laziness or forgetfulness or disorganization. I had no idea what to do about my fear.

Once I got more user-friendly with my fear, because I was going out of my way to confront it rather than avoid it, it was interesting to see how little power it really had. My fear turned out to be just like a big dog with a huge bark and menacing fangs that, when faced down, whimpers and licks your hand, wagging its tail to win your approval. These days when I think about these kinds of calls, I can still feel the fear buzz around the inside of my chest, almost like a little electric shock. I just carry the pain of my fear buzz straight to the phone and get the calls over with.

When we find ourselves blaming anyone or anything, we can change the focus from the object of our blame back to ourselves and any feelings we might be having at the moment. One clue is that fear is painful. IT HURTS! Even a little fear gives a certain buzz around the heart or stomach area or in the throat. Breathing is usually more shallow. Today I still have fear, but I have a different relationship to it. For one thing, it is now invited rather than uninvited. I have welcomed my fear back into my life. Fear is no more to me than the roller coaster I rode when I a kid: "Whew, I was scared to death, that was a good one!"

A good way to get in touch with repressed fear is studying things we hate to do. Hate is simply fear projected onto some object. For instance, although I don't mind at all filling the dishwasher, I "hate" to empty it. Sometimes when I remember that hate is just projected fear, I focus my awareness on any fear that might be going on by taking my focus off how much I hate emptying the dishwasher. Sure enough, I can always catch that little electric buzz, or at the least the tight throat and the shallow breathing. This awareness has elevated emptying the dishwasher to a whole new experience. Once we get in touch with little fears, we can go on to bigger ones.

I used to hate it when my husband started yelling at me about something. When I took the focus away from hating my husband to checking out my gut level of fear, I got in touch with a whole mother lode of repressed fear. This was also true about those sudden, unexpected loud whoops and calls, not directed at me at all, that he lets loose while watching a football game on TV. They can still set bolts of fear swooshing through my entire body.

Ultimately I began to understand that it was not so much that the yelling filled me with fear. It was more like the yelling was a flashlight that illuminated a lot of unfinished, repressed fear that had been raging around inside of me since childhood and brought it to my attention so I could let it finish. My husband's yelling, which I used to hate, turned out to be a great gift. We don't have to arm ourselves *against* fear, but rather *with* fear and *by* fear. When we willingly undergo our fear, we understand that fear is a power source that comes from the inside—it is not caused by an assault from the outside. Once we are no longer children and have "separated" from our parents,[6] no one can *put* fear in us; there is no law of psychology, biology, or physics that would allow for that.

The pain of fear is like any other kind of physical hurt in that it is an automatic primal-mind defense mechanism that makes it possible to know immediately that we are in danger or have just cut ourselves on a piece of barbed wire. Psychic feelings of pain also alert us to problems we need to fix, but the connection between the problem and the psychic pain is not as easy to see as a cut on the leg. Also, our leg doesn't periodically hurt unless we have a bodily injury, unlike our mind, which can be overcome by painful feelings that can be activated accidentally.

When we attend to our wound, our cut leg stops hurting. Unless we attend to our thinking process, our mind will keep on hurting, even in the absence of any real problem. Our whole lives can be fear-based when we do not use our fear to impel us to action but, instead, let the fear itself manage our lives.

What can we do? We can train ourselves to *undergo* these painful feelings of fear and let them subside on their own while we direct our thoughts to distract our attention from them. We can consciously choose a rational, higher-mind, substitute thinking or a substitute behavior to put in place of the irrational, primal-mind one. Remember, we can only think one thing at a time. If we are thinking something *rational*, then the *irrational* thought will have to wait in the wings.

Otherwise we will try to escape our painful feelings by repressing them or projecting them in the form of hurt, blame, and complaint. Hurt is fear directed inward, blame and complaint are fear directed outward. All rote projections of feeling are irrational. The way to change irrational thinking or irrational behavior is first to recognize intellectually that it is irrational.

Unfortunately, our own irrational behavior is difficult to see. There is quite a hidden reluctance on anybody's part to "know thyself" due to the strategies of the primal mind to protect the status quo. When I first began my quest, long-standing habits of behavior did not, at my command, parade themselves for my perusal and judgment upon them. For any particular behavior of mine, I would be able to see it first only in hindsight and from a long distance away.

Suppose, for instance, that I decided to study particularly how I was always getting into trouble because I didn't have the courage to say no and disappoint someone. I would try to think about some examples. Usually the first example that would occur to me was pretty much ancient history; years ago, or months ago. Then as I pursued the behavior, I would remember situations that were more and more current, last week or last month. Then I would get to see it yesterday, or ten minutes ago. Then as I stuck to it, the primal mind, figuring the jig was up, would finally let me catch my self in the act.

Catching myself in the act did not mean that the fear that influenced the behavior in the first place would allow me to change it, then and there. I still had not yet fully paid my psychic dues. First I had to undergo the fear. By examining my fearful situations, I was beginning to question the reality of some of my "problems" by doing instant mental autopsies on my own thinking and behavior. When my awareness became current I could say to myself something like, "Wow, I am feeling really scared right now, and I am saying, 'yes' and I don't want to." When we are aware of what we are feeling and doing *at the moment,* we can more easily begin to direct our thinking beyond old patterns to choose different behavior based upon some moral imperative. It is hard to stop stealing if we do not ever see ourselves as a thief.

To help myself with the behavior of saying yes because I was too wimpy to say no, I prepared myself by choosing, ahead of time, some "scripts" that I could use to say no as gracefully as possible when the next occasion arose. Something like: "Normally I would say yes but things have been piling up and I hope you will forgive me if I beg off this time." I practiced them out loud in front of the mirror. It didn't seem so terrifying.

But the first time I said no instead of saying yes *was* terrifying. It was like dying. I know now what the mystics mean by "little deaths." We really have to die to our fears in order to triumph over them. Now, of course, there are people like my husband who have never been afraid of saying no. My answer to this is that some of us are afraid of spiders, and some of us are afraid of snakes. This side of enlightenment there is not one among us who is not afraid of *something*. The point is not necessarily to reconstruct who we are; the point is to "know thyself" by observing thyself in action.

How can we be wise about our fear of depression? When we are feeling depressed we can attach to these feelings the idea, by conscious learned association, that we are therefore functioning from the primal mind, over which we do not have direct control.

We cannot stop these feelings directly, but we can refuse to be moved by them if they do not accord with our chosen values; or refuse to act upon them, knowing that they are not necessarily objective reality. We can bear them, and suffer them, and use our higher mind in any small activity to alter the thinking that activated the unwanted feelings until they subside. The more we practice doing this, the more we will know what to practice. Also, when we remain aware, many things stop by themselves, we do not have to stop them.

It takes effort to consciously choose values and make sure that our behavior corresponds with them, because we have to *do something* with the principles of honesty, commitment, integrity, fidelity, love, honor, and courage. It is harder to choose to do something with principles, and easier to collapse into rampant feelings where we don't have to do anything but follow them around.

Unlike the primal mind, principles like courage and honor can do nothing with us. We can improve upon our principles, but they cannot improve upon us. This is what freedom of the will means; we can choose principles but they cannot choose us. We can wield them just like Excalibur, but they cannot wield us. It is only the primal mind that can *do us* in the form of mania, paranoia, or depression.

It is the same with our maintaining a common-ground connection to the world around us. We have to do something with the world. It can do nothing with us. When we feel alienated, it is up to us to activate our connection with the world, no matter how hesitant or faulty; regardless of how scary the idea is. It is hard to make a connection. It is easier to do nothing. But whether we acknowledge it or not, we remain the sole source of the world for ourselves, just as we remain the sole source of food for our body.

Nobody can eat for us, and nobody can provide us with a world. Our action is the switch that turns on the world. Whether we turn on the world with some action on our part is up to us. The world will not compel us. It may try, in the form of psychotherapy; but the only thing a psychotherapist can use to help us is us.

I remember one depressive episode when I had spent days without going out of the house—just glued by passivity to the unhappy furniture and the gloomy, vacant calm. My grandchildren were dropped off for a visit and they wanted to take a walk. I agreed with little enthusiasm in my heart. But after twenty minutes or so I realized, with surprise, that there was a "whole world out here" that I had completely forgotten. I had been thinking my sad little house was the whole world. I had forgotten there was a sky, and trees, and clouds, and houses in which there were probably some nice people living.

Maybe some of those people are even sad today too, I thought, just like me. I didn't even know I had lost common ground until I found it so solid beneath my feet again. I wished them well, all the people in their houses that were again part of my world, which made me part of theirs. I felt less lonely.

I promised myself that I would not forget common ground again, the wide world of trees and clouds and houses full of people.

Until we take a walk and look at the stars, talk to somebody, or find something to turn a hand to, the world remains alien, remote, and cold, with all its possibilities frozen. And therefore, we remain alien, remote, and cold, with all our possibilities frozen. This does not feel good. This is often called depression. Mike Wallace said about his depression, "All you focus on is yourself and how bad you feel."[7]

No, we can't decide to feel good as an act of will. Our only hope is to decide, as an act of will, to get up anyway, even if we don't feel like it, and take some small positive action. Run, or take a walk, take out the garbage, make the bed, volunteer to clean up the highway. Anything can be the start of our understanding that we are already connected to the world. Then, as a result of feeling hooked up with life again, good feelings can result.

William James said to "keep the faculty of effort alive in you by a little gratuitous exercise every day. That is, be systematically acetic or heroic in little unnecessary points. Do every day or two things for no other reason than that you would rather not do them, so that when the hour of dire need draws nigh, it may find you not unnerved and untrained to stand the test."

I make my bed every day because of William James's principle. One day I started to make my bed and didn't feel like it. So I started to quit. Then I thought of William James and said to myself, "Wait, I don't feel like it. It takes thirty seconds to make my bed. What a great exercise!" So from now on, I decided, I am going to make my bed every day, exactly *because* I won't feel like it. Our life doesn't work unless we do. We and life are absolutely simultaneous creations. We can't sit around and wait for our life to get fixed up, as if our life were some kind of rundown house. Life is not some place we live in, it is whatsoever we are doing RIGHT NOW!

If we refuse our food, we will starve. If we refuse our connection with the world around us, we will remain alienated, solitary, and depressed. If we do not consciously connect with present reality, we automatically fall into the cave of our primal mind where old, self-pitying, fearful, self-absorbed mind videos are continually playing. We don't choose to think them, they choose to think themselves, *on our time*, if we let them.

Depression is voluntary suffering, like watching horror movies. We just forget it is voluntary and that we have other options. Like a deer at midnight frozen in the headlights, we watch our pain. We don't have to. We can learn to stop thinking thoughts about our pain and direct our thinking to connect with some other thought that moves us away from our pain and our sense of isolation. Depression is not regular life. It is our own private hell of self-absorption. To get out of it we need to reconnect with the common ground of regular life in some small way.

Life is all of a piece; we will never find an empty spot or a hole in life where even the tiniest thing could get lost. So clearly there is no way for us to be lost, even though we feel lost. We are, each and every one of us, always in the hand of existence. Existence is not going to do anything to connect to us because existence knows we are already connected. We're the ones who don't know that. "Having never left the house, we are looking for the way home," goes an old Eastern saying.

When we are feeling depressed and alienated, it is not so much a matter of accumulating right ideas about how we might connect back up with life as it is a matter of ignoring the primal mind's *wrong idea* that we are unconnected. It is not so much a matter of risking effort as it is risking the uncertainty of reality by acting upon it in spite of our fear.[8] We have to risk acting in some other way than being depressed. We have to risk acting as if there is no such thing as depression when depression is at that very moment convincing us that despair is the only reality. We have to act upon some other reality than depression.

It is not so much a case of understanding some great truth about how to make ourselves happy as it is not believing, or at least not paying attention to the primal mind's insistence that we are unhappy. We cannot *become* connected to life because, as the old sages tell us, *we cannot become what we are already*. This is the reason all our grand schemes to seek meaning and purpose in life must inevitably end in failure. The problem with depression is not that we have no meaning and purpose in life. The problem with depression is that we have been trained by our culture to ascribe to depression the role of being the most interesting or compelling thing in our lives; more interesting and compelling than any effort to make something out of our day; more interesting and compelling than our own loved ones. We just need to recognize that this is never the case, objectively speaking (as everyone else around us can plainly see but us). So we should not make it the case subjectively speaking.

The good news is that we don't need any grand and glorious plans. We just need to experience ourselves as okay and connected by some small positive act that focuses us away from the primal mind's erroneous fear that we are not okay but lost and disconnected. This is the explanation, in terms of ancient wisdom, of the recovery of the depressed lawyer-turned-paperboy.[9] When we see we are connected with the smallest part of life, that small part is connected to something else, that is connected to something else, ad infinitum. We just need to recognize our fellowship with that first small piece. "Everything in Nature contains all the powers of Nature," says Ralph Waldo Emerson. "Everything is made of one hidden stuff." We can escape from our unawareness anytime we want by choosing any small conscious action or thought to reestablish our sense of present reality. "The only way to resumption," said S. P. Chase, Secretary of the Treasury under Lincoln, "is to resume."

We are not alone. We all suffer, whether or not it is readily apparent, one to another. I have a friend who suffers from depression. I told her once that I do not wish depression on her. But knowing that at times she suffers from depression helps me because it reminds me that I am not alone in my struggles. Our great literature tells us that. Goethe reminds us when he says, "To know of someone here and there whom we accord with, who is living on with us, even in silence—this makes our earthly ball a peopled garden."

If the world were run like summer camp (and maybe it should be), we could each have a bunk buddy assigned to us. Then when we needed to complain, blame, and moan about our lot, our buddy could listen, reassure us that we are really okay by him, and remind us that we seem to be overidentifying with our unhappiness instead of swimming, boating, crafting, hiking, or doing something interesting so that we could be having more fun at summer camp.

Eleven

AN EXCUSE IS NOT A TICKET TO ANYTHING

It isn't our great strength that enables us to exercise, it is our exercise that makes us strong. And it isn't discipline that makes us organized. It is the humble stumble and bumble of working on getting organized that makes us disciplined.

Since the late 1960s, psychology has been encouraging us to look to our feelings, those irrational bolts of current coursing through our bodies, as some kind of path to the true self. There is some truth to be gained from feelings, but only in the context of feelings as *defense mechanisms*, not feelings as *holy imperatives*. Feelings are our path, they are not our goal. We are supposed to be meeting our goals on a daily basis, not our feelings. By placing undue importance upon our feelings as the legitimate arbiter of our behavior, our society has become fearful and aggressive and, therefore, selfish, shallow, dependent, and depressed.

Psychology has done us a further disservice by giving our feeling-based, poor-behavior choices diagnoses of "mental illnesses"—such as narcissistic personality disorder, alcoholism, or manic depression—as if the negative things we do or feel are somehow beyond our will and therefore not our personal responsibility.

Negative behavior and negative feelings are not beyond our management if we assert conscious authority over our thinking. But, unfortunately, we will have little help from the psychological community as long as it continues to insist that addiction is a disease, and an excuse is as good as a virtue. My daughter elevates this to the height of the ridiculous when she half-seriously blames her rudeness on her "know-it-all" gene, and her forgetfulness on her car-key-losing gene.

As psychologists have elevated feelings to a higher status over behavior, it is no wonder that excuses, to the same degree, have taken on an importance not commensurate with any true value. We are being led to believe that a good excuse cancels a bad deed, or that having a good excuse for not doing something is the same thing as doing it.[1] We use good excuses to counteract the guilt we feel when we don't do what we are supposed to do. As we do less and less, and feel guiltier and guiltier, our excuses get bigger and better. Excuses are a kind of character pseudocyesis.[2] Excuses have reached full height in our culture by rising to the legitimacy of mental-health diagnoses.

But an excuse is not a ticket to anything. When excuses are seen to have value, and when feelings can dictate actions, life is complicated and terribly inefficient. Feelings come and go, and we can't plan on them because we can't call them up at will to do our bidding. What we don't realize is that feelings call themselves up and we do their bidding, unless we have already planned in advance how not to succumb to them.

Even when we know about such mind techniques as witnessing, or forced thought, we don't necessarily do them. One of the reasons we don't handle life's problems better than we do is that we have too many readily available excuses proving to us that we are just not "the right stuff." It's almost as if we wish to be deceived.

Many of these excuses come in the form of shared cultural beliefs and assumptions, which we never think to question. Josh W. said his college roommate had achieved great success because his "real genius" was his discipline. He could study for hours, day after day, without being distracted, while Josh, who deplored his own lack of discipline, admitted that he usually began studying for exams the night before.

Will J. said the same thing about his younger brother; that he admired his brother's discipline, how he organized his work and got things done, while Will insisted that he himself was deficient in this quality. Laura W. confided to me in a session, after a frenzy of missed appointments and deadlines, that she just didn't possess organizational skills and discipline like some people.

There is something fundamentally wrong with all of these remarks in that they are self-defeating as well as self-deluding. They are saying that if we possess discipline, we can be organized and motivated to plan our lives properly. This is totally backward. This is like saying if we have good muscles, we can exercise well. It isn't our great strength that enables us to exercise, it is our exercise that makes us strong. And it isn't discipline that makes us organized. It is the humble stumble and bumble of working on getting organized that makes us disciplined.

We say things in such a way that we obscure to ourselves that we have a choice. And then we sell this obfuscation to each other in the form of "self-sayings" that we accept as "givens." We say "I'm not very disciplined," and plunk ourselves down comfortably by the side of what we believe is some natural, God-given road of weakness upon which it was our fate to be sidetracked. But we aren't being sidetracked by God or fate. We are being sidetracked by our own language. What we are really saying when we say we aren't disciplined is, "I don't have a high regard for duty." If we are more precise about what we are saying about ourselves, we can more easily see what we are doing.

For instance, when we want to avoid making a decision we say, "I'm of two minds about it," and wait for the heads around us to nod their agreement with our perfectly acceptable conclusion. When we know very well that we can always come from two places within ourselves, our impulse or our principles, our primal mind or our higher mind. And it is always our one choice not to dangle ourselves in abeyance between those two places.

Today's psychological paradigm of compassionate acceptance leads us to call ourselves shy and sensitive when it would be far more helpful and accurate to say that we are fearful and resentful. How is this a problem? It is a problem because the cure for shy and sensitive is outgoingness and self-esteem. But outgoingness and self-esteem are not the cures for fearful and resentful. The cures for fearful and resentful are courage and self-responsibility.

We say "I don't like conflict" when the truer thing would be "I am a coward." Again, the problem is that the cure for conflict is peace and tranquility. Peace and tranquility are not the cures for cowardice. Pursuing our principles in the face of our fear is the cure for cowardice. Psychology does not agree with the great Roman naturalist Pliny, who says: "The great business of man is to improve his mind and govern his manners; all other projects and pursuits, whether in our power to compass or not, are only amusements."

We need to educate ourselves so we know the *real* rules and principles we can count on, what pitfalls we should avoid, what can insure our success or cause our failure. We can start with what we believe at the moment to be a negative influence, the "big problem" that prevents our progress, and question that belief. Depression is one of those beliefs for many people. But if we are stuck deep in depression, it is usually too hard to work directly on the depression itself. Better to start with something small, outside the field of psychology, where we aren't so enmeshed and defensive.

How about physics? I have often thought that, since we exist as physical beings, if what happens to us psychologically can't be corroborated by some law of physics, then we are simply fooling ourselves. For instance, getting organized and becoming a disciplined person is equally hard for everybody. We all have the same laws of physics governing us. One of these laws is the law of inertia: an object in motion tends to stay in motion, an object at rest tends to stay at rest. When we take an action, it is easier to continue in that direction because we are already moving in that direction.

If we are not presently organizing our life well and want to change, we will have to overcome the law of inertia. At this point, when the law of inertia is working against us, instead of for us, it may seem that other people are "disciplined" and we are not. However, this goes against what I call the Primary Human Principle: *to be human is to choose*. We can choose to move in any direction at will. We are not so bound, as are other creatures in nature, by our instincts. Neither are we bound by anything we have done in the past; compelled by the law of inertia perhaps, but not bound. The magnificent opportunity of choice is ours upon any instant.

There is great magic here for those who truly understand the enormity of our choice. The magnitude of it first occurred to me when I was speaking before a group of Presbyterian churchwomen. How had I missed it before now? The impact of the realization was so powerful I was dumbstruck. I fell silent with this gigantic lightbulb of sudden awareness flashing wildly all through me. Very quietly I repeated myself to the audience, not just for emphasis, but from the sheer joy of understanding it myself for the first time.

Here's what happened. This particular appearance had been

scheduled for several months. The night before, my husband asked me what I was going to talk about, and I said that I wasn't sure. He was taken aback that I had not written a speech. But I told him that it was not my intention to plan anything at all about what I was going to say. He felt that it was disrespectful of me to "wing it," and he was not wholly convinced even when I explained my position.

I used to plan speeches very carefully. But in 1995, when my book *Children of the Gods* won the San Diego Book Award, with no advance warning I was interviewed at length by reporters over the phone for two magazine articles. Shortly thereafter, I was interviewed for a newspaper article on video, again, without the possibility of advance preparation. During the course of these interviews I said things that I simply didn't know until I heard myself say them. They were very helpful things, which I was then able to apply profitably to my own life.

I began to realize that when I write a speech, my whole effort is spent in trying to remember what I have planned to say, with the effect that the speech is limited to what I already know. But if I am spontaneous and do not plan ahead what I am going to say, and simply let myself be led by something someone in the audience says or by something that occurs to me upon the instant, I always learn something important myself. Something magic happens at these times, and I learn right along with everybody else. There is something terrifying about speaking extemporaneously, to be sure. But a skier risks his very life for glory on each downhill run. Surely I can risk mediocrity for understanding.

During this particular speech, where I had been invited to talk about my books, I referred to the fact that "most of us, at some point in our lives, find that we have been going for a long time in the wrong direction." For emphasis I began a deliberately exaggerated march toward stage left, clump, clump,

clump. "But all we need to do," I stopped marching, "is choose to take just the smallest, tiniest baby step in the right direction," I turned on my heel to face the opposite direction and continued walking, "to turn our lives . . ." I was going to say, "to turn our lives around."

But as I turned on my heel toward stage right I suddenly realized the great impact of this tiny, baby step and finished instead, "180 degrees around!" Just think about the impact of that for those of us who have some longtime addiction or deep-seated failing that has been eluding our management. The smallest, tiniest step in the right direction turns us 180 degrees around!

People think wrongly that virtues like temperance and discipline are commodities that we either have or don't have. But temperance and discipline are not commodities, they are behavior choices that we have to make every single time. They are simply a series of small steps taken in one direction. People mistake them for commodities because, as behavior choices are made over and over again they become habits, and habits are seen as commodities because people believe that they can anticipate that we will do what we have done before. But this is only an assumption on their part, not an imperative on ours.

Habits can only be possibilities, because otherwise they would go against the Primary Human Principle: to be human is to choose. We possess freedom of will. Habits are only more than possibilities because we have the law of inertia and the defenses of the primal mind working for them. This is both the good news and the bad news. If we are in the habit of doing evil, and decide to change, we may choose at any moment to do some small good thing. However, if we are in the habit of doing good, it is possible to fall from grace in any small moment of weakness. But then this is the mystery and the drama of the human condition.

Since behavior choices are not predictable, behavior cannot

be controlled outside of a person's will to do one thing instead of another. Certainly behavior cannot ever be "cured" by doctors or drugs. The consequences of one's behavior can make it worth one's while to choose one behavior over another, but free choice always obtains. That is why all methods of parenting fail that don't provide very unpleasant consequences for behavior we wish to extinguish, and favorable consequences for behavior we wish to encourage.

That is why there is no cure for drug addiction or alcoholism. Not because they are such insidious diseases, but because they are not diseases in the first place. They are behavior choices. Depression and mania cannot be cured either by psychotherapy or drugs because they are also behavior choices. Both depression and mania begin with chemical impulses in which one does not have to wallow helplessly for very long. It does not matter that people insist that "they can't help it." It does not matter that the whole psychological community declares that manic depression (bipolar disorder) is a mental illness and is not a question of choice. The whole psychological community has a great unrecognized incapacity in this area. The whole psychological community is wrong.

Unfortunately, this situation will probably continue until Freud is totally rejected and replaced with neuroscience and his theory of the unconscious mind gets tossed out with the other Dark Age demons. Like demons, the id, the ego, and the superego are helpful figures of speech; and literature will continue to owe a great deal to Freud for these inventions that help us describe our strong primal feelings by personifying them.

But these figures of speech are not in charge of us. They should be ushered out of the doctor's office and the courtroom and directed to the library and the bookstore. Why? It is due to their influence that we expect our mind to take care of us, instead of understanding that we are supposed to take care of our minds. It is due to their influence that psychology seeks for ways to excuse and understand deviant behavior rather than to bring about compliance with common-ground established norms.

It is due to Freud's "pleasure principle of the id" that psychology is afraid of limitation. We are wrong to believe that limitations will cause us to lose the power of our individuality. Power is based upon limitation. It is limitation that produces Niagara Falls. If that same amount of water were not confined within a small rocky chasm, but allowed to just meander any which way upon an infinitely wide expanse of land, there would be no thundering falls. There would be no powerful fire-fighting equipment without water being limited to the small cylinder of the firehose. There would be no spray cans without the large expanse of air being limited to the small space within them.

It is due to Freud that we think psychological states of mind fund all human motivation, and that we can therefore cure behavior choices by healing the mind. We cannot. Drugs can't heal the mind. Drugs only influence the mind. While being treated for mania, drugs can so weigh us down by the extra gravity that we can barely lift ourselves up through all the cloud-soup heaviness to do anything. If we are being treated for depression, drugs can so wig us out with a watered-down mania that, in effect, we ingest our personality instead of creating it because we don't have to depend on the consequences of our actions to fund our feelings of well-being. With drugs, we just get a temporary feeling adjustment, we don't increase in self-knowledge or become sure of our moral strength by testing our mettle against the "dark night of our soul." In neither winning nor losing, we might well begin to wonder if we are even playing the game.

So why do some of us want Prozac to be the master of our fate and the captain of our soul? Because we are convinced that without Prozac or Xanax or Celexa, the chemicals in our brains will force us to feel things we can't stand to feel, and do things we don't want to do. It is my experience that the wide mood swings of bipolar disorder can be controlled by controlling our thoughts. The *belief* that we can't control ourselves when these mood swings occur may be the only reason we *don't* do it, not because we *can't* do it. It is a matter of practice. We just need to practice controlling ourselves instead of practicing not controlling ourselves.

Actually, the fact that drugs like Prozac can immediately make great changes in our personas and "self-esteem"[3] should give us a clue as to how easily manipulated the mind really is; how lacking in depth, awareness, and understanding its workings are; how susceptible to commands and insistence; how separated from objective reality, how duped by feelings, and how unimpressed with moral principle.

I used to drink beer when I was in college to relax and "be myself" at parties, instead of being all nervous and self-conscious. It worked wonderfully well. But when I stopped drinking after I had children (except for an occasional glass of wine at dinner), although it was difficult at first, I finally learned to *choose* to "be myself" and relax instead of being autonomically all nervous and self-conscious.

And that didn't just work wonderfully well. That was really who I *habitually* grew into. Advocates of Prozac for depression consider the persona and the self to be synonymous. I do not agree. While it is true that the persona may be a vehicle for the self, the self can decide if it wishes to be the passenger or the driver.

What is the hidden truth in all of this? Because we are human beings, and thus endowed with freedom of choice, not only *can* we all do whatever we want, we *must* do whatever we want. There is no other proven reality. And since we *must* do what we want, shouldn't we plan our wants carefully instead of letting our minds choose our wants at random—or letting

Prozac choose, or Xanax, or Zoloft? We can learn to understand the mitigating forces that work for us and against us; so that we can learn to ride them to our consciously chosen wants, instead of being ridden by them to our autonomically chosen wants.

But, make no mistake about it, we *will* have what we want. That is either our fate or our destiny. It is the destiny of the tulip bulb to bloom into a beautiful flower. But if the bulb ends up in a garbage disposal, it will succumb to its fate, instead of meeting its destiny. If we become proactive about our wants, we may achieve our destiny. If we let our wants just bubble up through drugs or autonomic thinking, we will likely succumb to our unwanted fate.

It need not be our fate to spend so much of our lives sunk in depression. The impulse to fear is caused by chemical imbalances that are automatically triggered by negative thoughts or other shadow images of the mind that are occurring, but of which we may not be aware. We can override these negative thoughts and frightening shadows, even if we don't know what they are, by consciously choosing positive or neutral thoughts as soon as we notice we are feeling bad. It's not that we access the higher mind so that it can *control* the lower mind. Again, what happens is that as long as our attention is engaging the higher mind, our attention will necessarily disengage from the primal mind because we only have one attention.

To use the analogy of electricity, we can think of our attention as an electric plug. A thought is an electric probe that activates our brain neurons; particular thoughts activate particular areas of the brain. If our thoughts are accessing our depression channel, we can choose the kind of electric plug (thought) that activates that other channel that doesn't contain depression.

Our attention can flip from one thing to another with lightning speed so that it seems like we are thinking many thoughts at once. We are not thinking them at once, just so rapidly in succession that it seems like it is all at once, the same way that individual dots in a photograph "appear" from a distance to be a solid picture.

In reality, we can think only one thought at a time. We can concentrate on a thought by choosing it over and over again, but we cannot hold onto a single thought for very long. Concentrating on a single thought, choosing the same thought over and over again, is not usual. We don't have to concentrate on a single thought for most of our regular lives, but we have the capacity to do so. This kind of repetitive thought choice is one of the ways we can achieve intentional hypnosis.

We can also achieve *accidental* hypnosis when our mind, on its own, chooses to think some depressive or manic thought over and over. But we can refuse these thoughts when we become aware of them. We don't have to think them. Sometimes we don't realize that our mind is choosing to think fearful thoughts over and over again until we realize that we are terribly depressed. When we understand the concept of thought choice, we can refuse the autonomic thought choices of our mind by choosing a new thought pattern of our own, whenever we realize that depression or mania is going on.

It is simply a choice between two things *for our one attention*, like a choice between two cars for one driver. If we choose to drive downtown in the Ford, the Chevy will have to sit, unused, in the driveway. Its motor may be idling noisily, but if we do not get in and engage the gears, it is just running itself, it is not running us. Since we can only think one thought at a time, just like we can only drive one car at a time, if we purposefully concentrate on some action or thought and thereby employ the higher mind, our primal-mind depression will have to wait, fully operating but unused, off on a side track in our mind. Our mind cannot "think us" if we do not choose to let it. It is somewhat like the old peace movement statement: "What if they gave a war and nobody came." But in this case we would say, "What if the mind gave a depression and we didn't go."

Long bouts of depression and mania do not occur because of a chemical "hit." Some of us may have wider mood swings than others, but we can all learn how to manage our own specific deviations from the norm, be it height, weight, or mood. We can negotiate a chemical hit quite effectively once we learn a few techniques. Wildly fluctuating brain chemistry is already part and parcel of the normal fight-or-flight response with which we are all familiar. There is research that corroborates this. Thus in the last decade a small cadre of scientists has been fighting to "bring a Darwinian perspective to medicine." These studies suggest, as my own work has shown, that depression is not an aberration; it is an evolutionary adaptation.[4]

For instance, the studies of psychologist Eric Klinger, of the University of Minnesota, "indicate that depression plays a crucial role in the process of disengaging from a goal," which may be folly to pursue. An example of this would be the extreme lethargy of a deep depression, in which people are much less likely to commit suicide than a less severe depression that is accompanied by a great deal of agitation.[5]

Dr. Randolph Nesse, at the University of Michigan, thinks that "depression may have developed as a useful response to situations in which a desired goal is unattainable" and thus it enables us to search for a more realistic goal. Nesse states that it might not always make sense to block depression's defensive properties with medication.[6]

I am convinced that the key factor in handling depression is the understanding that full-blown depression or mania occurs because of our failure to access the upper-brain functions of rationality and creativity in a timely fashion to manage a chemical hit, and therefore, by default, we fall into the unwitting use of the lower-brain states at the worst time, when the defense mechanisms of fear, anxiety, paranoia, and depression are in full force.

Of course nobody minds falling into the primal mind when there is ecstasy and excitement going on. But when there isn't a high there, and the lows get uncomfortable, we can simply make a quick exit by refocusing our attention on something else other than it. We can function from either the upper-brain higher mind or the lower-brain primal mind; that is what it means to be a sentient being. We are not *forced* to function by instinct and feelings; *we can choose to function by reason*. But we have to learn to make a conscious effort to do so. As Cicero the great Roman orator, tells us, "He only employs his passions who can make no use of his reason."

I took a different route from the doctors, not on purpose certainly, but as the scientist Louis Pasteur said, "Chance favors the prepared mind." By the hour, I spent years shut up alone in my room, accompanied only by my own silence. It helped me to understand what the mystics tell us about silence and truth: Truth is so small that silence is absolutely necessary. And truth demands a high price. We not only have to be willing to not sacrifice the truth for anything else, we also have to be willing to sacrifice everything else for the truth. What truth did I find? That the "I am" that might begin a sentence is far stronger than anything that could possibly be added to complete the sentence, including the sentence, "I am depressed."

The psychological community, with regard to manic depression, has been willing to sacrifice the truth about manic depression for a palliative. This may be due to the overwhelming presence of drug companies in the research lab. The clue to manic depression is not what happens, but what doesn't happen. It is the same ignominious clue that remains after the mathematicians sift through all the hurry and scurry of million-dollar quantum-physics experiments with quarks and other siftings of the very small, and find only one sure thing about the nature of reality: "Things that don't happen critically influence things that do."[7]

What is *not* happening in the realm of depression and manic depression is that we are not accessing our upper-brain functions as an act of will, which critically influences the dependence by default upon our lower-brain functions, the seat of our emotions. What we don't do is the *cause* of our autonomic over-identification and enmeshment with our feelings that we call depression and manic depression.

The fear caused by the fight-or-flight response is supposed to impel us to proper action. When it doesn't, we suffer from mania and depression. In mania, we are not suffering so much from bad behavior as we are suffering from lack of good behavior. In depression, we are not suffering so much from emptiness as we are suffering from lack of fullness. Seeing that the practical difference between these conditions is one of intention, not semantics—one of practice, not belief—is an experiential insight that can literally change your life. But it will never win you a Nobel Prize for science.

Depression is our overly passive response to a normal and necessary defense mechanism that, like the rest of our body, is a product of evolution. Depression is the chemically based result of the triggering of the anxiety and fear of the fight-or-flight response, which ends up convoluting upon itself in perpetual recurrence instead of leading to some forward action.

Depression doesn't lead to forward action because we have been educated by psychology to improperly translate its message. Before the upper brain evolved, there was no way to translate the message of our lower brain. There was also no need because there was no other option but the simple defense mechanism with a single message: STOP. Period. We did not have any option to translate the message. Now that we have the higher mind also, we have more options. We can access the newer developed part of our brain to help us deal with our more complex situation. But the more complex brain must be properly trained so that the message of the lower mind can be appropriately translated in terms of both the primal mind *and* the higher mind.

Feelings have no language except the language we give to them, according to the education of our higher mind by our tribe or our culture. The properly translated message of the feelings of depression is "Assert Yourself, take immediate action, do something, take a walk, do ten jumping jacks, sing 'Row, Row Row Your Boat,' use the upper brain." Instead, in the last few decades, we have taken to improperly translating it, "Give up, hurt, all is lost, do nothing, feel bad, life is miserable, confine yourself to the lower brain." So we get into the fetal position and drug ourselves. If we would insist upon forward action, the proper chemical homeostasis would be restored naturally.

Drugs can't do the work that needs to be done. For one thing, drug therapy could never be a *cure* for depression because, psychologically speaking, it provides only a first-level content change as opposed to a method such as Directed Thinking, which provides a second-level process change.[8] Depression and manic depression are not diseases to be cured by drugs. They are situations to be transcended by a process change in the way we direct our thinking.

There is one more tricky thing about truth that ancient seers have suggested to us. We cannot apprehend truth as an object. We can't *know* truth as an object, we can only *be* truth. That's the tricky thing about manic depression. We can't *know* the truth about manic depression, we have to *be the truth* about manic depression because the truth about depression is not a matter of opinion and knowledge, it is a matter of habit and practice.

We have to call upon our higher-mind functions in an adverse situation, when we are experiencing depression or mania. We have to make a conscious choice of positive behavior "on principle," whether we feel like it or not, whether we believe we are capable of it or not, and whether or not we think it will do any good. Our decision to do so eternally awaits us. It is not going anywhere. It will remain at our right hand forever.

Twelve

DEPRESSION JUNKIES

If we observe carefully, we can see that the instinctual mind is never brave. The instinctual primal mind is a wimp because it opts for status quo, for safety, rather than for principle.

I don't trust complicated situations. If you look through the skin of any of them, they all turn out to be devices to hide the truth. Or, at the very least, they tire one out so thoroughly that one ceases to care about the truth anymore. This is why problems are so big and easy to believe, and truth is so small and hard to see. This is the second major conclusion I came to after several years as a psychotherapist.

The first major conclusion was that the problems people brought into my office were, qualitatively speaking, not very different from one person to the other. More, or less, of the same. A small triumph gets us high; a failure or loss depresses us. This is normal. It is in the escalated overcomplexity of our highs and lows that the pathology lies.

Recently my friend Jack called to tell me that his wedding had to be postponed.

"What happened?" I asked. "Well," he said, "it's really too

complicated to explain right now without betraying some confidences but you'll understand later. I think maybe she really wants to get married up North with you know all her family up there because the first marriage didn't include anybody just a justice of the peace so she missed a lot and then she was abandoned with a three-day old baby practically on the hospital steps like that with no warning and she had the full responsibility of bringing up her son and it broke her mother's heart because she wanted the whole nine yards you know the white lace veil and all that stuff that you women are into instead of the small ceremony we planned down here . . ."

Jack continued in this manner for a full five minutes, deftly deflecting all my questions. I hung in there and tried my best to figure out what my friend was trying to tell me, until he wore me out, and I retreated to "Mmm, I see," "Oh, my," and "Uh-huh." Jack has had two novels on the *New York Times* best-seller list, so I am not quick to fault either his verbal skills or his intelligence.

No, there was something else afoot here, the old syndrome of a big amorphous, all-enveloping, arm-waving problem protecting its small, quiet, hard truth. This became evident a few weeks later when my husband and I met Jack and his fiancée for dinner. I murmured something about being sorry to hear about the postponement, and she replied simply, "Oh yes, I decided I just wasn't ready, but I'm ready now, and we've set the date for the twenty-first of May." In concentrating on a myriad of confusing and complicating details, Jack could avoid the realization that his bride had a temporary case of cold feet.

When we are in a place we don't like and we want to explain how we got there, our logic is likely to be complicated. Ask anyone who is having relationship problems to tell us what the trouble is and get ready to find a comfortable chair.

It is an automatic self-defense strategy of the primal mind to maintain the status quo, no matter how terrible it is and no matter how much we hate it. Thus the primal mind has us thinking in circles instead of focusing exactly on the simple problem itself. *We don't want to know the simple problem* because the primal mind doesn't want us to solve the simple problem and change the status quo, which the primal mind trusts because we have so far "survived" in it.

We complicate our problems by thinking in circles. The more complicated our lives are, the less power we appear to have over them, and the more reasonable it therefore seems to us that we have done nothing yet to solve our "big problem." Complication is a great excuse to delay action and wait around for something else to happen or someone else to change. If it were just a *little* problem, like we were afraid, or dependent, or angry, or embarrassed, or selfish, or unloving, or lazy, it would be clear to us that we need to get to work and improve ourselves.

Neurologically speaking, complication is accomplished by lines of thought moving randomly and autonomically from lower-brain fear strategies to upper-brain reasoning faculties by the process of learned associations. Different thoughts access different parts of the brain and thoughts recreate themselves and cause other thoughts to spark, like attracting like, neuron by neuron, with wider and wider participation by chance connections.

We always have the choice to direct our thinking by narrowing our focus toward some particular goal, or else we can let our thinking think itself and simply ricochet back and forth from one part of the mind to another—from the primal mind to the higher mind as a natural result of random chains of thoughts.

We can use the excellent logic and reasoning faculties of the higher mind on purpose, when we deliberately activate (think) a rational principle. Or we can let the excellent logic and reasoning faculties of the higher mind set into motion an irrational premise that chooses itself accidentally through learned associations stimulated by excitement, paranoia, depression, or other feelings and strategies of the primal mind.

Trusting our mind can be very dangerous because the primal mind is always afraid for us to risk our "security" by reaching for something else. Doing it the way we have always done it is just fine with the primal mind. This is the real factualness of our defensiveness: our primal mind is protecting us so we don't make a change in how we "have always done it."

This is how we become addicted to problems. This is how even the most life-threatening addictions, such as alcoholism, drug abuse, depression, and promiscuity, very soon become the status quo that it is the duty of the primal mind to protect. This is the neurological explanation of St. Augustine's warning, "A habit, if not resisted, soon becomes necessity." This is how we begin to conspire against ourselves, which is the situation described by that odd little proverb, "The left hand knows not what the right hand is doing."

Vice is a monster of such frightful mein
As to be hated needs but to be seen.
But seen too oft, familiar with her faces,
One first endures, then pities, then embraces.
                              —Alexander Pope

We allow ourselves to drift, first in little ways, and then into a total abandonment of our self to the primal mind. Our vast and unredeemable loneliness means only that we have forgotten our own self. We have forgotten "I am" and think only "hurt." In my own case, depression would come and drag me under, and then it would lift. It would come and drag me under, and then it would lift. I became accustomed to the periodic torture and went along with it. Could we say, therefore, that I became addicted to depression? I think so. But not as a disease; as a vice.

My old relationship with my depression certainly fulfilled

the description of addiction as described by English theologian and author William Paley: "If we would know who is the most degraded and wretched of human beings, look for a man who has practiced a vice so long that he curses it and yet clings to it; that he pursues it because he feels a great law of his nature driving him on toward it; but reaching it, knows that it will gnaw his heart, and make him roll himself in the dust with anguish."

I didn't want the depression, I wanted the good feelings! I was like the alcoholic who wants the good feelings alcohol can bring and hates the terrible things alcohol does to him. I wanted to feel good but, once I began focusing on the primal mind for the good feelings, I couldn't withdraw my focus from the primal mind when it began to anguish with depression.

If feeling good is the most important thing in our lives, we will be terrorized by the fear of feeling bad. If feeling good is not the most important thing in our lives, we can do what is important no matter how bad we feel. In making the switch from having to feel good to doing something productive, we start to feel less bad. This is because we focus our attention away from the painful strategies of the primal mind[1] (which are only useful when limited to their proper place)[2] and call upon the faculties of the higher mind,[3] which are never painful.

A woman who sought counseling was talking to me about her daughter who had been a brilliant and popular college student, interested in philosophy and literature; she was a talented pianist. She had joined the family real estate company and in just a few years was able to acquire quite a bit of property for herself out of her earnings. Luckily so, said the mother, for the income from these properties had been her daughter's sole support for the last twenty years, during which time her daughter had become almost a recluse and, without the income from property, would "probably be a homeless bag lady."

Although her daughter attended weddings and other family gatherings, she seemed to do so reluctantly and was so gaunt-looking, so sad and withdrawn, that it broke her mother's heart to remember the wonderful, outgoing, caring person she had once been. "What causes someone to change like that?" she asked me. "We've tried to help, but she just slips away from us every time. We don't have a real relationship with our daughter anymore."

I suggested that sometimes depression can do that. Without an understanding of how our mind works, a serious onset of depression can escalate into a lifelong habit, an addiction, a way of life that is self-perpetuating despair, ricocheting from primal mind to higher mind and back again. People who are in despair are not going to be close to anybody. They will be noncommunicative, noncommittal, and will not seem very caring because they are frozen in pain.

This is the trick of depression. We think we are frozen in ourselves, so we feel helpless to get free. How could we get free from ourselves? But our pain is only the workings of primal-mind strategy. And we *can* free ourselves from that. Somebody has to clue us in that we have a choice, that we can direct our thinking, that the mind and its feelings do not have legitimate authority over us.

The reason our addictions and compulsions seem to get stronger is that, as we succumb to them, our behavior forms those particular neural patterns we call habits. The first time we do something else, other than succumb to our impulses, seems harder because we are forging a new neural pattern. But as we choose the new pattern over and over, that too becomes a habit. The old neural patterns don't disappear, but the more recently and frequently used patterns, following the law of inertia, take precedence when we are proactive and get the laws of inertia and synaptic plasticity to work for us instead of against us. When we remain reactive and these laws work against us, instead of forging positive habits we saddle ourselves with negative addictions.

Addiction to anything, whether depression, alcohol, gambling, or sex, sets in because we turn down our wick of awareness on certain behaviors—so that we can more easily continue them and maintain what has accidentally become the primal mind's status quo. Or, as psychologist Nathaniel Branden puts it, "self-destruction is an act best performed in the dark."[4] The primal mind wants us to chain ourselves with voluntary ignorance to "keep us safe." *The primal mind is secure in our addictions!* This is how, if we go along the easy, habitual lower road of primal-mind feelings, we can expect to become our own monstrous worst enemy.

If we observe carefully, we can see that the instinctual mind is never brave. The instinctual primal mind is a wimp because it opts for status quo—for safety—rather than for principle. But that is its job. It wants to know the outcome of any action before allowing us to proceed.

This is the reason we fear the possibly better *unknown* so much more than the impossibly bad *known*. The primal mind has us autonomically erecting smoke screens that "save us" from "risking ourselves" in "hasty action" that might threaten our status quo, regardless of how bizarre or miserable that status quo might be.

We can see, therefore, how there are natural obstacles within our own mind that prevent clarity. Without clarity about where we are, it is hard to figure out what we should do next. We might say we want to "work on our marriage," or want "more space." Working on a marriage or having more space is not doable; these ideas are smoke screens to foment confusion so we don't make any real changes. Ideas are not doable, only specific actions are doable: going out to dinner once a week, sex twice a month instead of once, just-the-two-of-us evenings once a week, three compliments a day.

And what do we mean by space? Do we mean don't read over my shoulder; or don't expect any sex? Do we mean one hour by myself a week; or five days by myself a week? Separate beds? Separate bedrooms? Separate houses? If we don't know what we mean by space, how will our partner know how to give it to us, or even more to the point, how will we ourselves recognize that we have got it? The poet Jan Struther put it this way. "It took me forty years on earth to reach this sure conclusion. There is no Heaven but clarity, no Hell except confusion."

But clarity about our problem and "doing something about it" are terrifying to the primal mind, and so it has us going around in circles instead. This is how we get just as upset over a little problem as a big one, without establishing any hierarchy of importance to organize our necessary tasks. That is how, as forty-year-olds, we might investigate our childhood instead of our laziness for the reasons we are late to work every morning.

That is how we do not instinctively question ourselves closely as to what our real values are, in case we might put our higher-mind values first, over and above our primal-mind feelings, and change our status quo. *Oh, the primal mind hates heroes.* The primal mind loves it when we hang back, do nothing, lead chaotic lives, and complain a lot, because the original primal mind is by nature paranoid and cannot trust our johnny-come-lately upper-brain improvements to "save us." That trust is a function of the self, not the mind. It is the foundation of our freedom of will, and the reason we must direct our mind.

One of the problems is that we see only in general, philosophically, that life is fleeting and tentative. We do not see specifically, in any here-and-now experience, that life is fleeting and tentative and that we ourselves are not fleeting and tentative. We, in the form of "I am" are the most constant, changeless, solid presence in any experience. And yet, most often, the experience, in the form of painful feelings or complicated situations seems "bigger and more" than us.

The painful feelings of the fight-or-flight response that lead us into depression may be triggered two ways. Something may be wrong with the way we are living our lives and this trig-

gering alerts us that we have work to do. Or the syndrome may
be triggered by accidental neuronal connections based upon
learned associations, and it is a trick of the primal mind that
we *think* there is something wrong when we are perfectly all
right.

If a tiger is charging us or if we are about to go bankrupt,
yes, the primal mind is a great protector. Our fear causes us to
jump into immediate action to save ourselves. If we have real
problems we need to solve, the primal mind will keep agitating
us until we solve them. But the primal mind is not our best
help in the case of false-alarm depression because, to help us,
the primal mind would have to deny itself, which is not in its
capacity.

But it is well within our capacity to deny the primal mind's
faulty conclusion that pitches us into the intolerable pain of "all
is lost" when our objective reality is that we are fine. First, we
have to see clearly what are the trick strategies (defense mechanisms) of the primal mind that get us into the pickle in the
first place. Then, we can choose higher-mind tricks to manage
the thought traffic jam that has gridlocked into depression.

It is not easy because depression is like a hole suddenly
opening up in the side yard, a few steps away from the swing
set, and dropping us straight into Hell. We can hardly breathe
for the pain. We feel lifeless, empty of all vigor—like a kind
of collapsed balloon of the soul. Isn't it strange though, being
so weak and helpless, how strongly we insist we can't do anything, and how painful it is that nothing matters? If nothing
matters, then what is the difference if we get up and go to
work, or stay in bed? If nothing matters, why would we insist
one action is doable and the other isn't? If nothing really matters, why do we feel strongly about anything, and what is there
to be so upset about? And how come there seems to be so much
of this nothing-that-doesn't-matter that it overwhelms us? And
how can the nothing-that-doesn't-matter be so powerful it feels
like it's killing us?

When we are in the throes of it, the power of depression seems so much greater than our own power. But how can this be? How can we be done in by our own depression? What is this dark beast" that we know has to be us, and yet at the same time is trying to devour us? And if it's just a part of us, why can't we just turn the damn thing off?

A wise man once told me, "Enlightenment is just a deep understanding that there is no problem." We think we are not all right because it is the job of the primal mind to be worried and we, who cannot differentiate ourselves as separate from our agitated primal mind, therefore believe it is *we* who are worried.

The feeling that we are empty and lifeless and the feeling that nothing matters are temporary feelings occurring to our primal mind. These feelings are not a true representation of our reality. They are the autonomic fears of the primal mind when its chemistry is skewed by casual thinking and negative thoughts. The primal mind does not know any better. And we cannot teach it any better. But we can teach ourselves that we are not our primal mind.

The reason we feel so strongly is that we are more closely bonded with the primal mind than with our dearest loved one, even our own child. At her wedding rehearsal, my husband spoke of our daughter as "a piece of my heart walking around." We hurt when our children hurt, we are happy when they are happy, but we can see that they are not us. We can differentiate our body from theirs.

We hurt when our primal mind hurts, we are happy when our primal mind is happy, but we cannot see that our primal mind is not us. Depression is a chemical paradigm shift in our energy power source, our primal mind. It is something that happens to us. We are not supposed to be something that happens to it. But if we are not forearmed, that is exactly what occurs. Before we know it, we can become it.

There is a pathological defense mechanism at work here in

addition to the biochemical defense mechanism of depression itself, which gives us a double whammy. The defense mechanism gone awry is called *identification with the aggressor*. It was first recognized and named by Sandor Ferenczi, a close colleague of Sigmund Freud.[5]

Remember, all defense mechanisms are instinctual, autonomic in the sense that we do not have to employ them as an act of will, nor are we naturally aware of them. Our awareness has to be directed to them by an act of will, otherwise they go merrily on their way doing their own thing until overridden by another, usually autonomic, command. Actually, it is a triple whammy that works to strengthen depression. First the chemical hit itself, which is probably the result of fearful thinking, then the fact that we unwittingly, through self-talk, keep imagining to ourselves that we "feel terrible," which tends to set the feeling like cement, and, finally, the identification factor.

Identification with the aggressor works this way: The strongest instinct we have is the instinct for self-preservation. Of course we are able, through freedom of the will, to override this basic instinct with learned values of patriotism and self-sacrifice in acts of heroism. We are also able to override it with the learned values of committing suicide. Given the exceptions of the learned values of altruism, patriotism, and suicide, when we are overwhelmed by some attack against us, our feeling of complete helplessness triggers our instinct for self-preservation and initiates thoughts that we need and must protect any other possible source of power that might "save us" even if the only available source of power is the offending aggressor. This is another example of how separated the mind is from present reality.

This autonomic defense mechanism acquired the nickname "the Patty Hearst Syndrome," after the young heiress who was kidnapped in 1974 by a group of terrorists and then later joined them and helped them rob a bank. This is also partly the reason that women who are raped keep it a secret for years, rather than tell. Guilt is another reason. In any interaction within a particular culture to which shame ordinarily would be attached, says Ferenczi, there is a finite amount of guilt to be assumed. Whatever guilt the perpetrator does not assume will be autonomically assumed by the victim. Since we must hide our guilt to protect our status, we are further separated from our legitimate fellows.

Ferenczi formulated his identification theory after two decades of studying child-abuse victims who protected their predators instead of telling on them. But I think it is not out of line to apply Ferenczi's theory to the feeling of complete helplessness that we experience during a depressive episode, where we seem to be taken over by a force stronger than our own, even though that force is inside our own body. So from the first, depression seems to have power over us. And we can immediately proceed to make this worse.

When we become our own depression by identifying with it, by merging with it, and then trying to escape from it, we end up fighting ourselves. There is really no aggressor; there is only our fighting. We exhaust ourselves, and then, tired and defeated, we attribute overwhelming power to that which has defeated us. Our depression seems mighty and prevailing. But what has defeated us is not our depression; our own fighting has defeated us.

Thus it is that people who are more intelligent usually have the worst time of it since their whole intelligence is in league against them. But when people tell us to pull ourselves up by our own bootstraps it is really no more of an order of difficulty than what we are already doing to ourselves in reverse—pulling ourselves *down* by our own bootstraps.

Overidentification is the reason, I am convinced, that so many people have not learned to "take care of business" with respect to depression as they are able to do with other systemic pain, like a broken arm or leg. We do not let our arms and legs boss us around the way we do our mind. I mean, one wouldn't take to one's bed with a fractured bone and sigh disconsolately, "I'm so terribly broken."

We seldom ask penetrating questions about or otherwise investigate our depression because it is not easy to be objective about it while we are undergoing it. Mostly it seems like unbearable, unalterable pain. When it's over, we feel lucky to have escaped with our lives; we don't want to call it back for a chat.

But if we really study depression, our own depression, as I have trained myself to do, we find that although it looms wide and high, like an inescapable solitary confinement of hopeless doom, it is also as easily shifted away from as a movie. As powerful a phenomenon as it is, we can learn very quickly that depression is totally dependent upon our rapt attention to it. If we are depressed, there is one sure thing we know about ourselves; no one is sawing off one of our arms.

So if depression is dependent upon our rapt attention to it, how is it that we can become its prisoner against our will? We can't, if we know how to assert our will. In depression or mania, the fight for precedence is between us and our primal mind, however, not between us and our higher mind. We are not so identified with our higher mind. We do not have as much trouble distinguishing ourselves from our principles as we have distinguishing ourselves from our feelings.

Unlike the primal mind, we can more easily separate ourselves out from our higher mind, and our higher mind takes direction quite well. It is a hard-working, intelligent Marian the Librarian. It is the primal-mind guardian, rash Sir Lancelot, whose strategies must be rigorously contended with. Merlin, whom we all secretly hope lives in the penthouse of our cranial tower, is never there. He simply visits us when we invite him by our silence.

But we can only achieve silence if we wait quietly in the

library with Marian. If Sir Lancelot gets too noisy, we can get the librarian to show him the door simply by refusing to grant him an audience. He can then conduct his necessary but distracting antics, like the defense mechanisms of fear and depression, down in the basement, out of earshot, where he belongs and where it is easier to tune him out.

It is a continuing intrigue. Primal Sir Lancelot, the first mind system to evolve, mistakenly believes that as original "Godfather," he should be in charge of us. He is absolutely dedicated, and is not going to give way without cunning on our part to limit the overextension of his dangerous strategies, which we can do only by taking action to access the higher mind.

If, instead of moving to action, we pay attention to depression we will be doing the converse of successful positive affirmation. Depression is *successful negative affirmation*. It has been common knowledge for years to anyone familiar with hypnosis that the mind cannot judge whether any particular memory is from an imagined or a real event. Recently, Henry L. Roediger III of Washington University in St. Louis proved that, given a few bogus details and a little prodding, 25 percent of adults could be convinced they remembered childhood adventures that never happened.[6]

All of us are susceptible to memory contamination. That's the reason all those motivation seminars work, the ones that have us mentally visualizing our perfect golf swing or our successful speech. The mind, in retrospect, experiences these imaginings as real practice. Unfortunately, that is also how our own random imaginings and fears work *against* us. We actually "practice" and exercise our depression for years and then wonder why it is such a powerful, strong, habitual force inside our minds.

The reason that the mind cannot tell the difference between a real and an imagined event is that we do not retain memories in any kind of a facsimile storage-and-retrieval software system. Our memory is tentatively held in the always slightly different patterns of the firing of neurons that, once jump-started, are re-created and serially echoed throughout the brain, somewhat like a living tissue hologram of electrical arcing, "like" continually attracting and sparking "like" by learned association. Experience shapes the changing design of these memory circuits. The circuits are not only receptive to first experiences, but are modifiable by continued experiences throughout our entire lifetime.

What this all means, as far as our habitual addiction to depression goes, is that we are eminently capable of establishing new responses and new neural patterns for ourselves and bypassing depression by insisting upon making willed, rather than autonomic, connections between our behavior and our physical and emotional environment. We don't have to "peel ourselves" to uncover childhood neural response patterns that disturb us; we can simply forge new ones, which nourish us, and the old patterns will fade with disuse.

Jeffrey M. Schwartz has described how his obsessive-compulsive patients changed their own brain patterns by altering their behavior and thinking.[7] My experience echoes Schwartz's research. By exercising such thought choice, I learned to indirectly control my feelings by choosing my thoughts. That progress gave me the space *to start questioning my thinking as well as my feelings.* Why should we question our thoughts? Certainly *other people* will question our thinking. Doesn't it put us at a terrible disadvantage if we are the only ones in the world who do *not* question our thinking? Wouldn't this be a good example of "being unconscious"?

Contrary to Freud's theories, our thinking is not determined by unconscious values or habits. Harmful addictions, habits, and values, like thoughts, are never unconscious in the sense that they are unconscious of themselves, or that they make up some unconscious part of the mind. They are unconscious in the respect that we are not naturally aware of their workings. But we can train ourselves to become aware of them. Not so that we can change them. So that we can create new ones to replace them.

The connection between our emotions and our behavior is widely misunderstood even among psychologists, most of whom still believe in things like the disorders of obsessive compulsion and post-traumatic stress.

Already we don't act upon 99 percent of the things that we think, so it seems ridiculous to believe that there is any particular thought that can't be ignored if we earnestly desire to ignore it by thinking about something else instead of it. There is ultimately no specific behavior that can hold us prisoner. But doctors and counselors, who have bought the idea themselves, are telling us that we can't help ourselves.

Instead, doctors could be role-modeling for us how to question ourselves as to the rightness or wrongness of what we are doing by their personal judgment upon our lazy, unlawful, unethical, or ignorant behavior. If they wanted to be really helpful they could hand us a list of old proverbs and check off the ones they think we should commit to memory.

Doctors can be judgmental about our physical condition. They can say to us that our cholesterol is out of control, and our broken leg "is the worst mess they've ever seen," and we don't feel all hurt and defensive. Why can't we just as dispassionately hear from them that we seem to have a weak conscience, underdeveloped courage, and we are suffering from the symptoms caused by being selfish and self-absorbed?

I think we could hear that if someone was willing to say it. The trouble with the psychological community and manic depression is that these dedicated scientists are so bogged down in quantifying symptoms and conducting chemical experiments with predictions borne out to the most infinitesimal decimal place that they are overwhelmed with medical probabilities. A thousand medical probabilities cannot make one psychological truth. And there is no psychological truth that is stronger than its opposing moral principle earnestly employed.

The theory and treatment of manic depression is based on a list of symptoms and the alleviation of those symptoms. But they are missing the cause. *However many symptoms you kill, you will never kill the cause.* For today's orthodox psychiatrists to see the simple thing I see, they would have to abandon their whole existing body of "knowledge" about manic depression as methodized ignorance. They would have to view it in the same way doctors had to view their existing "knowledge" about malaria (that it was an infectious disease) *after* the mosquito was found to be the culprit. This is not likely.

What the doctors are observing is not depression itself, but depression exposed to their particularizing questions. Instead of the nature of depression determining the measurements they are taking, the measurements they are taking are determining the nature of depression. In a way this is not so different from physics. The difference is that the physicist takes this into consideration. The psychiatrists cannot because they cannot prescribe a medicine to cure a theory. They can only prescribe a medicine to cure an illness. What this means is that the doctors are treating a structure without knowing what it is the structure of. People innocently believe that mental disorders are diagnosed using the same scientific criteria as general medicine. Unfortunately this is not true. General medicine began to abandon appearance-based classifications a hundred years ago as being unreliable—symptoms must be validated by specific physiological pathologies. Mental disorders, however, are diagnosed today by the appearance of symptoms alone, even self-reported symptoms. Committees of psychologists and psychiatrists draw up lists of symptoms and give the lists "illness names." Then they vote these various illnesses "in" or "out" of their *Diagnostic and Statistical Manual of Mental Disorders* according to the prevailing prejudices of the day. People foolishly believe that the diagnosis and treatment of depression is based upon the neurobiological and psychological data of the patient. This is not true. The diagnosis and treatment of depression is typically based on the presence or absence of self-reported symptoms alone.[8]

So thousands of people take their depression into hospitals to be "cured." First they are given a brochure that states flatly: "No one knows exactly what happens in the brain to cause depression, but brain chemicals called neurotransmitters are probably involved." And then they are given chemicals that alter the balance of these neurotransmitters.

Truth escapes us when we look to find only what our own study is already set up to see. The study of manic depression is based on a causal relationship between brain chemistry and depression. There is other research that shows a causal relationship between *behavior* and brain chemistry. Why is this being swept aside as incidental? Because, to a scientist with an agenda, nothing is as so inconvenient as the truth. That's why we are now questioning repressed-memory syndrome and multiple-personality disorders. Even a doctor can be self-deluded when the alternative is unacceptable knowledge, either because it ruins the experiment, goes against "scientific evidence," or is politically incorrect. There is nothing more politically correct today than the idea that we are the victims of our behavior, that our behavior is not our choice.

I did not choose depression. Depression occurred because of my lack of choosing to go the way of being cheerful. None of this is easy. For instance, sometimes I think that I am never so phony as when I try to be authentic. Maybe there is no authentic person either. Maybe the best we can do is to *attempt to do what we would like to be*. With this in mind, I do cheerfulness. I don't know the secret of life but, to me, doing cheerfulness beats the heck out of doing depression.

I started in small ways to change once I had the intellectual understanding of what needed to be done. We do need to choose something small to begin with. Even full-blown manic depression started with small, *unwilled, rote* reactions to difficult situations (like not getting out of bed when we "didn't feel like it") that built habit patterns over time. Small, *willed, intentional* reactions to difficult incidents (like insisting we will get out of bed at the count of three) can extinguish negative habits over time by replacing them with new ones.

There is a reason that we won't be able to clean our whole house, but maybe we could make our bed or clear off the table. The reason is that we probably won't feel like doing it, so if we choose something small to do, we won't have such a big feeling about it that we will have to overcome. We can more easily step out over a small feeling than a big one. Any time we want, we can call ourselves a beginner and begin.

Thirteen

THE LAW OF OUGHT

We should never just wait around until something happens to get us out of our depression. We should just choose something to do, interesting or not, whether we feel like it or not, and invest some time and effort in it, and our interest in it will automatically accumulate on its own as the neural activity in our upper brain starts to light up.

Historian William H. McNeill reminds us: "What makes us different from other forms of life is our capacity to invent a world of shared feelings and symbolic meanings and then act upon them in concert."[1]

We cannot separate ourselves out of our emotional connection with our fellows very long and remain well-balanced because we need each other as part and parcel of our combined ongoing social evolution. The world we can best trust is the world we make together with others, not alone. This is how depression, wherein we tend to closet ourselves, gives us such a devastating feeling of loneliness, and the reason we must not take the line of least resistance and adapt ourselves to our own depression or mania. We must adapt, instead, to the regular, ongoing, evolving, give-and-take society of our fellows. Adapting to the world outside our own brain always involves some fear and discomfort, and therefore we will need courage and persistence to move forward. But go forward we can. And go forward we must.

McNeill points out clearly the importance of maintaining such fellowship: "The process of symbolic evolution does not appear to be fundamentally very different from biological evolution any more than biological evolution was fundamentally very different from the physical and chemical evolution of the cosmos that preceded and sustained it."[2] This was Adam Smith's idea as well, who claimed that morality was not a purely internal calculation, that we arrived at moral rules from our ability to imagine ourselves in others' shoes. Smith maintained that morality arose from its manifest utility of reflecting shared experiences over time; of developing a shared moral understanding.[3]

One need only read the *DSM IV*, psychiatry's mental illness bible, to get an idea of the crazy kinds of symbolic worlds we tend to create by ourselves. This is the reason that group therapy, wherein we think about others, is so much more powerful and steadying than individual therapy, where we just think about ourselves. Thinking about ourselves, when depression hits, is something we have to train ourselves not to do. The way we don't think about ourselves is to think about someone or something else.

Even primal-mind happiness has us thinking about ourselves; that is why it is so short-lived. "In vain do they talk of happiness who never subdued an impulse in obedience to a principle," says educator Horace Mann. "He who never sacrificed a present to a future good, or a personal to a general one, can speak of happiness only as the blind do of colors."

Our descent from happiness to depression is an arrogance, no matter that we are crawling on our knees in anguish, begging for help. The arrogance is that we got into this condition because we put ourselves above the mundane, petty little everyday duties that we would impose, for instance, upon our child or a "lazy" neighbor. We would like to say to them, "Stop thinking life is miserable, why don't you just get up and clean up your mess, or do something nice for somebody, whistle a tune, or do your work instead of sitting there whining and complaining? Just get going. Snap out of it!"

And don't we hate it when someone says this to us when we are in our death throes? Why should we impose upon ourselves the little annoying daily acts of self-denial and self-discipline that *ordinary* people have to do in order to keep themselves out of trouble? *We* can do our work all at once, when we feel good, with no effort at all. Why should we take a shower and dress and try to be pleasant when we feel so bad? How can *that* help? Our depression is BIG, BIG, BIG; all that little stuff isn't going to do us any good. Isn't it interesting that we don't consider that our taking a shower, getting dressed, and being pleasant might do *somebody else* some good?

When we're depressed, we can't see any moral purpose in life more important than our own selves and our own misery. This is why Directed Thinking is so valuable. It can move us from preoccupation with the painful worrying going on in the lower brain to the immediate relief that comes from being situated instead, neural-activity-wise, in the upper brain, which never worries because it does not have the capacity to worry.

In years past, sufferers of depression were coldly advised to go to the local hospital and volunteer to help people who had "real" problems. This was not such a bad idea.[4] Part of the "cure" was that one's depression would seem less serious than the terrible physical ailments and injuries that other people were suffering. And certainly a person suffering deeply from depression might find common ground with *any* fellow sufferer. University of Pittsburgh professor of psychiatry Ellen Frank, under a grant from the National Institute of Mental Health, is currently studying the efficacy of Interpersonal and Social Rhythm Therapy; a treatment she developed for manic depressive illness that focuses on helping patients to increase the regularity of their daily routines and improve their day-to-day relations with others.[5]

Finding common ground helps to decrease the painful emphasis on self. There are other societies where people don't suffer depression as we do, and these are generally societies that "place a greater emphasis on community than on self."[6] Many psychologists report that people who are in good relationships also tend to be less depressed for the same reason—less emphasis on self.[7]

It sounds preachy, I know: Don't think about yourself, yadda yadda. But however much it sounds preachy, to that extent the full terror of finding ourselves in a parallel universe of fearful aloneness due to depression is being obscured by our blaming somebody for annoying us by telling us we're not perfect when we already know that. Here's something we may not know. Where depression is concerned, thinking about ourselves doesn't make us bad people. Thinking about ourselves makes us lose our grip on solid reality. We become less able to differentiate between those possibilities that can become material fact (such as I will go jog now) and those that will remain immaterial fantasy (such as life is worthless).

Emphasis on self, which bubbles up from primal-mind initiative, makes us fear-based. That used to be a good description of me—fear-based. I was seldom a calm, nurturing, or loving person to be around. I had an ungrounded, tentative energy that was tight and insinuating. I was going ninety miles an hour even when I was sitting still. I would do breathing exercises while I "listened" to my seven-year-old read his favorite book to me. I read the paper and ate my breakfast while I nursed the baby. I was an impatient audience to anyone else's story, listening intently only for some pause where I could intrude my own.

A professor in a creative writing course criticized my work

as "suffering from an excess of slickness." My generosity had a pointed edge to it. My friendships sat uneasy upon my shoulders because although I became clever at hiding my neediness, the truth was that when I was alone, *I thought nobody was home*. I was terrified of being alone. Alone, I could too easily fall into the darkness of myself. Alone, it was hard to keep my act going so that depression couldn't take over.

At first the only thing that I knew to do about depression was ongoing busyness *to prevent it*. But I learned that creativity alone cannot cure depression. Anxious creativity is hollow-hearted, like any other activity is hollow-hearted that proceeds from a fearful, driven soul. Even with a lot of activity, one is still afraid; it's just that we keep ourselves too busy to notice it. There are some of us who must keep busy with new businesses, new houses, or new affairs because we fear the emptiness of "nothing going on" or "being alone." What would we do? We might start to feel bad!

I think this is the real connection between depression and creativity, a serendipitous rather than a genetic one. To escape the terrible pain, one moves. The greater the pain, the higher the jump. Some move in the direction of creativity. My main objection to drugging people for depression is that drugs limit that.

It may be that depression alone is responsible for the passionate creativity that has pushed our brain development and propelled us intellectually so far beyond any other living creature. But there are two kinds of creativity. Creativity that comes from fear doesn't cure depression—it barely covers it over. Creativity that comes from fear and ambition, or creativity that is not an end in itself, but is a means to some other end, is not the same thing as creativity for itself alone. Creativity for itself alone is not a cure for depression either, but it is so fulfilling that there is simply no room for depression. "Fearful" creativity is filled with self-conscious, rote thoughts about how well the finished product will be achieved or perceived—whether it will bring us happiness, wealth, or reputation—all nouns, roles, possessions. Ambitious or fearful creativity turns the focus from the task at hand to primal-mind anxiety and thus it never rises to the stature of present reality.

But in "pure" creativity we focus wholly on the task at hand. All thoughts are directed to the present reality of the work in progress. Pure creativity is not concerned with the created or the creator. It is always focused on the creating—a verb. Present reality is *always* a verb, like doing, being, wondering, writing, knowing.

When our creativity is a pure act of attention to the task at hand, we are always in present reality. A choice of awareness of present reality always displaces autonomic thinking. Awareness of present reality is like turning on a light in the pitch-black room of depression. "Where did the darkness go?" Involving ourselves in creativity is the result of chosen thoughts, or thoughts directed toward some goal, rather than autonomic thoughts of which we take no notice as our thinking goes on automatic pilot.

There were a few times in my early years when the process of creating was so compelling that I was taken over by creativity instead of by depression. It was never anything very remarkable. Once I bought ten yards of some fine white material with small black line drawings of antique rifles on it to make pajamas for my two little boys, ages two and five. It was about ten in the evening and I was feverishly working away at my task, short pajama pants, long pajama pants, short sleeves, long sleeves, all from the same material, and thinking how smart I was and how much money I was probably saving. Midway into the task I had this horrible letdown feeling that I was just wasting my time, and it probably would be cheaper to buy pajamas, and what difference did it make how cute they were, who was going to see them anyway? I was very tired. I was too tired to fight the depression that started to come over me.

There we sat, us old enemies, me and my depression; my depression just hanging around hoping I'd get the energy to take it up; me just waiting resignedly to get the "hit" when it came. Like mind-doodling, I picked up a small piece of the material and turned it over and over in my hand. I liked the soft, silky feel of it, and I thought the pattern was remarkable, wonderful. For a minute or two I became absolutely lost in the pure admiration of the design.

Then I shrugged my shoulders and I just accepted that I was probably wasting my time, and I was probably a fool, and I knew that not one single person in the whole world cared a thing about all these pajamas but me, and that for some reason I still cared anyway. I went back to my sewing. All the feverish stuff was gone and I felt calm and peaceful. For years afterward, catching sight of those dumb pajamas tumbling in the washer, or folding them out of the dryer, or putting them on my two boys gave me the greatest joy. "When men are rightly occupied," observed English essayist John Ruskin, "their amusement grows out of their work, as the color petals out of a fruitful flower."

Such a funny little light in the huge darkness of depression! Unfortunately, again and again, I was dragged out of my regular life into that dark painful horror of empty self plummeting into the pain. Until I wrestled myself away from my addictive subjugation to my feelings, I was dragged along whatever roads my feelings fancied to take me, uphill or down, depression or mania. Now I understand that full-blown depression is always avoidable and that I, alone, can *absolutely* count on saving myself from it, every time. Any ordinary person can do it.

Manic depression is no "genius disease" as psychiatrists claim, despite the fact that some of our creativity may turn out to be hugely profitable and find a wide audience. Genetic experiments in 1998 discovered a natural blocker in the female sex cell at the moment of conception that prevents the passing on of any genetic material responsible for the development of the lower brain, which houses instincts and emotions. There is also a natural blocker in the male sex cell that prevents the contribution of any genetic material responsible for the development of the upper brain, where intelligence and creativity reside. So it is impossible for one person to naturally pass on both the emotional and intellectual genetic inheritance as a single package. Genetic engineering can no doubt change this in the future.

It is as self-serving and dishonest for celebrity manic-depressives to label their own mood swings "genius disease" as it is for authors to talk about their "writer's block." This is laughable! Writers deserve no special consideration for undergoing universal experiences that they fully expect everybody else to "tough out" on their own. Why is "writer's block" any more credible than "plumber's block" or "auto-mechanic's malaise"? The answer is, of course, that it isn't!

The only difference is that plumbers and auto mechanics don't write about or get paid for ruminating over their angst and procrastination. R. L. Stine, the well-known *Goosebumps* series author, says that he has no trouble with writer's block because "I sit down every morning at 9:30 and don't get up until I've written twenty pages."

Manic depression, rather than being a disease, is caused by a series of poor behavior decisions based on feel-good, short-term gains rather than harder-done, long-term gains. Therefore, part of the cure for manic depression is simply to go out the same way we came in: Behavior decisions should be made that lead us to long-term gains, as opposed to making behavior decisions that lead to short-term gains.

For instance, manic-depressives are notoriously egocentric. All we want to talk about is *our* suffering, *our* needs, *our* work, *our* ideas, *our* writing, *our* childhood, *our* future success, because it gives an immediate sense of satisfaction and emotional release. But unfortunately it bores people to death and they want to run in the other direction as soon as they see us. Then we complain about feeling alienated.

So no matter how narcissistic our genes are, we have to force ourselves to remember to ask about the *other person's* writing, childhood suffering, complaints, and dreams of glory so that they will want to talk to us because it feels good for *them*, and maybe they will be willing to share a little bit of their lives and we might make a friend. Making a friend is a whole lot more valuable than making an "impression," which we can't have the fun of meeting for lunch.

The by-product of being interested in what the other person says is that the conversation is less predictable and ultimately more interesting, even though it will be hard to curb our selfish natures. (I'm still working on this.) But that is what willpower is: choosing long-term gains over short-term gains.[8] That's the simple truth about willpower.

Willpower is not some mythical force that we either have or don't have. Willpower is our decision to use higher-mind thinking instead of lazing around in the clutches of our primal mind. Sometimes just asking ourselves a question and clearly answering it is enough to make the switch to the upper brain: "So, I'm not jogging today because...?"

The psychologists are wrong and Shakespeare is right. "The fault, dear Brutus, lies not in our stars [or our genes, or our chemistry] but in *ourselves*" that we are so damn depressed.[9] Not too long ago a feature article about depression ran in our local paper. I was particularly struck by one woman who said she had suffered depression for twenty years. Nothing had ever helped her until about five years ago when she took up oil painting. She now teaches painting; she gives art shows. "Oh, no, I never spend a single minute being depressed these days," she claims, "I'm much too busy."

Now, I am not saying that we can cure our depression by taking up oil painting. If we have some pressing issues that we need to address, we had better address them or our primal-mind defense system is going to keep beating us up until we do. But, in the absence of legitimate problems, when our out-of-whack defense system activates unnecessarily, we can cure our depression by directing our thinking to oil painting or anything else that replaces the random negative thoughts that concentrate our mind on depression.

When we replace the anxious thoughts with neutral or positive thoughts, we switch our neuronal activity to the upper brain and the chemicals change and the painful feelings subside. Any neutral thoughts work to relieve anxious worry. If we can encourage ourselves in some new hobby, it will be easier to concentrate on thoughts about some ongoing fun project we have chosen to take up, rather than drumming up neutral thoughts out of thin air.

Of course, neutral thoughts out of thin air work too. The important thing, when we are just learning to direct our thinking, is *never to wait passively for negative thoughts and feelings to go away on their own*. We need to be more proactive and spontaneous when simple things come our way instead of intellectualizing everything first, as if we are looking for a guarantee that it will give us some kind of a "high."

In this respect life is like a game that we can simply refuse to play. Life can get "old hat," just like Monopoly and Parcheesi—kind of been-there-done-that boring and not worth the bother. Even today I find it a great temptation to continue reading my mystery book, and to refuse the children when they ask me to play a game with them. But I have learned to direct my thinking *past* that feeling of temptation to "not bother," and I join in anyway, whether I want to or not. Although there is still nothing inherently stimulating about any of these games for me, once we begin to play, interesting things happen just by chance. It's not that the games per se are any fun. It's what happens to us simply because we decide to play—funny, charming, and loving things that no one could predict ahead of time.

For instance, my grandchildren and I once put a puzzle together and after it was all done we were so disappointed that one jigsaw piece was missing. I found a piece of cardboard, put it under the hole where the missing piece should have been, drew the shape, cut it out and we all worked on coloring it with magic markers. It was far from perfect but now they are more than likely to ask for the puzzle "with the piece we made."

Years ago my husband was away for a year and a half on a management training course. We only saw him on weekends, and it became the custom for me and the three older children to play the card game Hearts every weekday evening after dinner, when homework was done and the baby was down for the night. The boys were ten and thirteen and my daughter was only seven at the time. All of us knew immediately if my daughter drew the queen of spades (which usually meant you were going to lose the hand) because, although she would sit up tall and keep a straight poker face, one little tear would slowly trickle down each side of her nose. It is one of my most treasured memories.

Could it be that there is nothing inherently interesting about life itself; it's just what happens, simply by chance, when we decide "to play"? If we direct energy and time toward some project, as a natural course we will become more interested in it and find it diverting to think about, and have fewer of our neurons involving themselves in depression.

Directed Thinking is the idea that we should never just wait around until something interesting comes along. We should just *choose* something to do, interesting or not, whether we *feel like it* or not, and invest some time and effort in it and our interest in it will automatically accumulate on its own as the neural activity in our upper brain starts to light up.

We don't need to get hung up on what *should* work. Directed Thinking is the idea that we simply use what *does* work. If one thing isn't working for us, we just quickly choose again. For instance, the idea that "Today is the first day of the rest of your life" has inspired many people, but it doesn't do a thing for me. One day I realized that it would be more helpful to me if I would think "Today is the *last* day of the first of my life" because I am much more careful and respectful of the "last" of anything. I am rather frivolous and wasteful if it's just the beginning and there's plenty more where that came from.

Something is always doable. This is the same idea that Henry James expressed so eloquently when he said: "To take what there is, and use it, without waiting forever in vain for the preconceived—to dig deep into the actual and get something out of *that*—this doubtless is the way to live."

But prevailing "wisdom" says that we can't do anything until we feel good about ourselves, until we love ourselves first. Then we will be able to feel alive and do something worthwhile. This is just psychologized nonsense. This is warmed-over self-esteem dogma that can spiral us into debilitating self-absorption with anxious despair at the tail end of it. Individual success and self-esteem is not the quick fix to all our problems. Self-esteem won't help society. Self-esteem won't help the family.

It won't even help the individual since the very concentration upon self that is necessary to obtain it is enough, sooner or later, to do us in depression-wise. Self-esteem is a very slippery slope. Self-esteem is only good for a technically proficient but ultimately a weak, disengaged, and mediocre personality. Why? Because self-love impairs our judgment upon those things that most concern us, and about which we would be better off to humbly seek our fellows' advice. With self-esteem we adapt more and more to our psychologized need to feel good, and we adapt less and less to the challenges in our environment.

Roy F. Baumeister, a professor in the department of psychology at Case Western University, and two graduate students reviewed nearly 200 studies of assault and murder, youth gangs, juvenile delinquency, rape, domestic violence, terrorism, oppression, and genocide. Their conclusion is that people who engage in those behaviors rarely suffer from low self-esteem. "To the contrary, people with poor self-images are less violent and less aggressive than people with inflated egos."[10]

"In our view, the heavily positive connotation that self-esteem has acquired in recent American thought is partly a result of biased and wishful thinking that simply refuses to acknowledge the darker side. As compared with other cultures and other historical eras, modern America has been unusually fond of the notion that elevating the self-esteem of each individual will be best for society.

"America is also, perhaps not coincidentally, one of the world's most violent societies, with rates of violent crime that far exceed those of other modern, industrialized nations . . . I'd advise people to become a better person," said Baumeister, "rather than just staying the same person and thinking better of yourself."[11] Child psychology author John Rosemond agrees: "Self-esteem is not installed, it is discovered. It is the realization on the part of the child that, despite fears, frustrations, even failures, she is capable of standing on her own two feet. Of surviving adversity. Of dealing successfully with the slings and arrows of everyday reality."[12] Self-esteem is worthless unless it has been forged out of competence. It can't be manufactured out of free-floating good feelings.

Karla Homolka, age twenty-nine, was convicted in 1993 of helping her husband rape, torture, videotape, and kill three teenage girls, one of whom was her own sister. She wrote a note to her prison warden about why she should be sent to a halfway house and then paroled: "I learned [in prison] to get rid of my mistrust, self-doubt, misplaced guilt, and defense mechanisms. I am now completely in touch with my inner feelings. My self-esteem is quite high."[13] Self-esteem in a psychologized society is simply an artificial, synthetic, and ultimately poor substitute for common-ground connection.

We have lost the small-town living that used to provide so much of our common ground. It began to disappear in the 1960s as the new Wal-Marts and Kmarts won all the business away from the small family-owned businesses. It wasn't only that people liked the lower prices, they liked the anonymity. They didn't want to take the time to chat with some geezer storeowner that they were so-and-so's son, that they were the ones who just moved to the white house on the corner of Ingleside and Elm. Young people didn't want to be recognized at the pharmacy counter. Immigrants especially didn't want anybody asking them questions. The new self-esteem needed its own space.

It is a cliché today that disenchanted marital partners bow out to seek "more space." But the idea of personal space was so limited in the early years of our culture that corridors did not begin to appear in the houses of the wealthy until 1700.[14] Before that one simply went through one room to get to the next one. No one had a door to shut out the rest of the family. Teenagers couldn't isolate themselves and slink away into their own private hell because there was always Grandma patting them on the head as she chatted by, or Aunty Sue dropping a fussy baby in their lap to soothe. Plus the fact that abodes were small and cozy to begin with, not the tract palaces you see today where lonely children can become rebel exiles in their own wings.

Our common ground has been disappearing in houses built to accommodate lavish interior decoration and giant TV sets, and communities that encourage dependence upon the automobile rather than up-close-and-personal cooperation with our neighbors. Now add the psychology of self-esteem and no wonder we are turning up lonely and depressed.

We need to find each other again. We have forgotten the simple joys of walking, and sitting on the front porch in view of our neighbors. We don't know each other's children. We need to get up and do something. We do need to reach out and touch somebody because as Conceptual Physics author Paul Hewitt reminds us, "You cannot touch someone without being touched in return." If we are in doubt as to what we should do, perhaps our focus could be on our duty to our fellow man in general to be friendly and interdependent, and our duty to the task at hand in particular. It is healthier to focus on something else, rather than to allow everything around us to focus on us.

The self-focus, which is encouraged in a psychologized, self-esteem society, makes relationships difficult. We bowl alone instead of in leagues. We use the golden rule with our neighbors mainly to measure them "up short" against our own success. We look in the mirror a lot. We think we have common ground when we have similar feelings. Feelings are located in the primal mind, and primal-mind feelings are *always* temporary. We should probably refer to finding commonality on the basis of the same feelings as *common sand* rather than common ground.

Concentrating on our own feelings, good or bad, is ultimately isolating because they situate us in the primal mind, where we experience ourselves as individuals, alone, rather than part of a group. Principles always lead us back out of our sense of powerlessness and aloneness into a sense of community because they provide a common ground for how we can best relate to one another, or how we can relate to those things that are also important to other people.

The misguided self-esteem precept that we need to love ourselves first before we can do anything worthwhile probably devolved from the simple reality that what we really love about anything—person, place, or thing—is our own investment, which colors our warmer perception of it. That's what sparks up our neurons—our own thinking and action. People wrongly believe that our interest comes first and *then* we can make an investment. Nope! Our neurons don't start to really sparkle at any great depth until after we get busy.

One reason why so many marriages fail is that we don't understand this. If we want to love something or someone, we need only to start making an investment of our time and energy in them. That's what bonding is. That's why "love" is a verb. We don't really love another person; what we love is our *interest* in the other person. As we expand our investment in them, we expand our interest in them, and we expand our love for them.

Love is our decision to invest ourselves in some specific other person by making them "special" to us. We make people special to us by doing nice things for them; by finding nice things about them to notice and to think about; by politely averting our eyes during their "ugly" moments (we all have them); by showing forbearance for their grievous flaws (we all have them); and by putting their interests ahead of our own, whether we feel like it or not. If we are not able to put someone's interests ahead of our own, the point is *not* that we do not love them; the point is that if we do not put someone's interests ahead of our own, we *cannot* love them because we will not be able to develop, thereby, the neuronal capacity to love them.

The opposite is also true. If we find we have developed an unchosen romantic interest because we have autonomically mind-wandered into making an investment in "the other woman," or "the other man" as the case may be, we can refuse to think thoughts about the person or situation. We simply choose other thoughts, direct our energy elsewhere, and before long we will find that as our investment has lessened, the associated neural activity fades and our interest cools.

But isn't this just denial? Doesn't denial of feelings take its toll in depression, anxiety, and migraine headaches? Yes. But we are not talking about denying feelings. We are talking about choosing one thought over another, and therefore causing different feelings to arise in response to the different thoughts. We don't want to deny feelings. But thoughts are different. They are very quick, bioelectrical. They are over by the time we are aware of them, so we can't really deny them anyway. What we are doing is just choosing to not think the thought again.

Feelings are biochemical instead of bioelectrical. When we are aware of them they already exist as ongoing physical changes in the body, and thus should be allowed to diminish and finish naturally. We can deny feelings by emotionally cutting off from them, yet they will still be reflected in our postures and in the chemical residue that can stagnate and ferment in the body.

Wilhelm Reich was the first one to call attention to our "skeletal body armor" caused by the contracted muscles and restricted breathing resulting from the habitual postures we take in response to fearful feelings.[15] The psychological responses of repressed feelings can become somaticized in the body. That is, physical postures that we take by shrugging or cringing, and mental postures that we take in avoiding or blaming can, over time, be reflected in changes to ourselves on a cellular level. Painful memories are thus stored in the tissues of our body and may be released during breath work or body work, such as therapeutic massage. We should feel painful feelings until they finish and we can effect a positive or neutral change of thinking that will then bring about *different* feelings. But just the choice of a single thought, one time, won't do the trick. It is the concentration on a train of thoughts, one thought chosen again and again, that we need to master. Directed Thinking takes effort and practice.

In a way, Directed Thinking is a sophisticated modern equivalent of old-fashioned duty, or at least it includes the understanding of the restorative power of duty. Duty is not the same thing as accomplishment. Duty is the question, "What ought we to do next?" The word "ought" is very out of fashion now, as is the word "should." In our present psychologized society, where feelings hold higher status over behavior, a popular maxim is: "I will not 'should' on myself," which is the most ridiculous oxymoron, though it makes the point admirably enough that we should not limit ourselves by saying I 'should' do this, or I 'shouldn't' do that. But I question that point.

Are the words "should" and "ought" really limiting? I wonder. What would happen if every time we were ready to do something (I will), we changed the "I will" to "I ought" just to see if we would continue, or would we change what comes after the word because our horizons suddenly widened? Maybe the use of "ought" would enlarge, rather than limit, our possibilities. Certainly the use of "I will" can have a tendency to mire us in alienating, self-absorbed, and unsocial behavior, which is extremely narrow in focus.

I can imagine changing the sentence from "I will have another drink" to "I ought to go home," or "I ought to quit drinking," or "I ought to think about my daughter, or my wife," or "I ought to get up from the table right now." Maybe the word "ought" is not the limiting factor it first seems to be. Maybe it is a magic wand that puts us in touch with our excellent higher-mind library of principles, our common ground with all that is ennobling to human existence. Maybe there is a "law of ought" like the law of inertia.

In earlier ages when people felt themselves slipping into the dark abyss of depression or insanity, they grabbed for duty to save themselves. Thus an eighteenth-century American clergyman, William Nevins, maintained, "It is one of the worst of errors to suppose that there is any path of safety except that of duty.

Philosophers of old did not have the advances of science that we have today, but they were certainly on the right track in their straightforward and simple reliance on humble duty, since modern neuroscience can now show us how duty "works" to eliminate falling into depression by stimulating neural activity in the upper brain. The nineteenth-century Catholic priest F. W. Faber anticipated neuroscience when he said, "Exactness in little things is a wonderful source of cheerfulness." How? Because concentrating upon being exact is higher-mind activity, and feelings of gloom do not reside in the higher mind.

Philosophers have always known that there is a connection between duty and mental and spiritual health, and that duty does not necessarily have a direct connection with happiness, wealth, or success. These wise men were always trying to capture this in their "hints" to us. The English theologian Richard Cecil defines duty thusly: "Duties are ours, events are God's. This removes an infinite burden from the shoulders of a miserable, tempted, dying creature. On this consideration only can he securely lay down his head and close his eyes."

William Paley was an English theologian, philosopher, author, lecturer, and scientist whose book *Natural Theology* had a great influence on Charles Darwin. This is what Paley had to say about duty: "No man's spirits were ever hurt by doing his duty. On the contrary, one good action, one temptation resisted and overcome, one sacrifice of desire or interest purely for conscience's sake, will prove a cordial for weak and low spirits far beyond what either indulgence, or diversion, or company can do for them." And were Paley writing that today he might well have added, "or some antidepressant pill."

American Unitarian theologian Theodore Parker tied the idea of duty to a sense of common ground: "Let us do our duty in our shop or our kitchen; in the market, the street, the office, the school, the home, just as faithfully as if we stood in the front rank of some great battle, and knew that victory for mankind depended on our bravery, strength and skill. When we do that, the humblest of us will be serving in that great army which achieves the welfare of the world."

And for those of us who are not sure what our "duty" might

be, Scottish author Thomas Carlyle assures us: "Do the duty which lies nearest to thee! Thy second duty will already have become clearer." The English statesman William Gladstone says that we and our duty are more or less coexistent: "Duty is a power that rises with us in the morning, and goes to rest with us at night. It is coextensive with the action of our intelligence. It is the shadow that cleaves to us, go where we will." English novelist Charles Kingsley adds: "This is the feeling that gives a man true courage—the feeling that he has a work to do *at all costs*; the sense of duty."

But in a psychologized society, primal-mind feelings are thought to be the legitimate arbiter of behavior, not higher-mind principles. In this kind of atmosphere, duty may not be seen as cosmic help but an unnatural, unnecessary hindrance to personal power and self-esteem. The battle within us still rages, however. The battle used to be between our impulses and our principles, and duty was the cure. Now the battle is between our doctors and our diagnoses (depression, mania, shyness, and compulsiveness) and self-esteem or pharmaceuticals are the cure.

This is a problem because morality is absolutely necessary to establishing the common ground that assures our survival as a species. In past eras there might have been a few "radicals" who discounted morality as an "unproved" necessary. Eighteenth-century author Samuel Johnson had this to say about them: "If he does really think that there is no distinction between virtue and vice, why Sir, when he leaves our houses let us count our spoons."

We can see the evolutionary roots of human ethical and moral systems in the behavior of animals. Researchers at Emory University claim that "sympathy, empathy and even rudimentary ideas of rights, fairness and justice are found in the higher primates and may be hard-wired into the human brain."[16] "In the neurosciences, personality is not so much a social construct

as it is a physiological threshold concept associated with phys-
iology and behavior features," said Michael McGuire, a UCLA
scientist whose work on brain structures and chemistry has
helped create a framework linking life scientists to social scientists.[17]

"Morality is not just an optimistic veneer," claims Frans de
Waal, primatologist and author of the book *Good Natured: The
Origins of Right and Wrong in Humans and Other Animals*.[18]
DeWaal relates instances of chimps showing indignation toward
their fellows who never shared their food and then expected a
piece of someone else's. Chimps "kiss and make up" after fighting, embrace to offer consolation, and have developed a system
of rules and justice.

DeWaal tells of two young apes in the research compound
who stayed out late and held up the dinner feeding of the other
apes being studied. The scientists kept the two apes apart that
night for their own safety but when they were returned to the
group the next day they still got a beating from the others.
That evening the two recalcitrants were the first ones to come
home.

Harvard University psychology professor Jerome Kagan insists, "The human moral sense, like a spider's web, is a unique
product of evolution that has been maintained because it insures
our survival." Kagan says the belief "that the self is ethically
worthy, like the ability to understand language, is universal."
Without this inborn "moral sense," he reasons, children could
not be socialized.[19]

And neuroscientist Antonio Damasio says, "It is apparent
that we must rely on highly evolved genetically based biological
mechanisms, as well as on suprainstinctual survival strategies
that have developed in society, that are transmitted by culture,
and require, for their application, consciousness, reasoned de-
liberation, and will power."[20]

Earlier generations had a high regard for the importance of

ceremony, civility, manners, and moral conduct. We should reconsider our present-day disregard for them, as they inform the totality of our emotional, social, and political life. United States Supreme Court Justice Oliver Wendell Holmes said that even the law itself was not based upon logic but rather "experience. The felt necessities of the time, the prevalent moral and political theories, intuitions of public policy, avowed or unconscious, even the prejudices which judges share with their fellow men."

Political theorist Edmund Burke said "Manners are of more importance than laws. Upon them, in a great measure the laws depend. The law touches us here and there, and now and then. Manners are what vex or soothe, corrupt or purify, exalt or debase, barbarize or refine us, by a constant steady, uniform, insensible operation, like that of the air we breathe in."

The two apes did not forget the lesson they had learned. The lessons we have learned are what distinguish us from one another. Our lower-brain primal minds are all very similar— the sealed unit of factory-installed defense mechanisms and feelings we were all born with. But since we are always changing or improving upon our principles and experience, our upper-brain higher minds can differ greatly from person to person.

We might think we suffer from depression because we have worse pain than other people. It seems logical to think that because we see ourselves suffering, and we see that other people don't suffer as much. In a way this is intellectual arrogance masquerading as helplessness, because our conclusion is based on the wrong premise that other people don't have the same capacity for pain that we do.

Everybody has a similar impulse to depression. Some people just do a better job of directing their thinking past it. It isn't that their depression isn't as painful. They simply make better use of other options in order to bypass their depression, which, if they didn't bypass it, would pitch them into the same interminable agony.

My editor told me about a young man in her office who is in his early twenties. One morning she heard him groaning to himself, or at least not addressing his comments specifically to anyone else in the room. "I'm having a bad day. I guess I'm depressed. This is not good." He bent over and put both hands over his face in seeming agony. But in the next instant he straightened up, shook his dark hair all around as if he were shaking water off after a dive in the swimming pool, and said resolutely, "Oh, well. Just have to get through the day is all. Get busy and it will go away."

"And that," said my editor, "was that." A short time later he appeared quite cheerful and involved with his work and made no other reference to his former doldrums.

After decades of dispensing positive-thinking advice to others, Dr. Joyce Brothers never realized what kind of pain people were talking about until she experienced her first severe depression after the death of her husband of thirty years.[21] The capacity, of course, had always been there. Few of us have the stellar distractions of TV talk shows and nationally syndicated columns like Dr. Brothers, but we can all learn to indirectly bypass depression and mania by learning to direct our attention away from focusing on them.

We can develop habits of proper mood control based on "rope tricks," which we can learn during intervals between depressive and manic episodes. In the lives of those with even the most severe cases of major depression or manic depression, there are periods of equanimity where there is a feeling of well-being. Depression and mania come and go; they are not static conditions but idiosyncratic ones, as in Dr. Brothers' case, or chronic repeat patterns as mine were.

We are all equal in the extent to which our passionate anger can rise up from the primal mind. The differences in our higher minds determine what kinds of things we will become angry about, and how we will direct our anger. Will our energy be invested in road rage or fighting injustice? Will we curse and throw obscene gestures or write a letter to the editor? We are all equal in the amount of pain we can suffer from our primal-mind depression; the differences in our higher minds will determine how long we will suffer it.

This is the reason children must be provided with proper input into their higher minds. Not only training in particular rules and precepts, which are the basis for our common-ground connection with society, but children should also be encouraged in earnestness. As part of my Girl Scout experiences, for a year I kept a small list of rules that I wrote down and checked off on a daily basis if I had followed them. Do one good deed every day. Tell the truth. Do my homework. Clean my room. My scout leader periodically checked in with me and encouraged me not to give up, to persevere in the ongoing task with the same enthusiasm I had started.

She was teaching me earnestness, a word I kept running into when I began my adult quest. Our early classic literature maintains that all things are possible through earnestness. "Earnestness alone makes life eternity," said the great Carlyle. "There is no substitute for thorough-going, ardent and sincere earnestness," said Charles Dickens. "Earnestness is the devotion of all the faculties," said American author C. N. Bovee. "It is the cause of patience; gives endurance; overcomes pain; strengthens weakness; braves dangers; sustains hope; makes light of difficulties; and lessens the sense of weariness in overcoming them." "Without earnestness," said Scottish author Peter Bayne, "no man is ever great or does really great things. He may be the cleverest of men; he may be brilliant, entertaining, popular; but he will want weight." Physicists say it this way: "The degree to which a particle is likely to wander in an indeterminate way from the straight and narrow is determined by its lack of mass."[22]

In my forties, I made a commitment to earnestness and

awareness. Well, more precisely, it was an earnest commitment to give a pure act of attention to the task at hand no matter what. I ran across a copy of *The Autobiography of Benjamin Franklin* around that time, and as it was very small, I used to carry it in my pocketbook because I wanted that kind of company. The company of a fellow pilgrim. Benjamin Franklin decided to embark upon a regimen of acquiring virtues at the age of twenty-two. He drew up his own list of thirteen virtues and kept a record of his successes and failures to follow them by way of a small graph, concentrating on one particular virtue each week. He had arranged them in such order that the acquisition of the first would aid in the accomplishment of the second, etc. (Listed below with Franklin's own spelling.)

1. Temperance: Eat not to dullness; drink not to elevation.
2. Silence: Speak not but what may benefit others or yourself; avoid trifling conversation.
3. Order: Let all your things have their places.
4. Resolution: Resolve to perform what you ought; perform without fail what you resolve.
5. Frugality: Make no expense but to do good to others or yourself; i.e., waste nothing.
6. Industry: Lose no time; be always employ'd in something useful; cut off all unnecessary actions.
7. Sincerity: Use no hurtful deceit; think innocently and justly; and, if you speak, speak accordingly.
8. Justice: Wrong none by doing injuries, or omitting the benefits that are your duty.
9. Moderation: Avoid extreams; forbear resenting injuries so much as you think they deserve.
10. Cleanliness: Tolerate no uncleanliness in body, cloaths, or habitation.
11. Tranquillity: Be not disturbed at trifles, or at accidents common or unavoidable.

12. Chastity: Rarely use venery but for health or offspring, never to dulness, weakness, or the injury of your own or another's peace or reputation.
13. Humility: Imitate Jesus and Socrates.

When we are ready to make a change in our life, any small positive thing has value. Then we can do another small thing. Then another. If we don't like where we are, we can take just one small step in the opposite direction. Is there any good reason not to do it? Not *feeling* like doing it is not a good reason for not doing it. Furthermore, we don't have to know *why* our life is in such a mess to begin to clean it up, just like we don't have to know how the car runs in order to get in it and drive to the grocery store.

Powerful feelings like depression can obstruct us from pursuing our chosen course. But here's another hint about choosing behavior that our present feelings seem to be preventing us from carrying out. Feelings are powerful; we can't, and shouldn't, stop feeling them. But feelings are very dumb and we can outsmart them.

I remember when my children were very small, I found myself escaping to the bathroom to spend an hour and a half taking a nice hot bath in the morning. I would have all sorts of plans and just soak them away and then be mad at myself for getting so behind. I just couldn't get out of the warm comforting tub and face my day. Quite by accident I found that although I didn't have the gumption to climb out of the tub all of a sudden, it was very easy for me, as I reclined in luxury, to take my big toe and flip the lever that opened up the drain. Once all the nice warm water ran out, I had no trouble at all getting up out of the cold tub.

Another time, when I lived in New Jersey, I signed up for early morning tennis at an indoor club and was supposed to leave the house at 5:30. Those cold winter mornings made it tempting to ignore the alarm when it went off. The whole first week went by and I just couldn't get out of bed. So Sunday night I decided that, come Monday morning, I would not turn off the alarm until both my feet were on the floor. Then I made a further decision that once both feet were on the floor I would not get back into bed. It worked like a charm.

Psychologists call this "successive approximations to a goal." Practically speaking, it is simply the insistence on our behavior being funded by a choice, which leads to the fulfillment of long-term goals, instead of our incipient intentions being derailed by primal-mind, don't-feel-like-doing-it fulfillment of short-term goals. We can measure our situation against the goals and values we have chosen, and if our situation doesn't support our values, we can initiate behavior to change our situation. This will automatically shake out our immature reactive behavior and behavior funded by hidden values because it will be incompatible with the new goals and values for which we have committed ourselves to be earnestly proactive.

We don't ever have to commit to something that seems more than we can do. Our mind, once directed, can be a marvelous, dedicated servant. But we shouldn't give it such heavy, huge commands that it's going to feel taken advantage of and balk on us. Even now, although I jog for forty-five minutes and then do exercises for forty-five minutes every morning, I never commit to forty-five minutes of either one. I commit only to beginning. To getting going. Only to that first step. Or to the first exercise. We should be pleasant and jolly our minds along for our normal daily lives, not drag them unmercifully and beat them with a stick.

Fourteen

THE MIND IS A
GIVEN; THE SELF
MUST BE ASSERTED

*We seem to be very afraid of "mind control" as it concerns
another person's power over us. But the worst mind control
of all is when our own mind is in control of itself, and we
are following after it like some kind of wag the dog.*

Depression is one of the universal experiences of life. The problem is that we seem less prepared for life than the smallest do-it-yourself project that sends us scurrying to the hardware store. For instance, no matter how smart and dedicated we are, we cannot sink a screw into a hard piece of solid wood without a screwdriver. With all the positive mental attitude in the world, on or off medication, with or without psychotherapy, a fingernail will not do the job. Nobody cries, or begs, or rages, or makes excuses about it. We just know better than to drive a screw with our bare hands.

Yet we think nothing of living our lives by our bare hands. We still use the screwdrivers, hammers, and saws that our great-grandparents passed down to us. But we have turned our psychologized backs upon the empowering principles and ethics they bequeathed to us; those common-ground golden-oldie rules that previous generations used to control automatic, instinctual reactions and base, primal behavior.

Our great-grandparents used willpower instead of Prozac and Zoloft. They valued conscience, responsibility, honesty, commitment, dedication, sacrifice, hard work, and courage. *And they practiced learning to bear suffering.* These concepts were universally taught to children, who naturally employed them as adults. These concepts had been tested and revered for thousands of years. People trusted their lives to them. In the 1960s we threw them all out.

Today most of us know nothing at all about how we came by the concepts and values that now conscribe our behavior. What is worse, we may not even know at all what those values really are. Still less do we know how the human psychological defense system works. Maybe it wasn't so necessary to know how to survive psychologically in the world when mankind was pitted against the woolly mammoth for physical survival. But science and technology have moved us way beyond that; our lives are exceedingly complex and fast-paced. We need to educate ourselves. We are making ourselves mentally ill.

We think we are at the mercy of our feelings. Most of the feelings we struggle with didn't used to be called feelings; they used to be called sins. The Greek theologian Evagrius Ponticus drew up a list of eight such feelings, which he called vices, to guard against: gluttony, lust, avarice, sadness, anger, acedia (spiritual sloth, from the Greek word *akedia* meaning "not to care"), vainglory, and pride.[1] In the sixth century Pope Gregory changed the list by combining sadness and spiritual not-caring, and merging vainglory and pride. He added envy to make up the now familiar seven deadly sins: pride, envy, anger, sadness, avarice, gluttony, and lust.

Strangely, in the last few decades, perhaps as depression as come to be thought of as a disease, "sadness" has been dropped from the list and "sloth" substituted. But sadness is one of the original seven deadly sins, although people of our psychologized culture would find it quite odd to speak of sadness as a vice, and quite alarmed if our plaintive cry of "nothing matters" would be condemned as the sin of "not caring."

If we are not going to be led around and laid waste by our feelings (the sloth and sadness of our unchecked defense mechanisms) or seduced and self-deluded by our excuses (our free passes to nowhere), we need some system of precepts, some game plan, or personal "code of the West" to live by. It also helps to have at our disposal some mind tricks that we can use when feelings like depression threaten to take over our brains. We need a plan to take charge of ourselves.

I began to see that neither my depression nor my mind was more powerful than I was, since I could decide and carry out any principle or action I chose, and neither my mind nor my feelings could decide anything on their own and carry it out without me going along. I learned that my mind is something that is happening to me; I am not something that is happening to my mind. I learned that I, myself, am not a thought in my mind since I could take any thought and empty it of all meaning; or cause the thought to disappear by thinking another thought; but there was no method by which I could empty myself of myself, or cause myself, the "I am," to disappear.

Now for those who insist that the mind is the seat of the self, and therefore believe it is an illusion that we can impose choice upon the mind because whatever we choose to think has to originate from somewhere within our mind, I will propose an exercise. Ask someone (outside of your mind) to propose to you some thought for you to think, and see if there is any impediment from inside your mind to your choice of thinking a thought that is an outside-the-mind choice. Of course there will be no impediment. We can choose to live our lives by principles.

By exercising thought choice, I learned to indirectly control my feelings. That progress gave me the space to start questioning my thinking as well as my feelings. Why should we question our thoughts? It is not crazy thoughts that make a person crazy. Everybody has crazy thoughts. What makes a person crazy is *believing* their crazy thoughts, accepting them as data. The point is not to believe our mind; the point is to direct our mind to do the thinking that makes rational, moral, economic, financial, or social sense. As philosopher Francis Bacon warns: "Whatever the mind seizes upon with particular satisfaction is to be held in suspicion."

If other people tell us to do things, we know that we darn well better check those things out against our own value system before we do them. The same goes for our own thoughts. If we get compelling ideas, or hear voices in our heads that tell us to do things, we better check those things out too against our value system before we do them. We shouldn't believe our own mind any more than we should believe someone else's mind. Ideas are not necessarily value systems.

Some people might think that there is something odd about taking intentional control and authority over our thoughts, as if there is something unnatural about it, as if it would take all our time and energy and turn us into a robot of some kind. Nothing could be further from the truth. What turns us into robots is letting our mind spiral us down into depression. We seem to be very afraid of "mind control" as it concerns another person's power over us. But the worst mind control of all is when our own mind is in control of itself, and we are following after it like some kind of wag the dog.

The strange story of John Nash seems to illustrate this. He was a 1994 Nobel Prize winner who spent three decades as a schizophrenic walking around the Princeton University campus with a zombielike expression on his face and "dead" eyes. He deciphered "secret messages" from the *New York Times* headlines and pasted them in a scrapbook, which he titled "Absolute Zero."[2]

He believed himself to be, at different times, a Palestinian refugee named C.O.R.P.S.E., a Japanese shogun, and the Biblical figure Job. He did not speak to anyone. He had a room in the home of his ex-wife near the college and was considered a harmless "crazy." Out of respect for his brilliant early work as a graduate student in the 1950s, he was allowed to wander the campus daily, and the students were told not to bother him and the tattered newspapers he always carried.[3]

How could such a brilliant man come to believe things like extraterrestrials were recruiting him to save the world? Later he would say that the ideas about supernatural beings came to him the same way that his mathematical ideas did, so he "took them seriously." He clearly follows psychiatrist Jamison's artistic profile of the self-centered, narcissistic but brilliant mind that finally succumbs to madness because of bad genes or chemical imbalances. But in the absence of any changes to his genes or his chemicals, what can account for John Nash's return to sanity?

After thirty years, he decided one day that any politically oriented thinking was a "hopeless waste of intellectual effort" because "nothing ever came of it," so he determined to not bother about any thoughts concerning politics in his "secret world." That led him to ignore thoughts about religious issues or "teaching or intending to teach" as being also "ineffectual." Fascinated by numerology, he began to study some of his strange ideas in terms of their mathematics and was offered the use of a computer, invented during his long sleep of sanity. He had to interact somewhat with the computer-lab people who instructed him in the use of the new technology. One day, out of the blue, he inquired about the daughter of one of the men who was helping him. It was the first step in his return to sanity. "I was so shocked," said the man, "I had no idea he even knew I had a daughter."[4]

The whole process of Nash's regaining his sanity evidently

remains a mystery to those who know him. I may not know the why of it, but I'm certain as to the how of it. When Nash *decided* to reject any of his thoughts, he was on his way back to sanity. When he began to direct his mind to do thinking about mathematics instead of entertaining the irrational political and religious thoughts about saving the world, he was no longer a complete prisoner of his mind; he had become its user. When he began to interact with the men in the computer lab, he found common ground in the larger world rather than being confined to his self-absorbed private world. Connecting with his fellows gave him the opportunity of hooking his mind back up with objective reality.

As he got more and more in the habit of *directing* his mind instead of *listening* to it, John Nash became completely sane. What makes Nash sane now is not that he no longer has irrational thoughts. He does have them, but as he says, the "noise level is turned way down." It seems the noise level is down because he doesn't pay attention to random thoughts and let them procreate themselves into self-hypnosis. He doesn't just let thinking go on by itself and then collapse into his private dream as if it is the real world.

The point is not that we *are* a mind. The point is that we *have* a mind. Further, we are the link between our mind and the objective reality of the physical and symbolic world we share with our fellow man. So when we say that we go insane and lose our mind, that is not exactly right. It is probably closer to the truth to say that *our mind loses us*. When we become too passive or too frightened, or for whatever reason we cease to maintain a healthy social intimacy with our fellows and refuse our role as an ordinary person in the normal workaday world we lose the common ground connection with objective reality, and therefore so does our mind. Now when we start believing in a mind that we have severed from its connection with our larger society, and therefore with its connection to objective reality, we are insane.

Relying upon our mind without cues from objective reality can get us into the same kind of trouble that pilots face who rely on their physical "senses" instead of their instruments during flight. My brother, who is a pilot, told me that when he first showed up for flying lessons the instructor took him up and proceeded to subtly maneuver the plane around, and then asked my brother if he could tell, without reference to the horizon, whether they were flying up, down, or sideways. My brother said he felt like he had a good sense of which way they were flying and told the instructor what he thought. He was wrong.

There are several flight instruments that give the same information and a good pilot constantly scans them all. If one is noncorroborative, the information must be taken from the other ones. Never should the pilot out of laziness or habit depend upon some "favorite instrument." Relying on his own senses, or a single instrument, and believing that he is climbing, a pilot can actually fly the plane right into the ground. We are the pilot of our minds, and we need to direct our mind using the guideposts of common-ground principles and feedback from intimate social interaction with our fellows. Alone, without the corroboration of these guideposts, we can experience cognitive vertigo and fly our mind right into insanity.

Of course there are accidents that result in physical damage to the brain, which means a part of the brain can no longer function, thinking-wise. We can lose our mind physically, but psychologically we cannot lose our mind. Psychologically, it is our mind that loses us. There are also rare genetic flaws that cause missing or extra chromosomes that result in retardation or toxic poisoning to the brain, but this does not include manic depression where the cognitive faculties are available, but not used, when, out of the laziness of easy rote habit, we rely on the uncorroborated impulse instruments of the mania or depression of our primal mind as if they are objective reality.

The mind has powers that the mind itself does not have the capacity to understand. The mind has limitations that the mind itself does not have the capacity to understand. The mind is not aware of itself as we may train ourselves to be aware of it, because the mind itself is not sentient. It is a thought-thinking, feelings-feeling machine. The main thing to remember about the mind is that the "lure of it" is not the "sure of it." An intelligent mind can rationalize everything, find excuses for everything. That is the duty of the mind, to make logical distinctions and connections between things. And it can do that perfectly, logically, and still be heading us in the wrong direction.

We *can* depend upon our mind's logic, we *can't* depend on its connection to objective reality; just like we *can* depend upon our plane to stay up in the air as a result of its properly functioning mechanics, but we *can't* depend upon it to go in the right direction. So, like steering a plane, we have to point the mind's logic in the right direction; where *we* want it to go. If the mind, in the fullness of its logic, directs us to be depressed; we can direct the mind, in the fullness of its logic, to make us cheerful. As Emerson says, "No house, though it were the Tuileries, or the Escurial, is good for anything without a master."

If we are engaged in some activity—fixing breakfast, mowing the lawn, reading a story, or working at our job—our thoughts are naturally directed by our attention to the task at hand. Once directed to the task at hand, our thoughts re-create themselves in helpful, orderly fashion through the process of learned associations, images, and other cooperative neural echo-response mechanisms in our brain. If we want to make ourselves a cup of coffee, the standard operating procedure just needs to be set in motion by reaching for the first item, coffee; then we automatically reach for the coffeemaker; search for the sugar and cream if we need it; find a cup; etc., etc.

The problem comes when our thoughts are not directed to some task at hand. The problem comes when our thoughts start coming unbidden by us and cease to be our obedient servants working in our best interest. Directed Thinking is the idea that we can learn to have complete intentional control over any thoughts that make us anxious, that cause us pain, or that lead us into action that may be destructive. The way we can have complete intentional control over any thought, and therefore any behavior, is by our simple intention to think whatever thoughts we want, or our equally simple refusal to think whatever thoughts we do not want to think. The way we refuse to think them is to think of something else *instead* of them.

Of course our lives don't normally go to extremes overnight. We may swing back and forth from implications of Dr. Jekyll to Mr. Hyde our whole lives.[5] But we must learn to watch what we are doing so that we have a clue as to which direction we are headed, so that we can see what principle it is, exactly, that is funding our behavior. Sometimes it is hard to see that "successful" may really be "antisocial," or "antifamily." "Profitable" might really be "unethical." "Making myself happy" might really be "ruining someone else's life," and "having a good time" may really mean "ruining my health." Sociologically, anthropologically, and psychologically speaking, antisocial, antifamily, unethical, or unhealthy are not ultimately profitable or successful. Very often they result in depression.

We are all born with creature impulses to keep us hip-hopping, by instinct, every which way the wind blows. We are not born with principles, we have to learn them. We are not born with a moral, common-ground code, we have to form one. We are not born with honor, we have to develop it for ourselves through proper discipline. Now and then we can check and see by our behavior exactly which principles we are using, or upon what moral authority we have decided to proceed. We are not just a mind having automatic thoughts and feelings; we are a self that has a mind.

So we must understand "principle" not just in the narrow sense of religion and philosophy, but in the broader context of anthropology, sociology, and neuroscience. This requires an inquiry into and an understanding of the basic constructs of such "givens" as happiness, abandonment, hurt, self-esteem, victim, forgiveness, popularity, and depression so that we can choose principles at the state of their lowest common denominator rather than "ingesting" them indiscriminately with tag-along hidden and false premises upon which these principles, and therefore we, founder.

We can indeed "call to heel" personal primal-mind impulses that may not be in our best interest and that may be at odds with our more abiding higher-mind principles and societal roles. This is not a matter of religion and ethics. It is a matter of anthropology and sociology because the survival of any member of a group depends upon a reciprocal relationship with the group. The mind, powered by impulses, is a given. The self, powered by choice, must be asserted. If the self is not asserted as a matter of principle or moral authority, random thinking and rote instinctual behavior can toss the self to the winds of chance that could throw it up on almost any shore—delusion, loneliness, addiction, mania, depression.

How does one assert the self? In contrast to present-day theories of self-esteem, asserting the self does not consist of having people tell us how wonderful we are. Nor does asserting the self consist in us telling other people how proud we are of our special selves. In earlier times we asserted the self by moving against our fear to honor our principles, no matter *what* people thought about us. Of course in earlier times we were also better acquainted with principles.

Courage, for instance, is acquired and strengthened by moving toward our chosen goal in opposition to our primal fear.

One might naturally assume that we would automatically know when we are afraid. But we will not be in touch with our fear if we have not learned to deal with our fear in a "business" way. Generally we play cat and mouse with our fear, and we play the part of the mouse. If we have not learned to deal with our fear, we will avoid it by believing that something else other than fear is going on.

In the case of trying to locate our hidden fears, our primal mind is not our friend. Our primal mind will see that our higher mind throws all kinds of logical debris at us to keep us from understanding that we are afraid, so that we will not upset our status quo by calling upon our courage. The primal mind's main purpose is to maintain our physical safety in the form of the status quo, which the primal mind reads as "not dangerous because we have already survived it"; although it might be perfectly miserable to actually live this status quo. Therefore, the primal mind cannot support courage.

One might well ask, "But isn't it primal mind emotion that allows soldiers to charge a machine-gun nest and win the battle when they know that they are going to die? Isn't *dying* upsetting the status quo?" The answer is: In such a case the impulse to fear has, through principles of patriotism and practice in warfare, led directly to *chosen* action—the pursuit of a goal in opposition to fear. This is how the system is *supposed* to work. By itself, primal-mind fear leads nowhere except to paranoia and depression. Only when fear is directed by the self toward forward action, according to the common-ground principles of the higher mind, can heroic feats of courage take place.

If our courage is weak, it will be hard for us to proceed with handling a difficulty that is causing us fear. Not realizing how fear is supposed to be used creatively to develop our courage, fear becomes a "hot potato" that we attempt to avoid by denying either the fear itself, or the situation that is causing it.

Unlike primal-mind fear, which comes unbidden as an autonomic defense mechanism, we must call upon our higher-mind courage, we must *will* our courage.

Once I was talking to a friend of mine who was going through a difficult ordeal. I said that over the years, when I had come up against something really frightening, it had helped me to think of the scene in Dickens's *A Tale of Two Cities* where the hero has offered himself up to be guillotined by switching places with the husband of the woman the hero loves. While he is waiting in line before that terrible instrument, a young seamstress who has also been sentenced to death expresses her fear to the hero. He tells her that there is nothing to worry about, it is just the time for courage, that's all. I have said that to myself many times; "Don't worry, it is just the time for courage, that's all."

My friend gave me a blank look and said that she had never thought of the word courage as it related to herself. She did not even know what it meant. I could understand her predicament. When my husband and I were seeing a psychiatrist together for our marital problems, the psychiatrist asked my husband what he expected of the marriage. He rattled off a list of his requirements with no trouble at all. But when the psychiatrist turned to me and asked, "And how about you, Mrs. Curtiss, what do *you* want?" my mind drew a complete blank. I didn't know how to think of "wanting something" as it might pertain to me. The very thought "wanting something" was frightening because my automatic reaction was, "Uh-oh, *now* what do I have to give up." I could not for the life of me recall that anyone in my whole life, up to that minute, had ever just out and out asked me, "What do *you* want?

I had no psychological framework to hang the idea of the kind of entitlement my husband was comfortable with, as my friend had no framework to hang any ideas about courage. Evidently my husband was better at above-board sharing; I was still stuck in covert manipulating to get what I wanted. Intellectually my friend and I both knew what courage and entitlement meant, but we obviously had never asserted ourselves to *take the risk* against our fear and apply them to our own lives. We had no practical experience as to the relevance in our lives of these two concepts, or one concept if you consider that fear to take one's space in the area of what one is reasonably entitled to shows lack of courage.

Where do we turn when our difficulties are great? Naturally we will be discouraged. It is in these times we must be especially careful. There are always powerful forces either at our command, or that stand ready to command *us* should we fail to exercise our strength in the face of them.

The law of inertia can work for us, as Shakespeare reminds us: "Refrain tonight and that shall lend a kind of easiness to the next abstinence." Or the law of inertia can work against us as we let ourselves slip into a bad habit. Those who want to discount the law of inertia as a paltry force in human behavior should think about this: The reason we are so loath to take that first small step on the proverbial journey of a thousand miles is that if we are going in the wrong direction, to take even the tiniest step in the right direction, we will have to turn ourselves around 180 degrees. That's a lot of inertia to overcome.

One device that can help make sure inertia is working on our side is self-talk, which comes to us by way of Emil Coue's work. Self-talk is another mind trick that can put either the "law of inertia" or "the law of ought" to work, for us or against us. We can self-talk autonomically and blow with the winds of chance, or we can self-talk *on purpose* and take control. Self-talk is that continuing conversation we are always carrying on with ourselves just below our level of awareness. It was Emil Coue's idea to replace autonomic negative self-talk with deliberate positive self-talk.

Modern motivational speakers' use of self-talk as positive

affirmation is different from Directed Thinking in that most motivational gurus who use this device concern themselves with changing the "subconscious programs that affect all behavior,"[6] rather than seeing behavior as a matter of conscious choice. Nor does motivational self-talk make a distinction between the mind and the self, or between feeling and thinking. The root idea for motivational self-talk in the manner of positive affirmations is to build our self-esteem and establish habits by changing the programs of the subconscious mind. It is basically a kind of hypnosis where the induction to trance is simple repetition.

Self-talk works this way: If we are driving in a country where the rule is to drive on the left-hand side of the road, we are probably saying to ourselves the whole time, "Keep to the left, keep to the left." If we are taking a difficult exam we may be saying to ourselves, over and over, "Oh, this is hard." If we have the flu, our self-talk is going, "Oh, I feel terrible, my head hurts." If we are feeling really good and direct our attention to our self-talk, we may find ourselves saying, "What a great day," or "How I love my new car." If we are depressed, our self-talk will probably be more like, "What's the use?" or "So what?" or "I'm done for," or "Why bother?"

Autonomic self-talk can have a huge effect on depression. Self-talk makes depression seem permanent while we are in it. But since human beings are not a stasis, but an ongoing act of creation, depression (like every other mood or temporary status of our existence) is *never* permanent.

We are unwittingly causing depression to hang around by our fearful thinking and negative thoughts about it, which are causing our brain to manufacture more chemicals. On its own, without our sustained interest in it and thinking about it, depression would be very short-lived. Depression actually needs to be maintained, to be constantly reinforced, or it will diminish. Any stasis has to be maintained by something. The flu has its virus, the headache has its stress. Depression has its chemicals and self-talk (repetitive thinking of which we are unaware).

The stasis of depression cannot be maintained by chemicals alone because both our autonomic or willed action or thinking can change our chemical balance. It is the thinking in our mind that determines what feelings we will be having. The thoughts come first; chemically induced feelings follow. Like the thought "lemon" that precedes salivating. So, too, with our brain chemistry as it concerns self-talk. If left to its own devices by our unawareness, self-talk can become an unintentional self-hypnosis and chemical factory to produce depression.

Self-talk that has not been upgraded to reflect the things we have learned to accomplish works against us. We won't know if we are saying to ourselves "I will" or "I ought" unless we make it a point to find out. We won't upgrade negative patterns of thinking if we don't know that they exist. If we don't know that we are angry, then of course we aren't going to help ourselves find peace of mind. If we don't know that our self-talk is saying, "I'm so stupid," we will find it hard to maximize our intelligence. If we don't know our self-talk is saying "I can't do what I want," or "I can't have what I want," we will not be able to create space for ourselves within the context of a relationship; because we will think we are the helpless victim of a "controlling person."

If our self-talk is nonstop, anxious, and fearful—"I don't have what I need," "I can't sleep," or "I'm not happy"—we will be depressed for "no reason" and therefore easy prey for drug companies and psychiatrists who want to sell us their latest brand of happy pills. There are some quite dramatic exercises to get us started on looking into our hidden self-talk, such as Nathaniel Branden's sentence completion exercises.[7]

My first experience with these sentence stems was at a seminar on self-esteem given by Dr. Branden that I attended in 1994. I had signed up for the course because I wanted to meet the well-known psychologist and perhaps talk him into commenting upon a book that I was writing. The first thing I learned was that I can't promote my own book at a lecture someone is giving to promote *their* book. Common sense should have told me that. But I had to learn the hard way that one gets short shrift from the lecturer under these circumstances, even if one is hoping for just a few words while the lecturing author is autographing the book for which one has just paid the requisite $22.95 plus tax, and stood in line for twenty minutes.

After my too short conversation with Dr. Branden, I started feeling bad, "intimidated," when I checked out my self-talk. It had been a long time since anyone had roused those old feelings in me, feelings that for years had been my psychic uniform. What's this? I thought to myself. How very interesting. What is going on? I decided to try Dr. Branden's sentence exercise when I got home. It gave me one of the most powerful insights I ever had and luckily I recently found that nearly ten-year-old scrap of workpaper I had stuck away in the bottom drawer of my bedside table and forgotten.

The exercise is similar to Fritz Perl's gestalt therapy, which is based upon the idea that we always have within us covert information that can be very helpful if we can make it available by acting it out spontaneously. We are wiser about ourselves than we know, and sometimes this hidden wisdom can be brought forward in playacting and free-association exercises, which reach down past our usual defenses. The idea with the sentence exercise is to choose the beginning of a sentence and then quickly supply various endings in "brainstorm" fashion— at least six, and no more than fifteen endings—in rapid time, without any judgment or overthinking, just off the top of the head. In Branden's presence I had obviously felt fearful so I chose the beginning stem: "I am afraid because . . ."

1. you don't like me.
2. you don't think I'm wonderful.

3. you don't think I'm extraordinary.
4. you don't think I'm special.
5. you won't give me any space.
6. you won't give me enough time.
7. you will brush me aside.
8. you will scorn my efforts.
9. you will not honor me as an equal.
10. I'm not good enough.

With number ten, I felt this overwhelming sense of IMPACT. My eyes teared. It felt RIGHT. I knew I had the answer and there was no need to go any further. And notice that all the other endings started with the word "you." Only number 10 started with "I'm." That observation alone is worth some thought. But what the answer meant, really, I had no clue. So I took the answer and made the answer into the stem of another question.

"I am not good enough . . ."

1. to save Mommy and Daddy.

WHAMMO! Where did THAT come from? Seemingly out of thin air but right between the eyes with the first one. Again, I KNEW I had the answer from my body language alone. The eyes teared, and this time a feeling of enormous RELIEF. The world stopped, and I was lost in the impact of this insight. My parents had been very unhappy, both of them and, as a little child, I could not help. I must have carried this feeling of help-lessness around all these years, my self-talk saying I was "not good enough" for whatever was going on that was really im-portant to me, as my parents had been really important to me. Through learned association, "things that are important," which were first associated with my feelings of helplessness about my parents, began to be subsequently associated with everything else that was especially important to me. And of course all "things that are important" were connected by learned association with my basic primal survival instincts. This is not Freud; this is Pavlov.[8]

My discomfort had nothing at all to do with Nathaniel Branden himself, of course, but I had known that from the very beginning. It was a great gift to have this understanding. Thanks to another exercise I had done a few years before in a hypnosis class, I suspected that this traumatic "fear-tagging"[9] occurred at about the age of three.[10]

These gestalt exercises can give us a "head's up" in knowing what kinds of things to check for in our self-talk. To get the knack of monitoring our self-talk, we can check in at odd moments to see what it is that we are thinking. If we have an earnest desire to know, and thus persevere, we will find out. Then, once the idea of surveillance has taken hold, we can tackle the more difficult moments of stress when such checkups on our thinking would least likely occur to us. This monitoring process opens up the possibility that we won't be limited just to what we are thinking, or just what we have always thought. Something else could also happen. Something new and different instead of the same old thing.

These ideas have been around for thousands of years. How is it that so many people still do not yet understand this simple truth: We have the power to choose any thought we want? How is it that so many people think we have to obey our mind by thinking whatever comes up ("I can't get up," "I can't be myself," "I'm too depressed to do anything") instead of directing our thinking ("I'm getting up at the count of five: one, two . . . ," "I'm feeling fine," "I have what I need"). Of course, in the beginning it may be a difficult exercise for us to think *on purpose*. It does take practice to break the habit of simply collapsing into whatever thinking our mind already has going on.

It is my experience that we can accomplish virtually anything that is humanly possible if we will just insist on the self-talk that positively reflects what we would like to accomplish. Sports coaches suggest positive self-talk to encourage players in competition. Since the human mind can only entertain one thought at a time, it stands to reason that to insist on the self-talk "home run, home run," rather than allow the fearful self-talk "I'm going to miss it," will probably influence our score for the better.

Many courses on how to pass achievement tests incorporate positive self-talk: "I know the answer; the answer is coming to me now." Motivational experts use positive self-talk to improve performance in all areas of life in the form of positive affirmations: "I'm going to sell this car," "I'm a worthwhile, lovable person," or "I can do it."

Maybe that's what accounts for King David's success—he probably sang those psalms continually, over and over, until they replaced the anxious worry in his mind. The Twenty-third Psalm is a wonderful thing to fill one's mind with. Probably why God liked him so much, despite his many faults, and saved him all the time. When our mind is filled with nothing but self-serving rubbish and whining garbage, God probably takes one look and thinks, "Why bother?"

We can forget we are responsible for our thoughts. Self-talk originator Emil Coue would take on a new patient only if he would agree to repeat one phrase over and over to himself as a daily habit; "Every day in every way I am getting better and better," which results in a positive hypnosis by simple repetition. Sigmund Freud, who studied Emil Coue's methods, got from him some vague idea of the "unconscious" mind as being different from "will."

But with Freud, self-talk, word association, and repetitive choice of thought became the "unconscious clue" to emotions and behavior, rather than being recognized as tools for the conscious, responsible manipulation (or mastery) of feelings and behavior by the self.

Thousands of books have been written that advocate some elaboration of on-purpose self-talk. It is the basis of Silva Mind Control, which was the basis for Mind Dynamics, which was the basis for EST (renamed The Forum) and NLP (Neuro-Linguistic Programming). Hypnosis, both medical hypnosis for use in operations, and stage hypnosis for entertainment, is based on this simple formula: the human mind can only entertain one thought at a time, we can choose any thought we wish, and the willful concentration upon that thought is sufficient to make the idea a reality for our mind.

Whole groups of people are taught to walk across hot coals barefoot by insisting on the self-talk and therefore on the idea that they are walking on "cool moss, cool moss." Tony Robbins, the guru of fire walks and founder of a $100-million-dollar-a-year motivational seminar business, based his whole empire on this simple reality—the mind can only entertain one thought at a time; we can choose that thought; and concentration upon that thought will bring about its fulfillment.

Remember the book *Inner Tennis?* Same thing. And all those best sellers by Wayne Dyer—*Your Erroneous Zones* and *Pulling Your Own Strings.* You bet! This simple idea is the basis for every motivational seminar and miracle medical cure that has ever been, and it has been available to anyone for the asking for hundreds of years. But it seems too good to be true for most people. If it's true, people think, why doesn't everybody do it? (We're talking here about the Western world only; the wise men of the Eastern world have long been engaged in the attempt to *transcend* hypnosis, not perfect it.) The difficult part of hypnosis is, of course, concentration. As concentration varies, success varies, but concentration is a skill that improves with practice.

Emil Coue's work in hypnosis was based upon the work of French doctor Franz Mesmer during the reign of Louis XVI. Mesmer was effecting such miraculous cures with his patients that the king decided to investigate him and enlisted the help of America's Benjamin Franklin, then ambassador to France, who denounced Mesmer's cures as the result of each individual's own powers of imagination, nothing more. Isn't it interesting that Franklin was not astounded that such miraculous cures could come about simply as the result of "mere imagination"? Or maybe Franklin was astounded and wanted to keep the true impact of that radical idea to himself. It would not surprise me if Franklin had later adapted some of Mesmer's techniques for himself, although Mesmer obviously would get no credit for it. On the other hand, Mesmer got some of his ideas from Paracelsus, and who has ever heard of him?

It is a continuing mystery to me why the political "establishment" always wants to kill its great teachers, run them out of town, or at least discredit them. It's generations later until we can see the wisdom of Pythagoras, Socrates, Mesmer, or Paracelsus, whose teachings, if not themselves, have survived their politically correct enemies.

Paracelsus was a maverick chemist and physician who spent most of his life battling the medical establishment and dung-sellers of sixteenth-century Europe.[11] He claimed he found better teachers among the company of witches, old wives, wandering tribes, and sorcerers than the "ignorant" professors in the well-known universities who taught, for instance, that silicosis (miner's disease) was God's punishment for the miner's sins. Paracelsus revered imagination, which he called "the Hidden Wisdom," above all else. He called the prevailing and politically correct medical reasoning of his era "the Great Public Folly."

Paracelsus's innovations became the basis of many modern medical techniques. For the treatment of wounds, he used antiseptic herbs that he got from the gypsies, at a time when the orthodox medical establishment insisted upon packing wounds with dried animal dung (being orthodox does not necessarily mean being correct). Paracelsus cured plague victims by a pill made of minute particles of their own excreta. Sometimes, warned by his disciples, Paracelsus would have to leave town in the middle of the night because the irate townspeople were threatening to burn him at the stake for his "heretical" ideas.

Paracelsus's gift to the Western world, via Mesmer, all the way down to Tony Robbins and Napoleon Hill (who wrote *Think and Grow Rich*) is that resolute imagination can accomplish all things. "Man is a star," said Paracelsus, "even as he imagines himself to be, such he is."

Wise men have been telling us for eons that the only thing we are really subject to is our own ignorance. But although the idea that we can direct our thoughts and change ourselves by the use of our creative imagination has been around a long time, because it seems too good to be true, people must write lengthy books and organize complicated and expensive seminars before anyone will act upon it.

Therefore it generally costs several hundred dollars, or several thousand dollars, for any of the thousands of both little-known and well-known courses based on this simple idea of thought choice. Having paid all that money, *then* the person has confidence in it. Just paying the money is, in itself, a hypnotic suggestion. The anticipatory self-talk by the seminar participant will run something like this: "If it costs that much, it must be true. They couldn't charge all that money, and all these people wouldn't be here if it wasn't true."

I suppose that proves the converse, doesn't it: "If it is that simple and doesn't cost anything, then *it can't be true* because everybody would be doing it already." That is what my father believed. That is evidently what my brother believes, along with Kay Redfield Jamison, Kathy Cronkite, Art Buchwald, William Styron, and Patty Duke, who are urging people to believe that we are not at fault for our poor behavior choices because we have a medical illness called depression or manic depression (bipolar disorder), which cannot be cured without prescription drugs. I think Paracelsus would qualify this as a Great Public Folly.

To be fair to all those high-priced motivational programs, however, the principles of self-talk and Directed Thinking, though simple, are not easy. After all, the idea that to lose weight one must eat less is certainly as simple as it is true. The idea that one can have a healthy body if one exercises is equally as simple as it is true. But millions of dollars are spent every year to help people carry out these very simple ideas because, although simple, they are not easy to do.

And so far, although obesity has reached medical-illness status, refusing to exercise is still called laziness instead of sitting-in-a-chair-disorder. I'm not denying that we may need help to bestir ourselves. I'm just shocked that the lack of be-stirring ourselves is called an incurable medical illness, absolving us from personal responsibility and necessitating dangerous medication. The doctors that are succumbing to this depression-as-disease model seem to be sacrificing good judgment for the good opinion of a psychologized society.

Just because we *don't* direct our thinking to alter our behavior and our feelings doesn't mean we don't have the *power* to do so. The seriousness of the trouble we get into, up to and including suicide, is not the proof that we have something wrong with our brains that incapacitates us. We can literally die from lack of life-affirming principles to live by. Failure to live responsibly is not a physical disease in need of drugs. Nor is it a clarion call to the health-care community to expand its mental-health services. It is a psychological ignorance in need of education. Better answers are out there. They have been out there for literally hundreds of years for those who will listen.

Fifteen

AND THIS IS YOUR BRAIN ON MANIA

We need to understand that "feeling" is something we are doing, not something that we are, or something that is being done to us.

When I had a handle on what to do about depression, I still had to figure out what to do about mania. What is mania anyway? As the up-half of manic depression, psychiatrists insist that it is a disease, a mental illness caused by a chemical imbalance in the brain. But how can that be when depression itself is not a disease? The depression that most people claim to suffer from is simply a bad habit. Major depression is a *very* bad habit. Mania is no different.

Like depression, mania is less a chemical imbalance in the brain than our unnecessary enmeshment with a necessary primal impulse. We need to understand that "feeling" is something we are doing, not something that we are, or something that is being done to us. We are supposed to use our feelings as a signal to propel us into some appropriate action, including mind tricks to avoid uncomfortable feelings, like the pain of depression, when we realize it is not rational to respond to them in any other way.

When we do not take action, however, we should understand how we therefore sustain feelings of depression, which
are unchosen to begin with, by choosing to pay attention to
them, instead of paying attention to some other thoughts or
action. Mania is the same—less a problem caused by chemical
imbalance than a lack of adequate coping mechanisms and
moral intentions. Lacking these mechanisms and intentions, we
remain more interested in our feelings than our decisions to
have those feelings, more interested in our thoughts than our
decisions to have those thoughts.

As a mood, mania is a chemical high accompanied by ex-
cessive positive imaging and the abnormal physical energy
surges that always accompany the excess adrenaline of the fight-
or-flight response mode. As a thought process, mania is our
projected "need and greed" taking precedence over all other
things. This thinking can lead to fantastical, often uncivilized
behavior when it is not ameliorated by discipline, common
sense, learned values, or societal mores.

Both manic and depressive behavior is founded in need and
greed, which is everybody's first instinct. Need and greed is
humankind's lowest common denominator, *our basic human nature that evolved from our primal survival instincts to seek food,
safety, and sex.* As evolved human beings, we are supposed to
advance to the use of higher-mind principles when we are agitated by primal-mind need and greed, not wallow in their
excesses like tearing beasts.

Yet, in the last forty years we have elevated need and greed
into a fashionable lifestyle as pop-psych best-sellers have us
outdo one another in *Having It All, Looking Out for #1,* and
How to Argue and Win Every Time. The television show *Survival*
is a good example of what we seem to prize these days, what
captures our attention now. Not our nobility, but our success.
Not *how* we win, *that* we win.

We do not need any more encouragement to be selfish and

self-absorbed. We all want, selfishly, to be "loved," or "saved," or "discovered," or become a millionaire. We all want, selfishly, to be extraordinary, whether it's making a fortune or healing the sick. The impulse to self-love is the primal jump-start of any human plan. The impulse to self-love is supposed to be controlled; first, by one's understanding of its existence, and then by principles, social considerations, and mature judgment.

Without principles and reasoned judgment, our self-interest will not become enlightened. Without this understanding, we can come to believe that our dreams are data, and our arm is as long as our imagination. In other words, we can become manic. Unfortunately, both mania and depression have increased in Western society as psychology and self-individuation have replaced philosophy and the community of small-town life. We have lost our common ground in our focus on the self as the center of our workaday universe.

When we are "so relentlessly centered on self," says David Blankenhorn, founder of the Institute for American Values, "all other structures of meaning and authority evaporate. 'What do I want?' becomes the governing question."[1] Mania is like having a crush on ourselves and our own ideas. We all have had the experience of a short-lived crush on someone who turned out to be a complete bum. But we don't see the "bum part" in the beginning. That's because when we "fall" for someone, we may attribute to them all sorts of wonderful qualities that aren't really there.

Having the capacity for such *motivating positive imaging* is both normal and necessary. God knows, without it, how would we ever fall in love and marry the eminently flawed creature we must someday wake up to? Without the autonomic process of positive imaging, how could we stand to look at ourselves in the mirror every morning? How could we buy those clothes that look so good in the store but turn into disappointing changelings overnight in our closets? "Were we perfectly acquainted with the object," said French moralist François, Duc de La Rochefoucauld, "we should never passionately desire it."

Positive self-imaging concepts are so interesting to me that I have developed a bad habit of staring at people. My children are always admonishing me to "quit staring, Mom, you're being rude." When I see someone who looks really outlandish in some way, I start imposing my own positive imaging on them, imagining in what "artistic" ways they might be seeing themselves "better" in their own mirrors than they appear to me "in real life." I find it fascinating.

Those of us who do not know that we buy things by selling ourselves on the positive images we project upon them, and who do not know that we fall in love the same way, will have a difficult time when we cease to project the positive and lament that we have been shortchanged. We can give away our clothes and buy new ones. But after the honeymoon is over and our initiating positive imaging wanes, the only way we can save our marriage is to substitute, in exact proportions, forbearance for the faults we refused to see in the beginning. Those of us who are very good at positive imaging will tolerate a lot more flaws than our less creative neighbor.

When positive imaging is not imposed on others for courtship purposes but on ourselves for self-aggrandizement, it can escalate into mania. The danger of mania is in not knowing when our positive imaging is so far off from reality that it ceases to be a *beneficial motivating force* and puts us in danger of either becoming an egocentric bore, a grandiose laughingstock, or a menace to kith, kin, and bank balance.

When we fall in love, "the other" temporarily becomes the all-important, desired one—the way nature gets us to fall in love and continue the species. In mania, we fall in love with *ourselves* and it is *us* and our *ideas* that become suddenly wonderful, necessary, and, thus, all important. If distressed, then we become the important one whose needs must be met now, and all others, even children, must do our bidding or be seen as subversive impediments to our welfare. Sometimes this results in violence.

The tip-off to mania is the high state of agitation or excitement, and exaggerated feelings of entitlement. We have the RIGHT to do what we WANT!! Many people think they have a right to yell at their kids even though it terrifies young children to see their parents turn into out-of-control monsters, when there is no real problem except the parent's own stress. Or the children themselves can go out of control, like those enraged school shooters, because they believe they have a right to punish the people who "hurt" them. Mania not only gives us a false sense of entitlement but a false sense of invincible power. We want to do it, and we can do it so we will do it.

Manic people often seem angry. Manic anger is nothing more than excitement and seeing something or someone as an impediment to what we "must have for ourselves immediately," or the "cause of our pain" who must be stopped immediately. Parents can get hyper and scream to quiet the children down so the parents can concentrate, or get to school or work on time. But parents have more history with self-control and can stop short of real danger, unlike children who have little experience with self-control, since parents are so afraid these days to hurt their children by painful discipline, which might upset their self-esteem. For children especially there need to be some "I oughts" that protect them from the impulsive "I wills."

Being mad about things without taking positive action to take care of ourselves is probably the cause of all our mental illness. Have you ever thought that there might be an important clue to recovery in the very fact that we use the term "gone mad" to describe an insane person; "madness" to indicate insanity? How can we stop getting mad about things? Getting mad is simply projecting our fear outward instead of acknowledging it and feeling it until it either subsides or until we can move into some positive action to take appropriate care of ourselves. It is painful to feel fear. That's why we repress the fear and get mad instead. And if we *get* mad often enough and long enough, we can *go* mad.

But we will not shoot up the office that fired us no matter how mad we get if we can maintain a healthy, common-ground connection to our larger community of fellows and avail ourselves of objective feedback from them. This is the best way to ensure that we will be encouraged to see that our anger leads to some action to take care of ourselves rather than letting it storehouse into madness. Such objective feedback also helps ensure that our action will create a positive solution for us without being destructive to others. Why should we care about being destructive to others when they have done us wrong? We do not want to put ourselves at risk of the laws of physics by initiating a destructive action and bringing down upon our own heads an equal and opposite destructive reaction.

"I wasn't thinking clearly," said Nathaniel Brazill, a thirteen-year-old honor student in Miami who received a ten-day suspension from his English teacher for throwing water balloons the last week of school. The suspension was to take place the following school year. He became more and more fearful, and thus more and more mad that the suspension would put him behind in his schoolwork and he would lose his honor status. He got so mad he brought a gun to school. When his teacher refused to give him permission to talk to a girl in the classroom, the boy held the gun up to the teacher's head and shot him. Dead.

"I thought I'd never catch up at the beginning of the next year," Brazill tearfully explained later. "All of my friends would leave me behind. I thought my future was ruined."[2] Do we warn our children that they must be aware of their manic thinking? That they cannot always trust their minds? That there might be information missing? Do we teach them moral principles that they can fall back on when their world comes crashing down around their ears? What principle might have helped Nathaniel Brazill? "Take your punishment like a man" might have helped. There is honor in accepting our punishment.

An immediate-gratification society imposes high expectations upon children for an exaggerated degree of requisite happiness. If no one has told children the facts of life, it may come as a complete shock to them that all human beings are supposed to be able to endure punishment, tragedy, abandonment, suffering, ridicule, failure, and fear. It may be a foreign idea to them that we are to exercise our courage in the face of these painful difficulties in order to strengthen our character and become a noble person.

Without this knowledge to protect them, without some self-affirming principles to provide a sense of common ground in their suffering with the rest of humanity (which connects them to objective reality), children will have no recourse except self-absorption, alienation, anger, and depression, which may even lead to murder or suicide.

Depression is unwanted fear turned inward (projected) upon ourselves instead of our using the impetus of fear to lead to some action based upon higher-mind principles. Anger is unwanted fear turned outward (projected against others)—using fear as an impetus to action funded by poor quality higher-mind principles. Excitement is wanted fear, which we are willing to feel directly without projecting it. We can thus indulge ourselves with fear and use it for entertainment in horror movies or on roller coasters. Wanted fear also seems, somehow, to be a component of mania. The impulse to fear is a great necessary but we have to be careful that it is harnessed for our use rather than projected unawares, or directed into destructive behavior. We do this by funding our behavior from principles rather than feelings. It is a lesson we can learn pretty fast whenever we decide to do it.

For myself, now that I have seen decades of poor consequences from my mind-flights of mania fueled by the tinder-box of excitement, I'm much better at patting some of my high-born ideas affectionately on the head and letting them go on without me. But it is hard to see ourselves, and painful. We must have the earnest desire to do so, to know thyself. Meeting ourselves unexpectedly in shoddy behavior that we are committed to become aware of is not fun, nor is it for the faint-hearted. The fainthearted can take the psychiatrist's little colored pills.

It is my own experience that, once I became conscious of it, mania was far more tractable than depression because I didn't need to get rid of the terrible pain. With mania, the feelings are not the problem; the nondirected, unwilled thinking that leads to automatic, precipitous action is the problem, and it is held in check by the "law of ought" and intimate, grounding relationships with friends and loved ones who will call us on our exaggerations.

Mania has no power of its own because it is only an idea after all. It is the idea that our feelings and thoughts can be trusted and should be immediately acted upon. If we just act on whatever feeling comes up, we produce more and more adrenaline and *can* get so drunk on it that we can lose sight of what we are doing. Except this is binge thinking instead of binge *drinking*.

Speaking of binge drinking, I don't think we should forget, in all this talk about depression as a disease, that many of the celebrity depressives, such as William Styron, also tell us about their history of alcohol or drug use. These synthetic mood enhancers can cause a worse chemical imbalance in the brain because its natural thrust toward homeostasis causes the brain to compensate for any introduced "high." Then, no wonder when the synthetics wear off, the brain's chemical balance further skews to low mood. Don't even try the "but which came first, the chicken or the egg" routine to justify this. Don't tell me the

reason for the drink or the drugs in the first place was a pre-
cipitating low mood. No one except a psychologist thinks this
way. No grandmother will buy it.

In my own case, I think it very well might be that because
I allowed myself to go so deep into depression, and to stay so
long in it, in order for my brain to achieve homeostasis it must
have had to churn out buckets of "up" chemicals. Then when
the up chemicals succeeded, finally, in achieving chemical homeostasis, it was more than I needed to just rouse me out of
depression. It was like Wow, now I can take on the World!
My personality would be jet propulsion compared to the horse-
drawn people I saw around me.

Shortly after I entered graduate school, I interested myself
in land conservation. Sounds innocent enough until I demanded
that my husband give me "my half" (according to the feminists,
at least) of our total net worth to buy some local wilderness,
which I was going to "save from developers." I said I had
worked just as hard as he had all these years and I deserved to
say how half our money should be spent. California being a
community-property state, I told my husband that he had no
choice; either he give me the money or I would get a divorce
and take him to court and get the money that way.

In six months I spent $500,000 and totally blew our retire-
ment account. After this my children began calling me The
Land Baroness. It's hard to believe I took that as a great compliment! I still own a 130-acre wilderness canyon, with a
stream, waterfall, bobcats, and a herd of deer, ten minutes from
downtown Escondido, which was to be the heart of my great
conservation project to save the city from urban sprawl. I put
a good face on it, but I can see now that it was not so much a
deep commitment to ecology as it was another manic episode.
And I can certainly understand why my husband doesn't find
the canyon particularly beautiful, and why, when he tries to
plan our retirement, he hates me.

He asked me once, "How could you do such a thing? How could you take the family's money and blow it all on a piece of worthless land? How could you be so selfish? What possible motive could you have had? What could you have been thinking? Just tell me," he pleaded, "I really want to understand." I said I didn't honestly know but I thought I did it for my soul. His very reasonable comment, as he slammed the door on his way out was "F—k your soul!"

And how did my more stable stockbroker husband let me get away with what really amounts to a case of financial suicide? Probably because we had been together so long. We started dating when we were fifteen, more than thirty years before. Over the years I had been startlingly correct about predicting things or telling my husband things that I had no way of knowing except through my visions, which I call "flashes."

Here's an example. My husband loves number games. He was very good with math and logic. I was terrible at numbers and I hated those games because I could never figure them out, and besides I didn't want to waste perfectly good thinking on something that wasn't productive. So, once at a party my husband began one of his amazing number puzzles and I said, "Wait a minute, if I can tell you the number, just guess it without you telling me anything, will you promise never to do one of these puzzles again?" "Yes," he said confidently, since what were the chances of my guessing one number out of an infinity of them. "Okay," I said. "But I don't trust you. Go in the corner and write down the number and fold it up and put it in your pocket." So he did.

"Okay," I said. "Seventeen." In a single motion he grabbed the piece of paper out of his pocket and threw it up in the air. I had correctly guessed the number. How is that possible? I don't know. I have a propensity for lucky guesses. I couldn't predict the weather just any old time, but if I got a flash and predicted it, it always turned out the way I said, and usually it was the opposite of the prevailing weather report.

I remember my son's wedding reception, which was to be held in our front yard in the early afternoon. At about 11 A.M. it was raining outside. I went to the front door, opened it, and stood on the front steps shaking my fist in mock anger at the clouds. All of a sudden I knew the rain would be over in time and told everybody not to worry. I was right as rain.

My husband had seen me make these predictions for years. He would start to tell me about someone he had just met and I would stop him, "Wait, I have a flash," and then I would go on to describe the person, whom I myself had never seen, and tell him something that was going to happen with him and that person in the near future and it always happened as I said.

One day I told my husband that I had a flash that the market was going to fail, and I wanted my money early Monday morning, no later. He was going to ignore me but by Tuesday the market was really off, and our stock was dropping at the rate of thousands of dollars an hour. So my husband got scared and liquidated half the stock and gave it to me. I had been so bizarre recently that he didn't really know what I was capable of doing. As it turned out, the market did plunge drastically. In a few days, whatever anyone had in the market was suddenly worth less than half of what it was before the fall, so my total net worth was suddenly twice that of my husband's and therefore, as manic as I was, I didn't look insane to anybody. I looked like a financial genius.

It's a funny thing about mania. We are not seen as manic if our crazy idea turns out to be right. Of course, being a prudent investor, my husband hung in and recouped many-fold over the market's fall during the following decade, although he still carries forward in his mind the missing funds I "stole from the family." I know that because when he's mad at me, he gives me the tally of what we "would have had."

Unfortunately, this was not the end of my grand plans. The last full-blown manic episode I can remember, and the one that finally opened my eyes to the possibility of my being manic, was starting a gift-and-collectibles store called Now and Then in Escondido, California. I had always been intrigued by the idea of owning my own store. One day I up and decided to do it.

Day One I rented a small store downtown on Grand Avenue. Days Two, Three, Four, and Five my daughter, her best friend, and I plastered and painted it. Day Six I bought glass display cabinets and a cash register. Day Seven I bought about $10,000 worth of merchandise in one day's shopping spree with my long-suffering friend Bobbi at the Los Angeles Gift Mart. Oh, I was in my glory. There was no little shadow of guilt this time about buying things in threes and sixes, or even dozens like I always did when I ran across a "bargain" so that I had enough to last. This was business. I was making money. Day Nine I bought a $1,200 full-page ad in the local paper with a come-on offer: Free Book ($10 value) with any purchase.

Now, about that free book. I had published a book and had 5,000 copies in my garage that I had not the slightest idea how I was going to market anyway. And one whole wall of my gift store was twenty feet of floor-to-ceiling card racks upon which rested some 400 dozen Earth Rider cards, thanks to the greeting-card company I had started within the last six months. I had to rent an office to house all the cards I didn't know how to market, due to the books already filling up the garage.

The other various and sundry items in the shop were leftovers from my foray into the antique business via buying at auctions and garage sales and selling at the swap meet in partnership with my son and daughter-in-law. I had decided to fund this partnership as a way for my son to make a living while he was going back to school and living in a tepee with his wife and two toddlers in my 130-acre wilderness canyon.

While living there my son wedged a claw-foot antique bathtub between two boulders by the side of the creek. He would dip the water out of the creek to fill the tub for the babies and then heat the water with a small fire of sticks he built under the tub. In the area of my son's wilderness bath the view was pristine due to the fact that all the overhanging dead branches and piles of old twigs clogging up the bubbling creek disappeared into the preparation of the Saturday night bath. My daughter-in-law says she still misses going to sleep to the sound of the singing creek and the sight of the bright stars twinkling down through the open top of the tepee.

The antique tub was the type of miscellaneous item we might pick up at moving-company auctions. We also bought unopened boxes that had been confiscated from people who failed to pay their storage fees. My part in this adventure lasted about a year, although my son and daughter-in-law helped support themselves for many years doing the swap meet while they built up their massage-therapy business. (They now own two hugely successful massage-therapy schools and were the first people in the country to mainstream massage therapy into the state college system.)

Here's that tricky thing again about mania that isn't mania if other people think it's a good idea or if, holy of all holies, it makes money. One Saturday, crazed with undue energy, I attended a storage auction and bought $1,000 worth of sealed cardboard cartons—contents unknown. Then came the frenzy of opening boxes and rooting through them to find things to sell. It was such a rush until the disappointment of finding mostly old canned food, rusty tools, and broken toys.

Sitting amid the scattered household debris of fifty opened boxes bulging their worthless contents out onto the parking lot until there was a pile six feet high in a circle around me, I was ready to cry with frustration, shame, and remorse for my foolishness. My son and daughter-in-law were standing nearby, with silent and concerned faces. But wait! There was one thing I hadn't opened yet. Like a Las Vegas gambler whose last pile of chips is on the red and the wheel is spinning, I was in despair about the money I had wasted and eyeing the last item with but little hope.

It was a huge, five-foot-high, old 1920s travel trunk. For this I had paid $65, thinking to repaint it. I forced open the lock with a crowbar. At the very worst I could fill it with blankets and sheets from the two or three boxes that had finally yielded up something of value. That trunk turned out to be filled with old sterling silver and carved ivory. Just the 200-piece nineteenth-century demitasse souvenir-spoon collection by itself was worth more than $5,000 in an antique shop. Hooray! Saved from craziness again!

Saved from craziness, if you just put aside losing $4,000 six months before on a multilevel marketing company called Pure Delight whose pitchman convinced me I could make $20,000 a month selling soy-based milk before the scheme went bankrupt. Saved from craziness if you don't consider the $2,000 worth of Wildlife Marble Plaques I had just purchased in order to "qualify" as a distributor. Don't you see, I could sell them right along with my cards!

Saved from craziness if you can ignore the $5,000 to move an old farmhouse from another location to an acre of land that I had bought a month or two before, "a real bargain at $47,000," that was adjacent to the 130-acre canyon. I had a grand scheme to remodel it and then rent it out until it might serve as a retirement house someday for my husband and me.

After I bought the property, I found out that I couldn't get an occupation permit because there was no legal access. You can see the house there today, the unlived-in house, the falling-down house, the house that remains mute testimony to my financial and real estate acumen. I ran out of money and my husband quite reasonably refused to bail me out.

The ad for my new store appeared December 17, 1987. I did about $1,000 worth of business in the next two weeks and hired a friend to mind the store. A distributer in London had just bought my card line with a $1,500 opening order, so since my rent was only $400 a month, I was feeling a little expansive. On or about January 1, I received an inch thick brown envelope from the government with forms I had to fill out for employees, forms for the Labor Department, Social Security, and State Tax Board, etc. etc.

It was the straw that broke the camel's back. I was overwhelmed by the thought of having to fill out all those forms, and the thought of figuring out employee compensation minus all the things I had to deduct; and then send in with more forms month after month to the various government agencies. I panicked. Swap meet, graduate student, counseling, book publishing, card company, gift shop plus the fact that I was already selling antiques out of two booths in two antique malls, where my husband was trying to tell me I was losing a little more money every month. Oh yes, and my husband had just served me with divorce papers; he was throwing in the towel. And now all these forms. I sank to the floor, the papers spilling all around me. "I just can't do it all," I wailed to my lone employee.

She was kind enough not to look me coldly in the eye and say, "Well, who the hell asked you to do it all?" Instead, she ventured in a soft, kindly voice, "Maybe there's something you could, you know, give up?" The next morning I called my small staff together—my daughter, her friend, and my friend—and made the following statement. "This is your two weeks' notice everybody. Now and Then is here and gone." I was in business this time for a little more than two weeks. I rented more booth space in a nearby antique mall and liquidated everything for about 25 cents on the dollar over the next two years.

To save moving costs from my failed store to the antique shop, I rolled four six-foot-high glass cabinets, one by one, three blocks down the sidewalk balanced on two makeshift dollies. The cabinets were heavy and unwieldy. I could have killed myself, or someone else, as they tipped dangerously going down the wheelchair access from the sidewalk as I crossed to the other side of the street. Walking by a store window I suddenly caught sight of this skinny, middle-aged lady, dark hair flying, skirts billowing, with the most intense, wild-looking eyes I had ever seen. Oh my God, I thought, that's me! What am I doing? I really am insane.

It was the beginning of my being able to see that the feeling of excitement that I always welcomed as a new lease on life, as rescue from depression, as the only way I felt good, was a kind of destructive, enervating craziness. I did not yet understand that maybe it had something to do with mania, like the *Diagnostic and Statistical Manual of Mental Disorders* indicated, even though by now I was also doing counseling eight hours a day for a clinical psychologist as part of my residency and was helping the doctor assess and diagnose his patients, using the latest version of this diagnosis Bible. I could see manic depression in some of *them*. But for myself, the final realization that I had been a classic manic-depressive all my life never fully dawned upon me until about three years after this store episode, until I was completely cured of it and could look back upon it.

There was no specific date or event to which I can attach this coalescence of insight. I think it is very possible that the state of self-understanding sufficient to see that you have once been totally, certifiably crazy, would by necessity treat such a realization as an anticlimax. I can certainly remember the wild, ecstatic joy with which I greeted the dawning of some of my other psychological epiphanies, those mind-popping, lightbulb flashing "a-ha" moments of insight. This was not like that.

I think that at one time I believed that I could be cured of my life and, somehow, I would then have a new and better one. I think Prozac can probably do that. I say I am cured from manic depression, but it may be closer to the truth to say I am cured of my ignorance about manic depression. Being cured of ignorance is not the kind of thing that has one turning cartwheels in the street. It is, to the contrary, a very sobering thing.

When I get those manic rushes now, I no longer experience them as pleasant. I experience them now as stress. I can now sense the pain in that kind of excitement. It is the same pain that comes with fear. And the euphoria, that oceanic feeling of oneness that is so overwhelming you want to run into the street and say "I love you" to mere passersby is just manic fool's-love. It is being drunk on self-love, not a loving way to be. But I could not see the slightest truth about this until I had figured out depression first, because mania was my "savior" from depression.

Essentially mania can be controlled by changing our old idea for a new one: the idea that feelings and thoughts should not be trusted, that they must be judged before they are acted upon. They should be judged by more objective standards than panic or excitement, or that oceanic feeling of urgency. I learned to avoid a lot of mischief by instituting a manual override that involves simply observing my agitated feelings instead of puppeting them. Yes, at first it is extremely painful to resist the impulse to "go for it." In a few years it becomes your own private joke with yourself and your family.

The trick to both mania and depression is to activate the Directed Thinking process, whether or not you believe in it. By that I mean, when I am depressed I do not employ mind tricks because I believe, at that moment, they will get me out of it. When I am depressed I necessarily think nothing will ever work again, that is what depression is—a painful feeling of total futility. However, as a discipline I have committed to employing mind tricks when depression hits, despite the fact that when I am depressed I know nothing will work. I do not give credence to my thinking at those times. I choose other thinking as a matter of commitment and discipline.

Mania is the same. I do not give complete credence to my manic thinking like I used to. Sometimes I notice the panic in someone's eye when I am bearing down upon them for a big hug. Sometimes I admit in the throes of having one that not all my ideas turn out to be wonderful. For instance, my daughter is looking for a moneymaking project. The other day I got a new idea for a board game and I wanted to say to her, "I have an idea that will make you Rich! Rich! Rich!" But I have decided not to say things like that no matter how much I think them true at the time. So I just said, "I have a new idea for a board game," period. (Okay, so I maybe did swear her to secrecy so nobody would "steal the idea.")

Sometimes it is enough for me to simply recognize the excitement of mania for it to subside. There are some things we can do out of ignorance that are simply not possible to continue once the light of awareness has been turned on. Sometimes realizing that my "great idea" may be nothing more than "disguised need and greed" is sobering in itself.

Psychiatrists like Kay Redfield Jamison believe that it is the chemically induced excitement that causes people to act out precipitously on inappropriate thoughts, and therefore people need drugs to balance the chemistry, to slow down the excitement. My own experience does not bear this out. With a commitment to moral imperative, and establishing habits to accord with them, we can train ourselves with simple exercises to ignore excitability at will and become aware of irrational thinking.

So I am not claiming that my manic irrational thinking is no longer going on. I have simply better learned to recognize irrational thinking as such. The difference between rational thinking and irrational thinking is similar to the difference between talking and singing. We are using the same machinery, just geared up a little differently.

Furthermore, I have decided that I will not accept irrational thinking as complete in itself; it must be subjected to more sober objective judgment before I act on it. And even if I mistake some irrational thinking for actual data, at least I have the intellectual understanding that the problem exists for me, so I can usually catch myself before I go too far and make a complete fool out of myself.

Unfortunately, it is hard for this culture to teach us how to be the master of our mania and the captain of our depression because the theory and treatment of manic depression is now the legal, court-protected, private property of psychiatrists and psychologists, who have divorced themselves from the other disciplines and are having affairs with the pharmaceutical companies. Psychiatrists have their own "real world" in which they must survive.

Many researchers believe that this is the reason Freud's research became corrupted during the time he advanced his well-known and now pretty much debunked seduction theory.[3] It seems he reworked his patients' actual experience of childhood incest by their parent perpetrators into the idea of *imagined incestuous desire* on the part of children for their parents. With this politically correct whitewashing of data, Freud did not have to go up against his wealthy and powerful Victorian colleagues, who had strong objections to his initial sexual-abuse findings.

There is also evidence that Freud tried to prevent the translation and thus the dissemination of Ferenczi's considerable medical case histories of child sexual abuse. The remnants of Freud's seduction theory can be seen in the psychologized fusion between sex and love in the last fifty years, a fusion that did not exist before in Western civilization, except as poet's flights of fancy, which only the most naive would care to emulate in their real life.

The combination of Freud's theories that has sex funding most human behaviors, and our psychologized cultural paradigm shift from goals and principles to roles and feelings has turned our emotional and love relationships into a competitive manic-depressive playing field. The reason we have such difficulty is that sex has been thrust forward as a role rather than remaining in the background of our lives as a biological goal.

Our natural sex drive has been twisted into an unnatural self-image that we term "sexuality," or "sexual orientation." We have subverted the physiological sex drive to be the handmaiden of psychological self-esteem.

In today's culture we are not a human being with a biological sex drive so much as a sexy person based upon our looks, our age, our clothes, our personality, our self-esteem, or how much money and power we have. In a society where most people would choose to be sexy and high rather than loveable and stable, sex and power naturally begin to seem more important than love and community. We have questions that no one seems to be able to answer. How do I know when it's "real love"? What about romance, stars in my eyes, and soul mates?

The desire for a soul mate is a misapprehension. We must each relate to the cosmos alone, not through another person. Any soul mate we may find will devolve into a person with flaws, and unless we understand this our search will last forever. The mystics have always told us that love is the basic material we are all made of, what the universe is made of, and when we chip away all that is not *us*, we are all revealed as *being* love—not being *in* love, being love itself. When we become revealed *as love* we no longer have stars in our eyes, we are the very stars themselves. So, according to the wise men, real love has nothing to do with some specific other person; that is the reason it can only be given, not received.

Young girls do not understand the powerful chemical imbalance in the brain we all call "falling in love." I can well understand how young girls can fall in love with someone over the Internet, or with their high school soccer coach, and run away at the age of fourteen or sixteen to be with their "true love." Most of us don't understand that we activate these powerful feelings ourselves, autonomically, when our mental checklist for a love object has been surreptitiously filled in by the sporadic, wandering thoughts of inferior higher-mind programs of which we may not even be aware.

It's like a psychic dance card, hidden from our normal view. When all the blanks are checked off, the primal mind wants us TO DANCE! NOW! It is an ongoing war between our prehistoric genes, which are programmed to get us to mate indiscriminately at puberty, and modern life, wherein our long-term interests are best served by waiting for an appropriate time and person, and exercising fidelity when we commit to someone.

And if we don't intellectually understand we are supposed to resist these primal urges that come to all of us, we won't make the proper effort to do so. We have to understand intellectually that that we are not resisting the other person. We are resisting our own urges, which, if we had happened to take a job in another company, would be focused on an entirely different person than our current office "soul mate" temptation. It is not higher-mind ideals that have us believing that we should leave our own husband for some married man with children at home. It is primal-mind mating urges that will end sooner or later and dump us off in the same place we were before, vulnerable to someone new, or suffering the pain of our new significant other looking over our shoulder at the greener grass.

We wrongly think these strong feelings within us are caused by other people, and therefore we attribute great value to the greener grass. And these feelings, being innate strategies of the primal mind to get us to mate and continue the species, are tied to our survival instinct, so no wonder when we are "in love" we think it's more important than parents, school, friends, husband, wife, children. Anything else is naturally secondary to our very survival. And let us not imagine we are so wise or mature as to be immune to such foolishness or we will be in for a humbling experience when we find that we, too, are no more than a foolish, weak, sappy mortal.

Directing our thoughts is a great help here. When all else fails, we can remember that our feelings and thoughts are our own; it is only our behavior we owe to our fellows, and that primal-mind love, like primal-mind mania or primal-mind depression, *always* ends. The principles of marriage used to be strong enough to provide us some protection in these matters. But the institution of marriage has been so eroded in this era that it is barely hanging on as a sane, noble, common-ground, higher-mind harbor into which we may profitably steer our primal-mind sexual instincts.

Our feelings of "being in love" are just as strong as our desire to stay alive while hanging by our fingers to the ledge of a forty-story building. No wonder we are so clingy. That is the power of the primal mind—very strong and very dumb. That's why the gushing statement "we are so in love," which is the only basis for some marriages, is at the same time their death knell. Unless we have committed ourselves to some long-term principles, strategies, and mind tricks ahead of time, we are no more a match for the primal mind falling in love than for the primal mind falling out of love, and into depression. Certainly no sixteen-year-old girl is.

We have to remember that primal-mind love, like depression, is a feeling that is happening to the primal mind, *not to us*. The feelings of falling in love are so good we can mistake them for holy; just the opposite of the hell of depression. But primal mind love, like depression, is not necessarily our objective reality.

What can we do? We can keep adapting to our environment instead of to our fantasy thinking and runaway feelings. That is, if we are already married and get a crush on someone at work, buying new clothes, jogging, or dieting and other self-improvement activity would be okay behavior; E-mailing love letters and passionate kisses in the copy room wouldn't be adapting our behavior to our environment of being a married person.

Lauren M. was anxious and upset when she "fell in love" with her brother-in-law until she realized that her brother-in-law naturally had many of the same qualities and mannerisms as her husband, and her primal mind couldn't tell the difference between them. She found, however, that *she* could tell the difference, and she was determined not to be knocked off balance by the periodic rushes of inappropriate passion. Lauren learned to leave the rushes confined to her primal mind, where they weren't inappropriate. "I just ride them like a roller coaster," she said.

Lauren understood that she didn't have any need to act on her feelings because they really didn't have anything to do with her and her relationship with anyone else, *just her and her relationship with her primal mind.* With a little earnest effort, Lauren ceased to have trouble respecting and adhering to the appropriate distance between her and her brother-in-law.

Someone *may* be appropriate, and it *may* be a suitable time for us to hook up with a sexual partner. But that someone could as well be our brother-in-law, or a rapist, or a married man with three kids, and *we* could be thirteen years old! Our excited, happy primal mind, activated by the completed computer-generated checklist that we automatically clicked off when we were letting our thoughts wander, will not care about these little details that weren't on our higher-mind list; so *we* had better care.

We had better program a more complete checklist into our higher mind that has to be filled in before we are willing to dance for the primal mind. The primal mind can get us into a mess, but it is not good at getting us out of one. When the second marriage isn't any better than the first, when the pregnancy test comes out positive and the boyfriend is only fourteen years old, or away at college, or married to somebody else, the primal mind's solutions are pain, blame, paranoia, or depression. Not very helpful.

A highly psychologized culture is very confusing because we are bombarded by messages to be true to ourselves, but there is no distinction as to which part of ourselves we should be true to—our primal-mind urges or our higher-mind ideals. These are two entirely different paths. It is hard to see our own path clearly sometimes, but if we look at others we *will* see clearly that people who follow the path of the primal mind live a life of chaos and anxiety.

I, too, struggled with the idea of love, thinking for many years that the reason I was unhappy was that maybe I hadn't found my "true love." I learned that I was unhappy because I was depressed most of my life. First, it was necessary to come to grips with that. Then, from a mind state of better equanimity, I could begin to see that "true love" doesn't reside in some *other* person.

The clue to true love was the same as the clue to manic depression: *things that don't happen critically influence things that do*. True love had never happened to me because I was not doing anything for true love; I was waiting for true love to do something for me. Then I found out that true love had always resided in my decision to be true, and kind, and forbearing and loving to the person I had chosen to marry *whether I felt like it or not* at the moment. And then moments came when I did feel like it. I discovered that the person we are with becomes our soul mate if we get very good at true love.

My grandmother believed that. When my grandfather had been complaining gruffly that he was feeling bad "these days" because his work was not going well, my grandmother suggested that maybe if he would give her a kiss good-bye in the morning his day might go better. It is such a humble idea that the wisdom in it can be easily overlooked. I have noticed that wisdom does not adorn itself with finery. It walks softly and comes from a quiet place.

Sixteen

THE GREAT CULTURE DUMP

At the turn of the millennium, psychologized social mores have mirrored a skewed preference for the individual over the family when the interests of the two are not aligned. Legally and politically this has made us a society not of the den but of the lone wolf.

A root cause of the modern-day escalation of depression, anxiety, panic attacks, suicide, addictions, and other so-called mental illnesses can be attributed to environment and laid at the feet of the disappearing social structures of parenthood, marriage, family, and community that are no longer the main support of present-day culture. The loss of these structures has left whole generations of children growing up lonely, empty, and valueless; hungry for love and connection and a way to belong. Even good parents often find the whole society in league against their efforts.

In the last fifty years, psychology has become the corrupted Darth Vader of Western culture who, emboldened by power, caused a great disturbance in the civil continuum. Psychology succeeded in making itself the new moral authority by separating itself from the other disciplines and abandoning *principles* in favor of *feelings* as the legitimate moral compass. In a psychologized society, intent (image) is more important than result (substance). In a psychologized society, self-actualization is prized over self-sacrifice, and character weakness is excused as mental illness. This is not a hard sell! The cultural dominoes of Western civilization began to fall almost immediately.

In a psychologized society, it isn't just that we are no longer required to bear suffering. It becomes an act of self-betrayal *not* to leave our unhappy marriage and seek our soul mate or our "true selves." The traditional family has degenerated from a social institution to a psychological relationship; from a married man and woman with their own biological children to any kind of loosely gendered partners, haphazardly acquired progeny, or drive-in occupants of any single abode. The idea of marriage and family as moral principles sustaining a civil society has systematically devolved to the idea of marriage and family as psychologically sanctioned methods of securing happiness, legal rights, and government benefits for *individuals*.

Divorce, as the new "higher morality" over marriage, mops up any remaining traditional hold-outs by becoming not just a fail-safe for the troubled fringe of the marital Bell curve, but a universally hailed rite of passage to self-individuation. Self-individuation means that when we are asked to write down a list of the principles upon which we base our marriage, or indeed our lives, we are more than likely to write down a list of what we want rather than a list of what we should do. We used to adapt ourselves to the demands of our marriage vows. Now we are vowing to adapt marriage to our demands. So what?

So plenty! The abandonment of principles in favor of feelings has meant a total failure of this society, since the 1960s, to preserve and pass on our collective American culture as it was handed down to us. We have inherited this complex society from our forefathers, or have immigrated into it, but where are

the time-tested, life-enhancing principles of interrelating necessary to negotiate it? Psychiatrists claim that depression and
suicide are public health crises. They are not. *Depression and
suicide are on the rise because of our psychologized propensity to
adapt to our primal-mind feelings instead of using our feelings as
an impetus to adapt to our environment.*

And Darwin has shown us that those who do not adapt to
their environment do not survive. No individual species is more
powerful than the totality of the environment in which they
live; the fact of which some scientists are trying to remind us
as we chop down our few remaining rain forests and pour more
toxic chemicals into our already poisoned water supply. I try to
imagine what George Washington might say were he to travel
up the California coast today: "I never thought that in the name
of freedom you would cut down all the 4,000-year-old redwood
trees and make picnic benches out of them."

How can we human beings better adapt to our environment? By using our higher-mind reason. Sadly, even when we
access our reason today to fund our behavior, what do we find
there? The folded, spindled, and mutilated principles that make
up present-day moral relativism and situational ethics are not
doing the job.

This psychologized change in Western culture is based upon
the ethical autonomy of the individual. For 2,000 years ethics
had been based upon right and wrong as absolutes rather than
right and wrong as situational or personal judgments. The
problem is that the evolutionary advances of our brain have set
us up for acquiring higher-mind principles, so our very brain
structures are vulnerable, neurologically speaking, for con jobs—
our own as well as others'. If moral and ethical values of Western civilization are not going to supply our higher-mind principles, something else will. This is simply a biological and
neurological fact.

Sometimes that "something else" will be the precepts of a

temporary cultural imbalance like drug culture, recreational sex, or the Welfare State, and we will abandon our larger traditions in favor of the untried and the untrue. For those of us who have less education, training, and experience in the more universal common-ground disciplines of economics, sociology, and philosophy, the new principles forthcoming from cultural imbalances will take on more importance. Splinter groups spawned by these imbalances can provide a totality of mindset. Sometimes, drifting about in such a metacultural limbo, that mind-set may even be some shadowy conspiracy theory of our own fearful accidental construction as a result of random learned associations; and we will become depressed, manic, or suicidal.

The lack of a common moral framework is a huge problem for today's American society. We have sadly neglected ethics training since the 1960s, not only because parents have absented themselves from the home, but due to the rise of a secular liberalism that confuses morality and ethics with religion. It is society's job to see that children receive good input into their higher-mind systems so that succeeding generations can function according to higher-mind principles, rather than according to the baser self-preservation instincts and emotional impulses of the primal mind.

There is nothing prissy or goody-two-shoes about morality. Morality is an anthropological, sociological, neurological, and psychological necessity. Norman Lear spoke to a California audience in 1989 and cited a high school guidance counselor "who refused to tell students whether they would be morally obliged to return a wallet with $1,000 because he said he didn't want to *impose his values* on the students."[1]

Three decades of living in a psychologized society has resulted in what I call "The Great Culture Dump." Living by our feelings so effectively trashed what we have come to expect of a safe, sane, civil society. Future historians will probably mark the peak of this culture interruptus not by some momentous event but by a single cataclysmic word: self-esteem. Self-esteem is psychology's sacred cow. It is singularly responsible for the fragmentation of the family and for the alienation, tension, and anxiety that leads to the depression in our society at large.

The first result of self-esteem was the creation of "teenagers," a word that did not become popular until the 1930s. This was the first major assault upon the cohesive family unit. It separated out from the family a whole class of young people who remained dependent upon the family while at the same time growing in political and economic power.

For the first time in Western civilization, children who had not reached their majority or who had not emancipated themselves by leaving home and getting a job, could, while still getting lunch money from Dad, look outside the authority of the family for "rights" and "permission," which a psychologized society now considered the children's necessary legal support for their requisite self-esteem. A Culture Dump mother of a thirteen-year-old girl, for instance, can be barred from the examining room and told that the results of her child's gynecological examination is "none of your business, it is a private matter between your child and the doctor." This situation evolved to protect the child's "reproductive rights" from undue family pressure or punishment.

The interests of these two entities (family and individual) are bound to be adversarial at times, and it is our social mores that will dictate the laws and politics that will choose between them when these times arise. Since the 1960s, psychologized social mores have mirrored a skewed preference for the individual over the family when the interests of the two are not aligned. Legally and politically this has made us a society not of the den but of the lone wolf.

The second result of self-esteem, after the creation of teenagers, was the idealization of a female work force symbolized by "Rosie the Riveter," which plucked out post–World War II generations of women from their support of a traditional family lifestyle, further weakening the family. The third result of self-esteem was the separation of subcultures out of their support of mainstream society, which weakened our common-ground view of ourselves as one people. We no longer celebrate ourselves as Americans with a national tradition and a universal ethical base, we have divided ourselves into Native Americans, African Americans, or Asian Americans.

By partitioning ourselves into a growing number of separatist labels, we begin to lose the connection between who we are and what we *do* in the focus on who we are and what we *feel* about ourselves—what our self-image is. We become nouns instead of verbs. We stop actively happening to ourselves and become, instead, the happenings, passive results, and victims of our circumstances. I became a manic-depressive.

I was not a Culture Dump child so, luckily, I had a good classical education that ultimately provided the understandings I used to wean myself from psychology. When I was in high school, Virgil, Shakespeare, and Emerson were mandatory studies, and in college Plato and St. Augustine were requisite. This great literature helped me to think along the lines of heroic behavior and what was the "ultimate good." These books taught me that the "ultimate good" and the love and respect I longed for were somehow connected.

When I was a child there was still some talk of honor. As I recall, it started to fade with the popularity of Ayn Rand's *Atlas Shrugged* and Objectivism, and the pop-psych best-seller *Open Marriage* by Nena and George O'Neill. Sex, giving virginity the Bronx cheer, replaced baseball as the all-American sport, and marriage vows deteriorated from sacred trusts to impediments to personal growth and fulfillment.

Fairy tales in the 1970s for children no longer began: "Once upon a time there was a poor *but honest* woodcutter." In school libraries *The Wind in the Willows* was edged out by a series of popular children's horror books. Poetic lines such as, "I could not love thee, Dear, so much, loved I not honor more"[2] disappeared from English classes, to be replaced by "That was then, this is now," and "nice guys don't win."

The married heroines in 1970s women's magazine stories stopped fighting temptation and began to say yes! Yes! Yes! to their husbands' best friends. Men turned in their old wives for new. Mothers left home to seek careers and romantic love, abandoning their kitchens to McDonald's, their communities to The United Way, and their children to day care. Families were pulled apart and put together like Legos. Honor was laid to rest; the worship of happiness had begun.

Honor began to fold up her tents sometime in the late 1950s and by the mid-'70s it was gone entirely, swallowed whole by success, materialism, and self-esteem. The rise of happiness as the "greatest good" started in the speakeasies of the 1920s and was waylaid for a while by the necessities of World War II. The 1950s tried to circle the last of its intact family wagons. But the 1960s giggled and wriggled out of its straitlaced values, and the 1970s convinced any stragglers that happiness was the greatest good, the ultimate goal, and could be had for the taking.

Honor, based on personal commitment to common-ground principles, was old and boring.

Psychology, based upon individual happiness, was new and exciting. It rose to power swiftly because information channels after the 1960s were controlled by those who were the acolytes of the new psychologized political correctness. Scientific journals and much scientific reporting was skewed due to funding by pharmaceutical companies and journalists who were too willing to pounce on the latest "miracle cure."

News media are the primary source of health news for many

people and their stories are often inaccurate, misleading, and harmful. "News reports are filled with the latest breakthroughs, but they are often exaggerated by inexperienced reporters, over-eager editors, and self-interested scientists" in a communal over-dose of optimism.[3] What is the "scientific" message about depression? You feel bad because of a chemical imbalance in the brain; that balance can be fixed by drugs.

General information in newspapers, on TV, and in maga-zines was skewed by journalists whose commitments to their social and political agenda was more important to them than their professional detachment as reporters of objective fact. Their message? Subculture is better than American; whereas, for the original Founding Fathers of our country, minorities were "in general bad things; mostly identical to factions, selfish groups who have no concern as such *for the common good*."[4]

Because of this fear of minorities, the Founding Fathers set up an "elaborate machinery to contain factions in such a way that they would cancel each other out and allow for the pursuit of the common good."[5] In the Culture Dump "the common good disappears and along with it the negative view of minor-ities. It is now the very idea of *majority* which is understood to be selfish interest which therefore must be done away with in order to protect the minorities."[6]

We can see this factionized philosophical slant advanced in journalism today, which is probably the most trenchant example of how absolute principles, such as the common good and duty, can be eroded and subverted by self-actualizing them into moral relativism and situational ethics. Kara Briggs, president of the Native American Journalist Society, announced in an interview that her identity as a Native American was more important to her than her career as a journalist. "I was born into a tribe," she said, "not a newspaper."[7] I notice that she didn't say, "I was born in Idaho."

Journalist Lani Guinier has spoken nostalgically about the

exciting days when journalists were "part of the unpaid staff of the civil-rights movement," easily slipping ahead of their professional ethics the moral relativistic "activism" of news reporters.[8] But, you may question, isn't the moral issue of civil rights ultimately more important than mere objective newspaper reporting? And I will answer by saying that this is the very problem of moral relativism, "trashing" one principle in order to further another.

Solomon taught us this lesson with the parable of the two mothers claiming the same baby. The true mother would not "trash" the baby in the name of justice. A true society does not "trash" one principle in the name of another. It may be that one principle is more *germane* to a particular situation than another, and therefore should obtain—as it is with our legal system, which depends upon precedence—particular rulings subsequently applied to similar cases.

What principle is more germane to the profession of journalism—professional objectivity or civil rights? Which principle is more germane to the use of public libraries by minor children—the children's individual civil rights, or parental authority? Which principle is more germane to a strong society—protecting children from sexually explicit material and violent entertainment, or protecting sexually explicit material and violent entertainment? Culture Dump answers, based upon psychology, were different from pre-1960s answers to these questions, which had been based upon the principles of Western civilization.

For instance, the American Civil Liberties Union, in the name of freedom of expression, protects the interests of the pornography industry over community standards of decency by convincing the American Library Association to prevent parents from locking out porn sites on public library computers. Do you know what an eight-year-old will get when he wants to study the history of the White House and accesses whitehouse.com? He will get a porn site, with bare-breasted women heaving their nipples under his nose.

Principles of early-age sexual preoccupation are not good programming for children. It's not just that they are not mature enough to handle the consequences of early sexual experimentation. Researchers studied 8,200 adolescents across the country, from ages twelve to seventeen, and found that falling in love makes them more depressed, and more prone to delinquency and alcohol abuse than if they had avoided it.[9] Even setting such behavior aside, the undue excitement alone is a problem because it situates them in the primal mind and *doesn't* lead to action. Excitement can easily twist itself into depression from the random change of thoughts brought about by the chance connection of learned associations.

This is the huge importance of directing our thinking. Whenever we access our higher mind to fund our thoughts, we will be accessing different programs from those programs that may create themselves, autonomically, on their own, with their roots still damp from the primal mind fear and paranoia from which they sprung. This is the reason for the emptiness we feel after most entertainment today, for adults as well as children. Our primal-mind feelings are being overstimulated by special effects, without the accompaniment of our higher mind being inspired by courage, nobility, or wisdom.

These higher ideals are also missing in the educational system in our Culture Dump society. Well-meaning efforts to raise the self-esteem of subcultures stopped focusing positively on what they themselves did actively to contribute to mainstream American society and turned instead to the de-emphasizing, denigrating, and ethnic cleansing of mainstream Western-culture consciousness from the schools. To this end public schools have been politically corrected, social-agendized, and psychologized away from academic excellence and training in mainstream American ideals.[10]

In her 1999 book, *Losing Our Language*, Sandra Stotsky shows how multiculturalism and the intent of public schools to foster the self-esteem of black and immigrant children has been not only at the expense of their reading and language skills, but at the expense of their intellectual growth as well. Basic readers have been dumbed down in the way of sentence structure and grammar as well as content.[11] Self-esteem can be a very slippery slope.

Historical references and stories about national heroes and traditional morality that were such an integral part of the old elementary school readers until the 1970s are missing in Culture Dump readers, replaced by stories extolling the virtues of cultural separatism and the *virtue of emotional responses over analytical reasoning.*[12] The sleeveless triumph of image over education.

"Image is all" said Marshall McLuhan of "the medium is the message" fame. He was the first one to sense this cultural rift in our society when he put forward the idea in 1963 that we had made a paradigm shift in interest from "goals to roles." Neither McLuhan nor psychologists saw this as a moral loss to be remedied so much as a psychological progress to be embraced. McLuhan and psychologists should have been worried. For schools to elevate feelings over principles, emotion over reason, and roles over goals has proved to be disastrous.

In his 1972 book *The Identity Society*, Dr. William Glasser correctly identified the problem in the California public schools—that the students were intent upon their own self-image and self-identity. They were interested in roles rather than goals, and the schools no longer offered what they wanted. "They wanted to be accepted and treated as human, not as a group of children who had to learn reading and arithmetic quickly or be cast out of the system," sympathized Glasser.[13]

Unfortunately, the solution was to supply exactly what these psychologized children wanted. The schools chose to eliminate failure not by forcing children to learn the material, but by eliminating grades and other "competitive" systems that had always rewarded learning and competence on the basis of merit. Instead, psychologists instituted self-esteem programs based upon spoon-fed approbation, not awarded on the basis of achievement or any effort on the part of the child but simply on the basis of the child's supposed need for it.[14]

There are millions of depressed young people who have graduated from high school without the language or math skills sufficient to get them a decent job. *People are successful in jobs because they have skills, not because they have needs.* There are millions of people who are depressed because their education has not prepared them for moral struggle. People are depressed because they lack moral substance, not because they lack self-esteem. Most of the psychological establishment in the 1970s did not understand that the problem in the schools was the loss of basic principles that provided goals, and the solution was to restore the basic principles, not to encourage the switch from mission to image.

It was psychology that effectively undermined the public school system and left the students, in the absence of moral principles, to their own moral authority. The subsequent rise of gang culture, rap culture, Goth culture, alcohol culture, entertainment, and drug culture has replaced traditional work-ethic Western culture as the higher-mind input of Culture Dump children since the 1960s. Children are no longer proud to be American; they seek identity in subcultures. Children are not urged to be modest; they are urged to be cheerleaders. Children are not taught to be good sports; they are trained to win at any cost. Children are not instructed how to cooperate with authority; they are encouraged to sue it.

At the same time that education was falling prey to the Culture Dump, mothers of young children were being forced into the workplace as the working world ceased to revolve around the principle of a single paycheck to support the family.

A lifestyle of raising children and taking care of husbands, homes, and communities had always been considered difficult, but worthy. It was now seen as unintelligent and shortsighted because these activities do not assure a woman of money and power. As a result of changes in the workplace, family cohesiveness, and no-fault divorce laws, money and power are necessary to women in a psychologized society.

The trouble is that in order to get it, women have to do double duty. They must not just maintain their homes and children, they must also compete in the workplace by becoming, so to speak, "one of the guys." In the mad rush when millions of us women entered the workplace, the family and community experienced the most serious "brain drain" in American history.

For years women had been able to move more slowly and deliberately, more in harmony with the secret heart of the world. Women had understood, almost on a cellular level, that there is something else other than happiness—understanding; that there is something else other than success—grace; that there is something else other than knowledge—knowing; and that these things, being sacred and priceless, cannot be exchanged for commensurate value.

But in order to compete for men's jobs, women had to stop thinking and feeling like women. They ceased to be the caretakers of the enigmatic and intangible to opt for the pragmatic and material. Woman had to abandon their power base of moral and spiritual authority for a share of the men's power base of economic and political authority. We forget how much time and effort were once expended by women to nourish the quality of life inside their homes. We don't have the time or energy for those niceties anymore; for the extra touches. We must hurry things along. We used to light candles in the evening, for our family's pleasure, in the dining room. Now we light them late at night for ourselves, on the side of our tubs, for stress reduction.

A sense of mutual respect and cooperation among men and women used to be the mainstay of a stable Western society, wherein each gave up some autonomy in exchange for reciprocal benefit. "He is no true man who ever treats women with anything but the profoundest respect," said nineteenth-century French poet Jeande Alphonse Lamartine, "and she is no true woman who cannot inspire and does not take care to enforce this. Any real rivalry of the sexes is the sheerest folly and most unnatural nonsense."

This cooperative attitude died in the Culture Dump. The dominant mating regime used to be based on romantic courtship, leading to marriage. With marriage demoted from "goal" and "permanent" to "option" and "temporary," "a new, more loosely structured, less emotionally and sexually cohesive, far more temporary set of arrangements" was born between men and women.[15]

These new mating practices pit women and men against each other because they are both trying to hang on to their autonomy while getting the other person to "meet their needs." This is the principles way to see the present state of men-women relationships. The feelings way to see the present state of men-women relationships is described by the title of the pop-psych book by Jordan and Margaret Paul, *Do I Have to Give Up Being Me to Be Loved by You?*

Today's Culture Dump relationships are based upon feelings rather than principles and, since feelings are always changing, generally these relationships do not last, and end up in attitudes of hurt or revenge. Men get depressed and turn to violence, women get depressed and turn to deceit and dirty tricks.[16] Too many families are now simply revolving doors to depression because they all tend to break up within a few years. Children are no longer able to leisurely sink down their roots in their own front yard, where they might soak up some real nourishment; they are having to drag their roots down the highway to visit Dad. Today only 26 percent of families are made up of two parents and their biological children.[17]

Mom isn't home much either. Culture Dump children began coming home from school to lonely, empty houses. Culture Dump girls sought the arms of their boyfriends as a substitute for their missing fathers. Culture Dump boys being raised by their mothers were not getting sufficient socializing by the curbs of a strong adult male authority over them. They began to be in trouble, "socially, emotionally, academically and—given the high rate of medicinal dosing—physically."[18] "A social worker in a wealthy suburb of Boston reports that the women most urgently seeking male mentors for their sons are well-educated single-mothers-by-choice whose darling baby boys have grown into rage-filled teenagers."[19]

Self-esteem dogma proclaimed that divorce and day care were "just fine" for children because the primary thing to consider was that ultimately children could be happy *only if their parents were happy.* But this "trickle-down parenting" turned out to be a false and misleading premise.[20] Children who had been suffering from years of abandonment and neglect were becoming depressed. But this invisible suffering didn't alarm anyone greatly in the beginning because the depressed children didn't cause too much trouble until they reached puberty. I was not the only devastated Culture Dump mother who finally woke up to all of this as a result of my depressed, alienated teenager running away from home.[21]

Drug use, sexual promiscuity, and teen pregnancy began to rise in the late 1970s. Suicide clusters began to appear across the country. Sociologists identified the suicide victims as "middle-class white alienated youth living in suburban neighborhoods."[22] Psychology is little help with this. Here is one clinical psychologist's explanation of these suicides: "Kids who are vulnerable to suicide tend to have low self-esteem and a vague concept of who they are. Kids who commit suicide have real doubts about their capability to get along in the world."[23] This is not principle-based, task-oriented thinking. And people are starting to mistrust these kinds of psychological-theories-advanced-as-solutions.

I watched a TV special on suicide recently in which one of the teenagers, who had attempted suicide but was saved in time, explained her plan for avoiding another suicide attempt in the future: "I just try to concentrate on the important things, like just being happy I guess." I was horrified at the flimsy straw this poor child was counting on to save her life. Happiness indeed! When she searches her higher mind she does not find any principles of responsibility to her parents and friends, she finds no sense of duty to devote some of her efforts to her fellow man, no prophylactic determination to avoid self-absorptive and alienated thoughts. When she consults her higher mind she finds only a quest for happiness. This is what psychology has brought us to.

How much better we were served by our earlier philosophy. Thus Seneca counsels: "As the soil, however rich it may be, cannot be productive without culture, so the mind, without cultivation, can never produce good fruit." The older generation has been better served by an education rich in Western culture that spliced life-affirming and, as it now seems, life-*saving* principles onto our very bones. Thus, when he came face to face with suicide, veteran actor Rod Steiger said he didn't kill himself out of an ingrained sense of decorum not to leave a bloody mess behind for someone else to clean up, out of a sense of duty to his children. And comedian Phyllis Diller said she didn't commit suicide because she "didn't want to be a quitter."[24]

By the late 1980s teenage suicide had tripled. It was second only to accidents as the leading cause of death for America's teenagers. *Our children were growing up aimless, aweless, shameless and depressed.* Psychiatry stepped in to alleviate the depression that was causing the suicide by providing antidepressants. But antidepressants affect more than just depression in the psyche. They water down the anxiety, fear, and diffidence that are essential to our decision-making process and that act as a brake on impulsive, abusive, and violent behavior.

It is a bit confusing because it seems reasonable that we should try to eliminate these negative impulses. However, neuroscience tells us that without the properly functioning primal mind, our *higher rational mind* cannot function properly either, which is the lesson of Phineas Gage. The structures in the lower brain are absolutely necessary to bring our higher-mind reasoning to the point of decision making.[25]

And the unforeseen result of antidepressants, say sociologists, was that many teenagers impulsively began to "externalize their depression."[26] Instead of blaming themselves for their unremitting despair, teenagers began to rage out against others who "caused their pain."[27] "Only now that boys have started 'crying bullets,' as one psychologist put it, have we bothered to wonder what's wrong."[28] With the breakdown of proper reasoning faculties under the influence of psychology and prescribed drugs, the *depressive* suicide cluster victims of the 1970s and 1980s become the *manic* clusters of school shooters and sex parties of the 1990s.

This is understandable when we consider that as human beings evolved, we have developed societies that are less and less dependent upon individual, lower-brain instincts and more and more dependent upon the complex interactive principles of higher-mind reasoning. With the Great Culture Dump, too many of our children did not get the tried-and-true principles handed down to them by society, along with the higher-evolved environment to which they were expected to adapt. They are missing the tools they need to function. They are missing the tools they need to save their lives.

It is a recent idea in Western culture, for instance, that education should socialize children and make them feel good about themselves rather than to improve their character and train them in the literary, scientific, and ethical principles of their accumulated heritage. Thomas Huxley, the English scientist, writer, and educator wrote a hundred years ago: "Education is the instruction of the intellect in the laws of Nature, under which name I include not merely things and their forces, but men and their ways; and the fashioning of the affections and of the will into an earnest and loving desire to move in harmony with those laws."

In past eras we had been willing to live and die for the sake of ideals and values. Culture Dump children are now dying from *the lack of them*. One teacher put it this way: "A whole generation has grown up in a moral vacuum."[29] "They who provide much wealth for their children," warns Socrates, "but neglect to improve them in virtue, do like those who feed their horses high, but never train them to manage."

School shootings and similar tragedies in the last ten years seem to have had a coalescing effect, polarizing people's thoughts about parental involvement, violence, and missing ethics. We are beginning to realize our children have been shortchanged. The problem is not only that our children are armed with guns and early sexual indoctrination. The problem is that our children are *not* armed with principles. Ethically, psychologically, sociologically, philosophically, and anthropologically speaking, our children have been bombed back to the Stone Age by an explosion of decadence disguised as parental self-actualization, freedom of expression, and children's civil rights.

"Until the middle of the twentieth century, it was considered an obvious fact that children are prone to cruelty, aggression, and boundless egotism and that a major purpose of their upbringing is to restrain and redirect those impulses," writes Kay Hymowitz in her book *Ready or Not*, which decries the present-day failure of adults to provide moral guidance for the young. We no longer mold our children into the "independent moral actor demanded by a free society," says Hymowitz, but rather have become the allies, partners, and friends who "empower children, advocate for them, boost their self-esteem, respect their rights, and provide them with information with which they can make their own decisions."[30]

Part of the problem is that parents are no longer parenting. Part of the problem is that even when we do our job as parents, we no longer have healthy communities, a strong, stable, pre-existing viable national culture, or a shared moral understanding to induct our children into.

Just before the 2000 school year started in Tacoma, Washington, eight young boys, ages eleven to nineteen were arrested for stomping, kicking, and beating a young man to death "for the thrill of it" because "they were bored." Everyone in the neighborhood had known about this "bad bunch of unsupervised kids" hanging around the same street corner everyday, mouthing off to the passersby and threatening them with foul language and taunts. They grabbed a woman's purse and dumped it out all over the sidewalk. They hit a man on the side of the head with a two-by-four. Everybody walked on the other side of the street in fear of these boys because nobody seemed to know what to do about them, neither the police nor the neighbors. Now, of course, everybody wishes they had tried harder to do something.

In the 1950s most parents conformed to traditional rules of behavior and made sure their children knew what was expected of them no matter how much the parents' own personal lives might be otherwise falling apart beneath them. My parents both worked and my brothers and I had no one waiting for us at home either. Our parents were struggling with their own lives. Our mother wanted to divorce our father much earlier, but she didn't because of us children. She could not have made it economically on her own. Though my parents had equal educational qualifications, the workplace still had a defining preference for men since they were the breadwinners of a one-income family. My parents were unhappy with their lives and with each other, but they remained an intact family because a 1950s society set it up that way. It was expected of them.

My mother frequently screamed at my father, and my father customarily ignored my mother. But, by God, they did it from the places they faithfully took each night at either end of our dinner table. The whole family ate at the table even when the food upon it was so scarce that it would hardly merit being called "dinner" by today's standards. I can remember some meals consisting of nothing more than cut-up cubes of bread in a bowl of milk with some sugar sprinkled over it.

Our Ping-Pong dining table was the gathering place, the town square of our house. On weekends and holidays we sat at the table all the time to chat with each other. One or both of my parents would fix themselves a cup of coffee and sit down for a well-deserved break, and that usually attracted one or more of us children.

The dining room table was where my parents read the newspaper and the mail. Or we would all sit down for the treat of a half-gallon of ice cream for the family; in those days we had no freezer. Our one old hand-me-down couch, the single item of furniture in the living room, wouldn't hold us all and besides, it was usually full of coats and books we dumped on it when we came home from school. There were no closets in our house to hang clothes.

The reason the dining table was more important than the living room couch, the town square for most modern homes, is that there was no television in those days. We were our own entertainment and the stage was the dining table, and the show played like today's television sets, nonstop, whenever we were home. Sometimes the entertainment was clever and funny. In those days my father brought jokes home from the office (Culture Dump fathers just pass them along on the Internet).

The clean jokes were told with great dramatic effect "at table," and the wicked ones were whispered to my mother and we children knew better not to ask what the laughter was about. Sometimes the dining table conversation was educational, as we listened to our parents' views on politics and their worries about the job market. Sometimes it was heavy drama as periodic family tragedies unfolded.

My parents might have been inadequate and neglectful in some ways, but they punished us for wrongdoing when they found it, without even a passing thought about our self-esteem. My brothers got whacked, lectured, and grounded; I got smacked, lectured, and grounded. If some of our sins got by my parents, neighbors or teachers would clue them in. In those days parents could count on society picking up their slack because society reinforced the principles that mainstream parents were trying to instill.

Society in those days didn't allow juvenile delinquents to hang around street corners in gangs. Vile language was not tolerated in public in the name of freedom of expression. Society has changed. Society blames the parents of the Columbine shooters but, at the same time, society has almost sucked parents dry of influence over their children by offering them a tempting alternative culture contrary to most parents' mainstream morality, and by passing laws that restrict parental authority over them in the name of the children's "civil rights" or "freedom of expression." Thus, as a Culture Dump mother, I cannot find out from my child's school or library what books he is reading; or from the school counselor, who very well might know, if he is sexually active; or from the college I am paying for, what his grades are, or even if he is physically there or hasn't been to class in six weeks.

But as a child in the 1950s, I still had the whole of Western culture going for me. Classic literature (and Classic Comics as well) introduced me to important moral principles and gave me inspiring hero role models. Women's magazines espoused commitment to marriage, tempting affairs were resisted; or at least their consummation was accompanied by a requisite amount of guilt and suffering. In the movies, evil was punished, and nobility and heroism were rewarded. Today let some filmmaker or TV network produce an inspirational and patriotic film glorifying America, like Kevin Costner's *The Postman* or A&E's *The Crossing*, and all the critics will immediately pan it.

The critics are much more likely to praise the decadent and the deviant, as if it is some kind of sophisticated higher art form. This did not happen in the 1950s. My childhood innocence was protected by community standards. I did not see preteen "dudes" bulging out their jockey shorts in Calvin Klein ads or watch "cute" TV shampoo commercials dramatizing hairwashing as if it were an orgasm—Yes! Yes! Yes! (Does anyone think ten-year-olds don't *know?*) Recently an Atlanta mother complained of an underwear-clad talking Austin Powers spy doll her eleven-year-old picked up in Toys "R" Us that asked, "Do I make you horny, baby? Do I?"[31]

In 1999 some concerned San Diego parents tried in vain to remove from the walls of the public library a pre-Christmas art exhibit that featured large paintings depicting sexually deviant themes of old men leering at nude or partially clothed young children. The library opted for the artists' right of free expression. The pictures stayed and the parents had to cancel their children's recitals and reading groups. It's called *incest* when parents stimulate a child sexually for their own purposes. What do we call it when society does that?

Children today are desensitized to the violence and sex they are bombarded with even on the daily news programs. Recently a six-year-old girl and her five-year-old cousin killed her three-year-old brother on purpose. Smothered him to death. They had seen such things enacted over and over on TV.

Sex-wise, there's not much left to the imagination in the local movie theaters. But in the movies I saw as a child, even a married couple never so much as *sat* together on the side of a double bed because the implication was considered too provocative. Neither did movies engender distrust in authority by a steady stream of antihero and conspiracy movies where it always winds up that the "bad guy" is either head of the CIA, the U.S. Army, or president of the United States.

I don't know that any great literature has been inspired by thumbing our nose at authority or dropping our cultural pants and waving our genitals at each other. When did morality become a four-letter word? When did it become religious? Morality, before the Great Culture Dump, was not religious but societal. A sense of common morality once provided a safety network of expectations for us all. Since more of us conformed then, more of us also "fit in." Without this common-ground safety net, too many of us have become alienated and depressed. Paul Gilbert, a psychologist at the University of Derby in England, puts it this way: "For my money, the important thing really is recognition that the environment is key to many of these disorders. And if you really want to affect depression, it's nice to have therapies that work, and it's nice to have drugs that work. *But do we really want a society where we drive everyone mad and then give them drugs to get them out of it?*"[32]

The good news is that I am not alone in thinking we may be in a state of societal recovery from The Great Culture Dump. Social scientist Francis Fukuyama argues that "the values that began to subvert the Western world in the mid-1960s are rapidly losing ground ... in every Western democracy crime has advanced, family stability has declined, and trust in core societal institutions has eroded," but already the pendulum has begun to swing back.[33]

The good news is that in June 1999, Congress decided to give the states the right to hang the Ten Commandments back on school walls, and began considering limits on violent entertainment. Not that I think the Ten Commandments per se is any kind of panacea. I think maybe a series of proverbs would be more help behavior-wise, but at least this indicates some bow to Western tradition.

Congress also recently voted to change the amendment to the Constitution that allowed desecration of the American flag. Although some disagreed with the vote, saying the intent of the Constitution was to "protect the right of people to be obnoxious and offensive," the vote showed that we are changing our mind about that. We are not so sure anymore that our society benefits from guaranteeing the freedom of violence, obnoxiousness, and depravity.

Some back-to-order adjustments have already been set in place, says Fukuyama. "People feel intensely uncomfortable if they live in a society that doesn't have moral rules. Not everyone will obey them but over a large population, there is a tendency to spontaneously generate rules to control deviance and set limits on individual behavior."[34] Fukuyama sees a sign of a return to values in the popularity of radio personality Dr. Laura Schlessinger, who, with her 20 million listeners every day, may be singularly responsible for thousands, perhaps millions, of people re-committing to family and children.

I agree with Fukuyama. I remember seeing Schlessinger about ten years ago on the old Phil Donahue talk show and she was literally booed and vilified by the politically correct audience who told her she was "unrealistic" and to "get with the nineties, teenagers are not going to stop having sex." Audiences no longer do this; she is winning them over. Schlessinger has been a veritable Joan of Arc for the return of character, courage, and conscience. Even arch-feminist Gloria Steinem, who pinioned marriage with her immortal line, "a woman without a man is like a fish without a bicycle," recently became a blushing bride, at the age of sixty-six.

More good news. Welfare "as we know it" is no more, says

the *Wall Street Journal*, despite the fact that we had all but conceded that the welfare state was "an immutable fixture in the cultural scenery." "The end of welfare has changed people's calculations about the advisability of raising children out of wedlock" so illegitimacy rates are falling. Teenage pregnancy rates are falling too. Not as a result of the psychology of putting condoms in the schools to the tune of "there's no way you can stop kids from having sex so let's dole out the contraceptives, but as a result of the principle of abstinence, which is now being taught in schools."[35] Actually, the pregnancy rates are rising among the contraceptive users. "These data," insists the *Journal*, "underscore a significant shift in the moral pitch of our discussions of unwed motherhood once sanctified in venues like *Murphy Brown* as just another lifestyle choice."[36]

Some school ethics programs are even hesitantly coming to the rescue, starting to pick up the ball that parents have dropped in teaching values. For two years, a La Jolla, California, elementary school has been focusing on character and values. "We have to do it here," says the parent who pioneered the program, "because we have moved away from extended families and children are not often at the top of the list of parents' priorities, there is no one home to discuss with the kids how to behave. The schools must fill in."[37]

But they are doing it gingerly. The school principal at the La Jolla school was too frightened to call the new program "values" or "virtues" for fear that liberal parents would complain it was "religious," so the program is called "interactive skills."[38] There are programs now to teach the classics to the homeless in Indiana. Michael Newton, a homeless man in his fifties says, "Socrates makes it clear that you have to have the courage to examine yourself and to stand up for something. A lot of us have justified our weaknesses too long."[39]

Character First!, an ethics- and values-based teaching program that is a joint venture between the public schools in

Oklahoma City and a Christian organization, moved into twenty-one of Oklahoma City's sixty-four elementary schools in 1996, into thirty-three schools in 1997 and fifty-six schools in 1998.[40]

According to a report in a 1995 *New York Times Magazine* article, some educators have been recognizing the need for ethics training for several years now: "Last year the Mississippi Board of Education voted unanimously to develop a plan for the teaching of values. The New Hampshire Department of Education recently announced that a like-minded program would be set up in that state . . . similar efforts are in progress at the local level—in big cities like St. Louis, Seattle, Chicago, and San Antonio."[41] However these programs are hesitant because Culture Dump teachers themselves have not received a classic education in ethics and values.

I foresee a problem with the teachers not knowing the difference between universal moral issues such as greed, pride, and anger and emotionally charged societal problems such as abortion and homosexual marriage. It is basic training in the more timeless concepts found in "the seven deadly sins," old proverbs, and the wisdom of the Greek, Roman, and French philosophers that they get as young students that civilizes people and allows them to grapple as adults with their society's problems of war, slavery, overpopulation, abortion, genocide, infanticide, or euthanasia. Had this same educational climate existed 200 years ago, Thomas Jefferson might have been so narrowly situated in primal-mind anxiety and depression about his personal connection to slavery that he wouldn't have been able to proceed into action by writing the Declaration of Independence.

Should elementary school children be discussing how they *feel* about bigotry or should they be taught ways to handle fear and jealousy? Should school children be discussing how they *feel* about slavery, or should they be taught the philosophical concepts of freedom of the will and the "golden rule"? Should they be discussing how they *feel* about homosexuality, or should they be taught the difference between feelings and principles, between impulse and volition, between short-term goals and long-term goals?

What does it mean that a seven-year-old will know what a lesbian is before she knows what the proverb "a stitch in time saves nine" means? Which would be more helpful to her behavior in school? Should children be talking about how they *feel* about racism, or should they be taught the principles of hard work, civility, kindness, personal responsibility, courage, and respect for authority and how these principles can empower them to meet their goals for earning love and respect? At least we are waking up that we need some kind of moral code to live by.

As a child I was very influenced by my father's stories, which taught me a kind of "code of the West." They were sprinkled with such phrases as "honor among thieves," "faithful to his duty," "stuck to his principles," "never gave up." I remember being punished three times in my childhood and I can see by these punishments that they were reinforcing this code of honor.

1. One Saturday when I was six, the little boy next door punched me in the stomach to make me get off the swing. I was hurt and frightened and didn't do anything to defend myself. Later on that same day I saw the boy with his back turned to me and rushed at him and knocked him to the ground. He started to cry and my father, who saw me do it, came up to me and gave me a good swat and scolding for it. I tried to explain that I was just "getting back" for the earlier attack, but my father insisted that there was never any reason to "shoot a man in the back" and not "fight fair," and what I had done was a cowardly act.

2. When I was six, my mother was bedridden with asthma and,

as my father worked, I was in charge of my three younger brothers all day. (Until I started school, at which time my parents got my grandmother to live in.) I also did the cleaning and the cooking as well as I could. I tried in vain to get my brothers to cooperate and help me with some of the work.

One day I got the idea to promise them a "surprise" if they would help me, and they did. Even the youngest, who was only two, did his share and together we got the house quite clean and tidy. When it came time for the "surprise," I told them all to turn their backs and close their eyes and I gave them each a fanny pat on the bottom. They ran crying to my father who had just come home, and my father said that if I promised them a surprise that I had to "be as good as my word" and give them "something nice." And he made me give them something of mine, though I don't remember what it was. There was no mention of the hard work I had done.

3. When I was fourteen, we moved from our old farmhouse to a house in a country-club neighborhood when my mother found a great no-down-payment opportunity. My parents bought all new furniture, joined a country club, bought each member of the family a set of golf clubs and ten lessons each from the club pro. Everything was bought "on time" and it took them ten years to pay everything off. I had always helped with the housework and usually did the dishes at night although no one had ever said I should, in order to help my mother who, since an insightful doctor had led her to believe her asthma was psychosomatic, had gotten up out of bed and gone to work in town. My brothers all played golf and never did the dishes as it "softened their callouses," which evidently were necessary to the game.

One night I was going to a party and I "announced" to my mother that I would not be "doing the dishes tonight" because I was going out and "didn't have time." I probably said it in a belligerent tone as I was always mad at my brothers for not helping around the house. But my father overheard me and said, "Young lady, you are not going out this evening at all. That is no way to talk to your mother and you *will indeed* do the dishes!" There was no mention of the work I had been doing all along to help my mother. I did feel hurt and unjustly treated at the time but that was not the point. The principle of justice was not the point. The germane principle here was my submitting to my parents' authority.

My mother's authority over me was supported by my father. And my father's authority over the family was supported by my society. I can see that these punishments, which were not based upon the psychology of self-esteem but the infraction of specific principles, taught me not so much to respect myself as to *respect others*. These punishments put definite limits on my behavior toward other people. Now, to be sure, there were other times when my father kissed and hugged me and praised me for things I did well and made me feel "special" so I also had a sense of achievement and personal power. Although depression made me feel the agony of helpless and hopeless fear, when I wasn't depressed I did not feel powerless to pursue my goals. A child must build their self-worth out of some adult's positive feedback at the child's efforts to do something right.

I was a Culture Dump mother who had five children approximately five years apart. Their upbringing spanned those twenty-five years that saw a complete turnaround from a society based upon moral principles and goals to a society based upon psychology and self-esteem. I found it hard during the 1980s to help my children develop a strong system of values because the changes of the sixties and seventies confused me, and left me with a lot of self doubt as to what the values of my society were that I was supposed to be passing along to them. One year I accepted one mode of thinking, and the next year, it was totally the opposite. For instance, there was much more arguing in front of the last two children because my therapists convinced me it was healthy to "express my anger."

But I have succeeded in re-educating myself so that I am no longer confused by the changes going on around me. I contemplate new ideas within the framework of a larger context of human society—no longer limited to simply the last thirty or forty years, no longer glued to the idea there is some kind of essential goal that it is necessary to win. What is essential is that my actions are based upon some moral principle rather than the likelihood of a successful outcome. Hesitantly muddling along to an uncertain destination has always been the case. The difference is that it is no longer terrifying. I have reached a credible and unwavering stability now, based upon principles, which was simply not available to me when I based my life upon psychology alone.

Seventeen

VICTIMS OF
HAPPINESS

If we didn't want anything we couldn't possibly be a victim. We are all really victims of what we want, which is how most of us become victims of happiness.

One of the reasons we don't lift ourselves out of despair and hopelessness is because we have committed ourselves, unwittingly, to some prepainted picture of how our life should be. And depression is not supposed to be part of the plan. When we understand, philosophically, that the process of depression is part of any normal life, we can decide to develop the skills to handle it. But it takes time and effort, and all our role models for depression show us "they couldn't do it without drugs." This does not set us up for character training but for medical treatment. We have changed, in the last fifty years, the way we look at real life.

In his book *Life the Movie* Neal Gabler posits that we have experienced a major paradigm shift of culture brought on by our new economic stability and our fascination with consumerism, feeling happy, and having fun. Our model for fun is the entertainment industry, and so, says Gabler, we are modeling our lives on movie scripts and celebrities. In our new prewritten life scripts, our significant others must make us happy and feed our self-esteem, and their challenges to us—if they come at all—must be weak and brief, not hard-fought and unremitting.

But then how do we encounter that intimate quotidian resistance so necessary to temper our soul in its bath of fire? Up against what must we be strong and prevail? Is it okay that we are all turning into the Duke and Duchess of Windsor?

King Edward VIII, known as the Duke of Windsor, assumed the throne of England on January 20, 1936. He was a hardworking, dedicated leader adept at diplomacy and interested in the plight of the lower classes. He abdicated the throne December 11, 1936 to marry Wallis Simpson, an American divorcée with whom he had fallen in love. Thereafter, until his death, he led a life of celebrity indolence consisting of yachting, cocktail parties, travel, and interior decoration.

Many claim that the sad-eyed but stiff-upper-lipped duke must have regretted his decision to defect from his duty as king of England to join the nightclub set. Critics blamed the conniving duchess for "vamping" the king and appropriating him as her own private meal ticket to a life of fame and fortune. Or was the duchess simply ahead of her time in modernizing the king's old-fashioned sense of duty and service into a commitment *to her alone*, the ultimate romantic fantasy role of happily ever after?

They spent the rest of their lives together, twenty-four hours a day, in seeming contentment, where they fretted about nothing more substantial than how the duchess was wont to break her nails eating pistachios unless the duke would gallantly crack them open for her. This is one kind of no-fault relationship where each person has the role they have chosen and can simply continue to play their part.

So what is wrong with this? So the king abdicated, so what? So somebody *else* can be king. So we get divorced, so what?

Somebody *else* can raise the kids. Why shouldn't we have what we want? Yes, but based upon what do we want it? Higher-mind *principles* or primal-mind *feelings*? If these are the lives of the times, it is also these times that see depression soaring. Psychiatrists' offices are filled with the new American "dukes" and "duchesses." Have we hollowed out our real substance and replaced the vagaries and hard realities of normal human conflict with the easy certainties of prescripted lives defined by happiness and lifestyle alone?

As Gabler puts it, most of us now think there is some image, some role in life that we now have and must maintain at all costs, or some better role that we deserve and must obtain at all costs—happy person, self-assured person, glamorous person, successful salesman, nondepressed person, more advantageouly married person, unabused wife.

Those of us who are married will imagine we might be better off divorced. Those of us who are single will pin all our hopes on getting married. Which means that we can either end up with a lifestyle of living "in the meantime," kind of halfheartedly, and looking over our shoulder for something better; or if we are wealthy and powerful enough and see it slipping away, we can simply write off the slippage like the movie stars do.

I had a friend once, who, at the age of forty-two, decided to leave his wife and four children to reclaim his bachelorhood. He got braces on his teeth; he bought a sports car and a fancy trailer for his even fancier motorcycle; he bought a yacht in which he intended to take up residence, "perhaps sail around the world." The last time I saw him he had a captain's hat, brass anchor buttons on his blue blazer, and an adoring girl-friend on his arm who "made him happy at last."

I told my husband that our friend seemed to think that life was some kind of a prolonged photo op. You set the scene with all the right props—clothes, recreational activities, and people who don't ask you to take out the garbage; and then you just "leap" into it—ta-dah! Pose! Snap! He didn't see what everybody else saw—that he had become a two-dimensional, rather shallow caricature of himself for having lost his roots and his depth when he dumped his problems and responsibilities.

Life is not a play or movie that we can jump into any more than we can jump out of our own skin. We are the play already. We can't change the scene and *then* be there because we *are* the scene. Life is a series of specific interactions we encounter one at a time. Life is not any particular role. Roles are just something shallow and temporary we ride on, like horses; they are neither our journey nor our destination. They will not, of themselves, make us aware, happy, nor save us from depression. They can, however, make us believe we are losers who are depressed because we are being denied what we deserve, or winners who are so arrogant we think we deserve whatever we can take.

As Ishmael in *Moby Dick* said, "in all cases man must eventually lower, or at least shift, his conceit of attainable felicity; not placing it anywhere in the intellect or the fancy; but in the wife, the heart, the bed, the table, the saddle, the fire-side, the country."

When we identify ourselves with roles instead of goals, we end up labeling ourselves as successes or failures. We see ourselves as commodities that must be protected against loss of value, instead of understanding that we are evolving beings who must continue to risk ourselves and fail in order to learn. Roles are interchangeable; people are not. We are more solid than our roles, which are only important to the extent that we make use of them. Roles must be constantly nourished by our energy since they have none of their own. The queen must service the crown with honor in the same way that victims must service their perpetrators with want.

If we didn't want anything we couldn't possibly be a victim.

We are all really victims of what we want, which is how most of us become victims of happiness. And we transfer that onto other people and think we are victims of them. We get to thinking "they owe us" what we need. Now we can be totally frustrated because we have *no* power to make them give us what they owe us.

We have no power to get other people to do what we want. Ultimately we have only the power to take care of ourselves. We can look at chronic adverse situations as projects instead of insults and decide in advance what a reasonable response on our part would be: if they do "x," then I am going to do "y."

I can remember how difficult it was for me, at first, controlled by my primal mind and frozen in depression the way I was, to withdraw my attention from what my husband was "doing to me" and say to myself: "Okay. In this adverse situation, what can I do to take care of myself?" I had no idea that the main reason taking care of myself had always been so difficult was that I simply never got around to thinking about it. Complaining about my husband was so easy and natural that I never could tear myself away from it. Committing the above sentence to memory and "tagging" it to the feeling of helplessness as a reminder (so that the sentence would come to mind whenever a feeling of victimhood came over me) is one of the first triumphs of Directed Thinking.

Since the primal mind depends on habitual rote behavior to maintain the status quo, the primal mind keeps the knowledge of our habits from us like privileged information, on a need-to-know basis only. This is the reason we don't see specifically and clearly how we make ourselves victims.

Of course the primal mind doesn't give two hoots if we are in constant touch with our opinions about anything, or our values, because we don't live according to our values and our opinions unless we have made a conscious effort to form habits that correspond with them. For instance, most of us think that lots of television is a bad idea, but if we were to write down the hours of television we watched in a year, we would probably be unpleasantly surprised. I, personally, have the highest regard for order. I would not be proud to show you my messy garage.

When we see how we are fooled and confused by our relationship with our own mind, we should suspect that our relationships with other people will not be less complicated. It is simply human nature to see our negative situations in terms of someone else's shortcomings, someone else's betrayal, or something the other person is not doing for us. We generally think of our hurt and our anger from the paradigm of victim consciousness—what someone else has done wrong, rather than in terms of self-inquiry, *what we are not doing right*. None of us is completely free from this kind of "learned helplessness."[1]

Gina M. recently told me about an argument she had with her husband many years ago that started out with his raging and complaining and justifying his failures and his angst on the fact that he had had such a tough life. His father had been an alcoholic, his parents had divorced when he was young, and he had to work his way through college. He was going on and on in a litany she had heard many times before when Gina suddenly leaped up angrily and started waving her own arms all around.

"Well," she said icily, "I want you to know that I had warm and loving parents. They never divorced, and they were always kind and generous to me. They helped me with my homework and paid my way through college. All my life, whatever I have done, I have had nobody and nothing to blame my failures on. I have always had to accept absolute and complete responsibility for every single thing I have ever done in my whole life and I think *that's* tough!" Her husband looked at her in amazement and sat down quietly, "I never thought of it that way."

We have to catch ourselves red-handed before we can understand what our deep-rooted habits are, before we "get" that the problem is not what another person is doing to us, the problem is *what we are not doing for ourselves!* Unfortunately there are real child victims. But once child victims reach adulthood, they are no longer victims in the same way that they are no longer children—no one is responsible for them and no one is going to save them.

We read about those remarkable children who transcend terrible abuse and become wonderfully nurturing parents themselves, dedicated and compassionate. They seem to have this theme in common: At some point they reject their abuser as the source of anything good or trustworthy, and accept totally, some as young as three years old, that their own salvation is entirely up to them. At this point they no longer connect to the world through their abuser but directly access what they need from their environment, a much more cosmic view of human existence because although they may continue for some time to be a physical or legal victim, they are immune to being a psychological victim. You do have to expect something from somebody in order to be able to be disappointed or emotionally "hurt" by them. They learn early what we all must learn sooner or later. Our life is up to us. And we are up to life.

The idea that someone is coming to save us is a most insidious addiction, warns nationally renowned psychologist Nathaniel Branden. It is the kind of comforting self-deception that drains the very lifeblood out of us. Dr. Branden said that a member of one of his therapy groups once challenged him on this by saying, "But that can't be true, Nathaniel, because *you* came." "Yes," said Branden, "but I came to tell you that no one is coming."[2]

That *no one is coming to save us* is a frightening thought if we really entertain it. It means that nothing is going to happen unless we do it, *all by ourselves*. But how about the people who are supposed to help us, like husbands and wives? Shouldn't we be able to count on them? Of course we want to count on our significant others. But in whatever areas they are not forthcoming, and for whatever reason, we can encourage and cajole only so long before we will simply have to admit that in these particular situations we have obviously been abandoned.

Maybe we need to bear the pain of that abandonment in order to take our space fully in the world as an emancipated adult, no longer a slave to vague and false hopes. When we free ourselves from the anchor of our vain hopes, we too can rise to a more cosmic bird's-eye view of things. We may see that what we're all doing here in this earthly existence, in a way, is sharing with one another our mutual abandonment.

If cosmic abandonment is our basic human condition, then all we have is each other, so we should be careful not to blame our natural state on each other and become victims of each other's flaws. When we take care of ourselves, the other person's flaws are *their* problem, not ours. Sometimes we can be a loving help if we don't get sucked into someone's problem by making it ours to fix.

At one time I considered my husband controlling and verbally abusive and myself more like Mary Poppins—"practically perfect in every way." I now see my husband as manly and short-tempered, with flaws like me; two imperfect pilgrims following as best we can whatever light we see. One day I came home late and my husband had already started dinner. I came up behind him and asked pleasantly, "Whatcha cooking?" My husband turned on me like a jungle beast and growled nastily, "What's it to *you?*" Then he promptly turned his back on me and began stirring the pan furiously.

At one time I would have retreated—scared, angry, and despairing that I had married such a monster, gone up to my room, and gone into a depression. I have learned better. This time I gently eased my arms around my husband so as not to alarm him, laid my head against his back, and said very softly, "I'm sorry, I didn't mean to startle you, I just wanted to know what you were cooking so I could fix something to go with it."

"Oh," said the monster sheepishly, his four-year-old inner child shyly materializing before my very eyes, "I thought you were going to criticize me and tell me I was doing something wrong." Could it be that my six-foot-one, 230-pound husband was as frightened and traumatized by my blaming and criticizing as I was frightened and traumatized by his verbal abuse?

First I began to understand intellectually that we all function at the highest level of which we are capable at the moment. When I applied this concept to my own life, I found it reassuring. "It's okay," I would tell myself from the depths of some disaster I had gotten myself into. "This is just the highest level at which you can function right now, that's all." That's what I said to myself when it dawned on me that the Halloween costume I wore to class in graduate school was ridiculously inappropriate and made me look like a complete weirdo.

After a while I was able to extend this intellectual concept to other people. Even to my husband, but he is the hardest. It is hard to remember that our spouses don't owe us their perfection. We are much more accepting of our friends' imperfections. Except, isn't it interesting that we expect our friends to put up with *their* husband's faults and not go jumping around from marriage to marriage and disturbing our whole sense of social continuity?

I began to see that nobody "owed" me their good behavior, except for the children I was raising—not even house robbers. I could see that not even a murderer "owed" me not to kill me. It was 100 percent my responsibility to defend myself from such low-functioning behavior.

Once I understood that nobody "owed" me anything, I realized that I could still be injured, but I could only be a victim to the exact extent that I was trying to use someone, somehow, for my own purposes and therefore could blame them ("be

hurt") that they did not achieve my ends. In other words, I
could see how I could become the legal and physical victim of
a mugger without the necessity of becoming the psychological
victim.

But I could become a psychological victim by infusing someone's communication with malevolent intention. For years I
complained that my husband wasn't supportive of my efforts.
I no sooner brought up an idea for some business or moneymaking project than he could tick off six surefire ways it could
fail. I felt so hurt. Not that he was wrong, but that he wasn't
supposed to tell me how I could fail, he was *supposed* to tell me
how I could succeed! He was *supposed* to support me and encourage me! I thought that I was this wonderful, creative, positive person that somehow had got stuck with this negative,
mean-spirited husband who kept me from being successful because he was always discouraging my ideas and thus causing
me to have low self-esteem.

During the years I was highly psychologized, before I started
to use the principles of Directed Thinking, I could jab away at
my husband for hours with all the whys for his unconscious
betrayal of my efforts. You can imagine how happy and grateful
he was to come home every evening to another reason I came
up with to enlighten him.

Here are three of the dozens I was wont to pull out at a
moment's notice: (1) He was not respectful of my boundaries;
(2) He was afraid that if I was really successful I wouldn't need
him anymore and might leave him, so he wanted to keep me
dependent on him; (3) He had never separated from his mother
and therefore I became his mother and he unconsciously
wanted me to mother him wherein I became the extension of
himself and his needs rather than him seeing me as a separate
person with needs and desires of my own.

I was quite encouraged in this line of thinking by the
women's studies requirement of my graduate degree. One of

the questions on a final exam in one of my women's studies courses was to describe the insidious "primrose path" to "certain disaster" for those women foolish enough to get "seduced into it." The primrose path was opting to remain a wife and mother, staying home to raise your children.

Men, in a liberated woman's life, were really not to be considered central, and if they were to be tolerated at all they were to be supportive. This is where I got the idea that my husband was supposed to offer only positive reactions to me. And I can tell you that if he even raised one eyebrow at me, or tightened his lips, or just shrugged his shoulders the least little bit I felt betrayed. Then I got depressed.

Today I have an entirely different attitude about my husband's negativity. Compared to my rash jump-off-the-cliff daring, my husband is careful and prudent and that's probably why we were attracted to each other. God knows I needed that in my life if I only could have understood it years ago, instead of hating my husband because he wasn't my personal cheering squad. Now I quite fondly call him "the Great Preventer."

I tell him affectionately that I can see that his whole duty in life is to keep me from reaching the goal when I have this great "football" of an idea and I am running down the field with it. He is the guard (my husband says the correct term is lineman) whose entire life's purpose is to stop me. The upshot of this is that if I have enough faith, endurance, skill, preparation, and perseverance to get something past him, well, maybe it might have some merit after all.

Support is one of those psychologized ideas that doesn't pan out in practice because we try, and fail, to make it the viable third way between whining and working.

If, in the normal course of our intimate relationships, we get all hurt by what somebody is saying, how interested can we be in hearing "their truth"? If it is not their truth we want to hear, maybe we just want to hear "our truth." That makes us pretty controlling people. I have come to think that victims are the most controlling people in the world.

Being a victim is just so darn easy. It has immediate payback. We get to complain to all our friends, we get sympathy. Of course some people understand that pity is really a hidden kind of contempt, and they want no part of it. There is a huge hidden undertow in being a victim, and it isn't going anywhere good.

A lot of our confusion is caused by philosophical intentions that sound right but have no basis in reality. I'm as guilty as the next person for being taken in by some of these lofty-sounding ideas. In 1988 I wrote a book on forgiveness. Some of my thinking about forgiveness seemed helpful, even profound. But when I got to the end I realized that the whole idea of forgiveness on the part of the "victim" was bogus because any necessity to forgive is based on the wrong idea that we are "owed something" in the first place. We can only be a victim if we believe that our life is supposed to be made out of *what we have* rather than *what we decide to do about it*.

I learned a lot by writing that book. It put me in touch with my own experiences in quite a different way. I saw that life might be more than what I have and who I think I am. But until the veil of what I had and who I thought I was was pierced by failure and loss, I never saw beyond that veil. However, if we can't *accept* the failure and loss, then we see life through the veil of what we *don't have* and who we think *we should be*, which is like trying to look at the sky through a window and getting hung up by our own reflection in the glass.

The forgiveness book wasn't the first to meet such a fate. I had already written one about self-esteem with the same result. When I got to the end I realized that there was no earthly use for self-esteem. Any noble principle served us better than self-esteem and noble principles were to be had for the asking.

We can only think one thought at a time. If we are thinking about what somebody else should be doing for us, we can't think about what *we should be doing for ourselves*. Since we can only think one thing at a time, shouldn't we carefully choose what we think? Shouldn't we direct our thinking toward some goal of our own instead of thinking whatever bubbles up from the outdated goal of our primal mind to be secure in the misery of our victimhood? Otherwise we will become victims of our own mind as we have learned to become victims of other people.

Eighteen

DANCING NAKED IN THE MIND FIELD

Happiness is not a noble value to live by. Does it make us a faithful spouse, a good parent, or a trusted friend? And if we are not those, what are we? And if happiness does not help us to become those things, what is it?

As depressed as my father got, I never once heard him blame it on anyone or anything else. He did not understand it, he did not triumph over it, but at least he had the grace to own it. The psychiatrists convinced my brother that all his problems were the result of "double messages" from his mother when he was a child, which psychologically "froze" him in the "double-bind of paradoxical injunctions." They diagnosed him with manic depression, prescribed lithium, and secured him in the belief that none of his often outrageous behavior was "his fault."

I told my brother that no one can be stuck in a paradox because it is always possible to seek a third option. He said that a child can get stuck in a paradox, and that an adult can "get stuck" in childhood. When I refused to agree with him he suggested I read psychoanalyst Alice Miller's book *Prisoners of Childhood: The Drama of the Gifted Child and the Search for the True Self* [1] so I would understand why he was psychologically paralyzed.

Unfortunately, in the 1970s I did not lag very far behind my brother in my haste to absolve myself from the self-authorship of my life. Psychology is very seductive in disenfranchising us from self-responsibility, and, at first, I was not above falling for Culture Dump philosophy like everybody else. So for me, when the 1970s threw out honor as the greatest good in favor of happiness and individual fulfillment, my depression became not so much a moral failure on my part as the unfortunate consequence of inferior goods that had been foisted upon me at the cosmic supermarket in the form of inadequate parents and a flawed husband.

I did not buy the "disease" theory of depression like my brother did. But psychology did succeed in convincing me that my moods were the result of life's shortfall. Therefore, I reasoned, the way to control my moods was to manifest more of the goodies of life for myself, to demand more from life of the things I needed (yeah—deserved!) in order to be happy. This meant that the people around me should straighten up and "do me right" so I "wouldn't hurt." I was no longer ashamed of my depression. *It wasn't my fault.* It was my parents' fault, and my husband's. A best-selling book about depression at this time asked not *what's* wrong with you, but *who's* wrong with you.

At this point I did not understand that I was also manic. I just thought I was lucky, at times, to be fun-loving and free as opposed to uptight and inhibited. During depressive episodes I would attend family birthday parties only to excuse myself and lie weeping in a darkened bedroom. When I was in a good mood I would stay up all night, cleaning the house or, when I was in graduate school, writing.

My return to graduate school unknowingly landed me in the very maw of the machine that was turning out all this new moral relativism. It was during my graduate work that I completely succumbed to the self-absorbed "situation ethics" of pop psych, multiversity, alternative lifestyles, self-esteem, and feminism so prevalent in most colleges in the 1980s. I have since worked very hard to retrieve myself from this psychologized position. It has been a struggle.

As a graduate student in 1984, trying to "find myself" by expressing my feelings, I began to lose all sense of whatever little judgment I once had about the rightness or wrongness of my actions, which were not, unfortunately, now based upon the abiding principles of character, courage, and conscience, but on such psychological precepts as Primal Scream,[2] Penis Envy,[3] and the Peter Pan Syndrome.[4]

It was in graduate school that I learned that almost any behavior was to be treated with unconditional positive regard— bisexuality, promiscuity, having illegitimate children, drug use, group sex, teenage sex, alcohol binges—except for one thing. The only thing that was so reprehensible that it could get you kicked out of graduate school was *your personal judgment upon any of these behaviors.*

This is another reason the Culture Dump came about so quickly, this psychologized idea that we aren't to judge anybody's behavior. To the contrary, says social historian Fukuyama. "Gossip is one of the most important things that people do to establish communities and maintain informal moral norms. It involves this very basic human ability to make judgments about other people: who's naughty, who's nice, who can be relied upon, who's a rat. It's essential to the functioning of any society."[5]

Historian William H. McNeill also credits gossip with sustaining acceptable standards of behavior. We used to think twice about doing the wrong thing because we knew that we would lose all our friends because of it. People would talk; society would turn against us. In the 1950s the top box office star, Ingrid Bergman, left her husband to have an affair with a movie director. It was an outrage to public morality; her Hollywood career came to a screeching halt. It took Bergman almost five years to regain her previous stature.

Political scientist Christopher Wolfe of Marquette University says public morality consists of those laws and public actions that reduce the incidence of some acts, affirm the value of others, and therefore shape the conduct, habits, and character of citizens, and are basic to insuring the fabric of civilization itself. Wolfe warns that the Supreme Court in the last few decades has prevented communities' attempts to define public morality due to the court's promoting a right to privacy that mows down virtually all restrictions on adult sexuality and by making parental rights subservient to children's reproductive and contraceptive rights. Furthermore, the Supreme Court, by effectively redefining the term "obscene" down to practically nothing, has effectively erased the whole notion of public standards of propriety.[6]

The rationale for public morality, claims Harry Clor, a political scientist from Kenyon College, is that human beings have powerful irrational or unsocial inclinations that must be moderated to achieve self-control and civility, indeed, to achieve civilization itself. Unfortunately the customs and traditions that sustain good character have been undermined since the 1970s by legal protection for depersonalized sexuality and eroticized violence. The "celebrated nonjudgmentalism of contemporary America" and the privatizing and community-weakening dynamic that encourages people to act as "radically autonomous bundles of appetites" erodes self-control and moderation as much as does the dispensing of condoms to eighth-graders.[7] The moral outrage of our fellows used to be a governing force that kept us on the straight and narrow when we were tempted to indulge our more selfish, baser instincts.

In graduate school there was no straight and narrow; *moral outrage was the only sin.* In graduate school, personal judgment upon another person's behavior was not to be tolerated in any form. In graduate school our behavior was not the cause of our failure or despair. The instructor enlightened us that the goal

of psychotherapy was to learn how to express hidden and repressed feelings that were the unconscious cause of our failure
and despair.

Pillow beating for victims, in which the pillow represented
someone who had wronged us, was considered a good device
for getting out our hidden ire and learning how to express our
anger so that we would feel better. We were supposed to get
in touch with our feelings by talking about our fears, analyzing
our dreams, studying our perceived inadequacies, our hopes,
and whether we were happy or sad at any particular moment.
I got the hang of it after a while.

On a break from graduate school, I visited my teenage
daughter in Hawaii, where she was living on next to nothing
as a waitress. She had lovingly spent $15 on a floral lei to wel-
come me. I suddenly experienced this great pain that became
my whole focus. My daughter asked me what was wrong and
I said that I had always wanted a lei made out of plumerias
rather than the carnations she had just given me. The dear child
put her arm around me and let me cry out my pain on her
shoulder. In the immortal words of my mother: "What utter
crap!" But at the time I was following the political correctness
of the psychologists not to "repress my emotions," to "communicate honestly," to be "guided by my feelings," the perfect
breeding ground for a career manic-depressive.

Before too long, under this influence, my creativity degenerated into exhibitionism. Many of my heedless antics outraged
friends and lost my husband some of his best clients. I was
disciplined enough to jog and do yoga almost daily but, proud
of my body, when the euphoria of mania struck, I would suddenly get up and dreamily gyrate on the dance floor by myself
at formal dinner parties, or swim nude during backyard barbecues. One time I announced that I was going for a "skinny
dip" and one of my guests said that if I did her middle-age
husband would probably have a heart attack. Do you think that
stopped me? We never saw that couple again.

Once I fashioned a daring "sheath" dress, which I wore over black tights and rhinestone high heels to my husband's annual office Christmas dinner-dance. To make the dress, I cut a low neck and armholes in a dark green 40-gallon plastic garbage bag, which I cinched at the waist with a "perky" patent leather belt! Wasn't I the fun person! I couldn't imagine why some fuddy-duddy people in elaborate beaded gowns and tuxedos were offended!

My friends thought of me in those days as "driven" and distracted, a bit weird, like their own private, living soap opera they could check in on when they got bored. I was busy, busy busy, my children watching as my skirts ran by them. My days were exhausted in never-ending projects; I spent sleepless nights anguished by the fact that I was not happy.

It would have been incomprehensible to me, in those days, if someone had told me that one day I would take no more active, on-going interest in my happiness than I would in my digestive process. In retrospect I think my relationship with my children, although not perfect, was pretty okay. As for my relationship with my husband, I was extremely dependent, my understanding of commitment was more like security, and my idea of true love and happiness was really mania.

My experience with my family at this time was similar to all the mutually hurtful and anguished couples who would years later bring their problems to my counseling office. They could remember past arguments by how angry and hurt they were, but were very vague as to the exact point upon which they disagreed.

I remember clearly one unhappy family scene because I wrote it down to record the proof of how insufficient and unloving my husband and children were and, finding my old notebook years later, I saved it to remind myself how deluded and crazy I had once been. God help me, psychotherapy on top of manic depression had turned me into a come-alive, walking-around Tennessee Williams play.

Here is the scene. It is my birthday. I am looking to see how my husband and children are going to fail me this time. Why? Because somehow this has become my sacred duty. The women psychologists at the university encouraged me to take a dim who-needs-em-anyway view of men, One of our psychology texts was a book called *The Longest War*, which delineated centuries of abuse that women had endured at the hands of men.[8]

As if I needed any more encouragement to heap blame on my poor husband! My therapists have convinced me that I am codependent, have a lot of repressed anger, and I need to become more aware of my feelings. Codependent means that I let other people take advantage of me and it's not good for them either. I take all this to mean that I can only be happy if I register and track every tiny, insignificant hurt to its "cause" and exact an apology from the "perpetrator." In addition, I am already perpetually annoyed that my husband is of little help to me in the pursuit of my happiness, which pursuit is based upon strict adherence to psychological jargon.

After all, I am the one with A's in graduate school. He is the ignorant one who will never read the *Dance of Anger,* or learn the communication systems of Virginia Satir. I am the psychotherapist, among the top 20 percent who pass both the oral and written California state boards on the first try. He will never understand family dynamics or psychoanalytic theory. His failure to be a proper support is truly heartrending to me, the brilliant one, who knows everything there is to know about communication and human motivation.

Also let me say that I have just changed my name from Arline Curtiss to Dhira Starfield. That should tell you something right there. Now, here is the birthday party: As we are ready to go into the house where the children have prepared a little festivity for me, my husband turns to me and smiles, "Well, have you had a good birthday?" Did I smile back and say "Yes, thank you"? Perhaps give him a little hug and kiss?

Not on your life! I suddenly felt the thin veneer of my happiness fracture like eggshell around me as I slid helplessly into the abyss of my ever-waiting despair. The life just went out of me and I became as frozen as a stone. Then a furious, silent rage began to sear my soul from this latest assault. Who could put up with such a controlling person, such a bumbling oaf of a husband? And what, you may be wondering, was my husband's terrible crime?

The crime was that he had dared to start a conversation with a question! Hadn't I instructed him, time after time, that good communication meant that you have to share something about your own feelings first, *risk yourself* first? Hadn't I told him that he is trying to control me when he starts a conversation with a question, because by requiring me to answer him, he is making me less-than, putting me on the defensive?

No wonder I always get depressed, I thought. No wonder our relationship is a failure. No wonder I'm so unhappy. It's all his fault. How can I go on in the face of such a betrayal, and on my birthday too! I began to cry. I blew out the candles and cut the cake with tears streaming down my face. No one says anything about my crying because by now everyone is used to Mother being depressed.

My "great hurt" begins to fester as I see the situation in terms of nobody cares enough to ask me why I am crying. And because they won't ask me what is wrong I won't give them the satisfaction of telling them. Oh, I am a veritable wonder in communication! Why should I say anything to them—they are cruel and unfeeling and I wouldn't treat a dog the way I am being treated! *And on my birthday, too.*

Usually when I go this far into the victim mode I visualize leaving all my possessions behind and walking proudly away with just the clothes on my back, I want *nothing* from them, nothing! This is certainly irrational thinking, but it has nothing to do with chemical imbalance in the brain.

My brother says that he must be able to trust his own mind

and therefore he blames his manic depression on out-of-kilter chemicals in his brain and a destructive and unsupportive family, rather than simply wrong thinking, bad judgment, and weak character. I say that one's mind and thinking is the *first* thing one should question. Against what standard? Yes, that is the problem. What does one use to check out the validity of one's thinking? I had to figure that out in order to find sanity.

I tackled depression first as it was the squeaky wheel. Mania is a little different from depression because you don't know right away, feeling-wise, the minute you are into it. I know many, many people who take various drugs to combat depression. I have asked them if they have ever suffered from mania, and most of them say no. But my experience of them is that their drugs are allowing them to live a life of watered-down mania. They seem tense and brittle just underneath a very surface calm. And I think they believe, as I once did, that their manic moods are their good days.

I have witnessed depressed people in church meetings and at new-age encounter groups, "saved" by mania, who believed that the soulful gleam in their eye was love. Some of us have wider mood swings than others, but I am now convinced that if you suffer from depression, ipso facto, you also suffer from mania. I think others will be coming around to this notion very soon. Depression used to be a good way to tell if a child was in trouble, now, with so many children on antidepressants, mania may be the sole clue that something is wrong.

Antidepressants minimize depression, as well as fear and anxiety, which are our natural defense mechanisms against antisocial behavior. Vandalism, precocious sexual activity, and cruelty to animals by children is most probably mania. It may turn out to be that a child's long-range, carefully orchestrated plan to bomb or shoot up a school may be a case of full-blown mania! But depression has received all the attention; mania has been pretty much ignored.

Observing our own depression is duck soup because it hurts. Observing mania is really difficult, we have to be educated to it. Even with the wide mood swings I had, I never experienced myself as being manic. I didn't even see it in others as clearly as I saw depression. My father and brother only sought me out in their low moods, when they wanted to tell me of their suicide plans. The few times I saw either one of them "high," they could con me into agreeing with them because I didn't want to burst their bubble on the off-chance something good would come of their exaggerated claims. Mostly when they were high, they were out in the world being phenomenal. When I was "being phenomenal" myself, I thought that's what I was supposed to do too; go for the gold, right? It is natural to want a cure for depression because it hurts so bad we feel like we are dying. But it's hard to realize we need to cure ourselves of feeling so terrific.

I haven't studied anybody else's thinking from the inside as I have my own. But it seems to me that my thinking style is often very different from my husband's. When we talk, he sticks to the subject and confines himself to a few good points that answer the question at hand. He doesn't carry a point beyond its logical conclusion. Of course he's not perfect, either. He sometimes drags on about things that I think could very well go without saying, he has a nasty temper at times, and he can't envision a finished project from the sum of its pieces lying on the ground.

But neither will my husband's style of thinking get him into situations where he bites off more than he can chew. He is rational and linear. My style of thinking is often fanciful and chaotic and, as such, it can be downright dangerous. I was once talking to a friend and suddenly became painfully aware that I could barely contain my excitement about all the possibilities of the subject at hand. I could hardly verbalize all the terrific ideas I wanted to blurt out, and dance around with, and interrupt him because of. I realized with alarm, I don't *think*, I *brainstorm*. Remember the old 1960s slogan "Question Authority"? I realized at that moment that my slogan should be "Question Thinking."

Brainstorming is a very valuable tool. Used appropriately, it is responsible for some good novels, some great new inventions, and wonderful adaptations of old ones. But this kind of thinking is an irrational art form with high entertainment value. It does not concern itself with morality, feasibility, or even good manners, and thus has very little to do with proper conclusions.

If all a committee did was brainstorm, it would always be high on peak energy but little real work would get done. With brainstorming, one is supposed to set aside practicality, appropriateness, cost, etc. In fact, all considerations are set aside except the raw, creative, juicy idea that feels so good coming through. The dry work of sifting through the chaff for the kernel of wheat comes later. In mania, there is no later, sober judgment that precedes action. The middle piece of the equation for rational behavior is missing:

$$\text{Idea} + \text{sober judgment} = \text{action.}$$

I believe there are some of us who have learned to call upon our adrenaline reserves for this uncontrolled, breakneck mental speed, this racehorse type of manic brainstorm thinking. We can do amazing things with the mind; it is, after all, a tool for our use. For instance, years ago I took a course in hypnosis and learned to cure my migraine headaches by mentally constricting the blood vessels in my brain. My husband laughed at me until he tried it for himself with equal success. We have almost unlimited options for Directed Thinking, so there is no good reason to be led astray by nondirected, unchosen thinking, either depressive or manic.

When I finally realized that mania was causing me serious problems, it was obvious to me that I needed to distinguish somehow between rational, regular thinking and irrational brainstorming *before* I acted upon my latest "great" idea. The clue turned out to be extreme excitement. To put it a bit crassly, you would be having a whole lot more excitement if you were making love to someone new rather than a spouse of twenty years. That's about the level of difference between the excitement accompanying these two different thinkings. Also, rational thinking does not come without some doubt and uncertainty. *Doubt and uncertainty are totally absent in mania.*

Both thinking modes are good. We need to be capable of irrational thought because that is how human beings evolve as creative thinkers. But we have to know which mode of thinking we are in because they serve different functions. Not caring to know which mode we are in is analogous to not caring to know whether it is a car or a boat we are driving down the highway.

Not knowing if we are thinking rationally or are off on this other tangential mode of thinking is like not knowing whether we are astride a plow horse or a racehorse. If we think it's just a good old plow horse, and we don't know that it might take off at any moment, we won't take the proper precautions. And if we call upon it often enough, and let it feed at will, sometimes this "thinking racehorse" comes unbidden, throws us upon its back, and before we know it we are off and running amok, with our sober judgment barely holding on for dear life.

I am now committed to checking out my level of excitement and searching for some hint of doubt and uncertainty when I cogitate some new scheme. That is, I have learned to lift the veil of mania away from ideas like producing a video, or writing a musical comedy, and take another look. This helps to neutralize one of my main problems—grandiosity.

That not everyone is similarly troubled by depression or volatile mood swings need not discourage those of us who are. Some people seem to have acquired, early on, the knack of emotional checks and balances, and can work out any undue angst on the racquetball court or in the gym. They may be equally unaware of what their values are, but perhaps their unconsciously acquired ones serve them better. They seem more down to earth and levelheaded. My husband is that way, probably what attracted me to him in the first place. I said to him the other night, "I just realized something about you. You don't get depressed. You don't get crazy, wild ideas. And you don't have to worry about maintaining your sanity the way I do."

But I also remember an earlier conversation we had. It was one of those soft spring evenings when everything seemed to be perfect, a magic moment. All our five children were doing well, we weren't mad at each other for anything, and the house was all put to rights in preparation for a houseguest. My husband and I were enjoying a quiet glass of wine before dinner, just the two of us. We even had a John Denver CD on.

I sighed contentedly, turned to him, and said, "Are you one hundred percent happy right this minute like I am?" He gave me an odd look and said he couldn't remember ever being 100 percent happy. In his whole life. Couldn't even relate to such an idea. Didn't even know what I was talking about.

What if it is true, as poets and wise men have claimed, that a soul may climb the highest peaks of joy only to the exact extent that it is willing to descend into the lowest valleys of despair? Those of us who struggle with depression may be able to experience moments of passion and creativity that pass by our more stable brothers. Who among us will be so anxious for the doctors to rid us of our black holes if we understand that our stars may disappear as well?

It's a tricky thing about mania because when our manic ideas work, we don't look as crazy as we really are. I took an adult course in creative writing and in manic, start-at-the-top mode, sent the first essay I ever wrote to the *New York Times*. Within days I got a telephone call from someone on the staff who told me that they would be "proud to publish this beautiful piece of writing!" The essay was also picked up by the *Boston Globe* and published on its op-ed page.

When I took up the guitar and wrote folk songs, I flew to New York on a dare, without so much as a name, much less an appointment. I looked up the address of RCA and went straight there. I ended up with my songs under contract to RCA and later United Artists. My songs were published and produced as demo records although they never sold to any performing artists. Because these ideas gained some legitimacy and garnered some objective positive feedback didn't mean I wasn't undergoing severe manic episodes at the time I was doing them. I didn't make any distinction between my ideas except whether or not they appealed to me. I didn't judge them. I just did them.

It is truly a vicious cycle. When we are so identified with our feelings as "us," narcissism *is* the automatic, natural coping mechanism that alleviates the emotional pain of fear. Narcissism means that all other people are automatically relegated to class B, leaving us in class A all by ourselves. We become lonely there and, in our alienation from others, believe that it is other people who have frozen us out.

But that is not true. Other people have not frozen us out; we have withdrawn from them. We are unconsciously using the people in Class B to serve us somehow. When we get low and things are not working out for us, we think the people in Class B are cruel to us and we hate them. Or, if our narcissism happens to be working and we are feeling high, our relationship to other people is cooperative but condescending and controlling rather than warm and accepting.

Slowly, after I began counseling others full time, I began to understand that the high incidence of mania and depression I was seeing in my own life and in the lives of my patients was more sociocultural than biopsychological, more a matter of classical conditioning than chemical imbalance. All our suffering had a sense of biological and psychological unreality about it in the sense that, unlike describing a sore throat to a medical practitioner, we were terribly vague and indefinite about what was wrong with us. So much so that we usually didn't describe exactly what was wrong but exactly how we wanted our lives to be different.

Also, there was always some kind of claim or dueness involved, that this should not be happening to us, that we should be somehow exempted. By virtue of what? That we *deserved* better. I'm afraid that we Culture Dump Americans have been encouraged to consider more what we are owed than what is our duty. We feel "entitled" and when we don't get what we expect we turn anxious and aggressive, which ultimately turns into depression.

Recently a fourth-grader in Alcoa, Tennessee, hired a lawyer to force her elementary school to provide better fare in the lunchroom. She and her friends were fed up with pinto beans, cornbread, and salad.[9] The lawyer said he was "proud to represent" such "a spunky kid" for $1 (and a lot of free publicity).

A homeowner in Haverstraw, New York, had to be taken to court last year before she would put the "right" side of her picket fencing facing her neighbors instead of the raw, unfinished side. "If I'm buying it," she said, "I feel I should be able to see the nicer side of it."[10] We have gone socioculturally bankrupt because everybody has been intent on withdrawals; nobody has been wanting to make any deposits.

I remember a news story several years ago, the sad tale of two mothers rushing home to their children at the end of a hard workday. In a road-rage dispute one out-of-control mother got out of her car screaming obscenities at the other. She threw a Coke bottle at the "offending" car and then spat at the driver through her open car window. Instead of simply driving away, the spat-upon, out-of-control mother drew a gun and shot the spitting Coke thrower in the face—dead. One life ended, one life ruined. Children devastated. What are the higher-mind principles underlying such an event? Happiness? Entitlement? Self-esteem?

With no idea of real community, no love of duty, with no programming of principles into our higher mind that protect us, our higher mind can become nothing but a checklist of self-centered pursuits designed to bring us happiness and success; but focusing us away from common ground with our fellows, leading us into alienation and despair, and ultimately to depression. "The Internet is a perfect example of the modern idea of community. We want to associate but we want no restrictions on our behavior, we want complete freedom to enter or exit, we want the autonomy of our individualism."[11]

It didn't used to be this way. The trouble is that in a psychologized society all motivational speakers tend to focus us on how we can feel good about ourselves by going for our dream. A hundred years ago the speakers advocated order over ambition. Theologian Henry Ward Beecher told his followers: "The best part of one's life is the performance of his daily duties. All higher motives, ideals, conceptions, sentiments in a man are of no account if they do not come forward to strengthen him for the better discharge of the duties which devolve upon him in the ordinary affairs of life."

None of the role models we have today show us that we should judge our lives by the state of our integrity, not the state of our bank account; by our commitment to our primary responsibilities, not our commitment to whatever makes us happy. This self-centered mind-set is how we get addicted to judging our lives by the way we feel. I began to see this lack of earnestness in myself, evidenced by my inability to devote myself to anything by making an investment in it based on sound principles. I was always looking to "get rich quick" with an immediate cash flow to my feelings. Up until fifteen years ago I lived my life like a treasure hunt for happiness. I was a sucker for the latest guru or fad belief. If I could just be happy, then depression couldn't get me.

I really did think that happiness was the opposite of depression, so happiness had always been my goal. Happiness is not a noble value to live by. Does it make us a faithful spouse, a good parent, or a trusted friend? And if we are not those, what are we? And if happiness does not help us to become those things, what is *it*?

Depression is not the opposite of happiness. Depression is the opposite of awareness. The problem with happiness as a cure for depression, and its focus on the individual, is that we can become more interested in our public reputation than in private honor, drawn more to ambition than to study, more to amusement than to reflection. We can become sold on personal success and peak experience expectations by new-age gurus and gym-shoe manufacturers alike. We can focus more on *feeling* good than *doing* good.

The desire to feel good has implications of the "love me, love my dog" variety. If we try to go directly to feeling good, we are necessarily choosing to focus on our emotions and thus we hook into the primal mind, which isn't just all fun and joy. Once hooked into the primal mind, we can't just pick what we want from the menu; we are more of a captive audience for whatever the primal mind is serving up.

This is what English novelist Bulwer-Lytton meant when he said, "All the passions are such near neighbors, that if one of them is on fire the others should send for the buckets. Thus, love and hate being both passions, the one is never safe from the spark that sets the other ablaze." Rochefoucauld said the same thing; "The passions often engender their contraries."

We would do better to concentrate on some principle, small task, or positive action, and let good feelings come indirectly rather than to go looking for the Mr. Goodbar of happiness-in-the-raw. There is no greater oppression to the self than a puppy-love idolatry of happiness. *There is no greater freedom for the self than to loose ourselves completely from any requirement that we be happy.*

We need to separate from our habitual enmeshment with our thinking and our feelings, the same way we need to make that all-important separation from our enmeshment with our parents, not simply make an emotional cutoff from them because we can't handle the pain and trauma of the interaction. This is a psychological principle. Psychology is useful. Depression is useful. But psychology and depression must be confined to their proper limits by principles and ideals. To live an authentic life we need to learn to handle the pain of depression. We need the primal mind fully functioning, not straight-jacketed with drugs where we have the use of our talents, but we have lost our pilgrimage; where we are free from anxiety, but we have paid for our leaves with our roots.

We have forgotten how important ideals are. Carl Schurz, a nineteenth-century political reformer, reminds us, "Ideals are like the stars; you will not succeed in touching them with your hands. But like the seafaring man on the desert of waters, you choose them as your guides, and following them you will reach your destiny."

The trick to curbing depression and mania is a matter of living up to ideals and practicing principles; not drug therapy. Intellectually we have to get that we are not supposed to *be* our thinking, we are supposed to *use* our thinking. This is where the subtlety comes in. We think we already know this. But we don't really know its relevance to us—what it means for us, or we would be directing our thoughts toward some chosen purpose and taking responsibility for where our attention is focused. We would not be suffering from depression.

What do I mean by relevance? Remember the Magic Eye

books that asked us to look at a page full of dots, "unfocus" our eyes, and then, after a few minutes, the dots would magically reform themselves before our eyes into three-dimensional pictures?[12] Some people can see these pictures right away. Others can't unfocus their eyes and, from habit, concentrate on the dots in the "normal" way. All they see are the meaningless dots that make no sense to them. The dots have no relevance to people who can't focus their attention beyond the normal expectations of the flat page to see the three-dimensional effects.

Our mind is completely satisfied with the data that we know. This closure of satisfaction is the root of all our intellectual arrogance. There is no section in our mind set aside, marked, and reserved for data that we don't know; nothing to clue us in that something is missing and we need to educate ourselves in some particular way. There was nothing in their brain structures to alert the Columbine High School shooters that there was "information missing" from their higher mind.

We have nothing in our mind that directs us, for instance, as a blank stamp album directs collectors to search out the right stamps that "fill in" the printed boxes. If someone had not told me that they saw something else in those stereogram dots other than what I thought was there, I would not have tried to look at them in a different way. I would have been satisfied with my perception that they were just a page of meaningless colored dots.

Some of the ideas I came across in my search for a northwest passage out of depression seemed rather odd at first because they went against the usual lines of reasoning, or flew in the face of normal expectation.[13] But they were principles and ideas that came my way by means of reading the great literature of Western culture, so I tried them. As Bulwer-Lytton says, "Books are but waste paper unless we spend in action the wisdom we get from thought." I learned that the knowledge of life is not the same thing as the life of knowledge, which we can discover only by actually applying it to our lives.

I learned to unfocus my mind from my ordinary consider-ations in the face of these new ideas and "hang out" with them until I was no longer stuck in the dots of ordinary knowledge; I had leaped into relevance! I had achieved a unique under-standing, which was not my personal expected consequence of the information.

Culture is supposed to clue us in that we may be missing some information. Culture is supposed to present us with the principles and ideas that are necessary for our survival as a noble, respected, civilized person. We may not understand them at first, but culture is supposed to tell us that if we persevere in practice and focus our intentions, we will discover something wonderful and worthwhile in certain ideas and principles such as marriage, parenthood, family, work, friendship, responsibil-ity, loyalty, honesty, faithfulness, moderation, duty, politeness, and commitment.

But in a psychologized society based on self-esteem, everyone is a helpless victim of their circumstances, so people don't talk about "acting on principles." They talk about "making the world better," which is a euphemism for trying to adapt the environment to us, a nonpropitious, evolutionary tactic. This is the genesis of the ineffective War on Poverty, War on Drugs, the Welfare State, and pharmacology for mental illness.

After the shootings at Columbine, we heard that the young culprits had access to guns, felt alienated, were depressed, picked on, ignored, made fun of, ridiculed, pushed around, and desensitized to violence through video games, etc. The solutions put forward by psychologists were to *fix these problems.*

Initiatives immediately emerged to get rid of guns and vi-olent video games, to make students be more compassionate and nicer to each other, to have group meetings to help alien-ated students feel more comfortable at school, to install bully-awareness programs. In a culture based on principles, the initiative is for people to learn ideals and habits that empower them and strengthen their character so that they can handle the problems of depression, ridicule, being pushed around, being made fun of, and feeling alienated.

The deceiving thing about all this is that *the mind does not know what it is that it does not know.* We have to remember that. A culture based upon principles helps us remember. This is what Socrates meant when he said, "I do not think I know what I do not know." To some people this statement is simply nonsense, as meaningless as a page of Magic Eye dots. To others this statement is an alarm, a wake-up call, or at the very least a warning that acceptance speeches of any kind or sort should necessarily be extremely brief.

What relevance means for depression is this: There is nothing in our natural brain structures to alert us that depression is a feeling and not necessarily our objective reality; we have to program that information in before it is available to us. We know *what* we know about depression, but we don't know what we *don't know* about depression; and therefore we can dismiss out-of-hand places whereon we might stand to have the best possibility of the truth about depression finding us.

Nineteen

WORKING HARD AT KEEPING SANE

*I learned to raise my awareness and observe myself care-
fully when I was deep in depression, but not to the point
of experiencing myself, until one day my depression was
separated out, and I was alone, looking at it.*

Depression is not the central-core meltdown it seems. When we
focus on trying to feel good we are focused on the primal mind,
and then when the mood tide starts to turn, we are not in the
habit of nipping "downer" thoughts in the bud. "The chains of
habit," warns Samuel Johnson, "are generally too small to be
felt until they are too strong to be broken."

I remember the morning I woke in my usual state of despair, but when the escalating panic began its ascent, I said to
myself, "Wait, there is no requirement that I be happy." What
a sense of relief; some deep-down existential guilt seemed to
fade away in absolute surrender to that revelation. I didn't have
to be happy at all! I could just get up and begin my day as I
was, feeling terrible, lonely, panicked, in despair.

The pressure just melted away. It was like I called to all
those horrible feelings as if they were a bunch of pet cats;
"Okay, fellas, let's get about our day." I now sometimes use

this as one of my early morning meditations. There is such magic in it. "Wait, there is no requirement that I be happy." Sometimes I add, "There's no requirement that life has meaning either." I no longer think of myself as an existential vacuum that needs to be filled up before I can work.

If we are suffering from the lack of meaning and happiness; if we are panicked, terrified, feel like screaming, or want to slice a razor blade into our arm, it only means that our awareness of present reality and our upper-brain functions is turned way down. We can turn up the wick by the choice of any small purposeful thought or action such as repeating the phrase, "There is no requirement that I be happy in order for me to get up and begin my day."

I have come to see happiness and meaning as concepts that must have developed from our early primitive attempts to understand our primal-mind depression by describing it in negative terms, in terms of what was wrong, what we must be missing, or had lost, that might account for our pain. Meaning and happiness don't really exist; they are made-up ideas like imaginary numbers in mathematics.[1] Somewhere in our historical evolution, the negative descriptions took on the more solid prescriptive form of possessions thought necessary to cure our primal depression.

Skirting philosopher David Hume's warning that "you can't get an ought from an is," and following the law of supply and demand, million-dollar industries, in the form of religious cults, metaphysical schools, psychotherapies, pharmaceutical companies, and motivational empires have sprung up to provide us with the "missing" happiness and meaning. It's a wonderful business because we pay "up front," and when it doesn't work, we ourselves are blamed for the failure because of our lack of faith, our adverse reactions, or our pessimism.

Concepts like meaning and happiness vanish in the actual living of one's life because they have no basis in present reality.

They exist in the future. Present reality consists entirely of giving a pure act of attention to what is at hand. Again, this is the
basis for the transcendence of the lawyer-turned-paperboy. We
do not need happiness or meaning to "cure our depression."
We need only to understand its principles. Primal fear doesn't
need to be cured; it can't be cured. It's like dynamite. We don't
cure dynamite to keep from blowing ourselves up with it. We
learn its principles so we can "harness" it for our use. When
we learn to access the higher mind and direct our attention to
some task or goal, lower-brain primal fear will still be powering
us by compelling us to action, but we will not be in danger of
self-destructing along with the compulsion.

Wonderfully gifted authors like Tolstoy, who in describing
their own depression have perfectly delineated our own, help
us to understand the universality of depressive episodes. What
is also universal is the mistaken notion that the root problem
of depression is a loss of all meaning, and that to be "cured"
one must achieve meaning again. Lack of meaning is not a
problem. Lack of meaning is simply the signal that we are
focused in the primal mind. In the absence of all happiness and
all meaning, we still have all that we need, the choice to focus
on the upper-brain higher mind by directing our attention to
present reality, the task at hand. I have also come to understand
that reality never hurts. So if we are hurting, it is a good clue
that we are not in present reality.

> *I felt that something had broken within me on which my life
> had always rested, that I had nothing left to hold on to, and
> that morally my life had stopped ... All this took place at a
> time when so far as all my outer circumstances went, I ought
> to have been completely happy ... a good wife, who loved me
> and whom I loved ... good children ... a large property ...
> good health ... my name already famous ... I sought for an
> explanation in all the branches of knowledge ... I sought like*

a man who is lost and seeks to save himself—and I found
nothing. I became convinced, moreover, that all those who be-
fore me had sought for an answer in the sciences have also
found nothing. And not only this, but that they have recognized
that the very thing which was leading me to despair—the
meaningless absurdity of life—is the only incontestable knowl-
edge accessible to man.

—Tolstoy

Recently I woke up in the middle of the night to go to the
bathroom, and walking down the hall I realized the old Black
Cloak was well over me and I was so deep into depression I
felt like I had been hit with a sledgehammer. In the old days
I would have immediately started into habitual depressive
thinking—what does anything matter, it's all futile, what good
is anything, it's all over. When we really analyze these thoughts
they don't make any kind of rational sense, but habit will overcome intelligence every time; unless we make ourselves aware
of that habit.

Instead of thinking those old depressive thoughts, this time
I just naturally fell into the positive habit of singing "Mairzy
Doats." Half in my mind, half in a hoarse whisper, barely moving my lips (I was pretty groggy as it was three o'clock in the
morning). I continued with "Mairzy Doats" as my only thought
until I finished in the bathroom, walked back down the hall,
and climbed back into bed. I didn't stop singing in my mind
until I went back to sleep. In the morning when I woke up I
was quite cheery.

Betty D. told me that my ideas about depression started her
thinking about her mother and grandmother. "They were both
brought up on a farm and had a hard life. When I was a child
I remember how they always used to sing," said Betty. "They
would sometimes sing from morning till night, while they did

the canning or the washing. Some of the songs were long, sad ballads with verses that went on and on. Sometimes they would sing really loud. And they would rock too, and sometimes I would see them rocking furiously and singing almost in a trance. Now I realize all that singing and rocking must have been the way they distracted themselves and handled their depression. I am sure of it." I suspect Betty may be right about that. It makes perfect sense.

George S. is a rather beefy, formidable looking UPS driver who told me after a few sessions that he had figured it all out. "Yeah, I tell myself, 'Man, just don't go there, just don't go there in your mind'," he said. "Used to be when my wife and I had a fight," George continued, "I'd think about it all day and get lower and lower. I'd worry about the money if we got a divorce, how was I going to handle it. I'd sit around in the pain and think how unhappy and under stress I was. If one of my kids was in trouble, I would go over it in my head, how his life was ruined, how everything was a waste. Now I say to myself, 'Don't go there, you don't have to go there.'

"My family owns some land in Maine," said George, "on a lake. Instead of letting my problems go on, I control what I think. Sometimes I imagine me and my problems dumped into the middle of the lake and I swim for shore. Sometimes I almost drown but I always pull up somehow. If I turn negative and I get off track, and I go under, I always make sure that I save myself in my mind.

"Sometimes I think about how I would design the cabin I want to build there on the lake. I see everybody there, both my boys, my wife, everybody doing good, feeling good, nobody arguing, looking up at the trees, the blue sky. I still take all the hits, you know, but I just do what I can do and then I let it go. It's uncomfortable when things go wrong. I can stand it better now. Now I kind of plan ahead what I'm going to think. I don't go so easy into 'loser' thinking that brings me down."

Actor Rod Steiger, appearing on Larry King's show, says he got so down he considered getting a gun and shooting himself. His doctors told him that he had a "clinical depression caused by a chemical imbalance in the brain." That sounds so authoritative and unassailable. But, according to Steiger's own testimony, it wasn't the doctors who saved him from suicide, it was his own higher-mind ideals that had been influenced by 1950s values. "I couldn't believe I was so bound by convention under depression. I was afraid of making a mess. I was less concerned with killing myself than I was with what the people would walk in and see. There would be blood on the cat, on the card, on the flowers." And Steiger said he also considered his son, who was only two years old at the time, and his daughter. He didn't do it because of them. In the end, his higher-mind thinking was tougher than his pain. Steiger has marvelously proved my very point.

The psychology of depression is not as potent as our decision to handle it. Wanda T. came to an unpsychologized way of thinking about her husband's depression. Wanda told me that she had been very sympathetic with her husband for the complete duration of his six-month-long depression, the stress of which she blames for her own heart attack following her husband's recovery. When she recovered from her heart attack, she informed her husband that she would not stand by him again if he became depressed.

"From now on," she said, "if you feel bad don't tell me. I do not want to know. And I expect you to be pleasant from now on and have something cheerful to say, and not to make things anxious and stressful for me. There is nothing to be depressed about except being depressed, so you'd better not do it in front of me. If you have to be depressed, you can go outside and mow the lawn or clean out the garage." This was eight years ago and if her husband has had another depression, Wanda has not heard about it. Wanda was my first introduction to tough love for depression. At first I found it shocking and cold. Then I realized that I had already started to assume Wanda's exact attitude with my *own* depression.

William James, the "father of psychology," suffered terribly from depression. He would become famous for separating out psychology from "mental philosophy" and bringing the experience of human emotions to the scientific laboratory. But he would not find a cure for his own pain there. It would not be to science that this great scientist turned for salvation when depression threatened to overwhelm him. In his hour of need, this world-renowned physician used the simplistic device of repeating simple religious sayings over and over to himself:

> I awoke morning after morning with a horrible dread at the pit of my stomach, and with a sense of the insecurity of life that I never knew before, and that I have never felt since. It was like a revelation; and although the immediate feelings passed away, the experience has made me sympathetic with the morbid feelings of others ever since. It gradually faded, but for months I was unable to go out into the dark alone . . . I mean that the fear was so invasive and powerful that if I had not clung to scripture-texts like "The eternal God is my refuge," "Come unto me, all ye that labor and are heavy-laden," "I am the resurrection and the life," I think I should have grown really insane.

This self-talk repetition of prayer or nonsense nursery rhymes is simplistic but that does not mean it is easy. The tricky part is that since thoughts are very quickly over with, we have to keep choosing (concentrating) on the proactive thought, to fully wrest ourselves away from the strategies of the primal mind, which are also dependent upon lines of thought. We have to work at being sane, as Virgil warned us: "Oh, you who are born of the blood of the gods, Trojan son of Anchises, easy is the descent to Hell; the door of dark Dis stands open day and night. But to retrace your steps and come out to the air above, that is work, that is labor."

Moral principle is not necessary for the content of the repetitive self-talk used to shift us from one brain location to the other. Moral principle can give us the option of choice to restore our equanimity in the face of depression but the programs of the higher mind cannot be used *against* the primal mind to eliminate depression. The higher mind does not have that power. It is the *self* that has the power to choose the *use* of the higher mind over the *use* of the primal mind. All our power lies in that choice of one part of our mind over the other. We especially make a mistake by expecting vague philosophical concepts like meaning (that require no action on our part) to protect us like a permanent safety net against our primal fear. If we do that we will find, at times, only the yawning gap of nothingness beneath our feet.

This is the problem with psychologized thinking—that it traps us in a constant search for meaning since the focus is on feelings rather than principles. Everybody gets into a complicated why mode rather than a simple how mode. This does not encourage us to work hard at keeping sane. *Only principles tell us what to do next.* The most brilliant why in the world cannot do that. The most logical why is absolutely useless to us in any practical way because knowing is not doing; only doing is doing. The psychiatrists and psychologists who followed Freud have built their theories on the vague and shifting sands of wondering why. We do not need to know why our mind is the way it is, why it is afraid of water, why it likes to eat too much, why it doesn't want to have sex, in order to get the mind to do what we want.

Directed Thinking is built upon figuring out how. If we could describe Freudian psychology as the will to pleasure, Adlerian psychology as the will to power, transactional analysis as the will to okayness, logotherapy as the will to meaning, cognitive behavioral psychology as the will to logic, and pharmaceutical psychology (pharmacology) as the will to symptomatic relief, we could describe Directed Thinking as the will to a how.

Since my mood swings in my later years occurred more or less on a twenty-four-hour cycle, down in the morning and up at night, once I decided to study my moods, I had plenty of opportunity. It seemed to me that my unbalanced chemistry was stimulated by thoughts, and the reason I woke up so depressed was that I was unconscious when I slept and therefore couldn't control my thinking. I was further convinced this was true because if I took a nap *at any time*, even if it was in the evening and I was feeling good, I also woke up depressed. What thinking had got me into, I reasoned, thinking could get me out of.

At first I thought of the difference between feeling depressed and feeling good in terms of being conscious or unconscious, because Freud's model of the mind was what I was trained in. The minute I realized I was depressed, I would remind myself that I had "gone unconscious," and that any conscious activity on my part would *get me out of it*. I remember having an insight once that went something like this: "Oh, I get it now. Depression, being a defense mechanism, means it is unconscious, and any conscious thinking or behavior takes precedence over any unconscious thinking." I refined these concepts later but perhaps seeing depression as "going unconscious" was a necessary step. Ultimately I saw that I had to differentiate myself from my enmeshment with my *whole mind*, not simply from my depression.

I began to understand that if I was depressed I was never in present reality. I would test this out. When I got depressed I would ask myself questions about exactly what was wrong right now. My fears were always either regret or anguish about the past, about what I had lost; or anxiety about the future, and what I was not going to have. Any time I started to question myself seriously about my situation I could always see that *in this exact instant* I was really not so bad.

One of the mind tricks I created to help me to a more objective view of my moods was that when I was depressed I would visualize "saving some of it in my hand" to take into the next high, to remember how I was when I was down. This was not terribly difficult. And when I was really high I would "save some of it in my hand" to take into depression to remember how it was when I was high. This was much harder.

Since depression by its very nature is hopeless, it necessarily seems endless. Thus, it is hard to remember being high in the midst of a down, with the implication that another high will also come. But I insisted on doing the exercise and slowly, little by little, I got to the point where I could hold onto the idea of both extremes as being *temporary moods*. Switching from the idea of one mood to the reality of the other, back and forth, back and forth, regardless of which mood I was "stuck" in, I learned to feel my strongest feelings without losing my sense of objective reality that I was not my feelings, I was simply having them. I learned to raise my awareness and observe myself carefully when I was deep in depression, but not to the point of experiencing myself, until one day my depression was separated out, and I was alone, looking at it.

Elaine B., a brilliant computer scientist, told me about a similar device she uses now to lessen her self-identification with her mind. Since childhood she has often awakened in the morning with depression—an overwhelming dread that "something is wrong," that there is some fearful, nameless task crushing down upon her that she feels helpless to complete. She told me that she remembers having that same feeling once while standing in her crib, the joyless and dreary hopelessness of her existence. Just recently she found out that her younger sister, who bounds out of bed every morning with high expectations for the day ahead, often crashes with depression in the evening.

"Why my sister and I never talked about this before, I don't know," said Elaine. "But now that I know, I have a different attitude about my mornings. When the despair comes, I think about my sister and how she is at this very moment looking at this exact situation with hopeful expectation and pleasure. Since I learned that it is possible to choose my thoughts, I remind myself, 'No, wait. It doesn't have to be this way. I can *also* choose to look at things in a more positive way. Perhaps the day will bring something good. I can think about that.'

"And my sister now thinks of me in the evening. While she is in despair she knows that I am feeling calm with the day's work over, and the time to rest and be thankful. She has decided to see the evening through my eyes as I see the morning through hers."

It is not a chemical imbalance in the brain that causes us to be waylaid for long periods of time by depression. It is our lack of knowing how to handle that chemical imbalance. We need the impulse of fear to incite us to *any* action. It is our most important defense mechanism. Without the impulse of fear, we would be unable to function normally. In order to care about anything we have to be able to fear.

But if we become too fascinated by the negative thoughts, such as "I'm not happy," and dwell on them overlong, or if we become too frightened by the pain of the impulse of fear, we can freeze action. Then the impulse to fear will stagnate and, instead of inciting us to move forward thus becoming the means to an end, fear will become an end in itself. This is how we end up in depression.

The answer to depression is to access the higher mind at will so that we can stir ourselves to action and detour quickly around this painful stagnation when it occurs, instead of getting sucked into it. As Elaine saw her morning through the eyes of her sister, we can look at a despairing situation through the eyes of some principle. Or we can choose any other positive or neutral thought and keep repetitively thinking it. We can get off the track of suffering and onto another track of mind where we don't suffer.

We never know when fear will leap up out of the primal mind and terrorize us. When it happens, this is not the time to wonder why. This is not the time to look for meaning, for something to care about, to try to feel better, to zap ourselves with a pill. This is the time to switch our focus from the neural traffic jam going on in the primal mind and access our higher mind with some repetitive thinking in order to beef up the neural activity there. Depression cannot hold our attention if we choose to withdraw it. Depression cannot keep us from doing what we want. In my first efforts to pit myself against my depression, I began to see that being caught in primal-mind depression is almost like being trapped in a time warp.

It is like suddenly finding ourselves in a foreign country. We have jet lag or altitude sickness. We're homesick. Our regular language doesn't work. Nobody understands us. The food doesn't taste good. Everything is strange, different, unreal. And yet the pain of it is perhaps our most pungent reality; maybe the only thing in human existence that is not hearsay. We are forced to encounter it. But that does not mean that nothing can be done about it. What has begun in pain does not have to be continued in pain, and certainly does not have to end in pain. What has begun in pain may be changed by thinking. We may stand our ground, admit our mortal deficiency, and substitute some arbitrary positive choice.

We can't really let go of pain. We have to catch hold of something else that distracts us and then pain falls away on its own. Although pain is a construction of the mind, the self is not a construction of the mind. The mind is supposed to be a construction of the self. Pain does not have conscious choice;

only the self has conscious choice. Therefore, if we are insistent in properly employing the self, the mind's thinking will be reconstructed and the pain must ultimately give way.

How we think is how we are. Behavior and thinking are usually thought of as separate categories but, more and more, I view thinking as a *behavior done with our mind rather than with our mouth, arms, or legs.* Certainly behavior and thinking are different in their physical impact upon others. We might think of killing some annoying person without actually carrying out the thought, and the person doesn't get hurt. But I'm not so sure that the differences in the impact of thinking and behaving are so far apart with regard to the thinker. There have been numerous experiments of mental practice in sports, such as making free throws in basketball, that have been shown to be as effective as physical practice. My conclusion is that our thinking has a very powerful physical effect on us.

On a recent trip to San Francisco I visited the rocky island of Alcatraz, the twelve-acre former prison for hard-core criminals. It has now been turned into a tourist attraction and famous convict museum. I was fascinated by some of the taped interviews of the old inmates. Especially after I had seen with my own eyes the small, pitch-black solitary confinement cells. I have a tendency toward claustrophobia myself.

Sometimes when I can't get an aisle seat on a plane and end up in the middle seat, I have to concentrate really hard on the book I'm reading to keep the panic and crazy thoughts at bay. It would be so easy to start screaming, tear off my seat belt, and bolt into the aisle where I could breathe and wouldn't die! It would be the easiest thing in the world for me just to let go into a violent, crazy person trying to kick out the windows. When faced with things we are deathly afraid of, it takes a lot of effort, a lot of Directed Thinking, not to go crazy.

But I have decided not to go crazy on airplanes, as some of those convicts in Alacatraz had resolved that they would not go "stir crazy" in solitary confinement. One convict said that when he was in solitary, what he did was to tear a button off of his pants and flip it into the air. Then, in a place so dark you can't see your hand in front of your face, he would get down on all fours, like a blind man, and feel around until he found the button. He would stand up in the middle of the small cell and flip the button again. He would do that for hours and hours. That's how he kept himself sane. "A man in earnest finds means, or if he cannot find, creates them," said William Channing, a clergyman friend of Emerson's. "Earnestness," said novelist Bulwer-Lytton, "is the best source of mental power."

Another man who spent a long time in the total darkness of solitary confinement said that with a concentrated effort, he could imagine a movie screen emerging slowly against one wall. He would maintain a makeshift common-ground existence by conjuring up his friends and his family upon the screen and having long conversations with them. He would take trips to faraway places he had never even seen. "You can do it after a little practice," he said. "The colors were bright and pretty."

We can all do it. The way to intrude a positive choice into irrational craziness is to learn to replace the thoughts that are *not* contributing to the results we want with thoughts and behavior that do contribute to those results. There is a wonderful description of keeping sane in George Eliot's *Middlemarch*.[2] The town busybody is admonishing the newly widowed heroine to get herself a companion to live with her on her large estate.

"You will certainly go mad in that house alone, my dear. You will see visions. We have all got to exert ourselves a little to keep sane, and call things by the same names as other people call them by. To be sure, for younger sons and women who have no money, it is a sort of provision to go mad: they are taken care of then. But you must not run into that. I daresay you are a little bored here with our good dowagers; but think what a bore you might become yourself to your fellow-creatures if you were always playing tragedy queen and taking things sublimely. Sitting alone in that library at Lowick you may fancy yourself ruling the weather; you must get a few people round you who wouldn't believe you if you told them. That is good lowering medicine."

We need good lowering medicine. We also need good uppering medicine. Which way stability? We need to measure our thoughts against some common-ground standard, so we can judge which thoughts we should ignore and which thoughts we should act upon. We need to bravely face situations that are difficult and practice handling them. Then when we get it all figured out, we need to reassess everything as our situations change. *When all else fails, we need to remember what help there may be in earnestness.*

I recently took a trip during which my regular method of handling claustrophobia utterly failed. I have been successful with short trips, but this was a six-hour flight to Hawaii and I was stuck in the center of five seats on a fully loaded plane. At first I concentrated on my book, but little doubts kept creeping into my concentration until I started to panic. Every atom of my body was screaming, "I have to get out of here now." I forced myself to check that the seat-belt sign had been turned off, I excused myself by the other two passengers, and I bolted into the aisle. Saved!

I walked up and down for a while and did not have the courage to return to my seat. They served breakfast and though I was hungry, I still couldn't do it. I was miserable. My back started to hurt and so I sat down on the floor in the only available space I could find, which was near the lavatories. But the smell was terrible and people started giving me odd and annoyed looks for which I could hardly blame them. There were dozens of people perfectly fine in their seats. I was the only nutcase sitting down on the dirty floor where people were having to step over me. I began to feel ashamed for behaving so ignominiously.

When the aisles were cleared from breakfast, I walked up and down for a while longer and then I tried to sit in the pull-down stewardess seat but I was told it was against regulations. My back was starting to hurt again from standing and I started to think about my situation. I guessed I could stand up for another three hours. But what kind of a fake was I that I was writing a book about Directed Thinking and I couldn't even control my own claustrophobia? I began to study my situation earnestly, in terms of what was the fear about. Not *why* was I afraid but *what,* exactly, was I afraid of? I thought that I could control myself long enough to belt myself in for a landing, but I wanted to do better than that if I could. I didn't want to be a phony. Was I going to put my money where my mouth was or what?

I didn't try to search for anything rational. I knew that my terror was totally irrational. My former success with claustrophobia, I now realized, was limited. I could handle short flights in a three-seat flying situation. In a crowded auto I learned that I could control my panic if I could sit on the very edge of the seat or someone's lap, where my arms and legs were not confined, and lean into the space between the two front seats. Luckily I am not a large person, so I could usually maneuver a workable position. But this was the middle seat of five, in a totally full airplane, and I was terrified. Over the years I had just naturally avoided situations that were this uncomfortable. I was able to get aisle seats in airplanes. But not this time. I had received my comeuppance.

I was thinking about all these things while I was studying my situation on the plane. What exactly was I afraid would happen if I sat back down in the middle of those crowded seats? That I would flail my arms around and scream. Well, I thought, that is *just behavior*, isn't it, and I'm sure I can control my behavior so that I do not do that. Yes, I decided, I could depend upon my earnest commitment to not flail my arms around or scream. So what did that leave? *The terror.* Yes, I could do nothing to prevent the terror. I would feel like I was dying. I would feel like I couldn't breathe. Well, I thought, that is all *just feeling*, isn't it? I just have to stand the physical pain of that terror. I have to control my behavior and just feel the terror, just sit there quietly, even if I pass out, or *die* if that is my fate. I decided I could do that.

I sat back down, buckled myself in, and prepared to feel the most absolute terror of my life. I opened myself up to whatever pain would come. I was absolutely determined to bear the most unimaginably painful feelings, whatever they were. The most amazing thing happened. No terror came. Not even the smallest tinge of it. I completed the rest of the flight in total comfort. Now and then I invited the pain and terror if it wanted to come. But it never did.

I think the whole key was to separate the gestalt of panic into its plain, more user-friendly concomitants of behavior and feeling. Looking at the separate parts of my panic gave me a clue as to how to proceed. I saw the panic in terms of tasks to accomplish, rather than fear to succumb to. I could see that, although it might be difficult and painful, it was possible for me to control my behavior and keep myself from screaming or flailing my arms around. And it was possible to bear any pain that my feelings were going to inflict upon me. After all, they were *my* feelings, weren't they? What could my own feelings do to me, really? I know I can do that again. In two weeks, I would have to return from Hawaii. I determined to seek out the terror again and see what more work I had to do, or what new tortures my terror would teach me.

On my return trip, I found I had been given an aisle seat and I was tempted to let it go at that. But because I felt obligated to finish this story for my book, *however it turned out*, I told the clerk I was working on my claustrophobia so would she please give me the worst, crowded-up inside seat she could. Again I settled down quite prepared to feel the terror no matter what. In the beginning I got just a few tendrils of panic and again I opened myself up to whatever horror would be visited upon me. The tendrils of panic just faded out to nothing. I felt perfectly comfortable the whole trip. We can all make our life into something immensely satisfying regardless of the circumstances of it. With the earnest desire to do so. Anybody can do it with a little practice. The colors can be bright and pretty.

Twenty

THE VIRTUES OF DEPRESSION

Because in our ignorance, we are asking to be cured of ourselves, rather than doing the life's work we need to be doing in order to become ourselves.

I see the lines of suffering on my own face with the passing of years, and I eagerly search for similar lines in the faces of others that I might know them for fellow travelers. Depression has allowed me to see the truth about myself, for on my journey into that darkness I found I could not take the whole image of myself with me any more than I could see it in the mirror as a child. My attractiveness, money, possessions, accomplishments, personality, power, entitlements, enthusiasm I had to leave behind. Hope and meaning couldn't go with me. Nor a sense of time—no past, no future.

When I would come back from my trip to that netherworld, I would pick everything back up again. But over the years most things lost their reality because I could see how I was instantly vulnerable to the place where everything would disappear anyway. Except for the touch of a friendly hand—that could sometimes reach me. And small kindnesses from the people I love—

my husband, my children, a friend. A chord of music might reach me through the darkness, a bird's song, the sharp smell of cut grass, a joke. Problems and fear could easily make passage, as well as simple ideas and sparely worded principles. I became more interested in these things.

To help myself, I have studied the great thinkers of the past rather than my contemporaries. Perhaps society's pace when it was agrarian was better suited to an understanding of humanity in general rather than humanity as a particular lifestyle. Earlier society was more concerned with goals instead of roles, the anatomy of character rather than the sculpting of personality. Before the turn of the century most people lived on farms and accepted a relationship between undergoing fear at the onset of some difficulty and the development of one's character.

Difficulties were not always overcome. Crops often failed. Life was the way it was. We were supposed to persevere and grow strong. We studied nature to understand her ways. Adversity was considered not so much a thing to be avoided as to be somehow "got through." "Now therefore keep thy sorrow to thyself, and bear with good courage that which hath befallen thee," counsels *The Apocrypha*.[1] "He is not worthy of the honeycomb that shuns the hives because the bees have stings,"[2] warns Shakespeare.

Today even Nature's laws are less considered sacred principles to be understood than resources to be exploited, or technical obstacles to be overcome. Because we don't stay long in one place and get rooted in community life, we lose a sense of common ground with our fellows. We see ourselves separate from the workings of society. We expect society to protect *us* but do not see society in need of *our* protection. So we no longer "throw stones" at adulterers, perjurers, liars, cheats, bums, malingerers, dope fiends, and unwed mothers.

How do we improve upon our morality? Author Mark Caldwell said, "As Aristotle put it, only a blockhead can fail to realize that our characters are the result of our conduct."³ In other words, howsoever we behave, thatsoever we become. As a culture, if we are not careful to keep from lowering our standards and excusing ourselves from moral effort we will be in danger of becoming as shallow and pointless as the author of whom Gertrude Stein once complained, "There is no *there* there."⁴

In earlier times, adversity was the mechanism that forced us to improve our character. Seventh-century English poet laureate William Davenant said, "How wisely fate ordained for human kind Calamity! Which is the perfect glass, wherein we truly see and know ourselves."

It is especially hard in this day and age to see a connection between character and calamity. We just lump all types and manner of adversity under, "ugh," problems. We variously describe our problems as unusual, undeserved, and unexpected. Or we blame them on our failure to be well enough, or strong enough, or self-confident enough—none of which diagnoses seems to be terribly helpful. We expect our problems to be solved by the government, the psychologist, or some pharmaceutical company, as if they were specific, individual afflictions rather than general, normal work that we, as well as everybody else, need to do.

Doesn't it seem a bit odd that in this perfectly architected cosmos where no atom strays from its waiting and appointed course, that problems alone are thought to be mistakes? Problems alone are thought to be unnecessary, incidental, accidental, and somehow *in the way* of our lives? In today's society, problems do not lead to stronger character and self-understanding, they lead to migraine headaches and depression. In today's society, problems are not a call for self-responsibility and self-reliance; they are a call for Prozac or Zoloft.

People sometimes ask me why I stop depression since I maintain that it is so valuable an experience? Depression is of no use to me if I am undone by it, if I allow myself to be killed by the teacher. Again, let me use the analogy of electricity. Electricity is only valuable running through its proper wires in the walls. We do not want electricity dumped all over the floor so that we will electrocute ourselves. The extreme trauma caused by my depression is like being electrocuted. When I insist on depression returning to its confines by using mind tricks, or ignoring it, I am not destroying depression any more than I am destroying electricity by insisting that it keep to its wires. The impulse to depression remains a powerful presence in my life.

As the author of several children's books, I have been involved in the printing process the last couple of years. One day I was looking at a press proof of a color picture, and I knew there was something wrong. At first I didn't know what it was; everything was there but something was missing. Then I realized that what was lacking was the black ink. Later when I compared the two pictures, the one with the black ink and the one without, I could see that without the black ink the picture was faint, flat, uninteresting, shallow, and tentative. The picture with the black ink was strong, dramatic, definite, solid, and bold. That strong, deepening black ink reminds me of the defining effect that depression has had on my life. If I could, I would not erase depression from my life.

A similar sentiment about the virtues of suffering was suggested, strangely enough, by a German humorist, Jean Paul Richter, who said: "To love all mankind a cheerful state of being is required; but to see into mankind, into life, and still more into ourselves, suffering is requisite." And Goethe too honored suffering as a powerful force for transcendence when he wrote: "Who never ate his bread in sorrow, who never spent the darksome hours weeping and watching for the morrow— He knows you not, ye heavenly Powers." And a similar conclusion is echoed throughout Herman Melville's *Moby Dick*.

> For, thought Ahab, while even the highest earthly felicities ever have a certain unsignifying pettiness lurking in them; at bottom, all heart-woes, a mystic significance; and in some men an arch-angelic grandeur; so do their diligent tracings-out not belie the obvious deduction. To trail the genealogies of these high moral miseries, carries us at last among the sourceless primogenitures of the gods; so that, in the face of all the glad, haymaking suns, and soft-cymballing, round harvest-moons, we must needs give in to this; that the gods themselves are not forever glad. The ineffaceable and sad birth-mark in the brow of man is but the stamp of sorrow in the signers.

Understanding that suffering is an integral part of the human experience rather than suggesting methods to eliminate it has long been a tenet of Indian philosophers. So the eighteenth century master Subhadra Bhikshu tells us: "To be born is to suffer; to grow old is to suffer; to die is to suffer; to lose what is loved is to suffer; to be tied to what is not loved is to suffer; to endure what is distasteful is to suffer. In short, all the results of individuality, of separate self-hood, necessarily involve pain or suffering."

By insisting that life be improved and our problems erased so that we can be happy, unafraid, and accomplish more, we lose the opportunity to take on the very struggles that would allow us to improve and accomplish *ourselves*. If we are intimidated by people, how in the world are we going to work on that by sitting in a room all by ourselves? Or working only in offices with nice people? If we are intimidated by people, life itself will send "intimidating people" knocking on our door. As French novelist Stendhal says: "One can acquire everything in solitude—except character."

We seem to have no idea in this Culture Dump society how to handle fear and pain as a normal part of life. If we have hunger pangs, we don't go all hurt and helpless. We just go and get something to eat. How come when we hurt emotionally, we don't trust that we need to be up and doing something about *that*? Instead, we believe that we need to fix the pain itself before we can do anything. Imagine what would happen to our body if, instead of feeding ourselves when we were hungry, we kept deadening the hunger pangs, dousing them with chemicals, and pummeling them with electric shocks. We would soon starve to death.

And that is what is happening to our character. Instead of fixing our lives, we are fixing the pain that alerts us to the fact that there is something wrong with the way we are living our lives and we need to "take care of business." Theologian Pierre Teilhard de Chardin advises us that, "we are not human beings having a spiritual experience; we are spiritual beings having a human experience." When we talk about honoring the major commitments of our lives, shouldn't we include the commitment to our incarnation as a human being? It is not our body that is languishing for lack of food; it is our personhood that is languishing because we're not doing the work that is supposed to nourish it.

And, until we do that work, our spirit, self, or soul—whichever we call it—is going to be giving us holy hell. And we're going to hurt. And we can carry this hurt, sadness, depression, and anxious worry around to different doctors and therapists begging them to do something. And the best that they will be able to do for us is to write long lists of our symptoms, which they will keep in a big book on their desks. Then they will try to cure us of the name they have given to the list of our symptoms and we will feel comforted because they know what page our pain is on.

Oh, they can drug us into oblivion too, but they can't really help us, thank goodness! Because in our ignorance, we are asking *to be cured of ourselves*, rather than doing the life's work we need to be doing in order to *become ourselves*. And it is only our problems and our pain that can accomplish this by forcing us to do that work. Daniel Defoe echoes this idea in *Robinson Crusoe*: "It is impossible to make mankind wise but at their own expense, and their experience seems to be always of most use to them when it is dearest bought."

Life itself will select our battlefields for us. For Viktor Frankl, an Austrian psychiatrist captured by the Nazis, it was a concentration camp at Auschwitz. We are not forced to make a stand. Dr. Frankl could have given up, turned his head to the wall, and died, as many prisoners did. But he lived to write about his experiences in his bestselling book, *Man's Search for Meaning*.[5]

Dr. Frankl was thrown naked, bruised, bleeding, and shivering into a small, cold room so crowded with other naked men that there was not even space to sit down. His head was shaved completely bald. The hair on his arms, legs, and the rest of his body was brutally scraped off as well. Dr. Frankl relates that the guards left him the only thing that was impossible for them to take away from him—his naked skin and, as he would learn from this experience over the next few years, his moral freedom to make choices about what to think and what to do next.

Instead of any lingering resentment and blame as a result of his camp experiences, Dr. Frankl insists that it was this very suffering that taught him "to the bone" the most important lesson of his life. Dr. Frankl learned that he, that *any* human being, is more than just a biological and psychological mind and body, more than an accidental accumulation of reactions to his body, and to the events in his life; that he is never without *some choice of his own*.

Dr. Frankl believed that he survived because he had meaning in his life, he had an overriding desire to write a book. He noticed, also, that others who chose to survive in the camps felt responsible for someone else, which therefore gave their own lives meaning. Frankl was influenced in this by his study of

Nietzsche, who said that a man can always survive if he can find meaning in life; that if he has a *why*, he can survive almost any *how*.

I don't agree with Nietzsche's conclusion, though Dr. Frankl's description of his camp experience corroborates for me the idea that a human being is not just a physical and psychological system of techniques that need a particular structure in order to find meaning. But I would take that further and say that *a human being is meaning itself*.

Choice is what gives us meaning and since we are never without the one, we can never be bereft of the other. What we do is to deny that we have choice and then, of course, meaning disappears immediately. It is rather like killing one's own parents and then bewailing the fact that one is an orphan. I say that since we always *have* a how, we do not *need* a why. Again, as ancient mystics have said: "A result cannot have a purpose of its own." The necessity to search for meaning would make us the result of what we found.

Choice means that in the face of fear, courage can keep us from being forced away from our free choice of what to do or what to think next. In the face of temptation, integrity can keep us from being seduced away from our free choice of what to do and what to think next. Failure to make use of courage and integrity one moment does not limit their availability to us in the next moment, any more than our failure to look at the sky would cause it to disappear. No matter how we have messed up our lives, our inner choice remains and awaits us absolutely unchanged, undamaged, and imminently accessible to our will to choose it. "Achilles absent is Achilles still."

In Homer's *Iliad*, Hector slew Patroclus who was wearing Achilles' armor. Achilles had new armor made and slew Hector to avenge his friend Patroclus, saying to Hector that he should have remembered the strength and loyalty that Achilles bore his friend. Achilles told Hector that he should have feared

Achilles, seeing the symbol of his protection in the form of his own shield on Patroclus, despite the fact that Achilles was not present at that particular moment, in battle: "Achilles absent was Achilles still."

Our choice, unused, is our choice still. This means that no one can predict or need despair what he or someone else may ultimately become. Dr. Frankl learned that one of the most sadistic of his Nazi guards ended up in a Russian prison after the war. There he performed such kindnesses and acts of personal sacrifice that he was universally loved and considered almost a saint by his fellow inmates (many of them innocent political prisoners captured by the Communists) before he finally died of cancer.

Given the same exact horrific circumstances of a concentration camp, one man will respond by ingratiating himself with his captors and spying on his fellow prisoners. Another man will decide to share his last crust of bread with a dying stranger. Dr. Frankl cited many examples from his camp experience of the redeeming and restorative power of inner choice, like the young woman prisoner he spoke to shortly before she died. She was cheerful in spite of knowing that she only had a few days to live and told him that "she was grateful that fate had hit her so hard."[6]

She said she had led a privileged life before being brought to the concentration camp and had not taken spiritual ideas seriously. Dr. Frankl was alarmed when the young woman remarked that she often spoke to the tree outside her window, which she described as her only friend in her loneliness, and said that the tree spoke to her. At first Dr. Frankl was afraid that she might be delusional and having hallucinations, but when she told him what the tree said, he changed his mind and thought it was, instead, a profound thing, "like a poem." Through the small window next to her bed, the only thing the young woman could see was a single branch of a chestnut tree where there were just two blossoms. And what did the tree say to her? "I am here. I am here. I am life, eternal life."[7]

Dr. Frankl lost his wife and all the rest of his family to the Nazis. Rather than suffer the depression common to people who experience such personal loss, he learned to exercise authority *over himself* rather than trying to control his environment. He had a different point of view, a different paradigm from his camp mates. He watched men go crazy trying to decide which was the "right" line to get in when they were told to form two lines. Everybody knew that one line would go to the work camp and one line would go to the crematorium. Everybody also knew that there was no way to tell which was which. Even those who chose on the basis of "clues" or "inside information" often "sealed their fate" instead of saving their lives.

Dr. Frankl learned to refuse to become this kind of neurotic plaything of circumstance. The wrong line, of course, would mean his immediate death. The lesson he learned was that when all else fails, there still remains the dignity of accepting reality. Since there was no rational way to choose the line that would save his life, Dr. Frankl chose to treat the lines with indifference rather than fear. He learned to get in a line based on some *personal choice of his own*—seeing a friend or wishing to stand in the sun. Although he could not be responsible for the outcome of his action, Dr. Frankl could make sure that his action was in accord with his chosen principles; his action, therefore, coming not from fear but from earnestness.

There was little food and little rest in the camps. It was common to be irritable and depressed. Dr. Frankl could see that giving in to his physical condition (adapting to his emotions) was not as inevitable as one might at first think. He experimented with himself. He learned that he could despair, or he could make a small joke. He could choose to be angry, or he could choose to help somebody. Dr. Frankl saw that he was never left without some freedom of choice either of action or attitude. He saw that although he could not be responsible for the circumstances of his imprisonment, or the outcome of his action, he could learn to be responsible for his behavior and attitude in the face of those circumstances and despite those outcomes.

Isn't this what wisdom really is, self-monitoring our attitude? Dr. Allan Anderson, my favorite professor in graduate school, said it this way: "Wisdom is never a matter of the past but rather a knack of present self-testing of attitude as to whether one thinks he knows more than he actually does. Attitude is always at hand to energize present intuition, never *in* hand for conquest or barter."[8]

Dr. Frankl saw that he could deny all that was happening as if it were a bad dream and cease to be aware of his surroundings as many chose to do. When he chose, instead, to undergo the pain of his prison reality, he found that his courage and integrity were a continual and remarkable sufficiency for him. "The hopelessness of our struggle did not detract from its dignity and meaning. Suffering became a task upon which we did not wish to turn our backs."[9]

How ironic that it was in this environment, where all his basic freedoms were denied to him, that Dr. Frankl encountered his moral freedom of choice. Or perhaps it was not ironic at all. Like the young woman who died in the camp, Dr. Frankl had little food, few physical comforts, no physical freedom, no family. All those things that people normally count on were taken away when he was captured. What few things he had left must have become more obvious and dear. His deprivation and suffering became a microscope for this great scientist of the persona to focus for the first time on the very core of his own self.

Here was a world where there was no outside security whatsoever. Upon the merest pretext, a guard could shoot him or send him to his death in a dozen unpleasant ways. Dr. Frankl saw that although he could not successfully attack a guard for his brutality, he could, nevertheless, refuse to "cringe or to snivel" in the presence of that brutality.

Dr. Frankl said that he figured that he had a 70 percent chance of *not* surviving. Under those arid conditions, looking to get anything from life ceased to be as relevant, he said, as being able to measure up to what life was *asking of him*. He said he remembered a quote from Dostoyevsky: "My only fear is that I should prove to be unworthy of my suffering." The French novelist Albert Camus said something similar, "My only hope is that I will be equal to my sufferings."

Dr. Frankl says that he chose to survive his experience *because he had meaning* in his life; he wanted to write a book. He believed other people chose to survive because they also had some goal, or there was someone else they had decided to take care of who gave their life meaning. I think Dr. Frankl accomplished something else even more remarkable.

Without the distractions his life before prison had provided, bereft of old roles and old habit patterns, abandoning rational expectations as irrelevant, and without the normal hopes and fears that cause us to focus on the past or the future, Dr. Frankl was left with nothing but present reality. Dr. Frankl's incredible transcendence was the fact that he had the courage, while in fear of his very life, to accept present reality!

Why is it so hard to accept present reality? Because reality only comes with the absence of conditions. Once we decide to accept reality, we give up the anxious wanting of "something else" other than whatever it is that we have now got and the totality of existence is thus available to us. When we give up our hopes and dreams, we no longer live in the past or the future. This is the reason all the wise men tell us that "desire" (which is focusing on the future based upon past experience) is the cause of all our pain.

What could be more hopelessly desperate than a Nazi concentration camp to provide an environment where it is impossible to impose any conditions? Dr. Frankl has given us the clue to the greatest virtue of depression. It is impossible to impose conditions upon depression because one has to hope for something to impose conditions, and depression deprives us of all hope. A right relationship to our depression is the quickest path to present reality. There is no greater freedom than when we have stopped looking over the shoulder of life for "something better."

This acceptance of present reality is the single constant in the lives of those remarkable children who not only survive their abusive environments but go on to successful careers and loving families of their own making. What more perfect place than a hopelessly abusive parent who beats and starves you to provide a situation where it is impossible to impose any conditions?

The other important lesson that Dr. Frankl harvested from the hard ground of his concentration camp experience was this: If enjoyment of life and creative endeavor are impossible because of extreme circumstances (becoming physically abused, incapacitated, or somehow losing one's freedom), then the style and the dignity with which one suffers one's deprivations must provide the necessary meaning, beauty, and nobility for one's existence.

Harm and adversity would not be as relevant as the moral integrity we discover by undergoing them. Painful and bitter situations would not be as relevant as the creative thinking and noble behavior that can arise in the face of those situations.

Of course, one might argue that all of this talk about suffering is only meaningful if one is ultimately victorious. Suppose, for instance, that Dr. Frankl had died in one of those camps? Then all his great thinking would have just gone for nothing. Maybe not. Noble thoughts and deeds do not depend upon the circumstances of our lives. Noble thoughts and deeds depend simply upon our will to choose them. In this sense, suffering depression is as valuable as more positive circumstances. Maybe more valuable, since suffering tends to attract our deepest attention.

And, this being true, where is the space for hatred and bitterness toward our suffering? Where is the room for blame, for others or for ourselves? Where is room for the emptiness of dark depression? Perhaps the space for hatred and blame and depression is whatever space is not yet filled with our noble thoughts and deeds.

There is only one reason we ever suffer with depression. In order to suffer with depression, we must think about ourselves and our pain. If we don't think about ourselves and our pain, there is no way to suffer. Over the years I have shared my "green frog" story with others. One was a friend who told me she was going on vacation with her family. "What fun," I said.

"Well, I don't expect to have a good time," she sighed.

"Why not?" I asked with some surprise.

My friend told me that she never had a good time when she was away from home. She had never said anything to anybody about it, but she suffered from a kind of agoraphobia. She didn't really like to go out because she never knew when she was going to get that panicked feeling, and at least when she was home, she could always go to bed and sleep it off.

"I don't know," she said, "I feel slightly alienated from people most of the time, even my relatives. I never really have a good time anywhere. Mostly I feel strained and not close, like being with people is a chore instead of fun, even when it's supposed to be a party. I hate parties. I feel like I'm really on 'the outside' of things most of the time. When I go on vacation, I guess I'm afraid of getting a real bad depression. It's just assumed everybody is having a 'great time,' and when you're not . . . well, it's just hard to hide it when you're living in such close quarters."

I didn't have any idea that my friend had this kind of problem, so I shared some experiences of my own struggles and some of the things that had worked for me. This took place a few years ago and, as I write this today, depression has taken such a backseat in my life that it's hard to remember how much of my time and effort used to be focused on it, how much of my passion I once devoted to it.

But one never knows what lies ahead on one's path. Past may return as prologue, as I learned only too well from the return of my migraine headaches recently, after I was sure I "cured them forever" twenty years ago. While the sun is cheerful as daffodils and warm as melted cheese, it is hard to believe that you can still be frightened by the shadows of some cold, dark night yet to come.

I used to get migraine headaches that were so bad I would throw up. I remember remarking one time that migraine headaches were all the pain you could give yourself without passing out. My only hope was to get in a quiet, darkened room and try to get to sleep. Usually, upon waking, the headaches would be gone.

Then I learned a biofeedback technique—how to mentally constrict the blood vessels in my brain and send the extra engorgement of blood (which causes the pain) to my hands. The first time I did it, it took about three hours. Each time, however, I persisted with the exercise and the time involved grew less and less until it became an automatic reaction. I would no sooner feel a headache coming on, that familiar pain behind the eyes, and the process of constricting the blood vessels would seemingly begin on its own. The headache never had a chance to get going.

But recently I had a headache and it had been more than twenty years since the last one. I found I had "lost the knack" of constricting the blood vessels, and I got sicker and sicker. I began to throw up, and I felt some panic in my chest. I thought maybe I was having a heart attack and my husband took me to the hospital. The diagnosis—migraine headache! I was shocked. And scared. I had spent years suffering with migraines and years without suffering. Without suffering was definitely better. Should I take a course in biofeedback and learn to constrict the blood vessels again? What to do? What to do?

I didn't take another course. I *did* go out and buy some Advil to keep with me "just in case." What happened was that the next time I felt the pain start behind my right eye, I took it as a warning that I might be under stress, even though I didn't feel like I was, and I stopped doing whatever work I was doing and consciously relaxed. I was surprised to find that I was experiencing a lot of stress and anxiety that I didn't know about until I checked myself out. It wasn't until I relaxed my back that I realized my "back was up." It wasn't until I relaxed my jaw that I realized it was tightly clenched. When I relaxed, the pain stopped. It was quite an insight.

The next time I got a warning behind the right eye, I assumed stress and relaxed again. It has been almost a year now and the migraine headaches have not returned as I feared. I can see now that it was a kind of arrogance to "fix" a defense mechanism by fiddling with my blood vessels. Sure, I "fixed the migraines," but I was still *under stress*, which I'm sure affected me in other ways. Now I listen to the warning and remove myself from my stressful environment, or refrain from thinking stressful and anxious thoughts. Eureka! What is a migraine? It is a warning that we are under stress and should relax. I never thought I would live to see the day I would think of the migraine headache as a friendly reminder. But I no longer carry Advil with me.

I still suffer from periodic panic attacks, however, a couple of times a year. I have no idea where they come from. I can be watching a TV movie or wake up in the middle of the night and my throat will close and I will have trouble swallowing and breathing. I call it my "body fear." Some motivational gurus downplay anxiety attacks by saying there is no such thing because there isn't any anxiety "out there" to attack us. But those of us who are attacked by maverick neurons suddenly arcing in our own brains will have to disagree that we are not "under attack."

I have learned that "belly breathing" takes care of panic attacks in fifteen or twenty minutes. I just put my hand on my belly and make sure my belly goes out as I breathe in sharply through my nose. Then I exhale as I pull my belly in. I just concentrate, belly out, breathe in, belly in, breathe out. I concentrate on the breathing itself instead of the fear that I can't breathe: I find it helps to exaggerate the breathing out part— to give another long extra exhale puff to empty yourself out more—beyond what you first thought was your last bit of breath. When you are this empty you just naturally breathe in to fill up. I don't panic anymore over panic attacks. I just breathe. And of course, since I avoid thinking negative or anxious thoughts, pretty soon my calmer feelings reflect the peace ful thoughts about breathing.

Back to my friend who was going on vacation and worried about depression. I told my friend about my "green frog" meditation. I also said that my experiences with depression—with my dark side—had changed a lot in recent years as it seemed, more and more, to bend itself to my newfound authority over my mind. With the pressure off, I could see that I have never learned anything of value from my successes. It is failure alone that has been my real teacher. It is only the dark moments that have forced me to question myself. It's only the dark moments that have pushed me into becoming a person of understanding rather than a person of productivity and acquisition alone.

My dark side has shown me how fragile I am against the force of all existence, and that I need to walk carefully and reverently on my path, or I will hurt myself or someone else.

My dark side has taught me humility and silence. I see what a mystery life is, and in those transparent moments between my own darkness and dawn, I am filled with gratitude that I have been a witness to such beauty.

My good friend took along a notebook on her trip in which she was going to record in as agonizing detail as possible "How I Suffered on My Summer Vacation." We agreed to discuss it over a pot of tea when she returned. She was to choose a few positive thoughts and silly rhymes to substitute for unconscious or obsessive thinking when depression or obsession reared its ugly head. I also gave her a silver necklace of mine to take as a reminder that she had a friend somewhere out there who, at the very moment of her own suffering, might also be "fighting the good fight." She was not alone.

The necklace, like the notebook, was supposed to work as a kind of post-hypnotic suggestion. If she was "deep into it," my friend was to grab hold of the necklace and it would remind her to choose her thoughts instead of being a prisoner of her unwanted thoughts. She was to remember that feelings, which seem overwhelming at times, are not just feelings but defense mechanisms that have "turned wolf," leaped their bounds, and need to be rounded up and returned to their proper quarters by Directed Thinking. The necklace was to act as a trigger for her to come to and at any point begin to think positive or neutral thoughts that, sooner or later, would break the connection between her autonomic thinking and the depressive feelings that they were conjuring up.

As you may have guessed, when my friend returned, she said she had the best time of her life. When the first hint of depression appeared, she would hold onto the necklace, "kind of like it was a talisman," she said, to remind herself that she could choose her thoughts instead of sinking into depressive or panicky ones, and the depression itself just never materialized. Perhaps my friend began to consider as I had begun to consider: How terrible can this darkness be that "has such people in it?"[10]

I know that my experience of depression, in which I always felt completely alone, is responsible for a much more profound connection with people—a connection that I would otherwise not have been able to make. When I hurt, I stop, I listen, I look, and I learn. One of the meditations I use in the morning consists of the words my friend spoke to his son about the world having enough trouble of its own without his son's malingering. I too get about my business because I would be ashamed to be just another lazy shirker when good people are hurting through no fault of their own. If I can't do it for myself, I have taken it as a sacred trust that I must do it for the others. And it is not necessary that I feel good while I am doing it. And it is not a requirement that I be happy.

There are many meditations that I can use when I wake up to my chronic morning depression. And because these moods are so frequently recurring, I have been able to try a lot of things. They all work, from the sublime to the ridiculous. These simple mind tricks are much more powerful than my depression because there is absolutely no way that my depression can prevent me from thinking "One, Two Buckle My Shoe" if I insist upon thinking it.

I can't be so easily bamboozled by the hidden processes of depression anymore. Certainly I can't be bamboozled for very long. When I learned how to check up on my morning self-talk instead of just paying attention to the painful feelings it produced, I was shocked to see how my mind was so quick to latch onto and proliferate these skulking, downer thoughts: "The windows need cleaning," "God, that was a stupid remark I made last night," "Look at that dust on the lamp table," "I forgot to pay the Visa bill." It is only natural to keep thinking these thoughts rather than good ones: "My hair looked good yesterday," "I think Shelli liked my present," because we have no resistance to good thoughts. They don't cause tension. We agree with them. So they fall away from us like water off a duck's back and immediately disappear. Again, as physics tells us, there is no movement without resistance.

We hate our negative thoughts and this resistance causes a lot of tension and neural movement in our primal mind. Unless we move directly into action, this neural activity can self-perpetuate itself into depression. By replacing these downer thoughts with neutral ones, we lose our resistance and the resultant slide into depression. In a way it's like grandma's sage admonition: "If you can't say something nice, don't say anything at all." Except the idea here is "if you can't *think* something nice, don't think anything at all—just think 'One, Two Buckle My Shoe.'"

This is how my morning meditation works if I wake and find I am depressed. My first thought is one of abject despair and the terrible pain I am in. My second thought, which I have "tagged" with the first thought so I will think it as soon as I realize I am thinking I am in pain, is: "Okay, I remember, this is depression." If it isn't too bad I might check out my self-talk just to see what in the heck I have going on. But if I'm really deep-down desperate and in bent-over agony, I quickly choose something to think instead of whatever autonomic thinking that must have been going on without my awareness. I always have my list at the ready. I vary my choices from the list in the same way that I might choose a red M&M over a green one.

1. I sing "Mairzy Doats" in my mind.
2. I sing "Row, Row, Row Your Boat" or "One, Two Buckle My Shoe" in my mind.
3. I say "Green frog" over and over.
4. I pray for three people and send them healing. Another thing I noticed about depression is that it absolutely requires me to think about myself. When I direct my thoughts for someone

else's benefit, the subjugation to self-absorption is broken. In order to suffer we must think about ourselves. If we don't think about ourselves, there is no way to suffer. When I use this exercise, I always pray first for Christopher Reeve. (It was in happening to think about him one morning that resulted in the cessation of my depression and gave me the insight. So I am returning the healing.) The other two people vary. I told my aunt once about my meditation and she said she was looking for a nice condo, so I told her I would put her on the list until she found one she liked. Now my daughter tells me she could use some help finding a used car, so I'll put her on the list. I'm seeing a red one.

5. I do fast counting.

6. I laugh silently. Or, if no one is home, I might laugh out loud.

7. I remember my friend's words; "If you can't do it for yourself, do it for the others."

8. I remember that there is no necessity for me to be happy. There is no necessity for life to have meaning for me to live up to the commitments that I have made to myself. I often think of the Duke of Wellington when I think about meaning. Remember, he's the one who said: "There is little or nothing in this life worth living for, but we can all of us go straight forward and do our duty." This and my friend's statement return me to common ground faster than anything else I know.

In the very beginning I may choose one device and drop it for another. Very soon, however, I insist on thinking the thoughts I have chosen to think. I do not allow any feelings or other thoughts to get in the way of the thoughts I have chosen. I insist upon them. If I drop them for a second, I pick them up again and continue. I never give up. I do not stop until I notice that I am no longer in the pain of depression. However, I do not treat sadness as depression. If I am sad, I figure that is an okay way to be. Maybe it's *my turn* to hold up the world that way for a while. I carry sad along with me as an honest but quiet companion. Sad does not interrupt my work or my cheerfulness. There is a big difference between cheerfulness and happiness. Sometimes I feel great joy and happiness. Sometimes I am sad. I am always cheerful. Cheerfulness is not a feeling; it is a way of being. Cheerfulness is my sacred trust for the privilege of human companionship, without which I would be utterly alone in the cosmos.

I have learned from the great thinkers and wise philosophers of the past, from people who have successfully met their challenges and learned from them, and lighted the way for people like me—giants of humanity like Dr. Viktor Frankl. There are other nameless and numberless heroes who quietly make life work for them against tremendous odds. These people inspire me to follow their example: the lawyer-turned-paperboy; "the transcenders"—children whose horrendous upbringing, instead of leading to mental institutions, lead them to Rhodes scholarships, counseling careers, and college professorships.

Transcenders are the subject of a doctoral dissertation by Karen Northcraft, a psychiatric social worker from Evansville, Indiana. One of her subjects, Elizabeth, was too poor to afford a musical instrument, but she joined the school band anyway, playing whatever instrument was available. She had no shower facilities at home, and when the high school counselor complained she was dirty, Elizabeth made the school swim team so she could get a daily shower.

Poverty was not Elizabeth's only problem. She told of "bone-breaking" beatings by her aunt, who once "stripped her naked and dunked her in a vat of scalding water." Her uncle, when she was eight, got into her bed one night and began what was to be five years of sexual assaults. She made it to college only to be told she was "dyslexic" and "should drop out." But she persevered, earned a graduate degree, and became a family therapist. How did she make it?

Elizabeth said the turning point was when her aunt shaved her head in the fourth grade. Elizabeth had always taken secret pleasure in her long, blond curls. It was the "last thing" she could lose and it left her, like Dr. Frankl, with nothing but her bare self, and the choice of what to think and what to do next. It was the end of her innocence in thinking that she might expect anything from her aunt and uncle, so she could no longer be their "victim." Remember, we have to be dependent in some small way upon someone, hope for something from them, in order to be their victim.

In a rush of anger, determination, and pride, Elizabeth rebelled and cut the umbilical cord tying her to the family craziness. She was able to turn off and dis-identify with the abuse and seek ways to do things for herself. In today's management jargon, she got "out of the box." She was no longer confined to doing what would be the expected thing in that unholy environment—cringing, crying, complaining. When her aunt cut her hair, Elizabeth rejected her entire home environment; she was no longer part of it, she had transcended it.

Another of Northcraft's subjects did something similar. His mother was a schizophrenic. During an observation session at their home, the mother insisted the family's food "was poisoned." Her two still-in-the-box daughters believed their mother's delusions and ate nothing. But the little boy "ate heartily." When the social worker asked why, the boy responded, "Well I'm not dead yet." The boy grew up to be successful and happy, quite unlike his two neurotic sisters, who were unable to latch onto some principle that would help them differentiate themselves from the craziness of their environment. This is the same task we have, to differentiate ourselves from the craziness of our depression.

I have differentiated myself from the craziness of my mind because I have, over the years, lessened my enmeshment, my self-identification with my mind. When I think of how we self-identify with the mind I think of a butterfly that flys into a mirror and can never again be free because he continues to fly toward the reflection that he believes to be reality. I no longer believe I am my mind. I do not yield to depression. I do not take any drugs for depression or mania. My wide mood swings have not altered, nor has anything else around me changed in any significant way. My brain is the same; it is I who have changed. My mind is the same; it is my intentions that have changed. The world is the same; it is the paradigm from which I view the world that has shifted since I live now by principle rather than by feeling.

I cannot make it on my own; I cannot hold on to my sanity all by myself. But connected, finding common ground with others, I still have pain but I can stand it. I still get groundless feelings of grandiosity, but I can usually refrain from announcing them to the world. I still get the old feelings of primal-mind depression and mania, but I can separate myself out from the primal mind.

Someone asked Buddha, after he became enlightened, if he "was happy." His response was simply, "There is no pain." This side of enlightenment we will always have pain. We can do nothing about that; that is the job of the primal mind. We just have to make sure that the pain does not have us. We *can* do something about that. That is *our* job.

To do battle with depression, mine old enemy, I have had to call forth every ounce of willpower and courage, some of which I was not even sure existed until the exact moment I succeeded in employing it. And this is the wonderful thing. The study of this dynamic and mysterious phenomenon, up close and personal, and the continuing mastery of my relationship to it, has helped me gain an understanding of all life quite beyond what would otherwise have been possible. Being overcome by the darkness and the despair of depression can be like entering the gates of hell but, properly encountered, depression can become the doorway to your soul.

We need not be the dupe of our nature. I have changed myself. I finally put a face on the darkness and it was my own face. And I named the darkness and it was my own name. And I owned the darkness, and found I owned myself for the first time.

It's a big surprise. I thought I never would be really happy.
The thing that happened is,
One day I just gave up romance, and wealth, and happiness.
I got too old and tired to work for 'em anymore.
So I boarded up my door and sat inside with all my pain.
Some mornings, if the hurt didn't come all on its own,
I'd call it out again.
If hurt was all the friend I was to have,
 I meant to claim it good and plain,
  and Devil take the hindmost!
That pain, it was unbearable at first,
 but I didn't care.
I suffered out of spite!
Then the pain it started coming tolerable,
 then, comfortable. It spent the night.
Then, visiting was over and it moved home.
I got so used to seeing pain in my best chair
I got to love the damn thing, fair and square.
And here I am, I'm happy
Without a lick of happiness, romance, or wealth nowhere.

—CHILDREN OF THE GODS

ENDNOTES

CHAPTER 1

1. This is the most generally accepted yearly figure according to D/ART: Depression Awareness, Recognition, Treatment, National Institute of Mental Health (800-421-4211, National Mental Health Association 800-969-NMHA). *Parade* magazine, which conducts a yearly Depression Screening Day program, calls it "nearly 20 million people" (Dr. Isadore Rosenfeld, "When the Sadness Won't Go Away," *Parade* magazine, September 19, 1999).
2. Edgar Lucien Larkin, *Within the Mind Maze: Mentonomy, the Law of the Mind*, self published, Los Angeles, 1911.
3. C. Harry Brooks (with a foreword by Emil Coue), *The Practice of Autosuggestion* (New York: Dodd, Mead and Company, 1922).
4. Carl Sextus, *Hypnotism: Its Facts, Theories, and Related Phenomena*, self-published, Chicago, 1893.
5. Paul Foster Case, *The Tarot* (Richmond, VA: Macoy Publishing Company, 1945).
6. Richard Wilhelm, translated into English by Cary F. Baynes, *The I Ching* (Princeton, NJ: Princeton University Press, 1950).

7. Lao Tzu, *Tao Te Ching*, translated by D. C. Lau (New York: Penguin Books, 1963). Wing-tsit Chan, *The Way of Lao Tzu* (New York: Bobbs-Merrill, 1984).

8. Nisargatta Maharaj, *I Am That* (Durham, NC: Acorn Press, 1984).

9. *Heraclitean Fragments*, edited by John Sallis and Kenneth Maly (Tuscaloosa, AL: University of Alabama Press, 1980).

10. Raymond B. Blakney, *Meister Eckhart* (New York: Harper & Row, 1941).

11. V. S. Ramachandran, *Phantoms in the Brain* (New York: William Morrow, 1998). This is a continuation of the work of Maxwell Maltz (*PsychoCybernetics*) and Oliver Sacks (*The Man Who Mistook His Wife for a Hat*).

12. Antonio R. Damasio, *Descartes' Error: Emotion, Reason, and the Human Brain* (New York: Avon Books, 1994). I am indebted to neuroscientist Antonio Damasio for his informative work on the architecture of the brain, which helps to explain neuroscientifically much ancient wisdom, as well as explaining what I had been experiencing as I studied my own behavior.

13. "Learned helplessness" is a term that describes how we unnecessarily make ourselves victims of circumstances when there are other opportunities. The original work by Martin E. P. Seligman is out of print but is included in a new book: Christopher Petersen, Steven F. Maier, and Martin E. P. Seligman, *Learned Helplessness: A Theory for the Age of Personal Control* (Oxford, England: Oxford University Press, 1995). Dr. Seligman's work on "learned optimism" is well known; Pocket Books had a 1998 reissue of his *Learned Optimism: How to Change Your Mind and Your Life*. What may not be as well known is that Seligman heads a research endeavor of great depth and girth throughout the American academic psychological community, away from the old long-term gloom-and-doom therapy to a new kind of bottom line "positive psychology."

14. Brooks, *The Practice of Autosuggestion*.

15. The British Duke of Wellington (1769–1852). Known as "the Iron Duke." He defeated Napoleon at the battle of Waterloo during the days when generals rode into battle at the head of their troops.

16. Ralph Waldo Emerson (1803–1882), American essayist, philosopher, lecturer; leader of the transcendentalist writers in New England who flourished during the last half of the nineteenth century.

CHAPTER 2

1. Eric Berne, *Games People Play* (New York: Grove Press, 1964). This book, by the founder of transactional analysis, has divided up the spectrum of human interactions into a system of "games" and "authentic transactions." Ain't It Awful is a "game" wherein all the participants spend all their time in trading horror stories about their difficulties instead of getting to work to do something about them.

Thomas A. Harris, *I'm OK, You're OK: A Practical Guide to Transactional Analysis* (New York: Harper & Row, 1967). Harris succeeds in making the descriptive transactional analysis into the prescriptive Institute for Transactional Analysis with accompanying book. Transactional analysis is an excellent way of seeing the unreality of human interaction but it fails on the reality side due to Hume's old bugaboo—You can't get an "ought" from an "is." TA is also based upon Freud's model of the mind, which doesn't help the prescriptive side either.

2. The *Diagnostic and Statistical Manual of Mental Disorders (DSM-IV)* is a pretty fancy name for a book of symptoms. Published by the American Psychiatric Association, Washington, D.C., it is the universal reference for the diagnosis of mental illnesses. It is updated periodically by a task force of more than 1,000 professionals who facilitate interchanges between the American Psychiatric Association and other organizations such as the World Health Organization, the American Health Information Management Association, and the National Center for Health Statistics. The avowed purpose of the *DSM-IV* is to "provide clear descriptions of diagnostic categories in order to enable clinicians and investigators to diagnose, communicate about, study, and treat people with various mental disorders."

There is also a very interesting disclaimer. The guide states that diagnostic categories such as pathological gambling or pedophilia do not imply that the conditions meet "*legal* or other nonmedical criteria for what constitutes mental disease, mental disorder, or mental disability. The clinical and scientific considerations involved in the categorization of these conditions as mental disorders may not be wholly relevant to legal judgments, for example, *that take into account such issues as individual responsibility, disability determination, and competency.*" (Italics mine.) You will look long and hard to find the word responsibility mentioned anywhere besides the disclaimer in this 886-

page book. This is the way the system works: If you have the requisite number of a particular list of symptoms, say five out of seven, you are certifiably the possessor of the mental disorder that is the name of that particular list of symptoms. You may possess the requisite number of symptoms of several lists. That would make you certifiably the possessor of the mental illnesses that are the names of the lists for which you have the requisite number of symptoms. In 1994 Dr. Judd of the UCSD staff claimed to have "discovered" a new illness. He did so by taking the list of symptoms that already had a name and—keeping the same list—lowering the requisite number of symptoms to qualify for that illness. Then he simply renamed the list.

Dr. Paul R. McHugh, who as the Psychiatrist-in-Chief at Johns Hopkins University School of Medicine may be the foremost psychiatrist in the medical world, is a great detractor of the *DSM-IV*. McHugh claims that the original idea of the list of categories that turned into the *DSM* was to "isolate clear and distinct symptoms that separated indubitable cases of schizophrenia from less certain ones by creating a set of research diagnostic criteria." No one, said McHugh, ever claimed to have found the "specific features of schizophrenia—a matter, scientifically speaking, of 'validity.' " The original intent was to identify certain markers in schizophrenia that would enable comparative study of the disease at multiple research sites, a matter of "reliability."

Now, insists McHugh, this original effort has been subverted, due to escalating politics and self-serving interests of doctor-pharmaceutical coalitions, into a clinical method of diagnosis based upon flimsy "appearance-based classifications" rather than neurobiological or psychological data. Classifications appear and disappear not as a result of experimental science but by committee approbation, which relies extensively upon the "prejudices of the day."

3. Jonathan Sternfield, *Firewalk: The Psychology of Physical Immunity* (Lee, MA: Berkshire House, 1992).
4. Jerome Kagan, *Three Seductive Ideas* (Cambridge: Harvard University Press, 1998), 193.
5. V. S. Ramachandran, *Phantoms in the Brain* (New York: William Morrow, 1998).
6. Ibid, p. 56.
7. See pages 281–282 (de Waal's work)

CHAPTER 3

1. C. S. Lewis, *The Screwtape Letters* (New York: MacMillan, 1966).
2. Sandy Banks, "Life as We Live It," *Los Angeles Times*, October 9, 1998.
3. Antonio R. Damasio, *Descartes' Error: Emotion, Reason, and the Human Brain* (New York: Avon Books, 1994), 93. Since the sixteenth century, hypnotists have understood that the mind is a "yes" system and now neuroscience shows us the reason. The mind doesn't literally respond to a "no" because the signals of cooperating neural activity in the brain "never 'terminate' as such, because from the vicinity of each point to which they project forward, there is a reciprocal projection backward. It is appropriate to say that signals in the stream move both forward and backward. Instead of a forward-moving stream, one finds loops of feedforward and feedback projections, which can create a perpetual recurrence." There is no stop action per se, another course of action is set going that directs the ongoing action forward into another action as a continuation rather than a stop-go process.
4. I first got the idea of impulses stagnating, or perpetual recurrence (although I didn't label it with that term until I came across Damasio's work), when it was demonstrated to me by my friend John. He was in the last stages of Alzheimer's when I began our regular Monday morning visits to give his wife a respite. There were large gaps for John when it seemed there was no connection from one thought to another. Sometimes in the middle of a word he would totally "freeze action" as if he were a robot that had just run out of batteries. If we played a simple game of cards, sometimes he would put a card down and just leave his hand there; or he'd start to pick up a card and, instead, would just let his hand just hang above the table grasping at air. At first I thought he just "forgot" what he was doing until an incident one day in the shopping mall helped me see his action in a different light.

   He seemed to enjoy walking there, with the bright lights and activity, then we might sit down for a cup of coffee. One day as I directed him to a chair I suddenly realized that he couldn't stop walking to sit down. I didn't know what to do, as he was a big strong man and was dragging me down the aisle. Desperate for some solution, I got the idea of heading him gently into a wall. Like a mechanical man held fast with his legs still moving, John's walking continued, but the wall kept him from going anywhere. The action of walking soon ran down as, I assume, he then had the opportunity to initiate another action that was not "stuck" and could progress to sitting down. After that first time, we just used the "wall solution" as a matter of course whenever he got stuck in perpetual recurrent walking.

CHAPTER 4

1. Paul R. McHugh, "How Psychiatry Lost Its Way," *Commentary*, December 1999.

Post-traumatic stress disorder is another catch-all diagnosis where people claim that their difficult past experiences have incapacitated them and rendered them unable to live normal lives. People blame their post-traumatic stress on long court battles, a difficult boss, a hurricane, a house fire. Yet this is what Johns Hopkins Chief-of-Psychiatry has to say about it: Emotional distress before and after combat was known in WWI as "shell shock," lingering anxiety, a tendency toward nightmares, and "the avoidance of activities which might provoke a sensation of danger." What was added after Vietnam was the belief that—perhaps because of a physical brain change due to the stress of combat—veterans who were not properly treated could become chronically disabled. This lifelong disablement would explain, in turn, such other problems as family disruption, unemployment, or alcohol and drug abuse.

"Once the concept of a chronic form of post-traumatic stress disorder with serious complications was established in *DSM-III*, patients claiming to have it crowded into VA hospitals. A natural alliance grew up between patients and doctors to certify the existence of the disorder: Patients received the privileges of the sick, while doctors received steady employment at a time when, with the end of the conflict in Southeast Asia, hospital beds were emptying. Any skepticism was 'dismissed as hostile to veterans or ignorance of the mental effects of fearful experiences.' "

But, says McHugh, "those who were treated for post-traumatic stress did more poorly than those who were not treated. Israeli psychiatrists claim that long-term treatment in hospitals has the unfortunate tendency of making battle-trauma victims hypersensitive to their symptoms and, by encouraging them to concentrate on the psychological wounds of combat, distracts their attention from the 'here-and-now' problems of adjusting to peacetime demands and responsibilites."

2. Joe Sharkey, "Mental Illness Hits the Money Trail," *New York Times*, June 6, 1999.
3. Robert Langreth, "Depression Pill May Help Treat the Acutely Shy," *The Wall Street Journal*, May 3, 1999.
4. Michael W. Miller, "With Remedy in Hand, Drug Firms Get Ready to Popularize an Illness," *The Wall Street Journal*, April 25, 1994.
5. Ibid.
6. Ibid.
7. Anuradha Raghunathan, "For Shyness a New Name and New Treatment," New York Times News Service, May 21, 1999.
8. Paul R. McHugh, "How Psychiatry Lost Its Way," *Commentary*, December 1999.
9. Claudine Chamberlain, "Exercise Exorcizes Depression and Other Ills," ABCNews.com, September 7, 1999.
10. Greg Tkachuk and Garry Martin, "Aerobic Exercise Works as Well as Psychotherapy," *Professional Psychology: Research and Practice*, June 1999.
11. R. B. Jarret, M. Schaffer, D. McIntire, A. Witt-Browder, D, Kraft, R. C. Risser, *Archives of General Psychiatry*, May 1999.
12. Ibid.
13. Martin E. P. Seligman, "Building Human Strength: Psychology's Forgotten Mission," *APA Monitor*, January 1998.
14. Ibid.
15. *Newsweek*, October 9, 2000. Michael Norlen, "Healing Myself With the Power of Work," *Newsweek*, October 25, 1999.
16. Ibid.
17. "Behaviorist Brain-Function Change Claimed," Associated Press News Service, September 16, 1992.
18. Jeffrey M. Schwartz, *Brain Lock: Free Yourself From Obsessive-Compulsive Behavior* (New York: HarperCollins, 1996).
19. Milt Freudenheim, "Drug Firms Aim Ads at Mentally Ill," *New York Times*, April 8, 1997. "Using tactics that would have been unthinkable a few years ago, the pharmaceutical industry is increasingly marketing mental health drugs directly to consumers." Drug companies claim it provides information to help people overcome problems. Critics say

people may seek out doctors all too willing to prescribe drugs that may not be right for them. Eli Lilly is offering scholarships to schizophrenics who will try their new antipsychotic drug, Zyprexa. Critics say that could encourage people to risk ill effects of switching medicine and raise expectations that schizophrenics can cope with higher education, perhaps an unrealistic goal.

20. John Hendren, "Patients Demand Medicines by Name," Associated Press News Service, January 8, 1998.

21. "Drugs for Toddlers," Associated Press News Service, February 23, 2000.

22. Janine S. Pouliot, "If Your Child is Sad—Take It Seriously," *Parade* magazine, September 27, 1998.

23. Ibid.

24. Dr. Isadore Rosenfeld, "When the Sadness Won't Go Away," *Parade* magazine, September 19, 1999.

25. Ibid.

26. Kay Redfield Jamison, *Touched with Fire: Manic-Depressive Illness and the Artistic Temperament* (New York: Free Press Edition, Simon & Schuster, 1994). This is one of the most popular books linking manic depression with the "artistic temperament" or "fine madness" of famous people. Jamison is one of the foremost authorities on manic depression, admits to being manic depressive herself, and is on drug therapy.

27. Cheryl Clark, "Rewriting Bible of Mental Illness," *San Diego Union*, June 6, 1994.

28. Ibid.

29. "Psychiatry Professor Faulted for Consulting," Associated Press News Service, October 7, 1999.

30. Terence Monmaney, "Medical Journal May Have Flouted Own Ethics 8 Times: Research: Drug reviews by *New England Journal* did not disclose author's ties to firms. Editor concedes lapses," *Los Angeles Times*, October 21, 1999.

31. Ralph T. King, Jr., "Medical Journals Rarely Disclose Researchers' Ties," *The Wall Street Journal,* February 2, 1999.

32. "Paper: Drug Trials Fraught with Problems," *New York Times*, May 16, 1999.

33. Ibid.

34. R. J. Igneizi, "Means to a Mend: Researchers Are Recruiting Those with Ailments to Test the Efficacy of Treatments," *San Diego Union-Tribune,* June 1, 1999.

35. Ronald R. Fieve, M.D., *Moodswing* (New York: William Morrow, 1975).
36. Herman Melville, *Moby Dick* (New York: Modern Library Edition, Random House, 1950), chap. XVI, p. 69.
37. Robert Burton, *Anatomy of Melancholy*, first published 1621.
38. See Endnotes, chapter 3, note 4.
39. *Larry King Live*, October 28, 1999.
40. William Styron, *Darkness Visible* (New York: Vintage Books, 1992).
41. "Styron: A Memoir of Madness," *Los Angeles Times*, August 28, 1990.
42. Terrence Real and Phillip R. Slavney, *I Don't Want to Talk About it: Overcoming the Secret Legacy of Male Depression* (New York: Fireside, 1998).
43. Ibid.
44. Patty Duke, *A Brilliant Madness* (New York: Bantam, 1992).
45. Thomas S. Szasz, M.D., *The Myth of Mental Illness* (New York: Harper & Row, Inc., 1974).
46. Ibid.
47. Ibid.
48. Paul R. McHugh, The *Perspectives of Psychiatry* (Baltimore, MD: Johns Hopkins University Press, 1983).
49. Ibid.
50. Ibid.
51. Kevin Galvin, "Mental Illness Target of Campaign," Associated Press News Service, June 6, 1999.

CHAPTER 5

1. Antonio R. Damasio, *Descartes' Error: Emotion, Reason, and the Human Brain* (New York: Avon Books, 1994), 128. "In simple terms: The old brain core handles basic biological regulation down in the basement, while up above, the neocortex deliberates with wisdom and subtlety. Upstairs in the cortex there is reason and willpower, while downstairs in the subcortex there is emotion and all that weak, fleshy stuff." This of course is not the full story for the whole premise of the book is that the emotions of the lower mind are absolutely necessary for the higher functioning of reason, and in the event that the emotional area of the brain is physically destroyed, the higher mind cannot function properly either, regardless of the fact that the person, with his intellect intact, could pass an IQ test with flying colors. He still couldn't hold down a hamburger-flipping job.

Damasio concludes that there is a fundamental difference in intellectual activities and social activities, which we also see in idiot savants, such as the character portrayed in Dustin Hoffman's movie, *Rain Man*. Damasio claims that it is the feelings of the lower mind that provide the bridge between the upper and lower mind. This certainly corroborates ancient wisdom, which says that impulse provides the energy for reasoning. It is perhaps that bridge of feeling that must be the obstacle to overcome so that we can access the higher mind as an act of will when we are stuck in lower-mind depression. I claim that there is another bridge—which is to access the higher mind by changing thoughts, which thoughts then proceed to influence the lower mind so feelings change and with that change, depression disappears.

2. Ibid., p. 90. "My view then is that having a mind means that an organism forms neural representations which can become images, be manipulated in a process called thought, and eventually influence behavior by helping predict the future, plan accordingly, and choose the next action. Herein lies the center of neurobiology as I see it: the process whereby neural representations, which consist of biological modifications created by learning in a neuron circuit, become images in our minds; the process that allows for invisible microstructural changes in neuron circuits (in cell bodies, dendrites and axons, and synapses) to become neural representation, which in turn becomes an image we each experience as belonging to us." Unfortunately, we go beyond mere possession, and experience those images as us when we identify with our depression.

3. Jerome Kagan, *Three Seductive Ideas* (Cambridge, MA: Harvard University Press, 1999).

4. Paul R. Ehrlich, *Human Natures: Genes, Cultures and the Human Prospect* (Washington, D.C.: Island Press/Shearwater, 2000).

5. Gerald M. Edelman, *Bright Air, Brilliant Fire* (New York: Basic Books, 1993).

6. Heather MacDonald, "SSI Fosters Disabling Dependency," *The Wall Street Journal*, January 20, 1995.

7. Doug Smith, "Buchanan's Pick Had Checkered Career," *Los Angeles Times*, August 24, 2000, "Ezola Foster's Request to Seal Records is Rejected," *Los Angeles Times*, September 2, 2000.

8. Estes Thompson, "Derailed by Depression," Associated Press News Service, October 8, 2000.

9. Anne Krueger, "S. D. Judge Has Been a No-show for a Year," *San Diego Union-Tribune*, December 3, 1999.

10. Paul R. McHugh, "How Psychiatry Lost Its Way," *Commentary*, December 1999.

11. Ibid.

12. The principle of inertia: a body in motion tends to stay in motion, a body at rest tends to stay at rest.

13. Friedrich A. Hayek, *The Constitution of Liberty* (Chicago: University of Chicago Press, 1978).

14. Friedrich A. Hayek, *The Fatal Conceit* (Chicago: University of Chicago Press, 1989).

15. Lauren Slater, *Prozac Diary* (New York: Random House, 1998). A very literate firsthand account from a psychologist who has been on Prozac for ten years.

16. Joe Sharkey, "Mental Illness Hits the Money Trail," *New York Times*, June 6, 1999.

17. Henry Ward Beecher (1813–1887), American clergyman and theologian.

18. Damasio, *Descartes' Error: Emotion, Reason, and the Human Brain*, 34–39. In the strange case of Phineas Gage in 1861 and in more recently documented cases, physical accidents have caused such extensive neurological damage that the survivors have been left bereft of that portion of the brain that houses emotions, the ability to feel good or bad about anything. These cases indicate that emotions are necessary and unique human properties that grant us "the ability to anticipate the future and plan accordingly within a complex social environment; the sense of responsibility toward the self and others; and the ability to orchestrate one's survival deliberately, at the command of one's free will." Denied the capacity to feel emotions, we can no longer live as independent, self-motivated social beings even though the capacity for higher reasoning and intellect is left intact.

19. John Cloud, "Just a Routine School Shooting," *Time*, May 31, 1999.

20. Claudine Chamberlain, "Prozac Prosecution Rests," ABCnews.com, June 5, 1999.

21. "Prozac Trial Resumes," ABCnews.com, October 10, 2000.

22. Kramer, *Listening to Prozac*, 289.

23. Thomas E. Joiner, "Depression Can Be Contagious," *Journal of Personality and Social Psychology*, August 1994.

24. Chris Dowrick, *Depressed Doctors* (Priory Lodge Educators, 1996); Dr. Howard Thomas, *The Touch of the Master's Hand* (Thomas Books, 1987); Trish Crawford, "Depressed Doctors Are My Only Patients," *The Toronto Star*, February 18, 2000; W. D. Johnson,

"Predisposition to Emotional Distress and Psychotic Illness Among Doctors," *British Journal of Medical Psychology*, December 1991.

25. Nathaniel Hawthorne, *The House of the Seven Gables* (New York: The Heritage Press, 1935), 184.

26. A teacher who came in for counseling told me that one-third of her first graders are on some kind of medicine to control their moods.

27. Associated Press News Service, March 17, 1995. Judge Elizabeth Donovan ruled in Boston that John Locke was not criminally responsible for attacking a police officer because he was a manic-depressive who had stopped taking the medicine that controlled his condition. There are numerous criminal cases, up to and including murder, in which the defense claims not guilty by reason of Prozac.

28. During the Clinton impeachment I heard commentator after commentator say that one of the reasons people were so apathetic about the trial was that so many people are on Prozac.

29. Elyse Tanouye, "Antidepressant Makers Study Kids' Market," *The Wall Street Journal*, April 4, 1997. This article describes a family from Hudson, Ohio, who for seven years have had their four children on prescription antidepresseants, mostly switching back and forth from Prozac to Zoloft. The older girl started on them while away at college at age nineteen; then her sister at age eleven, her brother at age sixteen, and the youngest girl at age thirteen were all similarly diagnosed as depressed.

30. Sherrye Henry, "America's Hidden Disease," *Parade* magazine, February 12, 1995.

31. Kent Layton, "Mental Illness: Perception and Reality," *San Diego Union-Tribune*, May 30, 1996.

32. For further information on the debunking of these disorders read Nicholas P. Spanos, *Multiple Identities and False Memories* (Washington, D.C.: American Psychological Association, 1996), and August Piper, M.D., *Hoax & Reality: The Bizarre World of Multiple Personality Disorders* (Northvale, NJ: Jason Aronson, 1997).

33. Malcolm Ritter, "Psychologist says Tapes Challenge Story of Sybil," Associated Press News Service, August 17, 1998. Psychologist Robert Rieber of the John Jay College of Criminal Justice in New York had the tape recordings in his desk, forgotten for twenty-five years. Rieber says the tapes show that Sybil's psychiatrist was inadvertently "carving out the characters for Sybil to absorb by giving names to the various emotional states that Sybil experienced."

It may be that this particular investigator of the Sybil tapes was not also aware that, according to Psychiatrist-in-Chief Paul McHugh of Johns Hopkins University in a December 1999 *Commentary* article, Dr. Herbert Spiegel of Columbia University knew the patient in question and disputed her case with the author of the book *prior to its publication*. Spiegel thought the patient simply a high hysteric with role confusion. But the author insisted upon going ahead because "if we don't call it multiple personality, we don't have a book. The publisher wants it to be that, otherwise it won't sell."

34. Carol Ness, "Woman Sues Author over Self-help Book," *San Francisco Examiner* May 20, 1994.

35. "Psychiatrist Faces State Discipline," Associated Press News Service, August 14, 1998. Depressed after the birth of her second son, Patricia Burgus sought therapy from Dr. Bennett Braun.

36. Andrew Buchanan, "Teen Says Alcoholism Is a Protected Disability," Associated Press News Service, September 10, 1999.

37. "Messy Hair Can Mess Your Mind, Too, Study Finds," Associated Press News Service, January 26, 2000.

38. Raymond B. Blakney, *Meister Eckhart* (New York: Harper & Row, 1941), sermon 9: "How the Inclination to Sin is Always Beneficial," 12.

39. Kay Redfield Jamison, *Touched with Fire: Manic-Depressive Illness and the Artistic Temperament* (New York: Free Press Edition, Simon & Schuster, 1994), 74.

40. Ibid., 193.

41. Ibid., 56.

CHAPTER 6

1. Stephen Hawking, *A Brief History of Time* (New York: Bantam, 1988).

2. Robert B. Reich, *The Future of Success* (New York: Knopf, 2001).

3. Ibid.

4. Julie Stafford, "Knowing What Causes Stress Is Key to Your Control of It," Knight-Ridder News Service, May 29, 1997.

5. Norman Brown, "Feeling Down Is on the Rise," *Health & Fitness News*, May 1994.

6. Nathaniel Hawthorne, *The House of the Seven Gables* (New York: The Heritage Press, 1935), 193. Hawthorne ends this sentence ". . . which, if you once look closely at it, is nothing." What Hawthorne

says here is helpful in drawing our attention to Now. However I think Hawthorne errs when he thinks of Now in terms of a noun rather than a verb whose motion is necessarily suspended (disappears) by our describing it.

An example of Now in physics are quarks. The Now of present reality is not quantitative but it is ongoing in the form of Monday and Tuesday. The material universe is not quantitative but it is ongoing in the form of quarks. There are "Monday" quarks and "Tuesday" quarks and physicists have different tests to see which quark is which. However, whatever quark they test for is *always* the quark they find, and the quark is always destroyed in the testing of it. Does this mean that a quark "knows" which test is being conducted and turns into the right quark? And if it "knows" wouldn't it also know it will therefore be destroyed if it turns into the quark being tested for? Is this an example of love? Does this mean that the universe does not exist except as we look for it and whatever we look for we find? Is the thought father to the thing? And therefore, does this mean we are not so much discovering the physical universe as creating it? No wonder all the physicists are turning into mystics and seeking out sages like Dr. Anderson. And Dr. Anderson would tell them something like this: The changing physical universe is nondifferent from the Absolute, which is changeless. That is because the Absolute is always othering itself to itself. The physical universe is really apparent in that it exists for a time but only apparently real in that it changes, it exists *only* for a time. He would explain the destruction of the test quarks by saying that in the physical universe, for a thing to appear it must be accompanied by its own absence. Practically speaking, this is the reason we write on the *black*board with *white* chalk.

7. *He was right, dead right as he sped along*
   But he's just as dead as if he'd been wrong.
   —ANONYMOUS

   A wise old owl sat in an oak;
   The more he heard the less he spoke;
   The less he spoke, the more he heard.
   Why aren't we like that wise old bird?
   —EDWARD HERSEY RICHARDS (1874–1957)

8. Edmond Dantés is the hero of *The Count of Monte Cristo* by Alexander Dumas.
9. I am indebted to my Indian guru for the idea that darkness is the absence of light.

CHAPTER 7

1. "New Trial Set in Rap Slaying,"Associated Press News Service, October 5, 1998.
2. See Chapter 2, pages 30–31.
3. Maxwell Maltz, *PsychoCybernetics* (New Jersey: Prentice-Hall, 1960).
4. Napoleon Hill, *Think and Grow Rich* (New York: Fawcett Columbine, 1966).
5. Leslie M. Lecron, *Self-Hypnotism, The Technique and its use in Daily Living* (New York: Signet 1964).
6. L. Ron Hubbard, *Dianetics* (Los Angeles: Church of Scientology, 1976).
7. Rudolf Steiner, *Knowledge of the Higher Worlds and its Attainment* (New York: Anthroposophic Press, 1975).
8. Jose Silva, *Silva Mind Control* (New York: Simon & Schuster, 1977).

CHAPTER 8

1. It is true that some negative thoughts, if chosen again and again, can activate the neural activity in the lower-brain primal mind, which can result in a chemical imbalance that causes painful feelings and depression, but thoughts per se don't hurt. That's the great beauty of Directed Thinking in managing depression.
2. An example of a first-level change would be the following: In a marital conflict, a lonely wife insists that her husband give up one of his weeknight meetings to stay home with her. He agrees to do so. This is a first-level *content* change. The *content* of the marital situation has been altered so that the symptom of the wife's loneliness has been alleviated. But the *process* of the woman dealing with her loneliness by depending upon her husband has not changed.

   A second-level change in another marital conflict is as follows: The lonely wife of a man who travels a great deal decides to get a job. She becomes so busy with her work and new friends that her husband's long absences no longer trouble her. This is a second-level *process* change. Nothing about the original situation that disturbed the woman has been altered. Her husband still travels the same amount. But her process of dealing with her loneliness has changed so that rather than the problem being solved, it has been transcended.

3. My mother does not remember this event but she told me that she was sure it could have happened because at this time of her life she was under terrible stress, which resulted, a year later, in her becoming totally bedridden for two years with psychosomatic asthma. We have both cried over this scene many times. At first I was weeping for myself. Later my tears were only for my mother who must have endured a great deal to have been thus reduced.

   I gave this book to my mother in case she wanted me to delete any references that she found offensive. After all, outing one's own frailties is not the same thing as "being outed." But my mother, bless her heart, said that she loved the book and has never cared what anybody said about her as long as it was true.

4. Dale Carnegie, *How to Win Friends and Influence People* (New York: Simon & Schuster, 1936).

5. Ibid.

6. Ibid.

7. "Not a Real Criminal," Associated Press News Service, March 3, 1999.

8. See Endnotes, chapter 3, note 3.

9. Transactional Analysis (see Endnotes, chapter 2, note 1) as well as other communication systems such as those of Virginia Satir maintain that blame is not a real communication but a "game" wherein the object is not to communicate authentic feelings but to carry out some agenda, to shift responsibility or to defend oneself in some way.

10. See Endnotes, chapter 5, note 1.

11. Nathaniel Hawthorne, *The House of the Seven Gables* (New York: The Heritage Press, 1935), 397.

CHAPTER 9

1. See Meister Eckhart's statement about sin, pages 112–113.

2. See pages 211–217 in the chapter about how one gets in touch with one's fear.

3. See Endnotes, chapter 3, note 3.

4. Jason DeParle, "As Welfare Rolls Shrink, Load on Relatives Grows," *New York Times*, February 21, 1999.
5. Antonio R. Damasio, *Descartes' Error: Emotion, Reason, and the Human Brain* (New York: Avon Books, 1994), 112. "Now I can say that since different experiences cause synaptic strengths to vary within and across many neural systems, experiences shape the design of circuits. Morever, in some systems more than in others, synaptic strengths can change throughout the life span, to reflect different organism experiences, and as a result, the design of brain circuits continues to change. The circuits are not only receptive to the results of first experience, but repeatedly pliable and modifiable by continued experiences." Again Damasio corroborates the ancient wisdom that "habit is stronger than nature."

CHAPTER 10

1. Antonio R. Damasio, *Descartes' Error: Emotion, Reason, and the Human Brain* (New York: Avon Books, 1994). According to Damasio, there is not enough time in our attention span to consider all possibilities for any one decision. So over the years possibilities are "fear-tagged" or "fear marked" because these experiences have been negatively perceived. This way whole categories of fear-based possibilities are eliminated for consideration and decisions are based on a smaller number of categories of possibilities that are not fear-marked. Persons who experience physical damage in the area of the brain where the impulse of fear resides are unable to come to any conclusions and thus cannot interact in society.
2. Charles, L. Griswold, *Adam Smith and the Virtues of Enlightenment*, (New York: Cambridge University Press, 1999). Adam Smith believed that our desire to move in harmony with others comes from our ability to imagine ourselves in the same situations.
3. See Endnotes, chapter 5, notes 1 and 18.
4. Ibid.
5. I am indebted to my editor, S. Shafquat, for this observation about pain and bread.
6. When we are born we do not see ourselves as separate from our mother and it is only "little by little" that we disidentify and distinguish our separate selves from our caretakers. As long as we "identify" with someone, we can "take on" fear from them. When we are

fully functioning adults we no longer "take on" fear from others. For a further discussion of the "identification" factor see the work of Sandor Ferenczi.

7. Mike Wallace, documentary film: *Dead Blue: Surviving Depression.*
8. The New Age idea of risking reality is to "go with the flow" instead of "pushing the river." The Christian idea of risk is to "let go and let God." The human motivational idea of risking reality is illustrated by the story of the traveler in the dark who slips and falls over a cliff, catching onto a branch to keep from falling, he thinks, to his death. He clings all night to the branch that he thinks is saving his life only to find in the morning light that his feet are only inches from the ground below him, and he could have let loose at any time without coming to harm. The idea here is that we often go to extravagant lengths to protect ourselves when, in fact, we are not in any danger. The depression idea of risking reality is to act in some other way than as if we are depressed. In other words, act as if we do not believe that depression can prevent us from feeling okay at the very moment when depression is insistent that despair is the only reality.
9. See chapter 4, page 70.

CHAPTER 11

1. Elbert Hubbard, "Message to Garcia," *The Note Book* (New York: Wm. H. Wise, 1927), 139–142. This is a positively wonderful essay on the slow decline of self-motivation and the upsurge of dependence on excuses to prove "why a thing cannot be done" on the part of the young people starting out in the world.
2. In pseudocyesis a woman believes herself to be pregnant and displays all the symptoms of pregnancy, but she is not carrying a fetus.
3. Peter D. Kramer, *Listening, to Prozac* (New York; Viking, 1993). A psychiatrist's view of Prozac in terms of his patients' experiences with quick personality makeovers as a result of taking the drug.
4. Erica Goode, "Some Depression May Have Evolutionary Link," *New York Times,* February 9, 2000.
5. Randoph M. Nesse, M.D., "Is Depression an Adaptation?" *Archives of General Psychiatry*, January 2000, pp. 14–20.
6. Ibid.
7. Jim Holt, "Parallel Worlds," *The Wall Street Journal*, August 7, 1997.

8. For an explanation of first-level and second-level changes see End-notes, chapter 8, note 2.

CHAPTER 12

1. Antonio R. Damasio, *Descartes' Error: Emotion, Reason, and the Human Brain* (New York: Avon Books, 1994), 92. "As a landmark study of neuronal connections by E. G. Jones and T. P. S. Powell showed some two decades ago, nature does not let the sensory harbors talk to each other directly, and it does not permit them to talk to motor controls directly either. At the level of the cerebral cortex, for instance, each collection of early sensory areas must talk first to a variety of interposed regions, which talk to regions farther away, and so forth . . ." Which is why thinking is not necessarily doing.

2. Ibid., 128. "The apparatus of rationality, traditionally presumed to be neocortical, does not seem to work without that of biological regulation, traditionally presumed to be subcortical. Nature appears to have built the apparatus of rationality not just on top of the apparatus of biological regulation, but also *from* it and *with* it."

3. Ibid. It seems that the most prosaic function of negative feelings, such as those we experience in depression, is that they act as an automatic negative marker to eliminate categories of possibilities so that our higher-brain decision-making process functions efficiently. There is not enough time in our attention span to consider all the possibilities of any single proposed action. So whole categories of possibilities are automatically eliminated from our working memory because they have been negatively marked in earlier related experiences. This somatic "alarm" signal allows us to make an automatic "feeling choice," rejecting a huge number of "fear-tagged" options so that we make our final rational selection among fewer alternatives.

4. Nathaniel Branden, *Six Pillars of Self-Esteem* (New York: Bantam, 1994), 81. According to Branden, we become addicted to stimulants to avoid being tired or depressed and, "whatever else is involved what is always involved is the avoidance of consciousness . . . including the implications of a life-style that requires stimulants to be sustained. To the addict, consciousness is the enemy." If we know that to continue our behavior may cause us to lose our job, or our family, or our very lives, we must cease to have an honest communication with ourselves

and, in effect, become "functionally stupid" about our present reality in order for us to continue it.

5. Sandor Ferenczi, translated by Michael Balint and Nicola Z. Jackson, *Clinical Diary* (Cambridge, MA: Harvard University Press, 1995).

6. "Scientists Implant Falsified Memories," Associated Press News Service, September 5, 1998.

7. Jeffrey M. Schwartz, *Brain Lock: Free Yourself From Obsessive-Compulsive Behavior* (New York: HarperCollins, 1996).

8. Paul R. McHugh, "How Psychiatry Lost Its Way," *Commentary,* December 1999.

CHAPTER 13

1. William H. McNeill, "A Short History of Humanity." This article was based on a lecture, "Passing Strange: The Convergence of the Sciences in the Twentieth Century," delivered at The World 2000 conference in Austin, Texas, February 10, 2000, and published in the *New York Review of Books,* June 29, 2000.

2. Ibid.

3. Charles L. Griswold, *Adam Smith and the Virtues of Enlightenment* (New York: Cambridge University Press, 1999).

4. Michael D. Yapko, *Breaking the Patterns of Depression* (New York: Doubleday, 1997).

5. It was announced at the 1997 Second International Conference on Bipolar Disorder that Dr. Frank is also conducting a NIMH-sponsored study of women with recurrent depression, hoping to establish how biology, life stress, and different types of psychotherapy interact to affect the recurrence of episodes of depression. The first International Conference on Bipolar Disorder, sponsored by the University of Pittsburgh, was held in 1994.

6. Yapko, *Breaking the Patterns of Depression.*

7. Ibid.

8. I am indebted to Antonio Damasio for getting me to think of willpower in terms of long-term gains.

9. "The fault, dear Brutus, lies not in our stars but in ourselves that we are underlings." *Julius Caesar,* Act I, Sc.ii.

10. Roy F. Baumeister, "Violence Is the Darker Side of Self-esteem," *Psychological Review*, February 1996.

11. Ibid

12. This quote is from a recent column by this nationally syndicated child

psychologist and author of dozens of books, including *Parent Power: A Commonsense Approach to Parenting in the '90s and Beyond* (Kansas City, MO: Andrews McMeel Publishing, 1991); *Because I Said So: 366 Insightful and Thought-provoking Reflections on Parenting and Family Life* (Kansas City, MO: Andrews McMeel Publishing, 1996).

13. "In Their Own Words," Universal Press Syndicate, May 27, 2000.

14. Andrew J. Cherlin, "I'm O.K., You're Selfish," *New York Times Magazine*, October 17, 1999.

15. Wilhelm Reich, *Early Writings Volume One* (New York: Farrar Straus Giroux, 1975).

16. Reuters News Service, "Morality May Have Evolutionary Roots, Animal Studies Find," January 11, 1996.

17. Ibid.

18. Frans de Waal, *Good Natured: The Origin of Right and Wrong in Humans and Other Animals* (Cambridge, MA: Harvard University Press, 1996).

19. Jerome Kagan, *Three Seductive Ideas* (Cambridge, MA: Harvard University Press, 1998), 193.

20. Antonio R. Damasio, *Descartes' Error: Emotion, Reason, and the Human Brain* (New York: Avon Books, 1994).

21. Dr. Joyce Brothers, *Widowed* (New York: Ballantine, 1992).

22. Stephen Hawking, *A Brief History of Time* (New York: Bantam, 1988).

CHAPTER 14

1. Evagrius Ponticus (346–399), Greek Christian mystic who wrote the treatise "On The Eight Principal Vices."

2. Sylvia Nasar, *A Beautiful Mind* (New York: Simon & Schuster, 1998).

3. Ibid.

4. Ibid.

5. Robert Louis Stevenson, *The Strange Case of Dr. Jekyll and Mr. Hyde* (New York: Doubleday, Doren & Co. 1932), first published in 1886. A well-respected Doctor Jekyll begins to experiment with a drug in order to experience passions "unknown to him," but the drug begins to exert a strange addictive power over him and periodically turns the doctor into a grotesque evil alter ego, the brutal monster Mr. Hyde.

6. Shad Helmstetter, *The Self-Talk Solution* (New York: William Morrow, 1982), 69.

7. Nathaniel Branden, *Six Pillars of Self-Esteem* (New York: Bantam, 1994), 313–321.

8. Ivan Pavlov (1849–1936) is the father of classical conditioning. He found that by repeated association, an artificial stimulus could be substituted for a natural stimulus to cause a physiological reaction. He rang a bell every time he fed a dog and found that, after a time, the association was so strong in the dog's mind that the dog would react to the bell itself as if it were food. That is, the dog would salivate at the sound of the bell as it used to do only with food, whereas before the paired association the bell naturally elicited no such reaction. Pavlov believed that our acquired habits, as well as our higher mental activities, depend upon a chain of conditioned reflections brought about by association of one thing with another. For instance, if we are beaten with a broom as a child, the image of a broom is going to have more negative associations for us than for someone who wasn't beaten. A neutral stimulus, the broom, can elicit negative feelings in us due to its association with a negative event. If our father did the beatings some of the fear elicited will be associated with all men, etc., etc. This is why Directed Thinking is better for depression than allowing random lines of reasoning that bubble up on their own, with the great possibility that they will be contaminated by accidental learning from the fear of the primal mind.

9. For an explanation of fear-tagging, see Endnotes, chapter 10, note 2.

10. The hypnosis class exercise was a guided imagery visualization. We were to imagine a path along a river, through the woods to an old cave, which we were to enter and speak with the "wise person" we were to find there. The idea here is to seek our inner wisdom by personifying it in the form of a guru in a cave. Other people in the class got old Indians, shamans, witches, sages, etc. But after trying it three times I always got the same little girl in a white summer pinafore, crying inconsolably.

I was very discouraged with my exercise and told one of the other participants who said she thought it was magical, and maybe I should ask the child some questions. So I took my classmate's advice and found out the child was three years old and had been in the cave "as long as she knew" and she was lonely and was waiting for someone to "remember she was there and let her out." That little girl is no longer crying in the dark cave of my mind. She is now safe in my heart.

11. Books on Paracelsus:

Jolande Jacobi (ed.), *Paracelsus, Selected Writings* (New York: Pantheon Books, 1951).
Anna M. Stoddart, *The Life of Paracelsus* (London: John Murray, 1911).
Arthur Edward Waite, *The Hermetical and Alchemical Writings of Paracelsus*, 2 vols. (London: James Elliot, 1894).
Henry Pachter, *Magic into Science* (New York: Henry Schuman, 1951).

CHAPTER 15

1. David Blankenhorn is the founder of the Institute for American Values and author of several books on the family and American values, including *Promises to Keep: Decline and Renewal of Marriage in America* (Rowman & Littlefield, 1996), and *American Idea* (New York: Basic Books, 1996).
2. "Teen Killing Suspect Speaks to Paper," Associated Press News Service, September 12, 2000.
3. Jeffrey Moussaieff Masson, *The Assault on Truth: Freud's Suppression of the Seduction Theory* (New York: PocketBooks, 1998).

CHAPTER 16

1. Peter Steinfels, "Public Schools Should Nurture the Sacred, Norman Lear Says," New York Times News Service, November 22, 1989.
2. Richard Lovelace (1618–1657), "To Lucasta on Going to the Wars," 1649. He knows his new mistress will forgive him for his absence because he is not leaving for another woman but for his duty:

Yet this inconstancy is such
As you, too, shall adore;
I could not love thee, dear, so much
Loved I not honor more.

3. David Shaw, "Medical Miracles or Misguided Media?" *Los Angeles Times*, February 13, 2000.
4. Allan Bloom, *The Closing of the American Mind* (New York: Simon & Schuster, 1987), 3.
5. Ibid

6. Ibid.
7. William McGowan, "Among the Believers: Diversity, yes. Diversity of opinion, no." *The Wall Street Journal*, July 16, 1999.
8. Ibid.
9. "Romance Dangerous for Teenagers," Associated Press News Service, February 18, 2001.
10. David Blankenhorn, Harold Bloom, and Allan Bloom have lectured and written extensively on this subject.
11. Sandra Stotsky, *Losing Our Language* (New York: Free Press, 1999).
12. Ibid.
13. William Glasser, *The Identity Society* (New York: Harper & Row, 1972).
14. See John Rosemond, chapter 13, page 373.
15. Barbara Defoe Whitehead, *The Divorce Culture: Rethinking Our Commitments to Marriage and Family* (New York: Alfred E. Knopf, 1997).
16. Ibid.
17. "Married with Kids in 26% of Homes," Associated Press News Service, November 24, 1999.
18. Kathleen Parker, "Society Has Abandoned Boys," *Orlando Sentinel*, August 25, 1999.
19. Whitehead, *The Divorce Culture*.
20. A. B. Curtiss, "Sad Legacy of Neglected Kids: Trickle-down Parenting Doesn't Work," *San Diego Union-Tribune*, May 23, 1996.
21. John Rosemond, "Shift to Secular Philosophy Has Spawned Increasing Misbehavior," January 28, 1999. The question was asked of John Rosemond, the child psychologist and nationally syndicated columnist, "Why is it that although we work much harder at parenting than did our parents, we have had so many more problems with our children than they had with us?" Rosemond's answer was that parents before the 1960s thought of a child's behavior and especially misbehavior as a matter of right and wrong, to be met with by punishment that helped to affirm accountability. "For a child to exercise control over free will, he has to learn that 'free will ain't free.'" Parents today think of misbehavior as "... the product of either (a) stress, anger, low self-esteem, conflict or some other psychological condition, or (b) a biochemical imbalance, bad genes, allergies, etc. In either case, the child 'can't help it.' Therefore he deserves not punishment, but understanding." I would add to Rosemond's comments that the reason understanding does not bring accountability is because we do not live our lives by our opinions but by our habits.

22. Anne Hendershott, "We're Still Looking for the Easy Answers," *San Diego Union Tribune,* June 13, 1999. Hendershott is chair of the Department of Sociology at the University of San Diego. She specializes in youth alienation.
23. Ibid.
24. *Larry King Live,* October 28, 1999.
25. Antonio R. Damasio, *Descartes' Error: Emotion, Reason, and the Human Brain* (New York: Avon Books, 1994), 128. "The apparatus of rationality, traditionally presumed to be neocortical, does not seem to work without that of biological regulation, traditionally presumed to be subcortical. Nature appears to have built the apparatus of rationality not just on top of the apparatus of biological regulation, but also *from* it and *with* it."
26. Hendershott, "We're Still Looking for the Easy Answers."
27. Ibid.
28. Parker, "Society Has Abandoned Boys."
29. Roger Rosenblatt, "Teaching Johnny to Be Good," *New York Times Magazine,* April 30, 1995.
30. Kay S. Hymowitz, *Ready or Not* (New York: Free Press, 1999).
31. "Loose-talking Spy Doll Angers Boy's Mom," Associated Press News Service, June 23, 1999.
32. Randoph M. Nesse, M.D., "Is Depression an Adaptation?" *Archives of General Psychiatry,* January 2000, pp. 14–20.
33. Francis Fukuyama, *The Great Disruption* (New York: Free Press, 1999).
34. Melanie Rehak, "Questions for Francis Fukuyama: The Unselfish Gene," *New York Times Magazine,* May 2, 1999.
35. "Baby Talk," *The Wall Street Journal,* June 14, 1999.
36. Ibid.
37. Ethan Bronner, "Schools Feel Burden of Teaching Morals," New York Times News Service, June 3, 1999.
38. Ibid.
39. Ethan Bronner, "For the Homeless, Rebirth through Socrates," *New York Times,* March 7, 1999.
40. Lisa Miller, "Today It's Reading, Writing and 'Diligence' in Elementary Schools," *The Wall Street Journal,* October 25, 1999.
41. Rosenblatt, "Teaching Johnny to Be Good."

CHAPTER 17

1. Learned helplessness is a phrase coined by Martin Seligman, a past president of the American Psychological Association and author of many books on learned helplessness and learned optimism. Learned helplessness is a term that describes how we unnecessarily make ourselves victims of circumstances when there are other opportunities. The original work by Martin Seligman is out of print but is included in a new book, *Learned Helplessness: A Theory for the Age of Personal Control,* by Petersen, Maier, and Seligman (Oxford, England: Oxford University Press, 1995). Some of his other books are: *What You Can Change and What You Can't* (New York: Fawcett, 1995) and *Learned Optimism* (New York: Pocket Books, 1992). Seligman uses the differences in explanatory styles of people to train them to dispute their pessimistic thinking and come to more optimistic conclusions.

2. Nathaniel Branden, *Six Pillars of Self-Esteem* (New York: Bantam, 1994). I am indebted to Nathaniel Branden for the idea that one of the most cherished and deeply held trusts is that someday someone is coming to "save us." It's what makes us a sucker for cults and Internet relationships. It's an idea that we are so dependent on that we don't even want to know we have it. But it is an idea we must acknowledge and give up if we are going to take full responsibility for our lives.

CHAPTER 18

1. Alice Miller, *Prisoners of Childhood: The Drama of the Gifted Child and the Search for the True Self* (New York: Basic Books, 1996).

2. Arthur Janov, *Primal Scream* (New York: G.P. Putnam, 1970). We have an emotional bottom of despair, which we can finally "hit" and release ourselves from in an ultimate and final scream of cosmic anguish.

3. Penis envy is one of Freud's now outdated theories: When a little girl sees a boy's penis for the first time she believes herself to be cheated, and therefore she feels inferior and lacking and remains envious throughout her life.

4. The Peter Pan Syndrome concerns men who never grow up to responsibility. It is usually linked with its alter ego, the Cinderella Complex, which describes women who depend upon men too much.

5. Francis Fukuyama, *The Great Disruption* (New York: Free Press, 1990).

6. Christopher Wolfe, "Public Morality and the Supreme Court," a paper presented at the American Political Science Association convention in Washington, D.C., September 3, 2000.

7. Harry Clor, "Public Morality and the Celebration of Non-Judgmentalism," a paper presented at the American Political Science Association convention in Washington, D.C., September 3, 2000.

8. Carol Tavris, *The Longest War* (New York: Harcourt-Brace, 1984).

9. "Child Hires Lawyer Over School Lunches," Associated Press News Service, March 13, 1999.

10. Patricia Leigh Brown, "As Neighborliness Fades, Fences Turn Inward," *New York Times,* March 14, 1999.

11. Fukuyama, *The Great Disruption.*

12. Also known as Single Image Random Dot Stereograms. *Magic Eye: 3D Illusions* (N.E. Thing Enterprises, Kansas City, MO: Andrews and McMeel, 1993).

13. Kenneth Roberts, *Northwest Passage* (New York: Doubleday, Doran & Co., 1936). An adventurer struggles to find a northwest passage across America to the East, enduring physical suffering and failure, and thwarted by political bureaucracy. A Western artist endures ridicule and poverty to paint Indians in their natural state. "On every side of us are men who hunt perpetually for their personal Northwest Passage, too often sacrificing health, strength and life itself to the search; and who shall say they are not happier in their vain but hopeful quest than wiser, duller folk who sit at home, venturing nothing."

CHAPTER 19

1. The answer to the question, what number multiplied by itself is −4, if there is such a number, can't be positive, negative, or zero because none of these multiplied by itself can give a negative number. So for "convenience sake" in solving some square root math problems, mathematicians invented a system of imaginary numbers whose squares are negative numbers.

2. George Eliot, *Middlemarch* (New York: New American Library, 1964).

CHAPTER 20

1. *The New World Bible: With the Apocrypha* (New York: Cambridge University Press, 1972).
2. William Shakespeare, *The Tragedy of Locrine*, III, iii.
3. Mark Caldwell, *A Short History of Rudeness* (New York: Picador, 1999).
4. Janet Hobhouse, *Everybody Who Was Anybody: A Biography of Gertrude Stein* (New York: Anchor, 1989).
5. Viktor E. Frankl, *Man's Search for Meaning* (Boston: Beacon Press, 1959).
6. Ibid.
7. Ibid.
8. Allan W. Anderson, Professor Emeritus of Religious Studies, San Diego State University, from his speech May 7, 1985, upon the occasion of his retirement from SDSU.
9. Frankl, *Man's Search for Meaning*.
10. William Shakespeare, *The Tempest*. Miranda, who has been living on a deserted island with her father, sees other people for the first time and in her delight with them declares "O brave new world that has such people in't."

INDEX